BANKING LAW AND PRACTICE

For the Students of B.Com., B.B.M., B.B.A. and B.C.S.

K.P. KANDASAMI
Former Registrar
Bharathiar University, Coimbatore
and
Former Principal
Gobi Arts & Science College (Autonomous)
Gobichettipalayam, Tamil Nadu

S. NATARAJAN
Former Deputy General Manager
Department of Banking Supervision
Reserve Bank of India
Central Office, Mumbai

R. PARAMESWARAN
Head
Department of Commerce
T.S.A. A.S.T. College, Perur, Coimbatore

S Chand And Company Limited
(ISO 9001 Certified Company)

S Chand And Company Limited

(ISO 9001 Certified Company)

Head Office: D-92, Sector–2, Noida – 201301, U.P. (India), Ph. 91-120-4682700

Registered Office: A-27, 2nd Floor, Mohan Co-operative Industrial Estate, New Delhi – 110 044, Phone: 011-49731800

www.**schandpublishing.com**; e-mail: **info@schandpublishing.com**

Marketing Offices:

Chennai	:	Ph: 23632120; chennai@schandpublishing.com
Guwahati	:	Ph: 2738811, 2735640; guwahati@schandpublishing.com
Hyderabad	:	Ph: 40186018; hyderabad@schandpublishing.com
Jalandhar	:	Ph: 4645630; jalandhar@schandpublishing.com
Kolkata	:	Ph: 23357458, 23353914; kolkata@schandpublishing.com
Lucknow	:	Ph: 4003633; lucknow@schandpublishing.com
Mumbai	:	Ph: 25000297; mumbai@schandpublishing.com
Patna	:	Ph: 2260011; patna@schandpublishing.com

First Edition 1998
Revised Editions 2003, 2007, Fourth Edition 2009
Reprints 2013 (Twice), 2016 (Twice), 2018, 2020, 2022

Reprint 2023

ISBN: 978-81-219-2235-7 **Product Code:** H8BLW48BAIN10ENAD09R

PRINTED IN INDIA

By Vikas Publishing House Private Limited, Plot 20/4, Site-IV, Industrial Area Sahibabad, Ghaziabad – 201 01 and Published by S Chand And Company Limited, A-27, 2nd Floor, Mohan Co-operative Industrial Estate, New Delhi – 110 044.

PREFACE TO THE FOURTH REVISED EDITION

It gives me great pleasure in presenting this revised fourth edition of Banking Law and Practice to the student community as well as to the teachers of different Universities in India. Encouraged by the widespread response and suggestions given, I have ventured to revise the book. Wherever the materials presented are felt short and modifications are needed, I have made improvements to suit the requirements of the students and the faculty as well.

As usual, I have added many Indian case laws in appropriate places so that the students and the teachers on this subject will be well acquainted with the present scenario of banking practice in India.

I hope that this present edition will meet the requirements of the students who are preparing for their examination.

I shall be grateful to the readers if they are kind enough to send me their comments and suggestions for the further improvement of the book.

Gobichettipalayam. **K.P. KANDASAMI**

PREFACE TO THE REVISED EDITION

We are glad to place before you a revised edition of this book with additional information and material on 'Banking Law and Practice' for the benefit of the students, banking companies and depositors. Appendix and 8 sets of Model Question Papers have also been added for the benefit of Banking Law students.

Suggestions for improvement are welcome which will be source encouragement to us for making this book consumer friendly.

AUTHORS

PREFACE TO THE THIRD EDITION

In response to the increasing demand from the students of Banking Law and Practice, the third edition of this book is needed. As the subject BANKING LAW & PRACTICE has been one of the subjects of study for many undergraduate programmes, viz., B.Com., B.B.M., B.B.A., B.C.S. etc., the users of this book are very large and hence the necessity of bringing out the third edition of the book has arisen. Many errors that were found in the previous edition have been corrected and updated. Wherever necessary, improvements have been made to incorporate the recent changes and trends in Banking Law and Practice.

Suggestions, feedback and constructive criticisms from professors on this subject would help us to improve the quality of the book. We express our gratitude and thankfulness to the faculty members and the student friends for their encouragement and support. We also thank the publishers, S.Chand & Co. Ltd., for their co-operation and encouragement.

It is hoped that the present edition will meet fully the requirements of both the faculty members and the students.

AUTHORS

CONTENTS

1. INTRODUCTION 1 – 5

1.1. Evolution 1

1.2. Development of Banking in India 2

1.3. Meaning and Definition of Banking 4

1.4. Features of Banking 5

2. LAWS OF BANKING IN INDIA 6 – 10

2.1. Evolution of Banking Law in India 6

2.2. Reserve Bank of India Act, 1934 6

2.3. Banking Regulation Act, 1949 8

2.4. Banking Companies (Acquisition and Transfer of Undertaking) Act, 1970 9

2.5. The Regional Rural Banks Act, 1976 10

2.6. The Banking Companies Act, 1980 10

2.7. The Negotiable Instruments Act, 1881 10

3. RELATIONS BETWEEN BANKER AND CUSTOMER 11–41

3.1. Definition of Banker 11

3.2. Customer 13

3.3. Customer–Old View–Duration Theory 13

3.4. Customer. Modern View : Rejection of the Duration Theory 13

3.5. Banker-Customer Relationship 16

3.6. Special Features of Banker-Customer Relationship 20

3.6.1. A. Rights 20

3.6.2. B. Obligations 31

4. DIFFERENT TYPES OF ACCOUNTS 42–71

4.1. Demand Deposits 42

4.2. Opening of a New Account 45

4.2.1 General precaution to be taken by a bank in opening of a new account 46

4.2.2. Risk in opening accounts without proper introduction 48

4.3. Operating the Account 49

4.3.1. Cheque book 49

4.3.2. Paying-in-slip book 50

4.3.3. Pass book 50

4.3.4. Entries in pass book 52

4.4. Fixed Deposit Account 56

	4.4.1. Features of fixed deposits	57
	4.4.2. Legal position	61
	4.4.2. Fixed deposit receipt	61
	4.4.4. Advantages of fixed deposit	62
	4.4.5. Disadvantages of fixed deposit account	63
4.5.	Recurring Deposit Accounts	63
4.6.	Nomination	64
4.7.	Closure of a Bank Account	66
	4.7.1. Circumstances under which a banker close his curstomer's account	67
4.8.	Insurance of Bank Deposits	68
4.9.	Deposit Schemes for Indians Abroad	69
5.	**SPECIAL TYPE OF BANKER'S CUSTOMERS**	**72 –95**
5.1.	Minor	72
5.2.	Married Women	75
5.3.	Illiterate Person	77
5.4.	Trustecs	77
5.5.	Executors and Administrators	78
5.6.	Customer's Attorney	80
5.7.	Clubs, Societies and Charitable Institutions	80
5.8.	Drunken Persons	81
5.9.	Parda Woman	82
5.10.	Lunatics	82
5.11.	Hindu Family	83
5.12.	Joint Stock Companies	84
5.13.	Partnership	89
5.14.	Joint Accounts	92
5.15	Bankrupts	94
6.	**NEGOTIABLE INSTRUMENTS**	**96 – 116**
6.1.	Meaning	96
6.2.	Essential Characteristics of Negotiable Instrument	97
6.3.	Presumptions as to a Negotiable Instrument	97
6.4.	Types of Negotiable Instrument	98
	6.4.1. Promissory notes	98
	6.4.2. Bills of exchange	100
	6.4.3. cheques	103
6.5	Differences Between Promissory Note and Bill of Exchange	108
6.6.	Differences Between a Cheque and a Bill of Exchange	109
6.7.	Differences Between Promissory Note and Cheque	109
6.8.	Similarities Between Promissory Note and Cheque	110
6.9.	Differences between a Fixed Deposit Receipt and a Cheque	110
6.10.	Holder in Due Course	111

6.10.1. Holder for value 111
6.10.2 Holder in due course 111
6.10.3 Circumstances in which a banker becomes a holder in due course 112
6.10.4 Differences between holder and holder in due course 113
6.10.5 Rights and privileges of the holder in due course 113
6.11. Liabilities of Parties to a Negotiable Instrument 114
6.11.1 Rights of parties in special cases 115

7. CHEQUES 117 – 142
7.1. Drafting of Cheques 117
7.2. Crossing of Cheques 120
7.2.1. Origin of crossing 120
7.2.2 Object of crossing 121
7.2.3. Types of crossing 122
7.2.4 Double crossing 125
7.2.5 Obliterating a crossing 125
7.2.6 Parties eligibnle to cross 126
7.2.7 Liabilitity of the paying banker on crossed cheques 126
7.2.8 Advantages of crossing 127
7.2.9 Impact of crossing 127
7.3. Marking of Cheques 127
7.3.1 Marking of cheques meaning 128
7.3.2 Advantages 128
7.3.3 Procedure of marking cheques 128
7.3.4 Effect of marking 129
7.4. Material Alteration 131
7.4.1 Definition 131
7.4.2. Alterations (Immaterial) 132
7.4.3 Effects of material alterations 133
7.5. Endorsement 152
7.5.1 Definition of endorsement 134
7.5.2 Legal provisions regarding endorsement 135
7.5.3 Kinds of endorsements 136
7.5.4 Forged endorsements 137
7.5.5 Endorser's liability 138
7.5.6 Bankers practice regarding endorsement 139

8. COLLECTION OF CHEQUES 143 – 156
8.1. Capacity of the Collecting Banker 143
8.2. Precautions to be taken by the Collecting Banker 147
8.3. Negligence 149
8.3.1 Circumstances in which the banker held liable 149
8.3.2 Examples of negligence 152
8.4. Duties and Responsibilities of a collecting banker 152
8.4.1 Procedure for collection 153

8.5. Conversion 153

8.5.1 Collecting banker and conversion 154

8.5.2 Definition of the term conversion 154

8.5.3 Circustances when conversion is said to have been done 155

8.5.4 Liability of the collecting banker for the act of conversion 155

8.5.5 Instructions of the paying banker and collecting banker 155

9. PAYMENT OF CHEQUES 157 – 179

9.1. Paying Banker 157

9.2. Role of a Paying Banker 157

9.3. Duties of a Paying Banker 158

9.4. Precautions by the Paying Banker 158

9.5. Statutory Protection to the Paying Banker 170

9.6. Refusal of Payment of Cheques 175

10. LOANS AND ADVANCES 180–207

10.1. Liquid Assets of a Banker 180

10.2. Investment in Securities 184

10.3. General Principles of Sound Landing 185

10.4. Classification of Loans and Advances 187

10.5. Credit Information 190

10.6. Level of Advances 191

10.7. Secured Advances–Modes of Creating Charge 191

10.7.1 Lien 192

10.7.2 Pledge 192

10.7.3 Hypothecation 196

10.7.4 Difference between lien and pledge 198

10.7.5 Difference between pledge and hypothecation 199

10.7.6 Mortgage 199

10.7.7 Difference between hypothecation and mortgage 206

10.7.8 Difference between pledge and mortgage 206

10.8. Assignment 207

11. SECURED ADVANCES–TYPES OF SECURITIES 208 – 237

11.1. General Principles of Secured Advances 208

11.2. Types of Securities 211

A. Advances against goods 211

B. Advances against documents of title to goods 214

C. Advances against life policy 220

D. Advances against Real Estates 223

E. Stock Exchange Securities 224

F. Advances against Book Debts 229

G. Jewellery and buillion 229

H. Advances against government securities 230

I. Immovable Property 231

J. Advances against fixed deposit 232

K. Advances against supply bills 234

12. LETTERS OF CREDIT AND GUARANTEES 238–250

12.1. Types of Letters of Credit 238

12.2. The Liability of the Issuing Banker 240

12.3. Bank Guarantee and Letter of Credit 241

12.4. Advantages of a Letter of Credit to the Beneficiary 241

12.5. Guarantees 241

12.6. Contract of Indemnity 242

12.7. Distinction Between a Contract of Guarantee and a Contract of Indemnity 242

12.7.1 Essential Features of a contract of guarantee 243

12.8. Liability of the Surety 244

12.9. Rights of Surety and the Circumstances Under Which a Surety is Discharged 245

12.10. Obligation of Creditor (Banker) Towards Surety 246

12.11. Precautions Taken by a Banker for Granting Advances Against Guarantee 247

12.12. Termination of the Guarantee 249

13. PURCHASE AND DISCOUNTING OF BILLS 251–254

13.1. Advantages of Discounting of Bills by banks 252

13.2. Precantionary steps before advancing 252

Model Question Papers (8 set) 255–273

1

INTRODUCTION

The development of 'Banking' is evolutionary in nature. There is no single answer to the question of what is banking? Because, a bank performs a multitude of functions and services which cannot be comprehended into a single definition. For a common man, a bank means a storehouse of money, for a businessman it is an institution of finance and for a worker it may be a depository for his savings.

It may be explained in brief as "Banking is what a bank does". But it is not clear enough to understand the subject in full. The Oxford Dictionary defines a bank as "*an establishment for the custody of money which it pays out on a customer's order*". But this definition is also not enough, because it considers the deposit accepting and repayment functions only. The meaning of the bank can be understood only by its functions just as a tree is known by its fruits. As any other subject, it has its own origin, growth and development. Let us briefly trace the evolution of Banking.

1.1 EVOLUTION

It is interesting to trace the origin of the word 'bank' in the modern sense, to the German word "Banck" which means, heap or mound or joint stock fund. From this, the Italian word "Banco" meaning heap of money was coined.

Some people have the opinion that the word "bank" is derived from the French words "bancus" or "banque" which means a 'bench'. Initially, the bankers, the Jews in Lombardy, transacted their business on benches in the marketplace and the bench resembled the banking counter. If a banker failed, his 'banque' (bench) was broken up by the people; hence the word "bankrupt" has come. In simple term, bankrupt means a person who has lost all his money, wealth or financial resources.

Thus, the origin of the word bank can be traced as follows:

Banck - German (Joint stock fund)
↓
Banco - Italian (Heap of money)
↓
Bancus/ Banque - French (Bench/chest, a place where valuables are kept)
↓
Bank - English (common meaning prevalent today, i.e., as an Institution accepting money as deposit for lending)

In India, the Banking Regulation Act 1949, under which banks are regulated by the Reserve Bank of India, defines 'banking as an activity of accepting of deposit, which shall be repayable on demand from the depositor'.

The origin of modern banks is traced to three important sources. They are,

(*i*) the goldsmith

(*ii*) the money lenders, and

(*iii*) the merchant bankers.

The goldsmith by virtue of dealing in Gold, which is a very valuable item, had facilities for the safe keeping of valuables. He accepted for safe custody the money, another important valuable item, belonging to his customers. The goldsmiths began to lend the money knowing that all the depositors do not withdraw their savings at a time. The moneylender lent his surplus funds to the needy and earned the income by way of interest. The merchant bankers were primarily traders and had to oblige his customers by accepting their money for safe custody. He was doing the banking business as a side occupation. Modern banks retain all the characteristics of these three types of institutions.

Banking made its first appearance as a public enterprise in the year 1157 in Italy with the establishment of 'Bank of Venice'. The 'Bank of Barcelona' was started in 1401, the 'Bank of Genoa' in 1407 and the 'Bank of Amsterdam' in 1609. The Lombards who migrated to Europe and England from Italy were responsible for the development of modern banking.

When severe restrictions were imposed on them by the king Charles-II, their business was affected at large. The goldsmiths were gradually replaced by private bankers. After the Banking Act was passed in 1833 in England, the growth of joint stock commercial banking was accelerated. Foundations were laid for the growth of modern commercial banking during the 19th century.

1.2. DEVELOPMENT OF BANKING IN INDIA

Banking in India is indeed as old as Himalayas. But, the banking functions became an effective force only after the first decade of 20th century. To understand the history of modern banking in India, one has to refer to the "English Agency Houses" established by the East India Company. These Agency Houses were basically trading firms and carrying on banking business as part of their main business. Because of this dual functions and lack of their own capital (Agency Houses depend entirely on deposits for their capital requirements) they failed and vanished from the scene during the third decade of 18th century.

The East India Company laid the foundations for modern banking in the first half of the 19th century with the establishment of the following three banks :

(*i*) Bank of Bengal in 1809

(*ii*) Bank of Bombay in 1840

(*iii*) Bank of Madras in 1843

These banks are also known as "Presidency Banks" and they functioned well as independent units.

During the last part of 19th century and early phase of 20th century, the 'Swadeshi Movement' induced the establishment of a number of banks with Indian Management.

For example, Punjab National Bank Ltd in 1895, The Bank of India Ltd in 1906, The Canara Bank Ltd in 1906, The Indian Bank Ltd in 1907, The Bank of Baroda Ltd in 1908, The Central Bank of India Ltd in 1911 and many other banks were established on the same line. But most of the weak banks went bankrupt due to wrong policy decisions taken by the management and due to the severe banking crisis during 1913-1918, the period of World War I.

In 1920, the "Imperial Bank of India Act", was passed for amalgamating the three Presidency Banks. As such, the 'Imperial Bank of India' was established in 1921. It was given power to hold Government funds and manage the public debt. The branches of the bank were functioning as clearing houses (Agency for effecting settlement of funds among banks). However, it was not authorised to issue currency.

Even though the need for a Central Bank was felt in the 18th century, it could be materialised only in the 20th century. On the basis of the recommendations of the 'Banking Enquiry Committee', the Reserve Bank of India Act was passed in 1934. Accordingly, the 'Reserve Bank of India' was constituted in 1935 to regulate the issue of Bank notes, securing monetary stability in India and to operate the currency and credit system of the country to its economic development. Initially, it was constituted as a private shareholders' bank with a fully paid up capital of Rs. 5 crores. After Independence, there was a general attitude towards its nationalization. Thus, the 'Reserve Bank of India' (Transferred to public ownership) Act was passed in 1948. Accordingly, the entire Share Capital of the bank was acquired by the Central Government from the private shareholders against compensation and it was nationalised on January 1, 1949.

In 1955, the 'State Bank of India Act' was passed. Accordingly the 'Imperial Bank' was nationalised and 'State Bank of India' emerged with the objective of extension of banking facilities on a large scale, specifically in the rural semi-urban areas and for various other public purposes.

In 1959, the 'State Bank of India' (Subsidiary Banks) Act was passed by which the public sector banking was further extended. The following banks were made the subsidiaries of State Bank of India:

(*i*) The State Bank of Bikanur

(*ii*) The State Bank of Jaipur

(*iii*) The State Bank of Indore

(*iv*) The State Bank of Mysore

(*v*) The State Bank of Patiala

(*vi*) The State Bank of Hyderabad

(*vii*) The State Bank of Saurashtra

(*viii*) The State Bank of Travancore

In 1963, the first two banks were amalgamated under the name of "The State Bank of Bikanur and Jaipur". In 1969, fourteen major Indian commercial banks were nationalised. These banks are Allahabad Bank, Bank of Baroda, Bank of India, Canara Bank, Central Bank of India, Dena Bank, Indian Bank, Indian Overseas Bank, Punjab National Bank, Syndicate Bank, Union Bank of India, United Bank of India, United Commercial Bank and Bank of Maharashtra. And in 1980 again six banks were nationalised. These banks constitute the public sector banks while the other scheduled banks and non-scheduled banks are in the private sector.

1.3. MEANING AND DEFINITION OF BANKING

A bank is an institution, which deals with money and credit. Thus bank is an intermediary, which handles other people's money both for their advantage and to its own profit. But bank is not merely a trader in money but also an important manufacturer of money. In other words, a bank is a factory of credit.

Let us see the definitions of bank and banking, given by various authorities.

Crowther defines a bank as, "*one that collects money from those who have it to spare or who are saving it out of their incomes and lends the money so collected to those who require it*".

Dr. L. Hart says that the banker is "*one who in the ordinary course of business honours cheques drawn upon him by persons from and for whom he receives money on current accounts*".

Sir John Paget says that, "*no person or body corporate otherwise can be a banker who does not*

(*i*) *take deposit accounts,*

(*ii*) *take current accounts,*

(*iii*) *issue and pay cheques,* and

(*iv*) *collect cheques*

for his customers".

Sir Kinley says, "*A bank is an establishment which makes to individuals such advances of money as may be required and to which individuals entrust money when not required by them for use.*"

Prof. Sayers says that "*Banks are not merely purveyors of money but also in an important sense, manufacturers of money.*"

Although the above definitions have described the meaning of bank, none of them precisely defined 'Banking' incorporating its entire functions. However, an attempt has been made in Sec 5(1) (b&c) of the "Banking Regulations Act 1949" to define 'Banking' and 'Banking Company'.

According to Sec. 5(1) (b), "*Banking means accepting for the purpose of lending or investment, of deposits of money from the public, repayable on demand or otherwise and withdrawable by cheques, draft, order or otherwise*".

Sec. 5(1) (c) defines banking company as, "any company which transacts the business of banking in India".

Scheduled Banks :

Scheduled Banks are those banks which are listed in the Second Schedule to the Reserve Bank of India Act, 1934.

1.4. FEATURES OF BANKING

Dealing in money: The banks accept deposits from the public and advancing them as loans to the needy people. The deposits may be of different types – current, fixed, saving etc. based on various terms and conditions.

Deposits must be withdrawable: The deposits made by the public can be withdrawable by cheques, draft or otherwise, i.e., the banks issue and pay cheques. The deposits are usually withdrawable on demand.

Dealing with credit: The banks are the institutions that can create credit, i.e., creation of additional money for lending. Thus, "creation of credit" is the unique feature of banking.

Commercial in nature: Since all of the banking functions are carried on with the aim of making profit, it is regarded as a commercial institution.

Nature of Agent: Besides the basic functions of accepting deposits and lending money as loans, banks possess the character of an agent because of their various agency services.

LAWS OF BANKING IN INDIA

2.1. EVOLUTION OF BANKING LAW IN INDIA

Banking as a business has its own distinctive features when compared with all other trade and business. A banking company deals mainly with the money of large number of depositors who do not have any control over the affairs of the bank. Hence, there is a need for proper control over the banks. It is the responsibility of the Government to safeguard the interests of the large number of depositors. The Banking Regulation Act, 1949, is the most important Act enacted by the Government to protect the interests of the people. The provisions of this Act are in addition to those of Companies Act, 1956, and any other law like the Contract Act, the Negotiable Instruments Act, the Codes of Civil and Criminal Procedures, etc. The commercial banks in India are also regulated by the Reserve Bank of India Act, 1934.

Banking law in India, as we find today, is the outcome of the gradual process of evolution. The Indian Companies Act, 1913, was not adequate and therefore a separate legislation was passed in 1949 under the name of Banking Companies Act, 1949. This Act was based to a large extent upon the English banking law. Later in 1966, this Act was renamed as Banking Regulation Act. Since its enforcement in 1949, the Act has been amended several times to cater to the needs of the society and also to remove the loopholes. An important amendment was made in 1968 for the purpose of introducing "Social Control" on the banks. To take over the 14 major commercial banks in India with effect from July 19, 1969, the Banking Companies (Acquisition and Transfer of Undertakings) Act was passed in 1970. To meet the changing requirements of the many enactments such as the Public Financial Institutions Laws (Amendment) Act, 1975, the Regional Rural Banks Act, 1976, the Banking Companies (Acquisition and Transfer of Undertakings) Act, 1980, etc. have been passed.

2.2. RESERVE BANK OF INDIA ACT, 1934

The Reserve Bank of India Act was passed in 1934 to establish the Reserve Bank of India, which is the guardian of the banking system in India. As the Central Bank of the country, the Reserve Bank of India Act contains provisions concerning the commercial banks. The Act provides for the classification of banks into scheduled banks and non-scheduled banks. Accordingly, a scheduled bank is one which is included in the Second Schedule to the Reserve Bank of India Act, 1934.

As per the conditions laid down in the Reserve Bank of India Act, 1934, a bank satisfying the following conditions can be included in the Second Schedule.

(*i*) It must have a paid up capital and reserves of not less than Rupees 5 Lakhs.

(*ii*) It does not conduct its affairs in the manner detrimental to the interest of the depositors, and

(*iii*) It must be a state co-operative bank or a company defined in the Companies Act, 1956, or an institution notified by the Central Government in this behalf or a corporation or a company incorporated by or under any law in force outside India.

A Scheduled Commercial Bank enjoys certain advantages such as getting financial accommodation from the RBI, cheap remittance facilities from the RBI, clearing facilities, etc. In order to enjoy these facilities, a scheduled commercial bank has to fulfil the obligation of maintaining statutory reserves with the Reserve Bank. It is not obligatory on the part of non-scheduled banks to maintain statutory cash reserves with the Reserve Bank.

Being the central bank of our country, the Reserve Bank of India performs all Central Banking functions and as such it performs the following functions:

(i) The Reserve Bank of India, being the sole authority of issusing of currency in the country, not only issues currency but also regulates the issue of currency in India. This power empowers the Reserve Bank of India to regulate and control money supply in the country.

(ii) The Reserve Bank of India acts as a banker to both the Central Government and also to the State Governments. The Reserve Bank of India not only looks after the financial transactions of the Government but also manages the public debt of the Government. The Bank undertakes to accept money and also makes payment on behalf of the Government.

(iii) The Reserve Bank of India acts as a banker to the commercial banks by keeping and maintaining their accounts just like the private individuals keep their accounts with commercial banks. As a banker to the commercial banks, the Reserve Bank of India also acts as a lender of the last resort to commercial banks.

(iv) In order to maintain price stability, the RBI exercises its control over the volume of credit created by the commercial banks.

(v) The Reserve Bank of India has the responsibility of maintaining the external value of the Indian Rupee just like maintaining the internal value of the currency. It is largely concerned with the organization of a sound and healthy commercial banking system in order to have control over credit through appropriate monetary and credit policies.

(vi) The Reserve Bank of India is also concerned with the development of rural banking, promotion of financial institutions and development of capital and money markets in India.

Apart from the above functions, the Reserve Bank of India has also taken up the following promotional measures:

(*i*) The RBI has established the Bill Market Scheme in 1952.

(*ii*) The RBI has helped to establish financial institutions to provide credit to the agricultural and industrial sectors of the economy.

(*iii*) The RBI has promoted the establishment of Regional Rural Banks (RRBs) with the help of commercial banks to extend banking facilities to the rural areas.

(*iv*) The RBI has not only helpped the establishment of an Export-Import Bank of India to finance exporters but also helped commercial banks to open branches in foreign countries.

(*v*) The RBI encourages and promotes research in the areas of banking.

Many powers are given to Reserve Bank of India to control the commercial banks by the Reserve Bank of India Act, 1934, and the Banking Regulation Act, 1949. The powers are as follows:

1. As supervisory and controlling authority over banks.
2. As controller of credit.
3. As banker to the banks i.e. as the lender of the last resort.

2.3. BANKING REGULATION ACT, 1949

The law governing the working and functions of banks in India was passed in 1949 and named as the Banking Regulation Act, 1949. Before passing this Act, the banking companies were governed by the Indian Companies Act, 1913. Since banking as a business has its own distinctive features, it was felt necessary to have a separate Act concerning only the banking companies. Hence an Act was passed in 1949, regulating the banking companies. In order to cover the co-operative banks also, the name of the Act was changed as the "Banking Regulation Act, 1949".

The Banking Regulation Act, 1949, was passed in February 1949 with the following objectives in view:

1. Comprehensive Legislation: The Indian Companies Act, 1913, was inadequate and unsatisfactory to regulate and control the business of banking in India and therefore, there was a need to have specific legislation containing comprehensive provisions, particularly to the business of banking in India.

2. To Prevent Bank Failures: The bank failures were common in those days due to inadequacy of capital and hence prescribing minimum capital requirements was necessary. The Banking Regulation Act, 1949, was enacted to prevent such bank failures by certain minimum capital requirements.

3. To Avoid Cut Throat Competition: The Act passed aims for avoiding cut throat and wasteful competition among the banking companies. The Act also regulates the opening of branches and changing the location of the existing branches.

4. Ensuring Balanced Development of Banks: In order to avoid indiscriminate opening of new branches and thereby ensuring balanced development of banking companies, the system of licensing is provided in this Act.

5. Regulation of Bank Credit and Working of Banks: The RBI has been given powers to approve the appointment, reappointment and removal of the chairman, directors and officers of the banks. This will ensure efficient and smooth working of banks in India.

6. Safeguarding the Interests of Depositors: The Act protects the interest of the depositors and the public at large by incorporating certain provisions such as prescribing cash reserves and liquidity ratios. This would enable the banks to meet the demand of the depositors.

7. Strengthening the Banking System: This Act provides for compulsory amalgamation of weaker banks with stronger ones to facilitate strengthening the banking system of our country.

8. Controlling Foreign Banks: The Act contains certain provisions which restrict the foreign banks to invest funds of the Indian depositors outside India.

9. Providing Quick and Easy Liquidation: The Banking Regulation Act also provides for quick and easy liquidation of the banks if they are not able to continue further or amalgamate with other banks.

The Banking Regulation Act, 1949, as amended up-to-date is divided into five parts and contains five schedules. This Act is applicable to all banking companies including co-operative banks. The provisions of this Act provide for achieving the above mentioned objectives for which the Act was enacted.

2.4. BANKING COMPANIES (ACQUISITION AND TRANSFER OF UNDERTAKINGS) ACT, 1970

The Banking Companies (Acquisition and Transfer of Undertakings) Act, 1970, is yet another legislation passed in India to nationalize the 14 major commercial banks in India having deposits of more than Rs.50 crores each in 1969. As per the provisions of this Act the ownership of the 14 top commercial banks viz., The Central Bank of India Ltd., The Bank of India Ltd., The Punjab National Bank Ltd., The Bank of Baroda Ltd., The United Commercial Bank Ltd. The Canara Bank Ltd., The United Bank of India Ltd., The Dena Bank Ltd., The Syndicate Bank Ltd. The Union Bank of India Ltd., The Allahabad Bank Ltd., The Indian Bank Ltd., The Bank of Maharashtra Ltd. and The Indian Overseas Bank Ltd. has been transferred to the Government of India. The aggregate deposits of these banks were Rs. 2632 crores and the total number of branches of these banks were 4130. However the independent entity of these banks has been protected and they are allowed to have their business in their old names. Though the Act empowers the Government to reconstitute any of the acquired banks into two or more banks or merge one with another, nothing in this regard has happened so far.

The Act provides that the entire capital of the new banks stands transferred to the Central Government. According to this Act, the general administration and management of the affairs of each nationalised bank is vested in a Board of Directors consisting of not more than fifteen members. Further, the Act provides that the net profits earned by the nationalized banks are required to be transferred to the Government of India.

2.5. THE REGIONAL RURAL BANKS ACT, 1976

The Regional Rural Banks Act, 1976, was enacted on 9th February, 1976, with a view to developing the rural economy of India. The Act was intended for the development of agriculture, trade, commerce, industry and other productive activities in the rural areas. The Regional Rural Banks provide finance mainly to small and marginal farmers, agricultural labourers, artisans and small entrepreneurs. The idea of starting Regional Rural Banks was conceived by combining the strong points of both commercial banks and co-operative banks.

The Regional Rural Banks Act, 1976, provides for the establishment of a Regional Rural Bank by a sponsor bank with the assistance of the Central Government. As per the provisions of this Act, the sponsor bank has to assist and help the Regional Rural Bank by subscribing to the share capital of such Regional Rural Bank. Further, the sponsor bank has to assist in providing the required managerial and financial assistance. The general administration and management of the affairs and business of a Regional Rural Bank shall vest in a Board of Directors consisting of not exceeding 15 members.

2.6. THE BANKING COMPANIES ACT, 1980

The Banking Companies (Acquisition and Transfer of Undertakings) Act, 1980, was enacted to replace an ordinance promulgated on 15th April, 1980, nationalising six more banks. The banks taken over were commercial banks whose demand and time liabilities exceed Rs. 200 crores. The main provisions of this Act relate to the establishment of new banks, business, share capital and management of these six banks. The banks taken over were: The Andhra Bank Ltd., The Corporation Bank Ltd., The New Bank of India Ltd., The Oriental Bank of Commerce Ltd., The Punjab and Sind Bank Ltd. and Vijaya Bank Ltd.

2.7. THE NEGOTIABLE INSTRUMENTS ACT, 1881

The Negotiable Instruments Act, 1881, contains important provisions relating to the negotiable instruments in which the banks normally deal. The negotiable instruments mainly concerned are Promissory Notes, Bills of Exchange and Cheques. It came into effect from 1st March 1882 and the Act is divided into 17 chapters and contains 137 sections.

The Central Government and the Reserve Bank of India are the two main authorities in India, which are responsible for administering the different provisions of the various legislations passed in respect of banking companies. These two authorities have separate departments of banking to look after all matters concerning the banking industry in India.

3

RELATIONS BETWEEN BANKER AND CUSTOMER

3.1. DEFINITION OF BANKER

Before examining the relationship between banker and customer, it is necessary to explain the legal meaning of the two terms. Till passing of the Indian Companies Act, 1936, there was no satisfactory statutory definition in India for a banker. Lot of efforts have been taken by many authorities on banking to define what exactly constitutes banking. As the banks have been performing multifarious functions and services, e.g., dealings in stocks and shares, trusteeship, executorship, etc. alongwith banking business, even the best authorities have found it rather hard.

Banking, an Evolutionary Concept

Many attempts were made to explain the exact significance of the term "banker", but most of them had their own defects. In a broad sense, the term is used resembling that of the financier, the capitalist, the stock broker and even high bank officials. The earliest successful attempt was made by the United States of America, through a legislation which defined banking as follows:

By "banking" we mean the business of dealing in credits and by a "bank" we include every person, firm or company having a place of business where credits are opened by the deposit or collection of money or currency, subject to be paid or remitted on draft, cheque or order or money is advanced or loaned on stocks, bonds, bullion, bills of exchange, or promissory notes, or where stocks, bonds, bullion, bills of exchange or promissory notes are received for discount for sale. (Indian Finance and Banking, by Firdlay Shirras, 2nd impression, p.336.)

The above definition is more like a description and does not have precision. The term banker can be applied to the credit merchant only when he uses the credit and funds of others. Otherwise he can be called as a captalist, if he uses his own funds. The Japanese Bank Act of 1927 defined banks as "institutions" which carry on businesses of giving as well as receiving credit.

The use of the word "bank" has been prohibited in Argentina, Belgium, Canada, Denmark, Germany and Italy. But in Zurich, any person could use the word "bank" as part of his name until the passing of Federal law wherein the bank was defined as an institution which appeals to the public for deposits.

There was no statutory definition in England for this term. Hence many writers on banking law attempted to give the essentials of the concept which are described below:

Dr. Herbert L. Hart, *the author of the well known treatise on Law of Banking, says, "A banker is one who, in the ordinary course of his business, honours cheques drawn upon him by persons from and for whom he receives money on current accounts.*" According to this definition, the essential function to enable a person or firm or institution to be regarded as a banker or a bank is that of receiving current deposits against which cheques may be drawn. This view is supported in the judgment of Buckley J in the Birkbeck Permanent Benefit Building Society (1912). This view was supported in the memorandum issued by the Ministry of Labour in England, wherein the expression "bank" was considered to include only those institutions where "a substantial part of the business consists of the receipts of money on current account to be drawn upon by cheques." (Banker and Customer by S.E. Thomas.)

Halsbury has defined Banker as "an individual, partnership or corporation, whose sole predominating business is banking, that is, the receipt of money on current or deposit account and the payment of cheques drawn by and the collection of cheques paid in by a customer". (Halsbury's Laws of England, 4th Ed., Vol. 3, p.31.)

The above view was supported by another great authority, Sir John Paget. Based on the Brickbeck Building Society Case, Sir John Paget says, that *"no person or body, Corporate or otherwise, can be a banker who does not (1) take deposit accounts, (2) take current accounts, (3) issue and pay cheques, and (4) collect cheques crossed or uncrossed, for his customers.*" (The Law of Banking by Sir John Paget.) Sir John Paget further adds that a person claiming to be a banker must profess himself to be one, and the public must accept him as such ; his main business must be that of banking, from which, generally, he should be able to earn his living.

However, no mention is made of other important functions of the present-day banker, such as (1) agency services and (2) other general utility services. Hence according to English Law, a person claiming to be treated as a banker should perform the functions as given by Sir John.

In India, till the passing of the Banking Companies Act, 1949, no restrictions were imposed on the use of the term "bank" or "bankers" by money-lenders. However, mere meney-lending does not constitute banking business. (Bank of Commerce Ltd. Vs. Kunj Behari Kar, 1945.) The Banking Regulation Act, 1949, defines banking Company, "*as a Company which transacts the business of banking in India*" and the word "*banking" has been defined as accepting, for the purpose of lending or investment, of deposits of money from the public, repayable on demand or otherwise, and withdrawal by cheque, draft, order or otherwise,*" vide section 5 (b) and (c). Accordingly, a banking company is one which performs the above functions. No banking company shall engage in any form of business other than those referred to above.

3.2. CUSTOMER

A customer is a person with whom the banker has some regular and formalised banking business. The important feature in this regard is the nature of the transactions and not the frequency of transactions. The dealings with the banker should be of a banking nature and regular in order to make a person a customer of the banker. Some casual services rendered by a banker to a person which are not of a banking nature could not entitle that person to be treated as customer. In the case of new customer, bankers do take considerable care in order to verify the bona fides of the customer before they allow him to open an account. A person may have some banking transactions with the bank without becoming a regular customer, such as purchase of bank draft. A banker enjoys several important protections under the Negotiable Instruments Act when he acts for a customer and it is important for a banker to ensure that he does not recklessly treat all persons as his customers.

3.3. CUSTOMER–OLD VIEW–DURATION THEORY

The term "customer" of a bank has not been defined by any law. But some eminent authorities have expressed their views. As per the views of Sir John Paget, *"to constitute a customer there must be some recognisable course or habit of dealing in the nature of regular* banking business". According to this definition, to constitute a customer of a bank, a person has to satisfy the following conditions:

(*a*) There should be a habit of dealing between him and the bank.

(*b*) The transactions should be in the nature of regular banking business i.e., frequency of transactions should be there.

As such, a person does not become a customer of a bank immediately on opening an account, i.e., a single and isolated act or transaction cannot constitute a customer. There must be some continuity of transactions.

Since the emphasis is placed on the continuity of transactions, i.e., duration of the bank account, this view is called as "Duration Theory".

3.4. CUSTOMER—MODERN VIEW: REJECTION OF THE DURATION THEORY

The duration theory was rejected long back. The "duration theory" of Sir John Paget was exploded by Mr. Justice Bailhache in the course of his judgment in the case of Ladbroke Vs Todd (1914). The facts of the case are as follows:

A cheque crossed 'account payee only' and payable to Mr. A was stolen by Mr. B. Mr. B forged the signature of Mr. A and represented himself to be Mr. A. He asked the banker to open an account in the name of Mr. A. The account was opened without any reference being asked for and obtained. The cheque was cleared and the greater part of the proceeds were withdrawn on the next day. The true owner of the cheque, Mr. A, sued the bank for conversion.

It was held that the relationship between the banker and customer began as soon as the first cheque was paid in and accepted by the banker for collection, i.e., as soon as the account was opened. It was further held that the banker was negligent in opening the account without obtaining satisfactory references and was therefore liable to the true owner of the cheque.

Thus, according to the laws, at present, duration is not the essence of the banker-customer relationship. A person becomes a customer of a bank at the moment money is deposited by him with the bank and accepted by the bank for collection, i.e., as soon as the account is opened.

This view was confirmed in the following cases:

(*a*) Commissioner of Taxation Vs English, Scottish and Australian Bank.

According to Dr. Herbert L. Hart, the author of the well-known treatise, Law of Banking, "*A banker is one who, in the ordinary course of his business, honours cheques drawn upon him by persons from and for whom he receives money on current accounts.*" This definition is based upon the dicta given in a number of decisions, beginning with Foley vs. Hill (1848). According to this definition, the essential function to enable a person, firm or institution to be called as a banker or bank is that of receiving current deposits against which cheques may be drawn.

Lord Dunedin, who delivered the judgment of the Board of the Privy Council, said, "*The word 'customer' signifies a relationship in which duration is not of the essence . . . . A person whose money has been accepted by the bank on the footing that the bank undertakes to honour cheques up to the amount standing to his credit, is, in the view of their Lordships, a customer of the bank in the sense of the statute irrespective of whether his connection is of long or short standing.*"

(b) In Savory & Co. vs. Lloyds Bank Ltd. (1932), it was held and concluded that frequency of transactions is not essential to constitute a person as a customer and hence a single transaction may constitute a customer. The facts of the case are: The plaintiffs were a firm of London Stock-brokers. They had two clerks in their employment, viz., Perkins and Smith. The plaintiffs sent out a number of cheques drawn on their bankers, The Midland Bank Ltd., and made payable to named payees or bearer.

These cheques were handed over to their clerks Perkins and Smith for posting. Instead of posting them as directed, Perkins and Smith stole the cheques and took them to a London branch of Lloyds Banks Ltd., with instructions to collect them, that is, in the case of Perkins, the amount of the cheques should be credited to his account, which he had at a branch of the Lloyds Bank Ltd. at Walkington, and in the case of Smith, to an account in the name of his wife at the Red Hill branch of the same bank. The first of these cheques was received before Mrs. Smith, in fact, became a customer. The Plaintiffs subsequently discovered the fraud of their clerks and sued the defendants, the Lloyds Bank Ltd., to recover the amounts of these cheques, on the ground of conversion.

In conclusion, it was held that frequency of transactions is not essential to constitute a person as a customer; but his position must be such that transactions are likely to become frequent. It means that, as soon as the banker receives cash or cheque to be collected on the definite understanding that the cheque is cleared, the relationship between the banker and his customer is said to have begun.

(c) Great Western Railway vs London and County Banking Company - If there was no sort of account he was not a customer. A person who merely comes to a bank for depositing valuables in safe custody or to collect the proceeds of cheques across the bank counter, cannot be called as the customer, unless he has "some sort of an account with the banker".

(d) Ladbroke vs Todd - Mere opening of an account without the actual drawing of money was sufficient to constitute a customer. It was held that the relationship of a banker and customer begins as soon as the first cheque is paid in and accepted for collection and not merely when it is paid. In the course of his judgment in this case, Mr. Justice Bailhache observed:

"... *a person becomes a customer of a bank when he goes to the bank with money or a cheque and asks to have an account opened in his name and the bank accepts the money or cheque and is prepared to open an account in the name of that person; after that he is entitled to be called a customer of he bank*".

(e) In Central Bank of India Ltd., Bombay vs V. Gopinathan Nair and others, the Kerala High Court has observed as follows "*So far as banking transactions are concerned, a customer is a person whose money has been accepted on the footing that the banker will honour up to the amount standing to his credit, irrespective of his connection being of short or long standing.*"

Therefore as per Modern view to be called as customer of a bank, the following conditions are necessary:

(1) A bank account–savings, current or fixed deposits–must be opened by making necessary deposit of money or by paying cheques for collections.

(2) Duration and frequency of the account are not essential tests although they may be anticipated.

(3) The dealings between banker and the customer must be of the nature of banking business. Any casual service rendered by a bank to a person does not however make him a customer if he has no account.

(4) Since anyone can become a customer of a bank as soon as an account is opened for him, it is essential for a banker to ascertain the reputation and integrity of the concerned person, before agreeing to transact the business with him. It was held in the case of Savory & Co. vs. Lloyds Bank Ltd. (1932). But, however, in the case of opening of fixed deposit account, the bankers do not generally ask for references and therefore, it is contended that, to some extent, if a person opens a fixed deposit account, he cannot be a customer of the bank. If a deposit account is opened by means of a cheque to which the prospective customer has no title, the banker will not be entitled to claim protection if no enquiry concerning the customer is made

at the time of opening of the account. Hence normally no banker would open a fixed deposit account by means of a cheque.

Thus, a person who has an account in a bank is considered to be a customer of the bank, irrespective of whether his connection with a bank is of long or short standing.

3.5. BANKER-CUSTOMER RELATIONSHIP

Banker customer relationship can be divided into two categories as follows :

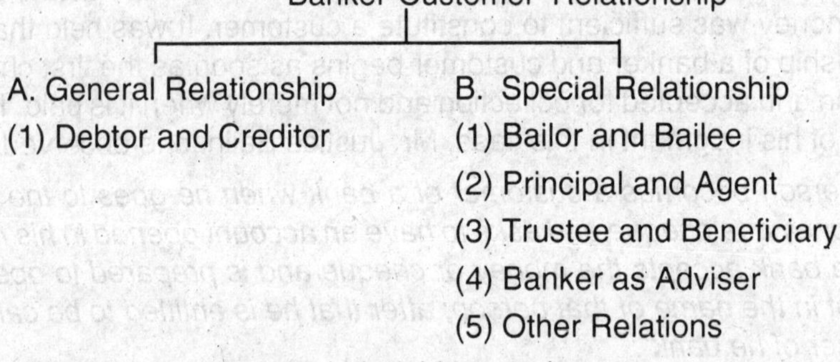

Let us discuss these relationships one by one.

A. General Relationship:

The general relationship includes the following:

1. Debtor and Creditor relationship: The relationship between a banker and his customer is mainly that of debtor and creditor. The respective positions depend on the state of account. Normally the banker is debtor and the customer generally keeps some amount in his account with the bank. In other words, customer's account generally shows a credit balance. But in the case of an overdraft the banker is a creditor. In the case of a loan account, banker is a creditor and the customer is a debtor. Thus Sir John Paget remarks: "*The relation of a banker and customer is primarily that of debtor and creditor, the respective position being determined by the existing state of the account.*"

On the opening of an account the banker assumes the position of a debtor. He is not a depository or trustee of the customer's money because the money deposited with the banker becomes a debt due from him to the customer. In other words, the banker does not keep it as it is and to give back the same notes or coins deposited by the customer. The understanding is that the money once deposited becomes the property of the bank and the banker is allowed to deal with the money in any manner he thinks it proper. As long as the customer's account shows a credit balance, the banker would be a debtor and in case the customer's account shows a debit balance, the banker would be a creditor.

This point of view was confirmed in the case of official Liquidator, Hanuman Bank Ltd. vs K.P.T. Nadar and others. In this case it was held that "the mere fact that a banker invites deposits, and is prepared to pay interest on them, is proof enough of his intention to make use of it as he likes and earn interest therefrom, so as not only to enable him to pay interest to his depositor but also to earn profits for himself. But even if the banker pays no interest on the money deposited, he is his customer's debtor and not a bailee, because he undertakes to repay on demand a sum equivalent to the amount deposited with him and the customer has no right whatsoever to claim the identical coins or notes deposited by him with his banker. The latter can pay the amount in any kind of legal tender". This fact has been established also by the decision given in following Indian cases; Dharmadas vs. Gangaderi, Subramanyam Chettiar vs. Kadireshan, Ichhars Natha Isher vs. Jiban.

In Velji Lakshamsey & Co. Vs. Dr. Banaji (1955), the Bombay High Court has thrown further light on the relation between banker and customer by holding that the relation between a banker and its customer is that of a debtor and creditor and any amount due by the banker to the customer cannot be claimed by the customer from the banker as a preferential creditor in case the bank is under liquidation. But suppose, the customer has given any specific instruction to the banker that certain amount must be paid to a certain person, then till the amount is paid as per the directions of the customer, the banker here acts as an agent and the agency would continue. Therefore the bank would hold the amount not as a debtor of the customer but in the capacity of a trustee.

Normally the banker is in the position of a debtor and the customer is that of a creditor. But when the account is overdrawn, the roles are changed; the banker becoming a creditor and the customer the debtor.

A depositor is an unsecured creditor as he has no charge over the assets of his banker. But when a loan is granted to him by a banker on some securities, the banker becomes a secured creditor of his customer. The position continues till the repayment of the loan by the customer. In the case of clean loans, however, the bank is in the position of only an unsecured creditor.

However, this debtor-creditor relationship is subject to the following peculiarities which are not there in similar commercial relationships, as the banker is a privileged debtor.

(1) Not time-barred: The deposit with a bank does not become time-barred on the expiry of threc years. On the other hand, an ordinary debt becomes a time-barred debt after the expiry of three years. The statute of limitations begins to run only when the amount becomes due. Based on the decision in the Joachimson vs. Swiss Banking Corporation case in 1921, the limitation period does not begin to run until the customer has made a demand for repayment.

(2) Creditor must demand payment: The debt due by a banker to his customer differs from ordinary commercial debt where demand for payment by the creditor is not necessary. In other words, the debtor (i.e. borrower) himself has to pay money to the creditor. But in the case of debt due from a banker, demand for payment is necessary. In other words, the customer who has deposited money in the bank (i.e. debtor) must ask the bank to pay money. He must demand payment; then only the banker has to pay. It was held in Joachimson vs. Swiss Banking Corporation that in the case of a debt due from a bank an "express demand" for repayment by the customer is necessary.

(3) Proper place and time of demand: When the bank accepts money on a current account, it promises to honour its customer's cheques in so far as the amount is sufficient and available. The obligation to repay the amount is limited to the branch where the account is kept. In other words, a customer can issue cheques on the branch of the bank where the account is kept. This view was expressed in' Clare & Co. Vs. Dresdner Bank '(1915). It was held that the bank is under an obligation to repay the amount at the branch where the account is kept and during banking hours.

The facts of the case are that the plaintiffs viz., Clare & Co. had an account at the Berlin branch of the defendant bank, i.e., Dresdner Bank., which has its head office in Germany, and a branch in London. They wrote to the London branch demanding payment of the balance due on the account at the Berlin branch and upon refusal to pay sued the London branch without having made any request to the Berlin branch to pay or to transfer the balance to London. It was held that locality was an essential part of the debt due by a banker to his customer and that his obligation to repay was confined to the place where the account was kept.

(4) Demand to be made in proper manner: Deposits are withdrawable by cheques, drafts, and order or otherwise. Demand for refund must be made by means of cheques or order as permitted by the banker. The amount should never be returned on oral instructions.

This point actually came for decision in Joachimson vs. Swiss Banking Corporation (1921), where it was held that in the case of a debt due from a bank, an express demand for payment by the customer is necessary before the debt becomes "actually and accruing due", on the ground that, othewise, the banker, by offering the money due to his customer, would summarily close his customer's account without notice and possibly injure his customer's credit by dishonouring his cheques.

B. Special Relationships:

(1) Bailor and Bailee Relationship: The bank becomes a bailee in case of the valuables or securities deposited with him for safe custody. It is his duty to preserve them properly and hand them over to the customer. The banker does not get the ownership of these articles. The ownership remains with the customer. In this case banks are acting as bailees. It is the duty of the bailee to redeliver the same goods to the bailor along with any profit or surplus that might have accurued from the goods so bailed.

It is to be noted that money deposited with the bank is not the subject matter of bailment because the banks do not pay the same coins or notes deposited, nor are they liable to surrender to the customers any profit made by them from utilization of the money so deposited. Except his obligation to honour the customer's cheques, the deposited money is entirely at his disposal.

(2) Principal and Agent: A banker also acts as an agent of his customer and performs a number of agency functions for the convenience of his customer. When banks undertake to purchase or sell securities, collect cheques, bills, interest, dividends etc., and pay insurance premium on behalf of their customers, banks act as

(3) Trustee and Beneficiary: In certain circumstances, when the banker acts as a trustee with regard to securities and valuables deposited for safe custody the banker's position is different. The funds or assets coming into his hands in the capacity of a trustee must be applied only for the specific purpose. But ordinarily, a banker is not a trustee or a bailee of the moneys deposited with him. He is a debtor and possesses complete freedom to use the funds.

For example, when a customer pays into his bank a cheque drawn upon another bank, such a cheque being received by the bank, he collects it on belhalf of the customer. So, he cannot acquire any by the rights of a holder for value i.e., he cannot have better title than that of the customer himself. On the other hand, if the deposit is made for a specific purpose, and the banker stops payment before applying it to such purpose, the depositor cannot claim the money paid and must content himself with his right of proofs as a general creditor (In re Barned's Banking Turner, 1857). But the case is different if the specific purpose has been partially carried out. In the case of Farley vs. Turner (1857), a customer of Bank A had £ 942 to the credit of his account. He paid in another sum of £ 707 with a written direction that £ 500 out of that sum should be forwarded to bank B, but before the bill became due, the bank A ceased to carry on business and the sum £ 500 was returned by bank B. The customer claimed back this £ 500, and it was held that, as the amount had been specifically appropriated, it belonged to him and not to the general creditors.

The position of a banker as a trustee or as a debtor is determined according to the circumstances of each case. For example, in case of a cheque received by the bank from a customer for collection from another bank as a bill for collection, the banker acts as a trustee till the cheque is realised and credited to his customer's account and thereafter he will be the debtor for the same amount. As a trustee, it is his duty to take care of the lockers and their contents.

(4) Banker as agent and advisor: When a banker buys or sells securities on behalf of his customer and renders other services, he is acting as an agent of his customer. Similarly, when he collects cheques, dividends, bills or promissory notes on behalf of his customer, the banker is acting as agent of the customer concerned.

(5) Other relations: The banker is a lessor, when he lets out safe deposit lockers. When the bank undertakes to render advice to corporate customers on financial matters and to manage their new capital issues, he acts as a Manager to the issue. The banker may undertake to make deferred payments or underwrite share capital or loans, or establish letters of credit or even act as an executor or administrator on behalf of his customer. In that case, he assumes the role of a guarantor.

The nature of relationship between the banker and the customer can be explained as follows:

Type of deposits and functions	Nature of relationship	
	Banker	Customer
1. Deposit account	Debtor	Creditor
2. Loan account	Creditor	Debtor
3. Safe Deposit Lockers	Bailee	Bailor
4. Collection of cheques / Instruments	Agents	Principal

3.6. SPECIAL FEATURES OF BANKER-CUSTOMER RELATIONSHIP

The special features of banker and customer relationship have the following rights and obligations:

Special Features of Banker-Customer Relationship

A. Rights	**B. Obligations**
(1) Bankers' Right of General lien	(1) Obligation to honour cheques.
(2) Bankers' Right of set off	(2) Obligation to maintain secrecy.
(3) Bankers' Right of Appropriation	(3) Obligation not to close the account of the customer without proper notice
(4) Law of Limitation	
(5) Bankers' Right to charge compound Interest.	
(6) Bankers' Right of Incidental expenses.	

3.6.1. A. RIGHTS

It includes the following:

1. Right of General Lien: One of the important rights enjoyed by a banker is the right of the general lien. Lien means the right of the creditor to retain the goods and securities owned by the debtor until the debt due from him is paid. It confers upon the creditor the right to retain the security of the debtor and not the right to sell it. Lien may be either (i) a particular lien or (ii) a general lien.

(i) Particular Lien: Particular lien confers upon the creditor the right to retain the particular security offered for the particular debt. Public carriers and craftsmen who have expended their labour, time and money on the goods and securities enjoy particular lien.

It arises in respect of transactions relating to the goods over which the right of lien is exercised. For instance, suppose Mr. A has given two pieces of cloth to a tailor for stitching two shirts. A can pay stitching charges of one shirt and ask that it should be given to him. The tailor cannot say that he could return both the shirts if the stitching charges for both of them are paid.

(ii) General Lien: In contrast to the above, bankers, factors, wharfingers, attorneys of High Court and policy brokers have a general lien.

General lien denotes the right of a creditor to retain any goods and securities bailed to him for a general balance of account. Section 171 of the Indian Contract Act, 1872, confers this right upon bankers, factors, wharfingers, and attorneys of a High Court. Thus a banker is entitled to exercise this lien on all securities placed in his hands as a banker by his customer. The only condition is that they should have been specifically appropriated.

The bankers can retain all the goods belonging to their debtors until the entire sum due to them has been paid. Since the banker has got a general lien he can retain all the articles belonging to customer until the whole amount due to him has been repaid.

For example, Mr. X, a customer, has borrowed Rs. 1,00,000 from a banker on the security of some Government Bonds, and a further sum of Rs.50,000 on the security of gold ornaments, Suppose the customer repays Rs.50,000 and asks for the return of the gold ornaments the banker can say that he would return the gold ornaments, and the government securities if the customer repays the entire sum of Rs.1,50,000 due to him. In other words, the banker can retain the security in respect of both the loans granted by him even if one of the loans is cleared. According to Indian Law, the banker can exercise his right of lien not only in respect of the securities that come into his possession but also in respect of the goods that may come into his hands. Banker's lien covers "all securities deposited with him as bankers by a customer unless there be an express contract, or circumstances that show an implied contract inconsistent with lien".(Brandao vs. Barnett, 1846)

The right of general lien enjoyed by bankers was judiciously recognized as early as 1864 in Brandao vs. Barnett and in that case it was decided that "*bankers most undoubtedly have a general lien on all securities deposited with them as bankers by a customer unless there be an express contract or circumstances that show an implied contract inconsistent with lien.*" This general lien on the banker is regarded as something more than an ordinary lien; it is an implied pledge. So far as Indian Law is concerned the position is clear. No agreement is necessary for creating lien. Section 171 of the Indian Contract Act 1872 has already conferred that power.

However, this right of general lien cannot go beyond the agreement. In C.R. Narasimha Shetty vs. Canara Bank (1990), the aggrieved customer, Mr. C.R. Narasimha Shetty, had purchased a vehicle under hire purchase agreement by executing a hypothecation deed. Though the entire loan due was paid by the plaintiff, a sum of Rs. 3694.90 was still due to the bank towards ground rent charges, seizure charges, etc. and also for the open cash credit limit of Rs. 50,000 sanctioned to a firm in which he was a partner and for which the vehicle was offered as a collateral security only. Under these circumstances, the banker exercised the right of general lien by seizing the vehicle. The plaintiff argued the case saying that no right of lien was available to the banker in respect of the debt due by the firm. If was held that thc banker could not exercise his lien over the vehicle for the cash credit dues of the firm, since the hypothecation deed had not given any right to the bank to seize the vehicle for the dues of the firm. The bank was directed to return the vehicle, of course, subject to the payment of Rs. 3694.90 only. Thus, it is clear that a lien cannot go beyond the terms of the loan agreement.

But in another case, Vysya Bank Ltd. vs. Akkem Mallikarjuna Reddy, the customer had obtained two gold loans and one crop loan. The two gold loans were repaid, but not the crop loan. Here the banker refused to return the gold jewels, exercising lien on them for the amount due under the crop loan. But the customer pleaded that the banker couldn't exercise his right of general lien on the jewels, and the jewels were deposited specifically for the gold loans only. It was held that the bank can exercise his general lien on jewels because there is an agreement "*to retain the gold ornaments for all the monies now owing or which shall, at any time thereafter, be owing to the bank in any capacity whatsoever.*"

No Agreement is necessary for creation of Lien: No agreement to create the right of general lien for a banker is necessary under the Indian Law, because such an agreement is implied under the terms of Section 171 of the Indian Contract Act 1872 so long as the same is expressly excluded.

Conditions to be satisfied for exercising Lien: No agreement is necessary to create the right of lien in favour of the banker. But certain conditions must be fulfilled to arise the right of lien. They are:

(*a*) The securities should have come into the possession of the banker in his capacity as a banker. That is, they should have been deposited with him as security for loan granted to the customer or for the purpose of being credited to his account. For instance, a banker cannot exercise his lien in respect of securities deposited with him for safe custody, because they are entrusted to him in his capacity as a trustee and not in his capacity as a banker.

(*b*) The securities should not have been entrusted to him for a special purpose. If the customer gives some securities specifically for a particular loan, he can take away the security after the loan is repaid. This is what is meant by the term "Express Contract" referred to in Brandao vs. Barnett. If securities are entrusted to him for a specific purpose, they become available to him only for that purpose.

(*c*) The lien does not arise in respect of documents or valuables left with the banker inadvertently. Suppose a customer has brought some securities with him for the purpose of offering them as security for his loan. But the loan is refused. If the customer has forgotten to take those securities with him and left them on the Manager's table, the banker cannot exercise lien over those securities.

(*d*) The possession of securities must have been lawfully obtained in his capacity as banker. For instance, the banker cannot exercise lien in respect of articles belonging to the customer obtained through the use of force.

(*e*) There should have been no agreement inconsistent with lien.

(*f*) The lien arises only in respect of articles belonging to the customer in the same capacity. For example, a customer has a credit balance in his account and the account of partnership of which the customer is a partner is in debit. The banker cannot exercise his lien on the credit balance belonging to the customer for the amount due by the firm although he is a partner of the firm. This is because the credit balance and the debit of the customers are not held by him in the same capacity. These are confirmed in Halesown vs Westmnister Bank Ltd. (1970).

Similarly, if a customer has a debit balance in his individual account and a credit balance in his trust account, the banker cannot exercise his lien over the credit balance in the trust account. But if there are no separate accounts and if the trust transactions are passed through the individual account, the bank can exercise his lien in respect of the trust securities also, because he cannot distinguish between the two catogories of the transaction.

(*g*) The banker cannot exercise his lien over the securities of the customer in respect of the amounts that may become due to him on a future date. For example, a banker has accepted a bill of exchange on behalf of a customer payable after two months. The banker cannot use the balance in the customer's account for meeting such a bill. Similarly, if a banker has granted a loan to a customer repayable after the expiry of a fixed period, the banker cannot exercise any lien on the securities of the customer even before the debt has become due for repayment.

(*h*) It has been decided that a banker can exercise his right of lien on securities deposited with him in respect of which he has the right to collect interest by filling in the coupons. But if a customer entrusts securities to the banker for safe custody, and he himself fills the interest coupons (which he entrusts to the banker for collection), the banker can exercise his lien on the interest coupons and not on the securities.

(*i*) A banker can exercise his lien even in respect of securities deposited with him for debts which have become time-barred. The Law of limitations is not a part of substantive law, but deals only with the procedure for enforcing claims. It does not lay down that time-barred debts are discharged. Hence the right of lien can be exercised even in respect of debts which have become time-barred.

Exceptions to the Right of Lien: However, a banker cannot exercise his rights of lien in certain cases:

(*a*) If the goods and securities have been entrusted to him as a trustee or as an agent of the customer, the banker cannot claim the right of lien on those properties.

(*b*) When a customer sends a cheque or a bill with clear instruction to utilise its proceeds for a specific purpose, the banker cannot exercise his right of lien on them.

(*c*) When some securities or documents are left with the banker by mistake or negligently, he cannot exercise the right of lien over such securities or documents.

(*d*) The banker has no lien on the credit balance in the personal account of the partners of the partnership firm. The reason is that credit balance on one hand and debit balance on the other do not exist in the same capacity.

Banker's Lien is an implied pledge : Normally a lien permits the creditors only to retain the possession of the property. But the banker's lien is of unique type because;

(a) It not only confers upon the banker right of retainer.

(b) But also the right of resale.

In other words, a banker is entitled to sell the goods or otherwise deal with the securities in his possession for the purpose of realising his dues. Hence, banker's lien is like a pledge and it is also defined as an "implied pledge". In case of pledgee the creditor enjoys the right of sale. Accordingly, banker has the power to sell goods and securities in case of default by the customer. Thus the banker enjoys the privileges of a pledgee and can dispose of the securities after giving proper notice to the customer. For this no separate agreement is necessary. However to be on the safe side, the banker takes a letter of lien from the customer. This right extends to all properties and securities except title deeds of immovable properties.

Thus banker's lien is in fact an implied pledge. Lien confers on the creditor the right to retain goods belonging to the debtor until his debt is cleared. But it does not give him the right to sell the goods and apply the proceeds towards the repayment of the debt. Pledge on the other hand gives the creditor such right. Since the banker's lien is an implied pledge, the banker has the right to sell the securities deposited with him if the customer fails to repay the loan within the stipulated time. If no time to repayment is fixed, he has to give a reasonable notice to the customer the intention to dispose of the security and apply the proceeds for the liquidation of the loan.

Thus banker's lien entitles him to sell the property that comes into possession, if the debtor (customer) commits default. The sale proceeds collected by the banker shall be applied to recoup the dues and the surplus is returned to the debtor. In case sale proceeds are not sufficient to cover the total claims due from the debtor, then the banker can recover the deficiency in a separate legal action.

The banker's lien is a composite of right of the following :

(*a*) Right of possession,

(*b*) Right of sale to recoup the dues, and

(*c*) Right to sue for the difference, if the sale does not yield proceeds to cover the whole amount of dues.

2. **Banker's Right to set-off :** The right to combine or set-off of accounts implies the right of a debtor to adjust a debt owed to him by his creditor. In other words, the debtor can pay only the balance amount after adjusting the mutual claims. A banker is also endowed with this right and as a result he can combine the debit balance in the account of a customer with the credit balance in other account of the same customer.

There was no unanimity of view regarding the point whether a banker has the right to combine accounts of a customer against amounts due from him to the banker, when two or more accounts were opened separately. According to the view held by some cases, such a right to combine accounts is exercisable by a banker.

This view was based upon the decision in Garnett vs. Mekerran (1872). In this case, a person had an overdraft with one of the branches of a bank and it was not cleared. After some years, the customer opened an account in another branch of the same bank. The credit balance in the second account was a little over the debit balance in the first. The bank combined the two accounts without giving any notice to the customer. This led to the dishonour of cheques drawn by the customer. As a result the customer filed a case against the banker for wrongful dishonour of his cheques. The court held that the banker had the right to combine the two accounts of the customer and set off the credit balance in one account against the debit balance in the other, as there was no agreement or usage obliging the banker to keep the account separate. It was also held that the banker need not give notice of his intention to combine the account, although it would be proper to do so. There was however no legal obligation on the part of the banker to give such a notice.

Some others opine that such right cannot be exercised without prior consent of the customer. As such, where a banker uses such right, the customer's credit may suffer if his cheques drawn on his credit balance are dishonoured (because of such combination of accounts). In the case of Greenhalgh vs Union Bank of Manchestor (1924) the judge observed, "*If a banker agrees with his customer to open two accounts or more, he has not, without the assent of the customer, any right to move either assets or liabilities from one account to other; the very basis of his agreement with his customer is that two accounts shall be kept separate.*"

That is, when the banker opens two or more accounts in the name of the same customer, he is not entitled to transfer assets or liabilities from one account to another without the consent of the customer. The very fact that the banker had agreed to open separate accounts obliges him to keep them separate.

In view of the conflicting decisions on the point, the banker is well advised to give prior notice of his intention to combine the accounts. Such a prior notice becomes unnecessary only if he can prove that he has the right to combine the two accounts by virtue of established course of business in support of his action. In order to avoid trouble, it is desirable that the banker should secure the right of combining the several accounts standing in the name of the customer by an express authorisation from the customer in this behalf. That is, by taking a letter of set off from customer who opens, in his own name, more than one account. Having done this, when necessary, the banker could combine them without liability to strike a balance by offsetting debit and credit balance of different accounts, (even where it is given by the letter of set-off will apply to existing debts only and not to future debts). To claim set-off, the credit balance of a private account against the debit balance of a joint account, the general rule is that there is no right of set-off between joint and separate debts.

For example,

(1) A's credit balance cannot be setoff against the joint debt of A and B unless (*i*) A has expressly agreed that it can be done or (*ii*) A and B have agreed to be both jointly and severally responsible for the debts in their joint names.

(2) The joint credit balance in the account of A and B cannot be set off against debt in either of the single names, unless both A and B have agreed that it can be done. Similarly the banker has no right to set off a partner's private account against on partnership account, unless there is an express contract to this effect. Where the partners have undertaken to be severally as well as jointly responsible for partnership liabilities, the bank can set off their credit balances against such liabilities. Likewise, the money held by a person in a fiduciary capacity (e.g., Secretary of an Association), cannot be set off against his private debt due to the same bank. If a depositor who has an overdrawn account (in addition to a current account with credit balance), assigns his debt to another person and notice of assignment is given to the bank, it can set off the overdraft against assignee's deposit.

Conditions to be fulfilled to set off : The right of set-off may be exercised subject to the fulfilment of the following conditions :

(*a*) Both the accounts of the customer must be in the same name and in the same right. The same right means that funds belonging to someone else but standing in the name of the account holder should not be made available to satisfy his personal debts. For example, the credit balance of a partner's personal account cannot be set off against the debt due by his firm or vice versa. Similarly, an overdrawn personal account cannot be combined with credit balance in the trust account maintained by the same customer.

(*b*) The funds in a trust account are deemed to be in different rights and therefore, a debit balance in a personal account cannot be set off against the credit balance in the trust account which may be in the name of the customer.

(*c*) The right of set-off may, however, be applicable to existing debts due from the customer and not to contingent debts or liabilities falling due at a future date. That is, the right can be exercised only against debts due on that date and not against a future debt.

(*d*) The amount of debts must be certain, for example, the credit balance of a guarantor cannot be set off against the debt due by the debtor unless the latter defaults and the liability of the guarantor is determined.

(*e*) This right of set-off is available to the banker only if there is no agreement to the contrary.

Circumstances under which the right of set-off arises automatically:

Under the following circumstances, the banker's right to set off arises automatically:

(*i*) On the death or insolvency of a customer.

(*ii*) On the insolvency of a partner of a firm or on the winding up of a company.

(*iii*) On receipt of garnishee order (he can first exercise this right of set-off and surrender only the balance to the judgement creditor).

(*iv*) On receiving notice of assignment of a customer's credit balance.

(v) On receiving notice of a second mortgage over the security charged to the banker.

3. **Right of Appropriation - (Clayton's Rule):** This is the right of a banker to appropriate the money paid by the customer to any one of the loans including a time-barred debt. But, however, once the customer gives specific directions regarding appropriation, the banker has no right to alter them. It is his bounden duty to carry out the instructions of the customer. In the absence of any such direction from the customer, the banker shall have the right to appropriate the payment to any debt or account according to his discretion. But the banker should inform the customer accordingly.

When a debtor makes a payment, he may appropriate it to any particular debt he likes. The creditor is bound to act in accordance with the appropriation made by the debtor. If the debtor has not appropriated, the creditor may apply the payment to any debt owing by the debtor. The creditor is conferred the legal right to do so. The creditor may apply the payment to any debt barred by the statute of limitations. But if neither the debtor nor the creditor has made any specific appropriation, then the law appropriates the payment in the chronological order. This is what has been laid down in the Clayton's case. It is said that the first item on the credit side, and the balance if any, has to be carried forward to the next item and treated in the same way.

Appropriation of Payments: Where the customer has more than one account, the banker would follow the instruction from the customer; the banker can credit the proceeds to any of the accounts and advise the customer accordingly. If any account shows a debit balance the proceeds may be utilized towards this account even if it is time-barred.

In the case of single account of the customer with the banker where overdraft facility has been allowed, the first credit into the account adjusts the first debit in the account. Thus the customer is not entitled to draw on the accounts the proceeds of the cheque credited until the overdraft is cleared. This is known as the Rule in Clayton's case and is incorporated in the Indian Contract Act under section 61.

In case both the banker and the customer have not used their powers, the rule given in Clayton's case would be applied. In this case, it was laid down that if no specific appropriation is made, whether by the debtor or the creditor, the law appropriates the payment by discharging or reducing the first item on the debit side of the current account by the first item on its credit side. Thus under this rule the sum first paid in is the sum that is first paid out. This rule is popularly known as the Rule in Clayton's case and vitally affects current accounts , especially when overdrawn. The facts of the case are as follows :

Clayton's case Devaynes vs Noble (1816) : A firm of bankers known as Devaynes, Davies, Noble & Co. has five partners. Devaynes, one of the partners, died and the surviving partners carried on the business of banking under the same name. The executors of the deceased partner objected to the continuance of the name of the Devaynes in the firm's name. After a year the firm became insolvent and all the customers (creditors) of the firm made their claims against the estate of Devaynes, the deceased partner.

N. Clayton was one of the creditors who continued to deal with the surviving partners by making payments to and receiving payments from the firm. At the time of death of Devaynes, Clayton's balance was £ 1713. During the next few days he withdrew several times and made payments and thus the balance was only £ 453 at the time of bankruption of the firm. A summary of the transactions between the firm and Clayton showed that the firm had paid him more than £ 1713 after the death of Devaynes. But Clayton claimed the balance amount £ 453 from the estate of the deceased partner on the following contention:

The withdrawals from the account after the death of the partner were paid out of the deposits made by him in the same period and thus the credit balance standing at the time of death of Devaynes was recoverable from his estate.

But these arguments were not accepted by the court and Clayton's claim was rejected. Sir William Grant M.R observed the general rule of appropriation as follows:

"*This is the case of banking account where all the sums paid in the form of one blended fund; the parts have no longer any distinct existence. In such a case there is no room for any other appropriation than that which arises from the order in which the receipts and payments take place and are carried into the account. Presumably, it is the sum first paid in, that is first drawn out. It is the first item on the debit side of the account that is discharged or reduced by the first item on the credit side*". Thus the first item on the debit side will be the item to be discharged or reduced by a subsequent item on the credit side. The credit entries in the account adjust or set off the debit entries in the chronological order. In other words, the payment should be used in the discharge of debts in order of time. The rule derived from the Clayton's case is of great practical significance to the banker.

Significance of the rule in Clayton's case: Where a customer owes more than one debt to the same bank and pays an amount which is not sufficient to completely liquidate any of the debts, then the appropriation of the amount can be made as decided in the Clayton's case, as follows:

(i) The debtor can indicate how the amount paid by him is to be appropriated, i.e., which particular debt the amount is to be adjusted;

(ii) In the absence of instruction from the debtor, the creditor can appropriate the amount according to his choice; and

(iii) In the absence of the above two, the rule says that the first debt is to be offset by the first credit.

The rule in Clayton's case applies to current accounts. It states the principle of appropriation of payment when there is no specific appropriation by the debtor or creditor.

For example, Mr. X has borrowed Rs.20,000 on 1st January, Rs.30,000 on 1st February and Rs.40,000 on 1st March 2001 from Y. In other words, X-the debtor owes several debts to Y (i.e. the creditor). Suppose the debtor (i.e. X) makes payment of Rs.15,000 to creditor-Y on 1st June. The debtor has the right to say which debt shall be cancelled or reduced by the payment he has made. He may apply the amount of Rs.15,000 towards reducing the third debt. The creditor is bound to make appropriation according to the instruction given by the debtor. Similarly, a customer may say that the amount he is depositing should be used to a particular bill or cheque. If he instructs so, the banker must appropriate the payment as directed by the customer.

If the debtor does not state to which debt the amount should be applied or appropriated at the time of payment, the creditor may appropriate the payment as he likes. He may use the amount paid to reduce or cancel any debt including time-barred debt. The creditor shall inform the method of appropriation adopted by him to the debtor. Then it cannot be changed. In other words, it is irrevocable.

Precautions to be taken: The Rule of Clayton's case is of great importance of significance to a banker. The rule of Clayton's case applies to an account which is still running. If the account is broken and a new and fresh account is opened, the rule does not apply to the old account. The reason is all deposits and withdrawals will be credited and deposited to the new account. So a banker should stop the operation of the old account and open new account in order to avoid the application of the rule in Clayton's case.

Similarly, when a partner dies and the firm has an overdraft, the banker should stop the account. This will make the estate of the deceased partner liable for the payment of the debt to the bank. A new account must be opened in the name of the surviving partners. The precaution will avoid the operation of the rule in Clayton's case.

When a guarantor dies, the banker must close the old account of the customer (i.e. borrower). This will make the legal representatives of the deceased guarantor liable for the payment of guaranteed debt in case of default. If the account is continued, the rule in Clayton's case will apply. According to this rule, a payment shall discharge the earliest debt.

4. **Law of Limitation:** A debt becomes time-barred if it is not repaid within three years after it is contracted. In other words , no action can be brought against the debtor in respect of the money due by him after the expiry of three years from the time of the debt. The amount deposited in a bank is also a debt repayable by the banker to the depositor (customer) but in this case the statute of limitations commences from the date on which the customer demands his money back. Thus although three years might elapse from the date money is deposited in a bank without any transactions having taken place, the debt due by the bank will not be time-barred.

In Joachimson vs. Swiss Bank Corporation, it was clearly laid down that the period of limitation does not begin to run until a demand for payment is made by the customer. In this case a partnership was dissolved on 1st August 1914, by the death of a partner and there was a balance of $2321 standing to the credit of the firm on that date. The balance was sought to be recovered six or seven years later. It was held that demand was necessary in order that the debt may become actually and occurring due and consequently the period of limitation began to run, not from the date of the debt but from the date of demand for payment. In India Article 23 of the Limitation Act of 1963 provides a period of three years from the time when the demand is made by the customer.

In the case of fixed deposits there is a difference of opinion as regards the date from which the statute of Limitation applies. According to some, it begins from the date of expiry of the period for which deposit is made while according to others, it begins from the date of demand for payment of the amount of fixed deposit. If the return of fixed deposit is made a condition for the payment of the amount, the period of limitation commences from the date of return of the deposit receipt.

In the case of loans and overdraft granted by the banker, the period commences from the date of the loan or overdraft, since they are loans and not amounts deposited with the banker. Under the provisions of Section 26 of the Banking Regulation Act, 1949, Banking Companies have to submit an annual return of all accounts which have not been operated for ten years giving particulars of the deposit standing to the credit of each such accounts. But in the case of money deposited for a fixed period, the period of ten years will be counted from the date of expiry of such fixed period.

A curious case on the point to law of Limitation came before the courts of England. In 1866, once Mr. X deposited a huge amount with his banker on the condition he could withdraw it any time after giving 14 days notice. Mr. X died and 61 years, thereafter, a legal heir of Mr. X came across the deposit receipt and filed a suit thereon against the bank. In this suit no question of Limitation arose because the bank could not prove any demand on the part of Mr. X after the lapse of this extraordinary time. However, fortunately for the bank, the court came to the conclusion that an inference of repayment could fairly be raised in the circumstances of the absence of all relevant entries regarding the deposit in the current records of the bank. The suit was therefore dismissed [Douglas vs. Lloyds Bank Ltd. (1934)].

In the case of fixed deposits to the effect of the Law of Limitation, opinion differs. It is felt by some that there should not be any distinction between fixed and current deposits, i.e., the period of limitation starts immediately when the customer has made a demand upon the banker asking him to pay the deposit in the fixed deposits also. But as per the views of others, the period of limitation will begin to run from the expiry of the specified time, if the customer has given notice to the banker to withdraw the deposit after a specified time. Though the latter view appears to be sound, the return of the deposit receipt is made a precondition to the withdrawal of the money, its return of the deposit receipt is fixed as the starting point of the period of limitation. Hence, until the demand is made, time does not begin to run even in the case of valuables left for safe custody.

In the case of overdraft granted by a banker to his customer, the period will begin at the time the overdraft is made use of. The reason is, that an overdraft granted by a banker is a loan and not money deposited with the banker.

5. Banker's right to charge Compound Interest: As creditor, a banker has the right to charge interest on loans and advances granted to his customers. It is the practice of the bankers to charge interest every half year but they can charge compound interest unless there is an agreement to the contrary. It is an implied right given to the bankers. The arrears of interest is also treated as a debt and bankers charge interest on this also.

6. Banker's right to claim incidental charge on unremunerative accounts: In the course of his relationship with a customer, a banker has the right to claim incidental charges.

As long as the relation of a banker and customer exists, the banker has an implied right to claim commission, interest and other incidental charges for the services rendered to the customers. They are not payable in cash, but are debited in the account as and when they become due. If a customer is unable to keep a remunerative credit balance, the banker in India charges Rs.10 to Rs.50 per half year. But in England in the case of unremunerative account, the customer is required to pay a certain sum per year or a certain percentage (from $\frac{1}{8}$ to ¼ per cent) on the turnover of his account during the year.

3.6.2. B. OBLIGATIONS

1. Obligation to honour cheques: Accepting of deposits of money from the public is one of the essential functions of a banker according to the definition of banking as given in the Banking Regulation Act, 1949. The bulk of the resources of the banks are mobilized by accepting deposits from the public. The most important statutory obligation of the banker is to honour the cheques drawn by the customers against their respective accounts. It is the duty of the banker to refund the money deposited by the customer whenever he (customer) demands by issuing cheques either in his own favour or in favour of third parties.

It is clearly mentioned in section 5 (b) of the Banking Regulation Act, 1949,that banking means – "*acceptance for the purpose of lending or investment of deposits of money from the public, repayable on demand or otherwise and withdrawable by cheques, draft, order or otherwise.*" Accordingly, banking business implies the receipt of deposits repayable on demand.

By opening a current account in the name of a customer the bank undertakes to honour cheques drawn by a customer, so long as the latter's balance is sufficient , cheques are in proper form and are presented in a reasonable time. The banker has also such an obligation even if there is not sufficient money to the credit of the customer if the customer has obtained an overdraft facility covering the amount of the cheque. According to practice, banks do not honour cheques presented six months after their ostensible date of issue. Such cheques are called 'stale cheques'.

The obligation of the banker to honour the cheques of the customer is a statutory obligation. Section 31 of the Negotiable Instruments Act reads as follows:

(*i*) The drawee of cheque, having sufficient funds of the drawer in his hands, required properly applicable to the payment of cheque, must pay the cheque duly required, to do so and in default of such payment he must compensate the drawer for any loss or damage, caused by such default.

(*ii*) This obligation may be extended by an agreement, express or implied to the amount of overdraft agreed upon. In the absence of an overdraft arrangement, the banker can dishonour the customer's cheque if there is no credit balance in favour of the customer, or if it is not sufficient to meet the cheque. The banker need not make a part payment of the cheque presented to him for payment (to the extent of the balance available); he can dishonour the cheque in its entirety.

(*iii*) Sometimes a customer may deposit cheque and bills for collection and credit to his account. He may draw a cheque on the banker in anticipation of such collection. The banker is not bound to honour the customer's cheque , if the customer's cheque and bills are not realised by the time the cheque is presented for payment. The banker must take reasonable time for crediting the funds before they can be drawn against.

Garnishee Order: The banker's obligation to honour a customer's cheques is extinguished on receipt of a court order known as the Garnishee order which is under order 21, Rule 46 of the Code of Civil Procedure, 1908.

Garnishee order is a judicial decree passed by a competent court on the banker, directing him to withhold or suspend payment of any money belonging to a debtor who may be found to have defaulted in satisfying the debts owing to his creditor. The creditor for whom it is issued is called 'judgement creditor; the debtor is called 'judgement debtor' and the third party on whom order is issued is called as 'Granishee'.

This order is issued in two parts:

(*a*) The court directs the banker to stop payment out of the account of the judgement debtor. It is an order called 'Order Nisi' seeking explanation from the banker as to why the funds in the said account should not be utilised for meeting the judgement creditors' claim.

(*b*) After the banker files his explanation, if any, the court issues the final order called 'Order Absolute' whereby the funds in the account are attached to be handed over to the judgement creditor.

Thus it is an order by the court served on a third party known as Garnishee directing him not to release any money due to the judgement debtor as the amount is attached by the court.

Effects of Garnishee Order: When Garnishee order is issued, the following will be the effect on the banker:

(*i*) The banker has to suspend operation of the account of the judgement debtor.

(*ii*) The cheques drawn by the judgement debtor on the Garnishee account should not be honoured after the order is issued on the bank.

(*iii*) When the order is made absolute, the balance available should be made over to the judgement creditor as per the direction of the court. If the customer's balance is not sufficient to cover the dues, then the banker has to pay whatever is available on the judgement debtor's account.

(*iv*) It restrains the banker from paying the debts due or occurring due (i.e. current account as well as fixed deposit account).

(*v*) The suspended account of the judgement debtor may be revived after payment has been made to the judgement creditors as per the direction of the court.

Thus on receipt of such an order, the banker is bound to pay the funds to the judgement creditors and his liability towards his customer is thus discharged. The banker is prohibited from paying amount due on the date of receipt of the Order Nisi.

Non-appliance of Garnishee order: The Garnishee Order is not binding upon the banker in the following cases:

(*i*) When the banker proves that judgement debtor identified as quoted in the order is doubtful.

(*ii*) When the judgement debtor's account with the banker is overdrawn and unused portion of the cash credit.

(*iii*) If the account of the judgement debtor is previously assigned to a third party and the banker has a due notice of it.

(*iv*) If the banker himself is entitled to a 'set-off' a debt due from the judgement debtors, then the banker is to be given the prior right to recover his dues.

(*v*) When the judgement debtor holds funds in trust and the banker is aware of this fact.

(*vi*) Joint account in the name of the judgement debtor and any other person cannot be attached in respect of a debt due from the judgement debtor alone.

(*vii*) In case of funds coming into the banker's hands subsequent to receipt of the Garnishee order, they are not attached.

(*viii*) In the case of a firm's account it is not attached by Garnishee order provided the order is issued against only one of the partners.

Thus the obligation of a banker to honour his customer's cheque is extinguished on receipt of a Garnishee order issued by the court under code of civil procedure.

Specimen form of intimation sent to the customer on dishonouring of the cheque:

Cheque No. ....For Rs.............................

Is returned for Reason No...

1. Effects not yet cleared: please present again.
2. Not arranged for.
3. *********************payee's endorsement required.
4. *********************payee's endorsement irregular.
5. Refer to drawer.
6. Drawer's signature differs.
7. Endorsement requires bank's guarantee.
8. Alteration requires full signature.
9. Cheque is post-dated.
10. Cheque is out of date.
11. Crossed cheque must be presented through a bank.
12. No advice.
13. Payment stopped by the drawer.
14. Payee's separate discharge to the bank required.
15. EXCEED ARRANGEMENT.
16. INSUFFICIENT FUND.
17. Collecting banker's clearing stamp required.
18. Others.

XYZ BANK LTD

DATE:

Asstt. General Manger

Consequences of wrongful Dishonours:

(1) A banker has the statutory obligation to honour his customer's cheques unless there are valid reasons for refusing payment of the same. In case the banker dishonours the cheque intentionally or by mistake, he is liable to compensate the customer for the loss suffered by him. According to Section 31 of the Negotiable Instruments Act, 1881, the words "Loss or damage" do not mean only pecuniary loss, but also a loss of credit or injury to reputation.

Thus, it is to be noted that the banker is liable to compensate the drawer not only for the actual monetary loss suffered by him but also for the loss of his credit or injury to reputation. It is more significant and it is the foundation on which his business depends. Therefore, he is entitled to claim not only the general damages, but substantial damages for such loss or damage suffered by him.

(2) Without appropriate reasons if a customer's cheque is dishonoured by a banker, he incurs the liability of paying damages for affecting adversely the customer's credit and goodwill. A customer has every right to claim substantial damages from a banker where he can prove in a court of law that his reputation has been spoiled even where he has not incurred monetary loss. The compensation payable need not have any relation to the amount of the cheque. On the other hand, the smaller the amount of the cheque dishonoured, the larger may be the compensation payable by a banker. In assessing the damage, the court will take into consideration various factors like financial positions, business reputation of the customer, custom of the trade in which he is engaged, etc.

Cases relating to this are given below:

(*i*) Gibbs vs.Westminster Bank (1939) – In this case, Mrs.Margaret Gibbons issued a cheque for £ 9 Sh.16 drawn on the Westminster Bank to her landlord in payment of rent. The cheque was dishonoured owing to a failure on the part of the bank to credit the money previously deposited by her. She was awarded only Sh.40 as nominal damages, since she being a non-trader was not entitled to recover substantial damages.

(*ii*) Davidson vs. Barclay's Bank Ltd. (1940). – In this case the plaintiff was awarded £ 250 as damages for the wrongful dishonour of his cheque amounting to just £ 2-15. In this case heavy damages were awarded since Davidson was a trader and injury to his credit worthiness on account of wrongful dishonour of the cheque for a small amount was considerable.

(*iii*) The banker can escape the liability if it is proved that the customer has nothing to lose either in financial terms or in the form of credit status.

Substantial damages would be awarded only to businessmen and traders because they are the persons who obviously suffer much from loss of reputation through dishonour of cheques.

In Sterling Vs. Barclays Bank, a cheque given by Mrs.Sterling was wrongfully dishonoured. Two cheques issued by her were dishonoured for want of sufficient balance. She was awarded reasonable damages but not substantial damages for the reason that traders in her business line did not attach much significance to dishonour of cheques issued by them.

Although a banker has the obligation to honour the customer's cheques, he has no similar obligation with regard to the payment of bills domiciled with him (that is trade bills made payable at the bank) unless there is an express agreement with the banker in that behalf or unless there is a recognized habit on the part of the banker to do so.

In the case of non-trader customers, the loss of credit or reputation is not to be taken for granted as a result of wrongful dishonour of their cheques. Therefore, they are entitled to only nominal damages. However, if it is proved in the court of law that they have sustained special damages, they would be entitled to recover the same as was held in the case of Canara Bank vs V.I. Rajagopal (1975).

In New Central Hall vs United Commercial Bank Ltd. (1959), the Madras High Court held : "*In case where a cheque issued by a trader-customer is wrongly dishonoured, even special damage could be awarded without proof of special damage or loss. The fact that such dishonour took place due to a mistake of the bank is no excuse, nor can the offer of the bank to write and apologise to the payee of such dishonoured cheques affect the liability of the bank to pay damage for their wrongful act*".

The liability of a bank for a wrongful dishonour of a cheque is towards the drawer and not the payee. The payee or the holder of the cheque cannot make the banker liable for dishonour as was held in the case of Meghiya Malsa Ltd. vs P.S. Commen (1963).

Conditions to honour cheques: Thus, the banker is bound to honour his customer's cheques provided the following conditions are fulfilled:

(*a*) There must be sufficient funds of the drawer in the hands of the bank.

(*b*) The funds must be properly applicable to the payment of the cheque i.e., if some funds are earmarked by the customer for some specific purpose, the said funds are available for honouring his cheques issued for such purposes.

(*c*) The banker must be duly required to pay. This means that the cheque must be presented before the banker at proper time, i.e.., within a period of six months from the date of issue.

(*d*) A banker is not bound to credit his customer's account with the amount of cheques or drafts drawn upon other banks, sent in for collection, before they are realized. The amount must, however, be credited to the customer's account with a reasonable time after realisation. The question what constitutes a reasonable time depends upon the circumstances in each case.

(*e*) There is no legal cause (ex. service of a Garnishee Order) which makes the credit balance or the agreed overdrafts limit unavailable.

(*f*) They are presented during banking hours.

Therefore, for wrongful disonour of cheques, the defaulting banker will be liable for the damages as under:

1. If a customer is a trader or businessman, he is entitled to claim heavy and substantial compensation for the damage done to his credit as a result of wrongful dishonour of cheques. It was decided in the case of Roline vs. Steward. He need not prove that he has actually sustained loss or credit standing has been adversely affected, because damage to reputation follows as a matter of course, when the customer is in trade or business.

2. In case of a customer who is a non-trader, the actual damages caused to his reputation must be proved to support the claim for compensation. The court may ask the banker to pay nominal or reasonable damages to the non-trading customer on the merits of each case (Gibbons vs. Westminster Bank Ltd.).

3. Even if cheques were dishonoured due to oversight or inadvertent errors on the part of bankers, substantial damages are to be paid to the customers in business (Roline vs. Steward).

4. Even if the cheque is for small amount, its wrongful dishonour may entail award of heavy damages (Davidson vs. Barclays Bank).

5. If it is proved that the customer concerned has nothing to lose either in financial terms or in form of credit status, then the banker may escape the liability.

Thus, if a banker dishonours cheque without proper grounds, the customer can claim damages for the injury caused to his credit. The amount of compensation is fixed by the amount of loss or damage suffered by the customer owing to such dishonour.

2. Obligation to maintain Secrecy: Another special feature of the relationship between the banker and customer is that the banker should not, except on reasonable and proper occasions, disclose matters relating to the customer's account. This restriction is imposed because the disclosure of customer's financial position may do considerable damage to his credit standing and business reputation. This obligation to maintain secrecy was judiciously recognised only in 1924 in the case of Tousier vs. National Provincial Bank of England. According to that decision, a banker should not disclose the condition of his customer's account except on reasonable and proper occasions. This obligation does not cease even after the customer's account is closed.

What is to be regarded as a reasonable and a proper occasion is a matter to be answered. Instances of proper occasions are disclosing the state of affairs to a proposed guarantor or under the compulsions of law. In case an overdraft is guaranteed, it would be appropriate that the guarantor has a right to be informed of the extent of his liability and the banker has every right to disclose to him the condition of the customer's account so far as it is necessary for the purpose. In the case of Robshan vs. Smith (1878), it was considered as an uncodified duty of a banker to answer the queries relating to his customer's general position and character, when asked by a person who is contemplating business relations with that customer.

But the legal sanction has been provided under section 13 of the Banking Companies (Acquisition and Transfer of Undertakings) Act, 1970. It orders the nationalized banks to observe (except as otherwise required by law) the practices and usages customary amongst bankers, and in particular not to divulge any information. This duty, according to Sir John Paget, exists not only during the existence of the customer's account but also after the customer's death; it is immaterial whether the account is in debit or credit.

Disclosure of information: According to section 13 of the Banking Companies Act, the duty of maintaining secrecy may be dispensed with under two circumstances. They are:

(1) Statutory necessity and (2) Bankers practices and usages. In Tousier's case it was agreed that the duty is not *absolutely qualified,* but it was asserted that the duty is a legal one 'arising out of contract'. Hence the banker will not be liable for disclosing his customer's account in reasonable and proper occasions. The learned judge in the above mentioned case has classified the 'occasions' under four heads:

(*a*) Disclosure under compulsion of law.

(*b*) Where there is duty to the public to disclose.

(*c*) Where the interest of the bank required disclosure.

(*d*) Where the disclosure is made by the express or implied consent of the customer.

(a) Disclosure under compulsion of law:

A banker is obliged to disclose particulars of his customer's account when he is compelled by court to do so. There are also provisions under the various other statutes which provide for similar powers as are vested in a civil court when trying a suit in respect of (i) discovery and inspection; (ii) enforcing the attendance of any person including any officer of a bank and examining him on oath; (iii) compelling the production of books of accounts and other documents, and (iv) issuing commissions.

It is the duty of banker to disclose information relating to his customer's account when the law compels him to do so. The following are some of the statutory provisions that fall in the category.

1. Section 131 of the Income Tax Act, 1961.
2. Section 285 of the Income Tax Act, 1961.
3. Section 240 of the Companies Act, 1956.
4. Section 4 of the Banker's Book Evidence Act, 1891.
5. Section 45B of the Reserve Bank of India Act, 1934.
6. Section 26 of the Banking Regulation Act, 1949.
7. Section 86 of the Gift Tax Act, 1958.
8. Section 94(3) of the Criminal Procedure Code.
9. Section 43 of the Foreign Exchange Regulation Act, 1973.
10. Section 29 of the Industrial Development Bank of India Act, 1975.

(b) Disclosure as duty to the public:

A bank is also justified in disclosing its customer's affairs on the ground of 'duty to the public'. The banker may disclose his customer's account to prevent frauds and crimes, for example, if a customer is trading with enemy country during times of war, the banker is justified in disclosing this in the interests of the state. Thus, in the following situations the banker can disclose the information in the interest of general public:

(*i*) His customer is engaging in the prohibited trading activity.

(*ii*) In case of breach of faith to the state.

(*iii*) His customer is having dealings with enemy countries.

(*iv*) His customer is violating the provisions of any law.

(*v*) His customer is receiving sizeable funds from a foreign country.

Thus in the abovementioned situations the banker must report to the Government and furnish necessary information in public interest.

(c) Disclosure on own interest of banks:

A banker will not make himself liable if he discloses the customer's account to protect his own interest.

(*i*) When a customer fails to pay money due to the bank, the banker has to file a suit for recovery of the debt. In such a case he has to reveal the state of the customer's account to the guarantor.

(*ii*) If the banker has to recover the dues from the customer or the guarantor, disclosure of necessary facts to the solicitors or guarantor becomes necessary and is justified.

(*iii*) The interest of the bank will involve disclosure of details of the customer's account particularly when there is a litigation between the two. When a banker makes a claim or brings an action against a third party (for example, a guarantor) disclosure is inevitable.

(*iv*) A case on the point of banker's right to disclose was well brought out in Sunderland vs. Barclays Bank Ltd. Mrs. Sunderland issued a cheque on Barclays Bank in favour of a dress maker. The cheque was returned alleging lack of funds. The real reason was that she issued a cheque to a book-maker which was honoured by the bankers. She complained about the dishonour of the cheque issued in favour of the dress maker i.e., to her husband. He directed her to take up the matter with the bank. She phoned up to the Manager. During the conversation Mr.Suderland interfered. The Manager informed him that the cheques drawn in her account were in favour of book-makers. Mrs. Sunderland brought an action against the bank. She stated that the bank was responsible for breach of duty in disclosing her account to her husband without her consent. The judge opined that the interest of the bank required disclosure and that disclosure was made with the implied consent of the customer. The Manager was right in thinking that the wife had no objection in explaining to the satisfaction of her husband.

(d) Disclosure on express or implied consent of the customer:

In case where a customer expressly authorises his bank to disclose his account to a third party, he may do so. A common instance is that where a customer gives a banker's reference, when the customer introduces a person to the bank as the proposed guarantor, the banker cannot be penalised for answering surety's questions. The banker gets an implied authority to disclose his customer's affairs.

When the customer gives the name of his banker to other businessman for the purpose of trade reference, the banker will be justified in giving answer to the reference made because an implied consent of the customer for such disclosure is presumed to exist in such cases.

In case the customer directs the banker in writing to intimate the balance in his account to his agent or employee, the banker would be justified in furnishing to such person, of course, the required information and no more.

In certain circumstances the implied consent of the customer permits the banker to reveal the condition of the customer's account to a person who guarantees the loan taken by the customer. Implied condition should not be taken for granted in all cases even where the customer and the enquirer happen to be husband and wife.

Trade Reference : The customer may himself give the name of his banker as reference to a third party. The banker can answer all such references.

Risks of unwarranted and unjustified disclosure:

If a banker discloses information unjustifiably, he shall be liable to his customer and to the third party as follows :

(*a*) Liability to the Customer : The customer may file a suit in the court of law against the banker for the damages suffered by him as a result of such disclosure. Substantial amount may be claimed if the customer has suffered material damages,

(*i*) if it can be proved that the information furnished is highly defamatory, and

(*ii*) he has suffered material damages.

(*b*) Liability to third parties : A banker is liable to third parties in the following situations :

(*i*) If he furnishes false information, knowing it to be false to a third party.

(*ii*) Such party relies on it and suffers losses. Such third party may ask the banker to compensate him for the losses suffered by him.

Since there is no contractual relationship between the banker and the third party, negligence on the part of the banker will not make him liable. Only if the charge of fraud is established against him, he can be held liable.

In answering enquiries from fellow bankers, he should exercise utmost care and should give only the general position of the customer as revealed by his account. He should not rely on rumours that may be afloat regarding the customer. If the banker gives false information regarding the customer, there is the danger of the customer suing him for damaging his credit. On the other hand, if he gives too bright a picture of the customer which is not justified by the state of the customer's account, the person who might extend credit to the customer on the basis of such report may sue him for misrepresentation. Therefore, the bankers must be very careful in answering the references made by third parties regarding the customer's account. He should give his replies in general terms only in order to avoid liability for defamation on the one side and misrepresentation on the other. Further he should reply to the references in utmost confidence.

It has been decided in Banbury vs. Bank of Montreal that the bank is not responsible for the statements made by the bank Manager and further that the bank Manager himself is not liable if he does not sign the letter. Sometimes, therefore, some bank Managers do not append their signatures on the replies to references replied by them. They further expressly state in the letter that the information is given 'in strict confidence' and 'without prejudice'.

When furnishing information relating to the customer, the banker need not make any enquiries regarding the customer. It is enough if he furnishes information on the basis of the entries made in his books of account. He should give only broad facts but should not indicate the customer's actual balance. If the customer happens to be a joint stock company, the banker should state whether it had formerly issued any debentures. He should particularly furnish such information when the bonds are in his own name.

3. Obligation not to close the account of the customer without proper notice.

Closing of accounts means the severence of the relations between the banker and customer by the withdrawal of the customer's balance in the hands of the banker, either by the customer's own act or at the request of the banker. The customer, if he so wishes can very easily close the account by drawing a cheque for the entire amount of his balance. But in view of the minimum balance that he is obliged to maintain under the rules of the bank, he has to inform his banker of his intention to close the account and return the unused cheques remaining with him.

But the banker should not close the account of a customer without giving sufficient notice. In the absence of such an obligation a banker may close the account of the customer at any time and dishonour all the outstanding cheques issued by the customer, thus injuring the latter's credit. That is why it is laid down that a banker should not close the account of the customer without giving sufficient notice. Further the amount standing to the credit of the customer does not become due unless it is demanded and hence the banker should not pay it off.

What constitutes sufficient notice is a question of fact. In Prosperity Ltd. vs. Lloyds Bank, it was held that a notice of one month was not sufficient in the circumstances of the case.

The facts of the case are : The plaintiffs launched a snowball scheme of insurance. Lloyds Bank agreed to act as banker to the company and to accept proposal forms and subscriptions sent in by would-be participants in the scheme. Many thousands of people in England and in other countries joined the scheme. The bankers reconsidered the question of their being the bankers for the company and decided to disassociate themselves from the scheme. Accordingly they gave one month's notice to close the account. It was held that in view of the widespread ramifications of the scheme and in view of the banker's being so closely involved in the scheme, one month's notice to close the account was insufficient . Although the company asked for an injunction restraining the bank from closing the account, a declaration was made to the effect that one month's notice was insufficient. Injunction was refused on the ground that an injunction is not appropriate for the enforcement of a contract of debt and that damages will be a sufficient remedy.

When the banker wishes to close the account, he usually sends a written intimation requesting the customer to withdraw his balance. He will not receive further credits in the customer's favour and allows the balance gradually to disappear if the customer refuses to close the account by withdrawing his entire balance.

QUESTIONS

1. Define the terms "banker" and "customer" and bring out the relationship that exists between them.
2. What is Banker's lien? When can he exercise such a lien?
3. Discuss the general relationship between a banker and his customer. Illustrate your answer with reference to a current account and a loan account.
4. What is meant by 'banker-customer relationship'? State some of the instances which do not come under this relationship and explain why.
5. State the special features of the relation between banker and his customer. Is the former bound to honour latter's acceptances?
6. "A banker is bound to honour his customer's cheques". To what extent is this true? Discuss fully.
7. What is the legal position of a banker if (a) he pays a cheque after business hours, (b) he irregularly dishonours a cheque drawn by his customer?
8. What is a garnishee order? What steps should a banker take on receiving such an order relating to one of his customers who has (a) credit balance in his account, (b) a fixed deposit for 6 months and (c) a deposit repayable at 7 days notice?
9. Is a banker legally obliged to maintain secrecy with regard to the state of his customer's account? In what case is a disclosure justified?
10. What precautions should a banker take when requested to give his opinion about the credit and standing of a customer ? On what occasions is he justified in disclosing the state of his customer's account?
11. State the Rule in Clayton's case regarding appropriation of payment. Illustrate the operation of the rule with suitable examples.

DIFFERENT TYPES OF ACCOUNTS

The banker solicits deposits from heterogeneous types of people in different walks of life having different forms of financial status. Thus he has introduced different kinds of accounts tailor-made to cater to their interests. They are :

- Demand deposits – popularly known as current accounts in India;
- Time deposits – known as fixed deposits;
- Savings deposits; and
- Combination of any two or three of the abovementioned accounts such as recurring deposits, retirement plan and cumulative time deposit accounts, etc.

4.1. DEMAND DEPOSITS

Demand deposits are popularly known as current accounts and are technically referred to as floating deposits. It includes savings bank deposits also. The banker is under an obligation to repay deposits on demand. Hence they are 'demand deposits'.

(a) Current Deposits: A current account is a running account between a banker and his customer. A customer can operate his current account any number of times during a working day. Thus, it has unrestricted operation. Current accounts represent a banker's demand liability, since they are to be repaid on demand. In recent years the ratio of demand liabilities of the Indian scheduled banks is on an increase in relation to the time liabilities. This proportion is not the same for all banks. It varies from time to time. As regards responsibilities thrown upon the bankers, the current deposits have been more important than the fixed deposits. By accepting current deposits the banker undertakes to honour his customer's cheques up to the credit balance in his account. The banker should exercise reasonable care on honouring customers' cheques. He will be personally liable where he pays a forged cheque. Similarly he cannot pay cash on crossed cheques across the counter. The banker has to supply the cheque form and pass book to the current account holder, free of charge. But now-a-days, some bankers charge a certain sum as bank charges. He has to keep sufficient funds in hand to meet the demands of his customers.

No interest is allowed on current accounts by bankers in India and in England.

A minimum balance is to be kept by the customer. This enables the banker to earn something on the minimum balance agreed to be kept. The banker's experience will teach him what proportion of the current deposits he must keep as reserve so as to meet the normal demands of his customers. Current accounts are generally opened by large scale businessmen, joint stock companies, institutions, etc.

Special features of current account: The current account carries certain privileges which cannot be enjoyed by savings bank account holders.

1. The basic objective of current account is to facilitate the handling of cash dealings and reducing the risks involved in it.

2. Current accounts do not carry any interests on the amounts of deposit.

3. Most banks charge incidental charges on such accounts which depend upon the balance kept.

4. Cheque book facility can be availed of by all the current account holders but only a few savings bank deposit account holders can avail this facility.

5. Third party cheques can be collected only through current account.

6. Overdraft facilities are available only to current account holders.

7. Other forms of loans such as cash credit can be availed only if current accounts are maintained. The loans and advances provided by the banks to these customers are made available through the current accounts.

Advantages to the customer of having a Current Account: Opening of a current account is convenient to the customer due to the following reasons:

(*a*) As cash, cheques and drafts are deposited in the bank's account, they will be perfectly safe.

(*b*) The customer can make his payments more conveniently by issuing cheques. He need not count cash at the time of making payments. This not only reduces errors but saves time.

(*c*) Payment to creditors situated at distant places is facilitated.

(*d*) Collection of cheques drawn on banks situated outside the place of business becomes easier.

(*e*) The paid cheque forms at the bank serves as a receipt. It can be referred to in case of dispute.

(*f*) Nomination facility is available for Current Account holders opened either individually or in joint names of depositors.

(*g*) Current Account can be transferred from one branch to another at the nearest of the account holder.

(*h*) If the cheques issued by the customer when passed cause a debit balance in the account for whatsoever reason, it would be deemed by the bank as an implied authority by the customer to the bank to pass the cheques and allowing a temporary debt / overdraft.

(*i*) Standing instruction for remittance such as insurance premium, subscription for clubs etc. will be carried out by his bank subject to levy of service charges in force.

However, the bank reserves the right to close unremunerative and undesirable current account after giving due notice to the account holder.

(*b*) Savings Deposits: Savings deposits have their origin in the trustee savings banks of England. These were institutions similar to banks. They were established for the receipt of money from the depositors. A depositor of such a bank could have only one account at a time. Main object of such banks was to encourage savings habit among the people.

In India, the history of savings banks dates back to 1833, when the trustee savings banks were organized in the presidency towns. In 1863-64 the management of trustee savings banks was transferred to presidency banks. In 1882, post office savings bank came into existence in a number of post offices in the country. Since 1958, even the post office savings deposits can be drawn through cheques.

Savings Deposits in Commercial Banks: While current accounts are usally meant for business people, savings deposits are popular with fixed income receivers, particularly to the middle class. Today commercial banks have found it to be profitable to accept savings deposits. To a commercial bank one great advantage in savings deposits is that it can maintain a little cash reserve to meet withdrawals on these accounts. Generally, there is a restriction regarding withdrawals on savings bank account. It may be in the form of restricting number of withdrawals during a month or a week or fixing a maximum for withdrawal during a stipulated period. Heavy amounts can be drawn by giving prior notice.

To inculcate banking habit among people, banks today permit withdrawal of savings deposit through cheques. To encourage more and more savings, attractive rate of interest (present 4.5%) is given on savings bank deposits. Generally interest is allowed on minimum monthly balances. Usually commercial banks and post offices allow interest on deposits received up to the end of first week of every month to enable those receiving salaries and wages to deposit their savings and earn interests. Banks are now providing such facilities to savings bank account holders as the collection of cheques and safe custody of their valuables. The important feature of this kind of deposits is that it promotes saving habit among fixed income receivers. They can deposit and withdraw even small amounts.

Special Features of Savings Bank Account: A savings bank account is meant for the people of the lower and middle classes who wish to save a part of their current incomes to meet their future needs and also intend to earn an income from their savings. It has the following special features:

(1) These accounts are intended to cater to the requirements of low income and middle class families who are having regular income.

(2) The banks mop up the savings of people through the savings bank accounts. That is the basic objective of savings bank accounts as it encourages developing the savings habit among people.

(3) Any person can open a savings bank account with as little as 100/- rupees.

(4) Payment of Interest: Savings bank balances carry some interest. At present interest allowed on these accounts is 4.5%; but it varies from time to time. This is more attractive than the current account where virtually no interest is paid.

(5) A depositor can withdraw as small a sum as Rs.10.

(6) Restrictions on withdrawals: In pursuance of the objective of the savings bank account, bank imposes restriction on the right of the depositor to withdraw money within a given period.

(7) If the banker is satisfied, the customer can get the use of cheque book facility.

(8) Accounts can be opened in the individual or joint names of depositors. Accounts can also be opened and operated by minors , provided they have completed 14 years of age and have the power of understanding.

(9) Savings bank accounts can be transferred from one branch to another at the request of the account holder.

(10) The minimum balance to be maintained in an ordinary S.B. Account is Rs.250. In accounts where cheque books are issued, a minimum balance of Rs.500 is to be maintained. Where the minimum balance in cheque operated accounts falls below Rs 500, a service charge of Rs.10 will be levied on each occasion irrespective of the number of days for which the position continues. But the minimum balance may vary from bank to bank.

Limitation of Savings Bank Account: The savings bank account has the following limitations:

(*i*) Restrictions on withdrawals: The banks restrict the number of withdrawals in any savings bank account.

(*ii*) Banks do not accept cheques or other instruments payable to third parties for collection in savings bank account.

(*iii*) When the cheque book facility is not provided, banks insist on the personal appearance of the customer for withdrawal of funds from savings bank account. That apart, pass books must accompany the pay order. This procedure causes inconvenience to the busy customers.

(*iv*) Interest also is not allowed on daily balance. It is calculated on the minimum credit balance maintained in the account between 10th and the last day of a month. So interest paid is negligible.

(*v*) Moreover banks do not wish to keep substantial balances in the savings bank account.

In spite of all of these limitations and restrictions, savings bank accounts become popular. These accounts render useful service in spreading the banking habit amongst the rural masses.

4.2. OPENING OF A NEW ACCOUNT

Before opening a new account, a banker should take certain precautions, i.e., the applicant who wants to open an account with a bank must be properly introduced to the banker. If the banker opens an account without proper introduction or shows carelessness in this regard, the chance of fraud or misrepresentation may occur. By making necessary enquiries from the references furnished by the new customer, the banker can easily verify and judge whether or not the person wishing to open an account is a desirable person.

4.2.1. General precautions to be taken by a bank in opening of a new account

By opening an account with the banker, a customer enters into relationship with a banker. The special features of a banker-customer relationship impose several obligations on the banker, e.g., honouring of cheques drawn by the customer, maintenance of secrecy of the account, etc. To safeguard the interest of banker, it is necessary that bankers should open only for honest, reliable, and responsible parties. Therefore before opening an account, the banker should observe the following precautions:

1. Application on the prescribed form: To open an account the customer is required to mention his name, occupation, full address, specimen signature and the name and signature of a person for reference. He also undertakes to comply with the bank's rules in force from time to time for the conduct of the account.

2. Introduction of the applicant: Before opening a current account the banker should obtain reference from respectable parties as to the proposed customer's integrity and responsibility. A bank should enquire from responsible parties given as references by the customer about the latter's integrity and honesty. If a bank fails to do this, it will result in serious consequences not only to it but also for other banks and the general public. By allowing a person to open an account without satisfactory introduction or reference, a banker would be inviting unpleasant consequence. By obtaining a cheque book, a dishonest person may use it for nefarious purposes. Further, if the person happens to be an undischarged bankrupt, the banker would be facing serious consequences.

What constitutes proper introduction?

(1) The banker should take reasonable care in accepting the introduction or reference from any person. Hence it is necessary that the person introducing the applicant who comes to the banker for opening an account must himself be a respectable person. This is because the opinion of the person introducing the applicant carries value if he himself commands respect and goodwill.

(2) The banker should take care to see the contents of a proper introduction; i.e., mere information about a person of his place of origin or birth of the prospective customer is not sufficient to the banker. If the introducer has not given any assurance about the applicant's business connections with him and that he was a bona fide customer of the introducer, then it cannot be a proper introduction. What is the duty of the banker in this regard was considered in the case of Indian Bank vs. Catholic Syrian Bank Ltd. (1980) and it was held that the bank was negligent in not

securing proper introduction of the applicant. It was further held that the bank ought to have made more enquiries than usual to test the integrity of the prospective customer before allowing him to open an account. In this case the applicant for opening the current account was introduced to the bank by a well known customer of the bank. But what has happened is that the prospective customer was informed to the bank Manager by the customer that the former was a man from Indore and he would like to open a bank account to enable him to do business at that place. The introducer has not given any assurance above the credentials of the person introduced. It was finally concluded that the banker should fully ascertain the true identity of the applicant and should not depend exclusively on the casual words of the introducer. Therefore, it was held that the bank was negligent in securing proper introduction of the applicant.

3. Safety against wrongful overdraft granted: At the time of opening an account although the banker may not intend to grant an overdraft to the prospective customer, at times an overdraft may be granted inadvertently. In such a case the amount can be realised only if the customer is a respectable solvent party.

4. Enquiries about the customer: Under common courtesy and practice, a banker has to answer enquiries from his fellow bankers. So a banker should retain sufficient information about his customer regarding the latter's financial soundness, nature of business in which he is engaged, etc.

5. Evidence of negligence: Omission to make enquiries regarding the new customer may make a banker guilty of negligence. He cannot claim protection under Sec. 131 of the Negotiable Instruments Act, 1881. In the course of his judgement in the case of Ladbroke vs Toold, Justice Balthackere said that "*the bank acted negligently for they did not make ordinary enquiries which ordinarily reasonable people should make in opening an account*". A contradictory view was given in a more recent case, Bapulal Premchand vs Nath Bank Ltd. (1946). In this case Mr. Justice Chagla held that 'it was not obligatory upon a bank to make enquiries as to the respectability of a customer in order to avail itself of the protection given to it under Sec 131 of the Negotiable Instruments Act". In view of these contrary ideas, it is therefore safe for a bank not to accept a person as a customer without introduction or some reference except in case of parties personally known to an office of the bank.

6. Specimen Signatures: Every customer is required to supply his banker with a few (usually three) specimens of his signature on the specimen signature cards kept by the banker. These cards are indexed and filed by the banker in an alphabetical order for future reference. A recent practice is bankers take specimen signatures of a customer at the top of the ledger sheet where the account of a particular customer is opened. The customer's name and address will also be written there.

7. Mandate for the operation of the Account: The banker should get from his customer a mandate if the latter intends operations on his account by another person. The mandate should clearly state the powers delegated to the person so authorised (mandatoree). His power to draw and endorse cheques does not give him powers to accept bills or overdraw the account. Specimen signature of the persons authorised to operate the account should be given in the mandate. Their particulars should be entered on the top of the ledger. Having opened a current account for a customer, a banker should supply free of cost a cheque book, a pass book and a pay-in-slip book to the latter.

8. Banker not concerned with the customer's title to Money Deposited : The banker is not expected to be concerned with the question of the customer's title to the money paid in by him, unless a notice, explicit or implied, is given to it. In case a third party deposits of money is paid into a customer's current account, the banker is ordinarily bound to accept. It is not necessary for the banker to know about the quantum of share of any one of the parties in the case of joint account in the bank. As far as the banker is concerned, the depositors are its creditors and it is the duty of the banker to pay the cheques drawn on him by the customer and allow operations on the Account in terms of their instructions.

9. Passport-size Photograph : In order to prevent impersonation and for easy identification, the banks, nowadays, insist upon the prospective customers to affix their passport-size photographs on the application forms at the time of opening accounts.

10. Proof of address: Nowadays banks insist upon the prospective customers to produce any one of the following to prove their residential address:

(*a*) Photocopy of the family card

(*b*) Photocopy of the voter identity card

(*c*) Photocopy of the passport

(*d*) Photocopy of the Driving licence

(*e*) A certificate from the employer in case the prospective customer is employed.

(*f*) Photocopy of the PAN (Permanent Account Number) Card.

With regard to opening of accounts, other points to be noted are:

(*i*) Once a deposit is made, it becomes the property of the bank.

(*ii*) In case the deposit made by a customer is the property of another person, say a trust, then the deposit does not become the property of the bank.

(*iii*) It is the responsibility of the bank for the safety of the deposits.

(*iv*) A banker may use his discretion either to accept or not to accept a deposit and it cannot be questioned (Faselli vs. Liggs National Bank)

(*v*) In case the money or cheque is entrusted to an employee of the bank to be credited to the account of a customer, and if it was misappropriated by the employee, the banker cannot be held liable for the fraud committed by the employee. (State Bank of India Vs. Shyamala Dey (1978)

4.2.2. Risk in opening accounts without proper introduction

If the banker opens an account without introduction, the banker runs certain risks which are as follows :

(*i*) The banker cannot avail of the statutory protection : Section 131 of the Indian Negotiable Instruments Act provides statutory protection to the banker, if he collects a bill or cheque etc., on behalf of a customer in case the latter has no title or defective title thereto. The collecting banker does not incur any liability to the true owner of the cheque or bill if the former has acted in good faith and without negligence. This means the banker should have collected the cheque or bill on behalf of a "customer", i.e., who has been allowed to open the account with proper introduction.

If a banker opens an account without introduction in the name of an undesirable person and if such person sends a forged or stolen cheque for collection and the banker does it, the banker cannot get the statutory protection available under Section 131 of N.I. Act, 1881.

(*ii*) Risk in case of Overdrafts : If a customer who is not properly introduced is granted an overdraft even by mistake or negligence, the banker may not be able to recover the amount. Under such circumstances of granting overdraft by mistake, the bank can recover the amount only if the customer is a respectable party.

(*iii*) Risk in case of undischarged insolvent : The deposits received by a banker from an undischarged insolvent without proper introduction carries the risk of attachment.

(*iv*) Issue of bogus cheques : A customer who is not properly introduced obtains possession of cheque books and may issue cheques without sufficient balance. As a result of the failure to make necessary enquiries, the banker may enable a dishonest person to obtain for fraudulent purposes, the possession of a cheque book and if such a person happens to be an undischarged insolvent, the bank might be placed in a difficult position by unknowingly allowing such a person to operate on his account with the bank.

(*v*) As per the directives of RBI, banks should immediately obtain introduction for all deposit accounts. Introduction is necessary for all types of accounts excepting that of a limited company. Also introduction is not required in case of opening a fixed deposit account because a cheque book is not issued under such account.

4.3. OPERATING THE ACCOUNT

After opening the account, the banker hands over to the customer (1) a cheque book, (2) a pay-in-slip book and (3) a pass book.

4.3.1. Cheque Book

The customer has to draw a cheque in order to draw money from the bank. The cheque may be in favour of the customer himself or in favour of a third party. The customer must exercise reasonable care to see that the cheque book does not fall into other hands. The customer must complete the cheque in all respects before issuing it. He must write the amount both in words and figures. The bank will dishonour a cheque if there is any defect in it.

This book contains blank forms of cheque which is used as an instrument by the customer to withdraw money from his account. The blank forms of cheque and their counterfoils are serially numbered. Every cheque book also contains one requisition slip to facilitate the customer to obtain a new cheque book when the old cheques are exhausted or about to be exhausted.

4.3.2. Pay-in-slip Book

When the customer wishes to deposit money into his current account, he will have to fill in a form called pay-in-slip form. If cash is deposited, the denomination of the notes paid in must be noted in the form. If cheques are sent for collection and credit, details must be given. Alternatively, the cheques etc. deposited may be sent along with a letter.

This book contains printed forms with perforated counterfoils to be filled in by the depositor himself or by his agent at the time of depositing cash, cheques, bills, drafts, etc., to the credit of his account. These forms are supplied by the banker free of cost. Separate forms may be used for cash and cheques or other instruments. Some banks have devised different forms, while others make use of the same forms with provision for both. The contents of the forms include information relating to the date of deposit, name and account number of the customer, amount to be deposited, the denomination of currency notes to be deposited, etc.

After filling in all such details on the foil and counterfoil, the customer hands over the same together with cash to the cashier who acknowledges receipt of the same by signing on the counterfoil along with the stamp of the bank and returns it to the customer. The foil retained by the bank is passed on to the clerk concerned who maintains the ledger for making necessary entries in the ledger of the customer.

4.3.3. PASS BOOK

The pass book is a replica of the customer's account in the bank's ledger. The pass book need not be presented along with the cheque for payment. The pass book may be sent periodically to the bank and the bank enters all the transactions as found in its own book in the pass book. The customer may compare the entries in the pass book with those in his own cash book and intimate to the bank any discrepancies so that they may be set right.

The pass book is a small handy book which contains the record of transactions in debits and credits between a banker and his customer. So, the bank pass book enables a client to check up his accounts to his satisfaction and to find out any discrepancy. It also contains rules and regulations governing current and savings accounts.

If there is any discrepancy, the customer should bring it to the notice of the bank and get it corrected. Entries in the pass book will be made only by the banker and the customer should not make any entry therein. When a pass book is lost, the banker will issue a duplicate. This will be marked "duplicate". For issuing a duplicate pass book banker collects some charges from the customer. Where a pass book is complete with entries, the banker will issue a "continuation pass book".

In the first page of a specimen form of a pass, we find the following:

Date	Particulars	Withdrawals Dr	Deposits Cr	Balance	Initials

The deposits by the customers are credited in the pass book, while the withdrawals are debited. The customer can verify the balance at any time. It is possible with the help of pass book to get a clear picture of deposits and withdrawals in a customer's account. In the first column, the date of the transaction is entered and in the second column are recorded the deposits (marked 'by') and withdrawal (marked "to'). The deposit amounts are shown on the credit amount column and withdrawn amounts are shown on the debit amount column. The balance whether debit or credit is written in the balance column. The pass book will usually have a thick cover page so as to withstand wear and tear and it has to move to and fro between bank and the client.

Statement of Accounts: In recent times with the mechanisation of banking accounts, the pass books are generally being replaced by statement of accounts which are daily or periodically sent to customer as agreed upon. But pass book has one advantage over this, as it gives a consolidated statements of the position of accounts. The statement of account also has columns similar to a pass book like:

Date	Particulars	Withdrawals	Deposits	Balance Dr / Cr	Initials

In the case of pass book, there is "passing to and fro" i.e. from the bank to the customer and from the customer to the bank; but statement of accounts is never returned to the bank but kept in the files of the customer.

According to Sir John Paget, the proper function of a pass book is "*to constitute a conclusive unquestionable record of the transactions between banker and customer and it should be recognized as such*". But unfortunately the pass book's position is not so satisfactory. According to Paget the entries in the pass book are conclusive and no discrepancy is to be found. But in view of the decisions which are given out in many cases, it is not correct to agree fully with Sir John Paget's view. In the case of Keptigalla Rubber Estates Company vs National Bank of India (1909), it has been held that the mere taking out of the pass book and its return without objection will not constitute a settled account between the banker and his customer. But if the pass book of certain business firm is returned to the bank after ticking entries in debits and credits, there is a prima facie evidence that the entries have been found to be correct and the account is settled.

But in U.S.A., in the case of Morgan vs United States Mortgage and Trust Co. (1913), the learned judge held that "*the depositor who sends his pass book to be written up and receives it back is bound to examine the pass book and vouchers and to report to the bank without unreasonable delay any errors which may be discovered.*" So it has been made obligatory on the part of the customer to examine his pass book and check the entries.

4.3.4. ENTRIES IN PASS BOOK

A pass book is a booklet in which the record of transactions of the customer is made by a banker for the use of the former. It passes periodically between the banker and the customer and hence its name. It contains a copy of the customer's account in the bank's ledger.

As to the question whether the entries in the pass book are binding on the customer and the banker, Sir John Paget is of the view that it is so. He says, "*The proper function of a pass book is to constitute a conclusive and unquestionable record of transactions between the banker and the customer and it should be recognised as such. After full opportunity of examination on the part of the customer, all entries at least to his debit ought to be final and not liable to be subsequently reopened, at any rate, to the detriment of the banker.*" The decision in the U.S.A. also supports this view. In Morgan vs. Mortgage Trust Co., it was held, "*The depositor who sends his pass book to be written up and receives it back with his paid cheques as vouchers is bound to examine the pass book as vouchers and to report to the bank without unreasonable delay any error which may be discovered*".

But the decisions in England and India hold a contrary view. In Keptigalla Rubber Estates Co. vs. National Bank of India (1909), it was held that there was no authority to the position that when a pass book is taken out of the bank by the customer is regarded as settled and binding on the other. The learned judge further added, "*Apart from authority, one has only to look at the facts of this case to see how absurd it would be to hold that the taking out of the pass book and its return constituted a settled account.*" However, in the case of trading concerns who maintain proper books of accounts with ticks placed against each item, it can be prima facie taken as binding on the customer.

The erroneous entries in the pass book may be favourable to the customer or to the banker. Both of them may, therefore, inform the mistakes or omissions and get them corrected. The legal position in this regard is as follows:

(a) Entries favourable to customer: It may so happen that mistakes committed by the banker turn out to be favourable to the customer. In such case, the entries in the pass book may form an evidence against the bank because the entries in the pass book are recorded by the bank. The customer is rightly entitled to believe them as correct and to act on the basis of such entries.

The following are the examples of the entries made in favour of the customer :

(*i*) double credits

(*ii*) credit of higher amounts

(*iii*) omission of certain debit items, etc.

By these entries, the pass book shows a higher credit balance.

In Akrokerri (Atlantic) Mines Ltd. vs. Economic Bank (1904), it was held: "*The pass book belongs to the customer and entries made in it by the bank are statements on which the customer is entitled to act*" [See also Mawji vs. The National Bank of India (1901).]

When the customer draws a cheque relying on a larger balance shown in the pass book by mistake, the banker has no right to dishonour such a cheque. If he dishonours, he may be held liable to pay damages for wrongful dishonour of his customer's cheque (Holland vs. Manchester and Liverpool District Banking Co. Ltd.).

A banker cannot recover the money wrongfully credited if the customer can show that in good faith and relying upon the accuracy of the entry, he had been induced to alter his position. In Skying vs. Greenwood, the bankers wrongly credited the account of a military officer. The officer (i.e the customer) relying on the pass book draws cheques in good faith and spent the amount. When the mistake was discovered, the bankers sought to recover the amount wrongly credited. But it was held that the bankers were not entitled to recover the amount on the ground that the customer relying on the statements sent by the banker adjusted his expenditure accordingly. In this case the customer was not a businessman and he did not maintain accounts. Besides he acted in good faith in order to take advantages of a wrong entry. In the case of a businessman as he is expected to maintain accounts But, it is very difficult to prove that he has relied on the entries in the Pass Book.

The banker may show or prove that an entry is made by mistake and have it rectified if the customer has not altered his position.

A customer cannot rely upon a fictitious entry, if made by a bank, which has not been communicated to him.

Sir John Paget felt that a pass book contributes a conclusive and an unquestionable record of the transactions between the banker and his customer. This implied an obligation on the part of the customer to check the entries in the pass book and report the error if any found. This view was upheld by American courts.

But this view did not find favour with the English and Indian courts. They did not agree with the finding that entries to the pass book are conclusive evidence of accuracy. Keptigalla Rubber Estates vs. National Bank of India is a case on the point.

The customer is entitled to believe that an entry in the pass book is bona fide even though it shows a wrong balance. He can draw a cheque for the higher balance and the banker cannot return the cheque (Skying vs. Greenwood). But the customer should prove two things:

1. He relied upon the banker and was not aware of the mistakes.
2. He altered his position by innocently drawing cheques.

As stated earlier, the modern bankers prefer to give statements in lieu of the old practice of giving pass books. The statements will not be returned to thc banker. There is no evidence of the customer checking the entries in the statements. There is no obligation on the customer to sign and return the confirmation slips sent periodically by the banker. Under such circumstance the legal effect of a wrong entry was under a cloud.

The decision of the Allahabad High Court in Kul Cushan vs. Allahabad Bank in 1963 was adverse to the banker. Fortunately for the banker, a decision was given by Kerala High Court in Essa Ismail vs. Indian Bank in the following words : "... *when confirmation slips are sent and signed by the customer he will be bound by the debits made*". As a matter of fact the Supreme Court goes to the extreme when it observed in the case of State Bank of India vs. Shyama Devi as follows : "*The employer is not liable for the act of the servant if the causes of loss or damage arose without his actual fault of privity ....*" Hence if a bank clerk embezzles and makes false entries in the pass book, the banker is not responsible.

The brief facts of the above case were as follows : A lady opened a Savings bank account in State Bank of India with the introduction by an employee of the bank, who was a close friend of her husband and a neighbour to her. The customer used to entrust with the said employee moneys and cheques for being credited to her account. The employee misappropriated the same and to cover up his fraud, made false entries in the pass book as if the moneys and cheques given to him were deposited in her account. When it came to light, it was pointed in the court of law on behalf of the customer that this employee had manipulated the accounts of three other depositors also and the bank had reimbursed those customers for the loss. It was argued that the entries in the pass book were prima facie sufficient to establish the customer's claim. The bank argued that the customer had entrusted the employee moneys from time to time for depositing in her account. In such a situation the employee could not be said to have been acting in due course of his employment. The Supreme Court, therefore, held that the employee acted as an agent of the customer and not acted as an employee in the course of his employment. The bank, therefore, was not held liable to make good the loss caused to the customer.

There are some exceptions to the abovementioned principle. If the customer maintains his account books and the bank regularly sends him the pass book, the customer cannot act on the basis of the above presumption. Normally a person spends that he presumes to belong to him, if the banker permits him to withdraw excess money on the above presumption as per the decision of the Madras High Court in Oakley Bowden and Co. vs. The Indian Bank Ltd. (1964).

(b) Entries favourable to Bankers: Entries favourable to the bankers may happen in the following ways :

(*a*) a credit entry is omitted,

(*b*) a credit figure is wrongly stated,

(*c*) any debit entry is erroneously made in the account of the customer.

These entries are favourable to the banker and against the customer. Under these circumstances, the customer is entitled to get the mistake rectified as soon as he happens to detect it. This right of the customer does not lapse even if he returns the pass book without raising objection regarding any entry or if he remains silent after the receipt of the pass book because it is not obligatory for the customer to examine the pass book. Therefore the customer is entitled to recover the amount wrongly debited to his account or omitted to be credited to his account.

The customer can any time demand that wrong debits should be set right and correct balance restored. This right does not lapse merely because he has returned the pass book without raising any objection as to the correctness of the balance.

Even where the customer returned the pass book to the banker after ticking all the items, it was held that the banker is entitled to infer the customer's acceptance of the entries there. (Chatterton vs. London and Country Bank).

However, if the customer acts in such a manner that the entries in the pass book are relied upon as a settled account, then his right to claim rectification will be lost in such a case.

(*i*) The negligence of the customer with regard to the entries in the pass book must be proved, and

(*ii*) As a result, the position of the banker must have changed to his disadvantage.

The legal view is mostly in favour of the customer and it would be very difficult to prove negligence on the part of the customer or any act by him rendering the entries in the pass book a settled account.

In a recent case in India, Canara Bank vs. Canara Sales Corporation and others, the following conclusions have been drawn :

(1) It is no duty on the part of the customer to examine his pass book and to report to the banker that payment has been made on a forged cheque and neglect in this regard, would not deprive him of the right to recover subsequently the sums paid on forged cheque.

(2) The implied contract as to settlement of accounts does not arise between a customer and his banker merely by reason of the banker sending the pass book to the customer with the accounts written up and the customer failing to point out any irregularities therein.

(3) The amount of a forged cheque can be claimed back at any time when it is noticed by the customer even though he has kept silence over it for a long time.

The modern practice is not to send periodical statements of amount of the customer indicating therein that the customer should verify the entries and report to the banker any discrepancies found. Here too it is not free from doubt if silence of the customer will render the accounts settled. Some banks send a confirmatory slip along with the statement of account requesting the customer to return the slip duly signed. But he cannot be compelled to do so.

The current account rules of banks nowadays impose a duty on the customer to carefully examine the entries and to examine the entries and to draw the attention of the bank immediately to any errors or omissions. They further add that the bank will not be responsible for any loss arising from the neglect of these precautions. For example, the monthly statement rendered by the State Bank of India to its current account holders contains a usual condition thus:

"Unless a constituent notifies the bank immediately of any discrepancy found by him in his statement of account, it will be taken that he has found the account correct".

If such rules form the basis of the operation of current accounts, then a specific duty can be deemed to have been cast on the customers. Return of pass book without any objection under such circumstances renders the pass book as settled or stated account. The customer will certainly be disentitled to claim rectification of wrong debts subsequently.

Limitation period for recovery of money paid under mistake: Limitation period is restricted to three years from the date of detection of mistake. However there seems to be no conclusive judgement on the date of recovery *i.e.* from the date of mistake or the date of detection.

To conclude, the position of pass book entries has been summed up by Mr. Sheldon as follows:

"*Just as the law would not sanction only attempt of the customer fraudulently to take advantage of an error in his pass book, to the banker's detriment, neither would it allow the banker to withhold money which he had received for a customer, even though the customer may not have pointed out the omission in his pass book.*" Since the legal decisions on the pass book entries are divergent, responsibility lies with both the banker and the customer. It should be the duty of a banker to take particular care in giving correct and up-to-date entries and return the pass book to the customer. Similarly, the customer should consider it his duty to verify the correctness of the entries made in the pass book and take the earliest opportunity to bring to the notice of the bank any discrepancy in the entries. There should be mutual co-operation and understanding between the customer and the banker in this regard.

4.4. FIXED DEPOSIT ACCOUNT

In addition to accepting money on current and savings deposits, bankers receive money on fixed deposit accounts, undertaking to repay the amounts on the expiry of a fixed period, or subject to a notice. Fixed deposits are also known as time deposits, being repayable only after expiry of a particular time or period. It is defined as a deposit of a definite sum for a fixed period at a fixed rate of interest. It carries relatively higher rates of interest because fixed deposits enable the banker to employ the funds profitably for relatively longer period since they are not refundable as and when customer likes. The banker need not keep liquid cash resources on such deposits unlike on current accounts. The term of deposit usually varies between three months and five years. People who can afford to keep their money with banks for a certain period without withdrawing it meanwhile, go in for fixed deposits.

The customer cannot withdraw the amount before the expiry of the period. A bank can use fixed deposits for lending or investment without keeping any reserve to earn income and so it pays interest on fixed deposits. The longer the period of deposit, the higher the rate of interest. For example, the State Bank pays 6% interest on one year deposit while it pays 9% on 5-year deposit.

People prefer to invest their saving in fixed deposit rather than in shares of joint stock companies. The reason is the investment in shares is risky and requires special knowledge.

Fixed deposits have grown in importance and popular in India during recent years. These deposits constitute major part of the bank deposits.

4.4.1. FEATURES OF FIXED DEPOSITS

The main features of fixed deposit are as under :

1. It is a certain sum of money kept with the banker for a specified period e.g. 15 days to five years or more. It is withdrawable only after the maturity of the fixed periods or subject to 'so many days' notice as the case may be. Often bankers permit the customers to withdraw their money prior to expiry of the fixed period as a sort of convenience and in such cases interest is foregone or premature repayment is allowed on a loan basis.

2. On the deposit being made, the banker issues deposit receipt acknowledging the claim of the customer on the bank.

3. The general relationship between banker and customer in respect of fixed deposit is that of debtor and creditor. The deposit cannot be deemed to be held in trust.

4. Not negotiable: Fixed deposit receipt is not a negotiable instrument. The banker should not pay the fixed deposit to any third party even if it bears the signature of the depositor for a mere endorsement of fixed deposit does not make it negotiable. The depositor has to execute assignment deed and notify to the bank in case he wants to transfer the deposit receipt to anyone else.

5. Fixed deposit accounts may be opened in the name of minors and they can give valid discharge for the deposit amount repaid to them.

6. Deposit receipt given by banker is exempt from stamp duty.

7. In case of insolvency of a depositor, the amount should go to the official assignee; in the case of death of a depositor, the amount should go to his personal representative, i.e., his legal heirs.

8. Loss of Fixed Deposit Receipt: A bank may impose a condition that the deposit receipt should be returned to the bank duly discharged before payment can be made. In such a case the depositor cannot claim money unless he returns the fixed deposit receipt to the bank. In Alkinawn v. Bradford Third Equitable Benefit Building Society, it was held that where the return of the deposit receipt is made condition for making payment, there would be no course of action until its return. However, in case of loss of deposit receipt, a court may exercise its equitable jurisdiction and allow the depositor to claim the money without producing deposit receipt (in Re Dillion). The court may not ask the depositor to execute an indemnity bond as a deposit receipt is not a negotiable instrument. A transferor cannot, give a better title to the transferee than what he has.

9. Law of Limitation: Where the fixed deposit receipt is to be produced for getting repayment of the deposit, the period of limitation will not begin to run till its return. Fixed deposit receipts usually contain a condition that they must be surrendered on maturity for repayment of the deposit. In other cases the law of limitation does not apply to a fixed deposit so long as interest is being paid on it or so long as it is being renewed. In case it is not renewed, the period of limitation begins to run from the date of maturity of the deposit, i.e. the date on which the depositor is entitled to be repaid.

In the case of fixed deposit account the law of limitation begins to run from the expiry of the fixed period. If the account is a deposit account repayable after the expiry of a specified notice of withdrawal, the law of limitation begins to operate immediately after the money is due to be repaid. If the account is a deposit account repayable on demand, the law begins to operate from the date when a demand for repayment has been made by the depositor.

10. Garnishee Order: A fixed deposit is attachable by a garnishee order as the order attaches all debts due or occurring due. The obligation of the banker to honour his customer's cheque is extinguished on receipt of an order of the court known as Garnishee order issued under Order 21, Rule 46 of Code of Civil Procedure, 1908. If a debtor fails to pay the debt owed by him to his creditor, the latter may apply to the court for the issue of a Garnishee order on the banker of his debtor. The banker is prohibited from paying any amount to the customer from the date of receipt of the Order Nisi.

Garnishee order attaches all debts due or accruing due. Deposits payable at a fixed date or repayable after the expiry of a specified notice are thus affected by garnishee orders. If the return of deposit receipt is a condition for obtaining repayment, then the Garnishee order does not operate on the deposit account.

A particular deposit can be attached by a court depends on the order of the court (i.e. Garnishee Order). The following deposits can be attached:

(*i*) a deposit repayable on demand.

(*ii*) a deposit repayable after the expiry of a fixed notice which has been given.

(*iii*) a deposit repayable at fixed future date or after the expiry of a fixed period.

So fixed deposits can be attached by the order of the court.

11. Donatio Mortis Causa : A deposit receipt can be given as a donation. The donee can claim the amount. So a deposit receipt may be the subject of a Donation Mortis Causa (Dubbin v. Duffin) gift made in contemplation of death and to take effect only in the event of death and the court will compel the legal representatives of the deceased donor. For the receipt of the fixed deposit receipt.

12. Disallowance of drawing of cheque: Cheque cannot be drawn by the customer on his fixed deposit account either to claim the interest accrued or withdraw the deposit money on maturity unless the banker is instructed to transfer the same to his current or savings account. In any case fixed deposit account cannot be operated upon through the issuing of cheques. But where a customer has given instructions to the banker to transfer the fixed deposit amount along with interest to the former's current account with the same bank, then cheques can be drawn.

13. Deposits in joint names: Bankers receive deposits in joint names also. In such a case both parties should join in for withdrawal except where one of them is deceased. In such circumstance banker can make repayment to any one of the survivor. According to English law, payment to any one of the joint depositors gives complete discharges to the banker. The same view was expressed in India in the case of Annapurnamma vs. Akkayya. This decision has been doubted in subsequent cases where deposits are in joint names, repayment condition will generally be in one or other of the following:

(*i*) payable to either or survivor; or

(*ii*) payable to the former or survivor; or

(*iii*) payable to no.1 or survivor (if deposits are in joint names of more than two).

When deposits are in joint names of husband and wife and it is provided that either of the parties can withdraw, and the wife happens to survive, then it may be said that the arrangement was made merely for the sake of convenience and consequently the survivorship cannot be excluded, then payment can be made to her. (Foley vs. Foley 1911). Thus deposit accounts may also be opened in the name of both parties. Here all the members should combine in withdrawal or due authority is given to any of them to receive payment on their behalf.

14. Rates of interest on fixed deposits: Interest at a specified rate is admissible on the amount held in the deposit account for the contract period. Interest is not allowed with expiry of the deposit period unless it is renewed. The rates of interest and other terms and conditions on which the bank accepts these deposits are regulated by the Reserve Bank of India. Fixed deposits are now classified into different categories with varying periods of maturity starting from 15 days. The creation of so many categories of fixed deposit with higher rates of interest for each successive category is to induce the depositors to take advantage of higher rates of interest.

15. Renewal before maturity: The Reserve Bank has permitted the bankers to renew an existing term deposit before maturity without invoking the penalty provided.

16. Payment of interest: The banks usually pay interest quarterly or half-yearly also at the request of the depositor. The depositor is required to present the receipt for the purpose of necessary entry regarding payment of interest and withdrawal of interest or the principal since cheques are not permitted. At the request of the customer the banker may credit the amount of interest or the principal to his savings or current account from which he may withdraw the same through cheques.

17. Interest on Overdue Deposits: A deposit which remains unpaid on the due date is termed as overdue deposit, and such deposit will not be eligible for any interest. However, interest on overdue deposits will be allowed provided the deposits are renewed from the date of maturity to a future date. Legally interest ceases to accrue on the overdue fixed deposit after the expiry of the fixed period, but the banks may at their discretion allow interest thereafter if the fixed deposit is renewed.

18. Payment before due date: Though a fixed deposit is payable at the expiry of the specified period, banker also permits encashment of such deposits even before the due date, if the depositor so desires. But according to the directions of the Reserve Bank of India if any deposit is repaid before the expiry of the period of deposit agreed upon at the time of the deposit, the interest on such deposit shall be payable as follows :

(*i*) First, the rate of interest applicable for the deposit on the basis of the period for which it remained with the bank is determined.

(*ii*) Then the said rate is reduced by one percent.

19. Advances against Fixed Deposit: If a loan is sought against F.D.R. by one of the joint depositors, the banker must require the loan application to be signed by other depositors as well or alternatively a letter of No Objections to the loan being granted to one of them may be taken from the rest of the depositors and the latter may be held as surety also.

The banker may also grant a loan on the deposit on the security of the fixed deposit receipt. But according to the directive issued by the Reserve Bank of India, interest on a loan against the fixed deposit receipt shall be:

(*i*) At least 2 per cent higher than the interest payable on the deposit, if the deposit stands in the name of the borrower either singly or jointly, and

(*ii*) In case the deposit stands in the name of person other than the borrowers, the rate of interest should be determined taking into consideration the purpose for which the advance is granted and the rate of interest chargeable will be the rate prescribed by the Reserve Bank for advances to the particular category of borrower such as agriculture, small industry etc.

20. Premature repayments: If one of the joint depositors requests the banker for repayment of the fixed deposit before its date of maturity, the banker should do so only after obtaining the consent of the other joint depositor/depositor. One depositor has no right to take back the amount before its maturity. If the depositor dies the legal heirs foreclose the deposit, the penalty of 1% need not be imposed.

21. Loss of fixed deposit receipt: Sometimes the depositors might have lost their fixed deposit receipt and request the bank to issue a duplicate one. A fixed deposit receipt is not transferable and not a negotiable one. Any other person, therefore, cannot claim payment of the amount covered by the receipt. However, customers request the banker for the issue of a duplicate one because banks stipulate that the receipt duly discharged must be surrendered for its repayment. The banker should take the following steps in this regard:

(*a*) A letter signed by the depositor/depositors informing the banker about the loss of the receipt and requesting it to issue a duplicate one should be obtained.

(*b*) A duly stamped letter of Indemnity must be obtained from the depositor/depositors to safeguard its own interest, in case the original receipt is also presented for payment

(*c*) A note to this effect should be made in fixed deposit ledger for future guidance.

22. Term deposit may be preclosed on the request of depositors. The rate of interest on such preclosed deposit will be 1% less than the rate applicable to the

period for the deposit has actually run as the ruling on the date of the deposit. However, no penalty will be charged on preclosure of term deposits.

23. If a deposit matures for payment on a public holiday, it becomes payable on the immediately succeeding working day. Interest in such cases is payable for the holiday also.

4.4.2. LEGAL POSITION

A banker is a debtor in the case of fixed deposit also. The reason is that he has borrowed money from the customers. The customer or depositor is the creditor. The banker has to repay the amount after the period of deposit is over. That is, he must pay the amount on the due date. But he is not bound to repay the amount before its due date. Thus in the case of fixed deposit, the legal position of the banker is "one of a debtor who is not bound to repay the amount before its due date". However some banks reserve the rights to repay the amount before the due date without giving notice. In order to exercise this right, the deposit receipt should contain this condition and the banker should have drawn the attention of that customer to it. The reason is that in such a case it becomes a contract between the banker and the customer. The banker cannot repay a fixed deposit before its due date without the consent of his customer.

A banker continues to be a debtor even if the deposit is not withdrawn after the period of deposit is over and interest is not paid after the due date. He does not become a trustee in such cases.

Opening and operation of Fixed Deposit Account: For opening a fixed deposit account, a depositor is required to fill in an application form wherein he mentions the amount of the deposit and the period for which deposit is to be made. He also gives his specimen signature. A fixed deposit receipt is thereafter issued to the depositor, acknowledging the receipt of the sum of money specified therein to be repaid at the expiry of the period mentioned therein along with interest at the specified rate.

4.4.3. FIXED DEPOSIT RECEIPT

When a fixed deposit is made, the banker issues a receipt which is known as Fixed Deposit Receipt. The receipt contains details regarding the name, address and description of the depositor, amount received, rate of interest payable, period for which the deposit is made, due date on which the amount is repayable and conditions attached to the deposit. It is generally marked "Not negotiable".

4.4.3.1. Features of Fixed Deposit Receipt

The fixed deposit receipt has the following features:

(*i*) Fixed deposit receipt serves as an acknowledgement of the deposit made.

(*ii*) It must be surrendered on maturity of the deposit for repayment. The return of this receipt is usually made a condition precedent for payment of the deposit.

(*iii*) The receipt obtained on the reverse of the F.D.R. on repayment of the fixed deposit serves as a valid discharge.

(*iv*) The fixed deposit receipt is not a negotiable instrument. It therefore can not be transferred by endorsement. However, the debt covered by it can be assigned like any other debt. Notice of assignment must necessarily be given to the banker.

(*v*) It can be transferred to another by way of assignment.

(*vi*) FDR as a security: A fixed deposit receipt can be offered as a security for an advance. But the banker should take the receipt after it is duly discharged.

(*vii*) Encashment of FDR: If the depositor wants, he can encash his fixed deposit receipt even before the due date.

(*viii*) Period of Intimation: Where production of the fixed deposit receipt is essential for repayment of the deposit, the period of limitation will not begin to run till its return.

(*ix*) Fixed Deposit Receipt and Donatio Mortis Causa : A fixed deposit receipt has been held to be a good subject of donatio mortis causa. In other words, a fixed deposit receipt can be given as a donation even though the receipt usually states that it is not transferable. As a result, on the death of the donor the gift will pass on to the donee.

(*x*) Stamp Duty: Fixed deposit receipts are exempt from stamp duty.

4.4.4. ADVANTAGES OF FIXED DEPOSIT

Time deposits are popular with the depositors in India for more reasons than one.

1. The rate of interest paid on fixed deposits is higher than those paid in any other kind of deposits; for example, a fixed deposit for a five, year period in a bank fetches as high as nine per cent whereas the interest paid on savings bank balance is as little as 5% per annum.

2. The deposits are insured to the extent of Rs. 30,000 that is, with the Deposit Insurance Corporation of India established on 1.1.1962 and later converted as Deposit Insurance and Credit Guarantee Corporation of India on 15.7.1978 which guarantees the depositors, repayment of balances in their accounts with the insured banks up to Rs.30,000 in the event of bank failure. Now it is raised from Rs 30,000 to Rs 1. lakh with effect from May 1, 1993. The scheme covers commercial banks, scheduled and non-scheduled co-operative banks as well as regional rural banks. This provides a measure of safety to the customer.

3. Interest paid on deposit by bankers is exempt from payment of Income Tax under Sec. 80 L of the Income Tax Act up to Rs. 12,000. This is an advantage to income tax assesses.

4. Fixed deposits are exempt from Wealth Tax also. So Fixed Deposits are favoured by rich people to avoid liability under the Wealth Tax Act.

5. In the event of any necessity arising the bankers give loan or sanction overdraft facilities up to 90% of the deposits at a rate of 2% more than the interest payable to the depositors.

6. Bankers pay interest on fixed deposits monthly for the deposits exceeding Rs. 3000. This is most attractive for pensioners and old age people who have lost their monthly Income on superannuation.

7. Bankers also like fixed deposits because they are not liable to repay the deposits before the expiry of the agreed period. They can safely invest these deposits and without necessity of keeping idle cash reserves.

4.4.5. DISADVANTAGES OF FIXED DEPOSIT ACCOUNT

1. An amount once kept in fixed deposit will be repaid by the banker only after the expiry of the agreed period. So in between if there is any demand for money, the customer will be in difficulty, if at all he wants he can take a loan from the banker or under extraordinary circumstances withdraw the deposit by waiving interest.

2. In these days of inflation, a depositor who gets back his deposit after a few years will get only the nominal value of the money originally deposited but not its real value.

Since the advantages overweigh the disadvantages referred to above, fixed deposits are popular.

4.5. RECURRING DEPOSIT ACCOUNTS

In recent years, a new type of savings account has been introduced by banks in India which is known as Recurring Deposit Account. This is intended to inculcate the habit of saving on a regular basis in order to take the advantages of getting higher rate of interest than that of savings deposit account. Under this deposit account, a customer is required to deposit a fixed sum, generally a multiple of Rs.50 or Rs.100, every month for a specified period. The rate of interest on this account is almost equal to that of fixed deposit account, i.e., 6 per cent to 11 per cent compound interest payable for period ranging from 1 to 10 years.

This is another form of savings bank account. Some banks refer to these accounts as cumulative time deposits accounts (C.T.D Accounts). This is devised to provoke the customer to save on a regular basis. Inducement for such a regularised saving comes in the form of higher rates of interest.

The recurring deposit account provides a person with an opportunity to build up his saving through monthly deposits. Accounts may be opened by (i) a person in his own name; or (ii) two or more persons (with joint names), the amount being payable to all of them jointly or to either or any one of them or the survivor or anyone or more of the survivors amongst them, as per the instructions given by them; or (iii) a minor jointly with his guardian; or (iv) a minor in his own name provided he is old enough to comprehend the transactions, say 14 years of age.

Recurring deposit accounts may be opened for monthly deposits of Rs.5 or exact multiples thereof for a specific number of months, ranging from 6 months to 120 months but in multiple of quarter year.. The instalment for any calendar month must be paid on or before the last working day of that month. If the depositor fails to deposit the monthly instalment, a penalty at the rate of Rs.1.50 paise for every Rs.100 per month for deposits up to 5 years and Rs.2 for every Rs.100 per month for deposit of over 5 years is charged. When the depositor prefers to adjust the penalty out of maturity payment, grand total of penalty arrived at should be rounded off to the nearest multiple of 50 paise. If the depositor opts for paying penalty now and then, the amount to be charged as penalty should be rounded off to the nearest multiple of 50 paise. A loan against recurring deposits accounts may also be allowed to the extent of 75% of the amount standing to the credit of the account, including accrued interest.

The rates of interest allowed on these deposits are the same as allowed for corresponding periods in the case of fixed deposits. The banks also allow the depositors to close down the accounts before the agreed period but only lower rates of interest will be allowed.

As in the case of fixed deposits, recurring deposits too can be offered as security for grant of loans or overdrafts. The benefit of section 80 L of Income Tax Act can also be had in the case of Recurring Deposits.

Notwithstanding any instalments paid in advance, recurring deposit accounts will mature for payments one month after the last instalment are paid or on the due date which- ever is later. In the case of premature payments the bank pays 1 per cent below the rate applicable to a recurring deposit of the period for which the deposit has actually been made. But if it is closed within 3 months of opening the account, no interest is payable.

4.6. NOMINATION

The nomination facility enables the bank to make payment to the nominee of a deceased depositor of the amount standing to the credit of the depositor: That is,

(*i*) return to the nominee, the articles left in the Bank's custody by a deceased person.

(*ii*) release to the nominee of the hirer, the contents of a Safe Deposit Locker, in the event of the death of the hirer.

Who can nominate?

(*a*) Bank account holders having Deposit account in their individual names or in joint names of two or more individuals.

(*b*) Individual customers who have deposited articles in safe custody with the Bank.

(*c*) Bank customers hiring Safe Deposit Lockers in their individual names or in joint names of two or more individuals.

(*d*) A person lawfully entitled to act on behalf of the minor, in respect of the Deposit account or articles left in safe custody or kept in the Safe Deposit Locker with the Bank in the sole name of the minor.

How to nominate?

Specific forms are provided for availing of nomination facility. The account holder/customer will have to fill in the relevant form. The Bank will acknowledge in writing to the concerned account holder/customer the receipt of the nomination form and the nomination will be registered in the books of the Bank.

Features of the nomination facility:

(*a*) Nomination facility is available to account holders having current accounts, savings bank accounts, and all types of term deposit accounts.

(*b*) Nomination can be made in favour of one person only. The Depositor has the option to execute a mandate authorising the Bank to indicate the name of the person in the Pass Book/Deposit Receipt.

(*c*) Nomination favouring the minor is permitted on the condition that the account holder, while making the nomination, appoints another individual, not being a minor, to receive the amount of the deposit on behalf of the nominee, in the event of the death of the depositor during the minority of the nominee.

(*d*) Nomination can be made only in respect of the deposit which is held in the individual capacity of the depositor and not in any representative capacity such as Director of a Company, Secretary of an Association, Partner of a firm, Karta of an H.U.F. (Hindu Undivided Family) and the like.

(*e*) In the case of a deposit made in the name of a minor, the nomination shall be made by a person lawfully entitled to act on behalf of the minor.

(*f*) A nomination will continue to be in force even on renewal of a Term Deposit unless specifically cancelled or changed.

(*g*) In case of Joint accounts, on the death of one depositor, the surviving depositor/depositors can change or cancel the nomination.

The new section 45 ZA in the Banking Regulation Act, 1949, provides the following for the facility of nomination by depositors in banks :

1. By nominating a person in the prescribed manner, the depositor allows the banker to pay the amount of the deposit in the event of his death.
2. In the case of a joint account, all the depositors together may nominate a person whereby in the event of death of all the joint depositors, the amount standing to their credit may be paid to the nominees by the banker. The nominee's, right to claim the amount of deposit arises only after the death of all depositors and the nominees, right cannot be more than that of the depositors.
3. A nomination can be effected in favour of individuals only and associations, societies, etc cannot be nominated.
4. Nomination facility is available to all types of deposit accounts.
5. On the death of the depositor/all the joint depositors, the nominee is entitled to all the rights of the depositor/all the joint depositors to such deposit, to the exclusion of all other persons. The above was decided in a recent case, viz., Smt. Parvati vs. Central Bank of India (1989). The High Court has decided that premature closure of the fixed deposit account by the nominee on the ground that section 45 ZA (2) confers all rights of the depositor in relation to the deposit on the nominee.
6. If the nominee happens to be a minor, the depositor may also appoint any other person to receive the amount of the deposit in the event of his death during the minority of the nominee.
7. The nomination may be varied or cancelled by the depositor in the prescribed manner.
8. By fulfilling the obligation under nomination, the banker is fully discharged from its liability in respect of the deposit.

9. There shall not be any claim by any other person other than the nominee for the payment the deposit by the banker.
10. The banker is not bound by any express notice of the claim to such deposits by any person other than the nominee.

The above provisions of the Law facilitate expeditious settlement of claims in the accounts of the deceased depositor and minimize the hardship that may cause to the family members on the death of the depositors.

Legal Status of the Nominee : It is necessary to understand whether the nominee becomes absolute owner of such deposit or the claims of the legal heirs of the deceased. It was decided in the Supreme Court in Sarbati Devi vs. Usha Devi (1984) in connection with nomination made in the case of an insurance claim. In this case, the wife of the deceased policy-holder was the nominee. But his mother and minor son claimed their shares from the life insurance money received by the deceased person's wife from L.I.C. The Supreme Court held that " *A mere nomination made under Section 39 of the Insurance Act does not have the effect of conferring on the nominee any beneficial interest in the amount payable under the life insurance policy on the death of the assured.*"

"*The nomination only indicates the hand which is authorised to receive the amount; on the payment of which the insurer gets a valid discharge of its liability under the policy. The amount, however, can be claimed by the heirs of the assured in accordance with the Law of Succession governing them.*"

Thus it is clear that the nominee cannot be the absolute owner of the amount received by him. The Law of succession will still prevail over the provisions relating to the facility of nomination as provided in the Banking Regulation Act, 1949.

4.7. CLOSURE OF A BANK ACCOUNT

The relationship between a banker and his customer arises out of a contract between the two and continues so long as both of them so desire. This relationship may be brought to an end if either one of them desires so by giving notice of his intention.

Following are the circumstances under which a banker can close or stop the operation of the account of a customer:

(*i*) A customer can close his account with the banker at any time he feels like without giving any reason. The banker should close the account with immediate effect on his returning the unused cheques.

(*ii*) If an account remains unoperated for a very long period, the banker may ask the customer to close his account. If a customer could not be traced after reasonable efforts, the bank usually transfers to an "unclaimed Deposit Account" and the account is closed. Similarly, the banker may close the account of a customer if the latter is found "undesirable" for valid reasons.

A customer is deemed to be undesirable under the following circumstances :

(*a*) When a customer is convicted for an offence of forging the cheques or Bills, (*b*) When a customer issues cheque when there is no sufficient credit balance in his account, and

(*c*) When a customer does not return the loan taken from the bank or does not repay the overdraft.

In such case, the banker must give the customer sufficient notice before closing his account.

(*iii*) When a banker learns that the customer has turned out to be a lunatic or insane or has died, the banker must stop the operation of the account.

(*iv*) If the customer is declared bankrupt, the banker must stop the operation of the account.

(*v*) When the bank receives a Garnishee order from the court attaching all the funds of a customer, the banker is bound to close the account of the customer automatically.

(*vi*) When the banker has received a notice of assignment of the credit balance in the account of a customer to a third party, the banker is bound to pay the amount to the said third party and must stop the operation of the account.

4.7.1. CIRCUMSTANCES UNDER WHICH A BANKER MAY CLOSE HIS CUSTOMER'S ACCOUNT

The banker-customer relationship commences as soon as an account is opened at a bank and this relationship continues as long as the parties concerned are willing to act as such. It will be terminated with the closure of the customer's account either by own act or at the banker's request. The account also may be closed by operation of law.

Following are the circumstances under which a banker can close his customer's account:

1. Mutual Agreement
2. Notice by the customer to the bank
3. Notice by the banker to the customer
4. Death or lunacy or insolvency of the customer
5. Granishee order by the court
6. Assignment made by the customer of his credit balance

1. By mutual agreement: An account of a customer can be closed by the banker paying the balance to him. In case of overdraft, account can be closed after it is cleared by the customer.

2. If the customer gives notice to the banker to close the account for any reason, the banker has to comply with such notice and the account is to be closed with immediate effect. A customer at his discretion can easily close his account in a bank merely by drawing a cheque for the entire balance. A banker cannot prevent a customer from withdrawing his balance and closing his account.

3. Notice by the banker: The banker himself may give notice to the customer of his intention not to act as the latter's banker, if the banker feels that the customer is no longer a desirable person as a customer. The banker regards a person who is convicted for forging cheques or bills or who issues cheques without sufficient funds as undesirable person. It is essential for the banker to give due notice to the customer of his intention to close the account before he actually stops the operation of the account. If the customer does not close the account after the expiry of the period of notice given by the banker, the latter can treat the account closed and return the balance to the customer and demand the return of the unused cheques.

4. On receipt of notice of the death of the customer, the banker must stop the operation of the account because the authority of the customer terminates as soon as he dies. The lunacy or insanity of a customer results in automatic termination of relationship since the lunatic is incompetent to be a party to the contract. The banker's authority to pay cheques is revoked. The banker should rerain himself from making any payments on the accounts until he receives an order from the court or he has a proof of customer's recovery. The banker should not rely on rumour but should have fairly conclusive evidence of customer's insanity. The banker can make payments only to such persons as they have the legal credentials.

Upon insolvency of a customer, his account must be closed because insolvent customer cannot give effective mandate against the banker. Therefore, the banker shall not pay his cheques, bills or undertake any other dealing on his behalf since the property rights are all automatically transferred to the 'Trustees in Bankruptcy' or to 'Official Receiver'.

5. If a Garnishee order is issued on the bank attaching all the funds of the customer, then the account is automatically closed, so as to be applied for payment to the judgement creditor as per the direction of the court.

6. A notice of assignment to a third party, of the balance standing to the credit of the customer has an indication to the bank to close the account. The balance so assigned has to be paid to the assignee since the assignor cannot operate the account

Thus the account of a customer with a banker should be closed or its operations suspended under varying circumstances stated above.

4.8. INSURANCE OF BANK DEPOSITS

An important and unique feature of the Indian Banking System is that deposits of the public with the banks are insured up to Rupees one lakh in each account. This had been introduced by the Reserve Bank of India and Govt. of India after the failure of the Palai Central Bank, a scheduled commercial bank in Kerala, in 1960. The failure of this bank had shaken the public confidence in the banking institutions. In order to instill confidence in the banking system, the Deposit Insurance Corporation of India was established by an Act of parliament to insure the deposits in the banks and the scheme came into existence with effect from January, 1962. The corporation was renamed as Deposit Insurance and Credit Guarantee Corporation with effect from July 15, 1978.

Features of Deposit Insurance : 1. The scheme of deposit insurance applied to all banks including non-scheduled commercial banks, co-operative banks and Regional Rural Banks. Hence all these banks are called as insured banks.

2. The insurance cover is available to all deposits made by the public except the deposits of the Central and State governments, foreign governments and the commercial banks.

3. The insurance cover is limited to the deposits held in the bank up to Rs lakh. This means that every account of a depositor in every insured bank is insured to the extent of Rs. 1 lakh only. Previously, i.e, up to April 30, 1993, the insurance cover was limited to the extent of Rs. 30,000.

4. The Corporation reimburses the depositors in the case of failure of the bank or the bank is amalgamated with another bank and defaults in paying fully the balances due to the depositors in case or by crediting the same fully to the transferred bank. For example, if X Bank on its merger with Y Bank gives credit to the extent of 50% of the deposit, a depositor having a credit balance of Rs 1,00,000 will get credit of Rs 50,000. The balance of Rs 50,000 will be reimbursed to him by the Corporation.

5. The rate of insurance premium is 5 paise per annum for every hundred rupees of assessable deposits. It is payable by the insured banks and not by the depositors at half yearly intervals. Assessable deposits are those deposits to which the cover of insurance is available, i.e., up to Rs 1 lakh in each account.

6. The Corporation maintains two funds, viz, (a) Deposit Insurance Fund and (b) General Fund. The income from insurance premia is credited to the Deposit Insurance Fund and is invested in Central Govt. securities. Income from such investments is credited to and the losses, if, any are debited to the Revenue Account of the Fund. The General Fund meets all other expenses of the Corporation.

4.9. DEPOSIT SCHEMES FOR INDIANS ABROAD

A good number of Indian citizens and foreign born Indians livc abroad and they are earning and save a good amount of money. In order to attract their savings and to bring them into our country in the form of bank deposits in India, the Govt. of India have formulated a scheme by which certain concessions and incentives are offered to remit money to India for investment. Banks in India are operating two types of accounts for them, viz. 1. Rupee Accounts and 2. Foreign Currency Accounts.

To open an account under any of the above schemes meant for Non-Resident Indians, one has to qualify as a Non-Resident Indian by fulfilling any one of the following conditions :

1. He is an Indian citizen, who stays abroad for employment or for carrying on a business, or vocation, or for any other purpose in circumstances indicating an indefinite period of stay outside India.
2. He is an Indian citizen working abroad with international organisations like UNO, IMF etc.
3. He is an official of Central/State government and public sector undertaking deputed abroad for temporary assignment.

4. He is a person of Indian origin. A person is deemed to be of Indian origin if he at any time held an Indian passport or he or either of his parents or any of his grandparents was an Indian and a permanent resident in undivided India at any time. Spouse of a citizen of India or of a person of Indian origin is also deemed to be of Indian origin even though his/her parents are non-Indians.

These accounts can be maintained with banks which are authorised dealers in foreign exchange or which are specifically authorised in this behalf by the RBI. Permission of RBI is not required to open these accounts.

1. Rupee Accounts : There are three types of accounts that can be opened in the names of non-Resident Indians :

(a) Ordinary Non-Resident Rupee Accounts (NRO Accounts): This is just like an account opened by a resident Indian to which local funds are credited. These funds do not qualify for remittance outside India. These accounts can be maintained in any form, i.e., fixed accounts, current accounts or savings account.

(b) Non-Resident (External) Accounts Scheme : Indian nationals abroad are permitted to open accounts in India under the accounts scheme. The accounts are maintained in Indian Rupee and are in the form of savings, current or fixed deposit accounts. The balances available in these accounts are freely repatriable at the prevailing rate of exchange. The money in these accounts can also be invested in the units of UTI, NSC, govt securities, etc. Interest on these accounts is tax free. These accounts can be opened by non-resident Indians or aliens of Indian origin and foreigners are not permitted to open such an account. The greatest drawback in this scheme is that there is exchange risk as the amount is repatriated at the current exchange rate. The fluctuation in the exchange rate has to be borne by the depositor and hence it is a disincentive to the Indian nationals abroad.

(c) Non-Resident (Non-Repatriable) Rupee Deposit Scheme (NRNR) : Under this Scheme, which came into force on 15th June, 1992, accounts are opened in Indian rupees with the authorised dealers by remitting funds in freely convertible foreign exchange from abroad. The features of the scheme are as follows :

1. Authorised dealers are free to fix the maturity period of deposits between 6 months and 3 years at a rate of interest prescribed by the banks which would be higher than those on domestic deposits.
2. On maturity of the deposit along with interest accrued thereon will not be repatriated outside India at any time.
3. The deposits may be renewed, transferred or shifted to another bank. But if the amount is withdrawn or invested in other schemes, it will not qualify for renewal under the scheme.
4. These deposits will not be considered as part of net demand and time liabilities for the purpose of Cash Reserve Ratio (CRR) and Statutory Liquidity Ratio (SLR). Hence they are free from any reserve requirements.
5. Lending against these deposits is not considered as part of net bank credit for the purpose of determining priority sector lending.

6. Authorised dealers may allow premature closure of the deposits and levy penalty for premature withdrawal as per their discretion.

2. Foreign Currency Accounts : Foreign Currency (Non-Residents) Accounts Scheme, 1993: Under this scheme banks permit exchange rate guarantee to the depositors. Deposits of one year and above up to 3 years are permitted and these deposits mobilised need not be surrendered to the RBI. The loans under the scheme are not subject to the lending rate stipulations of the RBI. These deposits are accepted in five currencies, viz, US dollars, UK Pound sterling, German Deutsche Mark, Japanese yen and EURO. At present the RBI has permitted the banks with effect from 16th April, 1997, to determine interest rates on such deposits subject to the ceiling prescribed by the RBI.

QUESTIONS

(1) Explain the legal position of a banker with regard to a fixed deposit.

(2) Discuss the formalities which a banker has to observe before opening a new account.

(3) What are the risks in opening accounts without proper introduction.

(4) Discuss the legal position of a Pass Book?

(5) "The Pass Book by itself cannot be relied on as a settled Account" – Do you agree ?

(6) What are the main features of a fixed deposit account ?

(7) Explain the circumstances under which a banker can close the account of his customer.

(8) What steps the banker should take if the customer refuses to comply with the banker's request to close his account?

(9) What steps should a banker take to close the account of an undesirable customer?

(10) What are the rules and regulations governing the opening and conduct of Non-Resident (External) Accounts.

(11) Who is a Non-Resident Indian? What is the procedure to be followed for opening:

(*i*) NRO (Non-Resident Ordinary) Account

(*ii*) NRE Account

(*iii*) FCNR Account.

(12) What is nomination? Who can nominate and how to nominate? What are the advantages to the customer by nomination?

(13) What are the features of nomination facility? Explain the legal status of nominee?

5

SPECIAL TYPES OF BANKER'S CUSTOMERS

The primary function of a commercial bank is to attract deposits of money from the public. The bank does this by opening accounts. An account in a bank can be opened by any person who (i) is legally capable of entering into a valid contract and (ii) applies to the banker in the proper manner, i.e., he follows the procedure laid down by the banker and accepts the terms and conditions stipulated by the latter under the provisions of the Indian Contract Act, 1872. Certain persons like minor, insolvent, lunatic and drunkards are incompetent to enter into valid contracts. So they cannot open and operate the account with the bank. Some persons like trustee, agent and executor have only limited power to enter into contract. The bank must take necessary precautions in dealing with such persons in order to safeguard its interests. Institutions like clubs, societies, colleges etc., partnership firms and joint stock companies also open account with the banker. The bank should take special care and precautions while dealing with such special types of customers. The present chapter discusses the legal position of the special cases of a bank's customers and the necessary precautions that a banker should take while dealing with them.

5.1. MINOR

According to Sec. 3 of the Indian Majority Act, 1875, a person, who has not completed the age of 18 years, is a minor. If he is under the court of wards, the age of majority is 21 years. That is, if a guardian of such person or property is appointed by the court before he completes 18th year, he remains a minor till he completes his 21st year. According to the Indian Contract Act, 1872, a minor is not capable of entering into a valid contract and a contract entered into by a minor is void except a contract for supply of necessaries of life which is regarded as a valid contract.

It was decided in the leading case of Mohori Bib vs Dharmadas Ghose that all contracts entered into by minors are void. Hence so long as a minor is a party, contracts for monies lent or to be lent for goods supplied or to be supplied and accounts stated are absolutely void. But contract with a minor will be valid if they are for necessaries of life or for the benefit of the minor and suitable to the standard of living of the minor. The case where the contracts involve recurring rights and liabilities such as partnership contracts with minor are voidable.

A minor can effectively discharge his duties as agent since an agent does not require contractual capacity. He can also be a witness to a signature. More than all, he can be a beneficiary in any contract and enforce it in his favour.

Natural guardianship of Minor:

Usually the banker encourages opening of Savings Bank Accounts in the name of the minor represented by his natural guardian. It is essential that the father alone should be the natural Guardian. Only if the father is not alive or available, the mother of the minor will be the natural Guardian. If both of them are not available, the court of competent jurisdiction can appoint a Guardian. The bank should record the date of birth of the minor to take action on his attaining Majority. On attaining Majority, the account shall stand in the name of the customer alone. His specimen signature will be brought on record and the minor shall be allowed to operate the account independently. Thus the guardianship can be summarised as follows:

(1) Boy or unmarried girl – father is a guardian; if father is not alive – mother.

(2) Illegitimate boy or illegitimate unmarried girl- mother; if not alive – father.

(3) Minor married girl – husband.

(4) If both father and mother are not alive, the person appointed by competent court.

(5) Father and mother as above do not include step-father and step-mother.

(6) Parsis/Christians – Same as above.

(7) Muslim: Father is a natural guardian and on death of father, the sequence being:

(*a*) Executor appointed by father's will.

(*b*) Father's father.

(*c*) Executor appointed by will of father's father.

(8) Mother as guardian for opening of accounts: As per the guidelines of R.B.I., Banks can open Savings Bank and Term Deposit Accounts in the names of Minors with mother as guardian while father is alive. However, no overdraft or loan against such deposit can be allowed without the father's consent.

In a landmark judgement on the guardianship of mother as guardian of a minor, the Supreme Court, in the case of Githa Hariharan & another vs. Reserve Bank of India (1999), held that in all situations where the father is not in actual charge of the affairs of the minor and the minor is in the exclusive care and custody of the mother or for any other resason, the father is unable to take care of the minor because of his physical and/or mental incapacity, the mother can act as natural guardian of the minor. The court further held that the definition of 'guardian' and 'natural guardian' do not make any discrimination against the mother and she being one of the guardians mentioned in Section 6 of the Hindu Minority and Guardianship Act of 1956, would undoubtedly be a natural guardian as defined in the Act.

The Supreme Court further classified that the words 'the father, and after him, the mother' do not necessarily mean 'after the lifetime of father'. Here it is emphasised that 'after' means 'in the absence of' and the word absence refers to the father's absence from the care of the minor's property or person for any reason whatsoever.

(9) Testamentary guardian for Hindu minor: A Hindu father by will can appoint a guardian in respect of minor or property. Such a testamentary guardian will act as guardian only after the death of father and mother.

If the minor customer dies, the balance in the account will revert to and in favour of the Guardian. But if the Guardian dies, the balance will be available to the minor only on attaining Majority. Of course it is open to the court to appoint any person as a guardian instead of the deceased.

Sometimes the banker advises the opening of joint accounts in the name of the minor and the Guardian. On attaining Majority, the minor too will be allowed to operate the account.

Minor as Agent: Since the minor can effectively function as agent, he can overdraw on his principal's account. The latter is bound by the same. But the banker should see that the minor acts within the authority granted to him by his principal. Even if an advance is granted to a minor on the guarantee of a third party in as much as the contract between the creditor and the minor, *i.e.* principal debtor is void; the contract of guarantee too will be void. The banker cannot in any event recover the money even from his customer. If the minor acts without authority or exceeds his authority, the banker should blame himself. The agent will be personally liable and the agent being a minor the banker cannot proceed against.

Minor as Partner: There is nothing to prevent a minor from becoming a partner in a firm and transacting business on its behalf. However he cannot be held liable for any debts of the partnership incurred before he attains Majority. On the other hand, unless he expressly repudiates the contract of partnership within six months of his attaining Majority, he will be regarded as having ratified the agreement and will become liable as a general partner for all debts incurred by the partnership since he was admitted to the benefits of partnership.

Precautionary measures:

A banker should therefore be very careful in dealing with a minor and take the following precautions:

1. The banker may open a Savings Bank Account (and not a Current Account) in the name of the minor in any of the following ways:

(*i*) in the name of the minor, to be operated upon by the natural guardian of the minor or guardian appointed by the Court.

(*ii*) in the name of the minor, to be operated upon by himself, if he has attained the age of 14 years.

2. The bank records the date of birth of the minor as given by the minor or his/her guardian on the attainment of maturity .The account of the minor in the name of the guardian should be closed and the balance paid to the minor or to be trans-

ferred to a new account of his/her own name in case of a joint account. The minor is also permitted to operate the account and his signature is taken on the account opening form.

3. If the father of Hindu minor dies, his mother becomes his natural guardian. After the death of the mother during the minority of the boy, there is either the testamentary guardian or the guardian appointed by the Court. The banker may return the money to such guardian.

4. In case the minor dies, the balance in the account is permitted to be withdrawn by the guardian and in case of joint account the balance will be held at the absolute disposal of the guardian.

5. No risk is involved if an account is operated in the name of a minor so long as the account is not overdrawn by the minor. But if an overdraft or advance is granted to a minor even by mistake or unintentionally, the banker has no legal remedy to recover the amount from the minor.

6. If an advance is granted to a minor on the guarantee of a third party, such advance cannot be recovered from the guarantor because the contract of guarantee is invalid, on the ground that the contract between the creditor and the principal debtor (minor) itself is a void contract.

According to Law a minor cannot enter into a valid contract and he cannot undertake a liability upon himself. Thus he cannot default. Surety's liability is a secondary one and does not arise, if the liability of the primary debtor does not arise. In Edavan Nambiar vs. Moolakai Raman (1957), the Madras High Court also upheld the above viewpoint.

Suppose a minor enters into an agreement by representing himself as major and later on claims such a contract as void on account of his minority at the time of entering into contract, the minor must restore the benefit derived by him under the agreement as decided in the case of Arooran Sugars Ltd. vs. State Bank of India.

7. A minor may draw, endorse or negotiate a cheque or a bill but he cannot be held liable on such cheque or bill. He cannot be sued in respect of a bill accepted by him during his minority. Such bill or cheque, nevertheless, will be a valid instrument and all other parties will be liable in their respective capacities. The banker should therefore be very cautious in dealing with a negotiable instrument to which a minor is a party.

8. A minor can be admitted to the benefit of partnership with the consent of all the partners; but he will not be liable for the losses or debts of the firm within six months. After he attains majority, he should repudiate his liability as a partner; otherwise he will be held liable as a partner of the firm from the date he was admitted to the benefit of the partnership.

9. A minor may be appointed as an agent to act on behalf of his principal. But the minor agent cannot be held responsible to his principal. The principal may be held responsible to the third parties in respect of the acts of his minor agent. Therefore, all his dealings with the banker will be valid and binding on his Principal.

5.2. MARRIED WOMEN

A married woman can enter into a contract in her own name. Such a contract will bind any property which she has acquired either as streedhan or otherwise.

Hindu married women are governed by the Hindu Succession Act, 1956. The status of married women of other religions is governed by the Indian Succession Act, 1925, and by the Married Women's' Property Act, 1874.

According to Indian Contract Act, a married woman has the right to enter into contract to acquire and sell property, to lend and borrow money etc. In other words, she has all the rights which a man has. A Current Account may be opened in the name of married woman. A married woman has power to draw cheques and give sufficient discharge. In the case of an overdraft, the banker will have no remedy against her if she does not have a separate estate. Even if she has separate property, the property may be so settled upon her that she is entitled to the income as it falls due but may not touch the corpus or the anticipated income. A married woman cannot make her husband liable except for the necessaries of life.

The married women are competent to enter into contracts. A banker may open an account in the name of a married woman and she can enter into contracts and bind her separate estate.

In case of a debt granted to a married woman, the banker has no legal remedy against her unless she has separate estate. Therefore, while granting a loan to her, the banker should examine her own assets and ensure that the same are sufficient to cover the amount of the loan.

A married woman can open a joint account with her husband. In such a case a banker should obtain clear instructions as to who is entitled to operate the account and to whom the amount is payable in the event of the death of any one of them. In the absence of clear instructions, the banker should not pay the amount standing in the joint account to the widow on the death of the husband, because the question of inheritance is involved in all such cases.

A banker should be very careful in granting an overdraft to a married woman. The reason is that he cannot proceed against her unless she has a separate property of her own. Even if she has property it must have been endowed in such a way that she can enjoy income from the property but has no right to sell property.

A married woman cannot make her husband responsible for the debts incurred by her except in some cases. If she is authorised to act as an agent of her husband, then the husband can be made liable for the debts.

Her husband can be made liable for the debts of a married woman in the following cases:

(*a*) If the loan is taken with his consent or authority and

(*b*) If the debt is taken for the supply of necessaries of life to the wife in case the husband defaults in supplying the same to her.

But her husband can escape from liability if he can prove that his wife was already well supplied with the necessities of life or that he can prohibit her from borrowing in his name. So a banker will not have any risk in dealing with a married woman so long as the account shows a credit balance. But if an overdraft is granted to her, he may find it difficult to recover the amount.

Precautionary measures:

A banker will have to keep the following precautionary measures while granting a loan or an overdraft to a married woman:

1. The husband of a married woman is not liable for debts contracted by her except in so far as they are for necessaries or for household purposes. So the banker should not lend money to a married woman simply because her husband has sufficient property.

2. If she does not have separate property, there will not be sufficient security for overdrafts granted to her. It may be difficult to recover money from her.

3. If she has separate property (Streedhan) the banker must find out the nature of her right to that property. She may not have the right to sell the property, although she may enjoy the income therefrom.

4. If a married woman applies for loan, the banker must examine whether there is any undue influence exercised by her husband. She should be apprised of her liability for the loan she contracts. She may be advised to consult her lawyer.

5. If there is a joint account in the names of husband and wife and if there is clause to the effect that in the event of the death of one party, the balance should vest in the survivor, the banker's position will be safe.

5.3. ILLITERATE PERSON

The banker can open an account in the name of an illiterate person who cannot sign but the banker can take his thumb impression as a substitute for signature. The banker should also take his recent photograph attested by a First Class Magistrate for the purpose of identification. While drawing cash from the bank, such persons should come to the bank and get cash in the presence of a witness in the office of the Bank Manager.

Illiterate persons cannot sign their names but affix their thumb impression. In such cases the bank may permit the opening of a Savings Bank Account or Fixed Deposit Account by an illiterate person by taking thumb impression instead of his signature. The bank should also insist on a copy of the photograph affixed on the account opening form. Withdrawals from this account will be allowed only if he comes personally to the bank and puts his thumb impression in the presence of some responsible officer of the bank.

5.4. TRUSTEES

Section 3 of the Indian Trustees Act, 1882 defines a trust as "it is a relationship which arises where a person holds a property for the benefit of certain other persons or for some objects allowed by law." The real benefit accrues not to the trustees but only to the beneficiary or the objects for which the trust is created. The person, who has settled the property, is the authority of the trust and is known as a 'settler'. A trustee is a person entrusted with the responsibility of managing an estate for the benefit of a person or persons according to the trust deed or will. That is, the person in whom the property is vested is the trustee. He is so called because of trust or confidence reposed in him. The document through which the trust is created is called 'trust deed'.

Precautionary measures:

While opening an account in the names of persons in the capacity as trustee, the banker should take the following precautions:

1. The banker should thoroughly examine the trust deed, appointing the person as a trustee.

2. He must also inspect the official probate or letter of administration.

3. He must acquaint himself with the names of the trustees, their powers, functions and the property vested in the trust.

4. In case of two or more trustees the banker should get clear instructions in writing of the person or persons authorised to operate on the account.

5. The banker should obtain specimen signature of person or persons authorized to operate the account.

6. A trust is an office of confidence. The trustees cannot delegate their power. They must act personally. The banker should insist on all the trustees signing cheques in the absence of such instructions.

7. The banker must see that the trust funds are not misapplied.

8. The banker should not allow transfer of trust funds to the personal account of the trustee.

9. The banker should not lend to a trustee as he does not have general power to borrow.

The banker should take all possible precautions to safeguard the interest of the beneficiaries of the trust, failing which he shall be liable to compensate the latter for any fraud on the part of the trustee.

5.5. EXECUTORS AND ADMINISTRATORS

Executors and administrators are persons who are appointed to conduct the affairs of a person after his death. The executor is appointed by the testator (person making a will) to execute his will after his death, whereas an administrator is appointed by a court for the execution of a will if the executor is not named in the will.

If the testator had executed a will and appointed persons to look after his affairs after his death, the appointees are known as executors. But if there is no such mention in the will or if the person dies intestate (i.e. without leaving any will) the court may appoint a person to administer the estate of the deceased. They are known as administrators.

In the case of executors, their powers and duties are mentioned in the will. The only thing is that the will should be probated, that is, certified by competent court as a bona fide document.

In the case of administrators, who are appointed by courts, their powers, duties and responsibilities will be defined by the letters of administration issued by courts.

On the death of a customer, his account is automatically frozen and the banker should not allow further operations. The executor can be allowed to operate the same on production of probate obtained from the court. In the case of an administrator the banker should insist upon the letters of administration issued by the court of competent jurisdiction. In either case the account of the deceased must be closed and a new account should be opened indicating the trust character of the account of the deceased, that is, as executors or administrators of the estate of the deceased.

When the appointees are more than one person they shall have a joint interest in the estates of the deceased. The banker may allow operation of the account by one or more upon the authority in writing by all the executors or administrators. But this authority is revocable and in case of revocation all the executors and administrators should operate the accounts jointly.

Precautionary measures:

The banker should take the following precautions while dealing with executors and administrators:

(1) On the death of a customer, the banker must stop payments from his account. The executor should be permitted to operate the account of the deceased after he has obtained the probate from the court. The administrator is authorised to do so after securing the letter of administration. The banker should examine these documents before the appointed person is permitted to operate the account.

(2) When two or more persons are appointed as executors or administrators, they shall have joint interest in the estate of the deceased and this interest is not capable of division. Then they should open a joint account with the bank. In such cases, the bank should obtain clear instructions regarding the operation of the account. One or more executors may draw cheques on the account but a letter of authority signed by all of them stating the name/names of the persons who will operate the account, is taken by the banker.

(3) The banker should be very cautious in conducting the account of executors/administrators so as to prevent them from misappropriating the funds of the deceased.

(4) The banker cannot exercise his right of set-off against the credit balance in the executor's personal account in respect of a debit balance in the account of the deceased.

(5) The banker should not permit transfer of funds from the estate account to the personal account of the executor.

(6) On the death, insolvency, insanity or resignation of any of the executors or administrators the bank can honour the cheques issued by him and can continue to operate the account, unless otherwise provided in the will.

(7) The executor/administrator may pledge the property of the testator to obtain an overdraft from the banker. The executor may do so only if he is permitted by the will. Hence the banker should examine the will before granting any loan to the executor or the administrators and they must jointly sign the loan document.

5.6. CUSTOMER'S ATTORNEY

A customer may appoint an attorney to deal with his bank account. The power of attorney may be either special or general. In the case of special power of attorney, the person so authorised gets power only for some limited purpose mentioned e.g. sale or purchase of property, etc. In the case of general power of attorney, the grantor of powers authorises the other person to act on his behalf in all matters concerning his business.

Precautionary measures:

While opening an account in the name of an attorney for a person, the bank should take the following precautions:

1. The banker should get a copy of the registered document attested by a Notary Public and keep it for his own record.

2. The banker should see that the power of attorney is in force at the time of opening the account. If it is for a specific period, the period must be noted at the top of the account so that the account does not continue beyond such period.

3. The banker should take note of all the terms of the power of attorney which are likely to be of concern to him at any time.

4. It must be seen that specific power is granted for opening and operating a bank account by the attorney himself.

5. The banker should note down the name and address of the person who has granted the power of attorney.

6. The account opening form should be signed by the principal and the signature of the attorney must be attested by him.

7. The banker should not accept any conditional power of attorney.

8. The banker should note that the death, insolvency or insanity of the principal revolves the authority vested in the agent and the latter ceases to act as agent of the principal.

5.7. CLUBS, SOCIETIES AND CHARITABLE INSTITUTIONS

Clubs, societies, charitable and religious institutions, libraries, schools etc. are not engaged in trading activities but their object is to render service to the public. These associations may be registered under the Societies Registration Act or the Indian Companies Act.

Precautionary measures:

Before opening an account for it, the banker should observe the following points:

(1) Incorporation: A society gets the legal recognition as an entity separate from its members only after its incorporation. Thereafter it is empowered to enter into valid contracts and to sue or be sued. The banker should, therefore, ensure that the applicant society is a properly incorporated body. The unregistered society cannot be sued in law.

These institutions may be registered or incorporated under the Indian Companies Act or the Co-operative Societies Act or the Societies Registration Act or under the Trust Act. If it is not registered, the organization does not have legal existence and hence it will have no rights to contract with the outside parties.

(2) Constitution: A registered society is governed by the provisions of the Act under which it has been registered. It may have its own constitution, charter or Memorandum of Association and rules and byelows etc. to carry on its activities. A copy of the same should be furnished by the society to the banker. The banker should ensure that these rules are observed by the persons responsible for managing the society.

Every organization should have a constitution of its own in the name of bye-laws or rules or Memorandum of Association and Articles of Association. These documents enable the banker to know exactly the rights and powers of the organisation. This will help the banker to deal with such organisation properly.

(3) Resolution of the Managing Committee: For opening a bank account, the Managing Committee of the Society must pass a resolution,

(*a*) appointing the bank concerned as a bank by the society.

(*b*) mentioning the name/names of the person or persons who are authorized to operate the account.

(*c*) giving any other directions for the operation of the said account.

A copy of the resolution must be obtained by the bank for its own record.

(4) Death or Resignation: In case the person authorised to operate the account on behalf of a society dies or resigns, the banker should stop the operation of the society's account till the society nominates another person to operate its account.

(5) While granting loans to such non-trading club, the banker should examine the borrowing powers found in the constitution of the club. A resolution must be passed by the Managing Committee for this purpose and a copy thereof be received by the banker.

(6) Transfer of funds: The banker should take care in case of personal accounts. If the person authorized to operate the society's account is also having his personal account with the same branch of the bank, the banker is under an obligation to ensure that the funds of the society are not being credited to the personal account of the said person or the office-bearer.

5.8. DRUNKEN PERSONS

One of the conditions of a valid contract is that it must be entered into between persons who are of sound mind. A person is said to be of sound mind if at the time he makes it, he is capable of understanding it and of forming a rational judgement as to its effect upon his interests.

If a person alleges that as a result of intoxication, he was incapable of understanding the nature and terms of the contract, which fact was known to the other party, he may invoke the protection of a court of law in setting aside the contract. The onus will be on the party who sets up the plea of disability to prove that it existed at the time of the contract. It should however be known that if a negotiable instrument in the meantime has been transferred to a holder who takes it in good faith and for value, the drunken person cannot deprive the holder in due course of his right under the instrument. It follows that banks have to be careful in getting documents executed by persons while they are in a state of intoxication.

A drunkard is a person who is under the influence of alcoholic drinks or drugs and stands on the same footing as a lunatic. An agreement made during drunkenness is void. The bank should not honour cheques of a person who has written and issued them under the influence of liquor. However, it is very difficult to judge whether the person is so intoxicated that he is not capable of understanding the applications of issuing the cheque. When customer presents his own cheque when he is drunk, the bank should not make immediate payment. Therefore it is better and safer that the bank should insist upon such a customer getting a witness (who is not drunk) to countersign before making any payment against the cheque.

5.9. PARDA WOMAN

As she remains completely secluded, a presumption in law exists that,

(*i*) any contract entered into by her might have been subject to undue influence and

(*ii*) the same might not have been made with her free will and with full understanding of what the contract means.

Thus a contract entered into by pardanashin woman is not a contract free from all defects. The other party to the contract shall have to prove that the contract with her was free from the abovementioned defects in order to enforce the same. The banker should, therefore, take due precaution in opening an account in the name of a pardanashin woman. As the identity of such a woman cannot be ascertained, the banker generally refuses to open an account in her name.

Therefore, a contract entered into by a pardanashin woman is not a contract free from all defects. The banker should, therefore, take due precaution in opening an account in the name of such woman. Usually the banker refuses to open an account in her name as the identity of such woman cannot be ascertained.

5.10. LUNATICS

Lunatic is a person of an unsound mind and hence he is incompetent to enter into a valid contract under the Indian Contract Act, 1872, since a lunatic does not understand what is right and what is wrong and hence a contract entered into by him is void.

Precautionary measures:

1. If a lunatic applies to the bank for opening an account, the bank should refuse to open an account for him.

2. When a person who has an account with bank has become insane or lunatic, the bank should suspend operation of the account and the bank is, however, entitled to debit the account of the lunatic customer in respect of all cheques honoured by the bank before getting the notice.

3. While suspending the operation of the account of any customer on the ground of lunacy, the bank must have sufficient proof (doctor's certificate or a court notice) of his lunacy.

A person of unsound mind can avoid a debt if he or his legal representatives can prove that he was of unsound mind at the time of borrowing. On receiving an express notice of a customer's insanity, it is customary for the banker to stop all operations on the account and await a court order appointing a receiver. It may be stated that reliance on hearsay would be dangerous. The bank should take care to ascertain the correct position. In case a person suffers from temporary mental disorder, it is customary to obtain a certificate from two reliable medical officers regarding his mental soundness at the time the advance is made. It is always safe to avoid lending to persons who fall in this category.

5.11. HINDU FAMILY

A joint Hindu family possesses ancestral properties and carries on ancestral business, the ownership of such property passes on to the members of the family according to the Hindu Law. While dealing with the account of a joint Hindu family and granting it a loan, the banker is naturally faced with a difficult task of ascertaining the rights of the members of the joint family.

Precautionary measures:

The following legal precautions should be taken by the banker in this regard:

1. The family business and its assets are managed by the eldest male member known as the Karta. According to the law, the Karta has an implied authority to take a loan, execute necessary documents and pledge the securities on behalf of the family for the purpose of the business of the family. However, to be on the safe side, the loan documents should be executed by all the adult male members of the family or with their consent by the head of the family in his capacity as its Karta or Manager.

2. The power of the Karta to borrow money on the security of the family property is subject to one limitation i.e. the loan is taken for the purpose necessary for or beneficial to the family. He can take a loan and pledge the property of the family for the purpose of meeting the needs of usual business of the family and not for any speculative business or for starting a new business. Other coparceners will not be liable for a loan contracted for a purpose other than the interest of the family business.

(*i*) The Manager of a joint Hindu family has power to alienate joint family property, so as to bind the interests of both adult and minor coparceners in the property, provided that the alienation is made for legal necessity or for the benefit of the estate *i.e.,* the payments of debts incurred for family business or other necessary purpose constituting a legal necessity.

(*ii*) The burden of proving legal necessity to support alienation is upon the alienee.

(*iii*) The alienee can succeed in (ii) above not only on proof of legal necessity but also on the proof that the alienee made reasonable enquiries and was satisfied as to the existence of legal necessity. In case of a dispute on his point the burden of proof the bank was satisfied before granting a loan that the loan was sought for the benefit of the family business lies on the banker himself. He should, therefore, be very careful in ascertaining the purpose of the loan sanctioned on the security of joint family assets.

3. If there is a minor coparcener in a joint family, his guardian must sign the documents on his behalf. When the minor coparcener attains majority, he should also sign the documents to give his assent to the undertaking given by major coparceners.

5.12. JOINT STOCK COMPANIES

The capital of joint stock companies is divided into shares. People who purchase these are the proprietors of the companies concerned. But a joint stock company is a separate legal entity. It has a separate legal existence, apart from that of the shareholders. Although some shareholders may die or become bankrupt, the company is not dissolved.

The liability of the shareholders is limited. A shareholder cannot under any circumstances be called upon to pay anything more than the face value of the shares allotted to him. If the assets of the company are insufficient to discharge the debts of the company, it is the creditors of the company that have to suffer, since the liability of the shareholders is limited. A shareholder of a company can sell his shares to others without the approval of the company or that of other shareholders. They cannot get any money from the company. On account of the transferability of the shares, investment is fixed from the point of view of the company, but is liquid from the point of view of the shareholder.

The management of companies is entrusted to directors elected by the shareholders from among themselves. Since the number of shareholders is very large, it is not possible to give the right of management to all the shareholders. Hence the management is entrusted to certain persons called directors elected democratically by the shareholders. The directors will have to manage the affairs of the company keeping in view the interests of the company and of the shareholders subject to the conditions, rules and regulations prescribed by law. The establishment as well as the management of companies takes place according to the laws in force in the country. The law generally prescribes what should not be done, and penalties are levied for the infringement of the law; but in the case of companies, the law prescribes what should be done.

Precautionary measures:

The precautions which a banker should take at the time of opening an account in the name of a company and in conducting transactions thereafter are described below:

Opening a bank account in the name of a public limited company:

(1) Before opening an account in the name of a public limited company, the banker must satisfy himself that the company has been duly incorporated. The procedure for incorporating a public limited company is prescribed by the Companies Act. At least seven persons must sign the Memorandum of Association, Articles of Association and submit them to the Registrar of Joint Stock Companies. The Registrar issues a Certificate of Incorporation. A company which has obtained the Cer-

tificate of Incorporation is deemed to have completed all the formalities connected with the issue of that Certificate. It is a conclusive evidence of the formation of the company. The banker must therefore examine the Certificate of Incorporation of the company before opening an account in its name.

(2) The banker must then examine the Memorandum of Association and Articles of Association of the company. In the Memorandum are mentioned the name of the company, place of registered office, objects, capital, liability of the shareholders and the willingness of at least seven members to form themselves into a company. In the Articles are laid down the rules for the internal management of the company. If the company does not submit a separate Articles of Association, provisions of Table A in the Act will apply.

These documents are of utmost importance in the conduct of the affairs of the company. The company must pursue only the objects mentioned in the Memorandum of Association. Anything done which is not sanctioned by the objects clause of the Memorandum of Association is *ultra vires* the company. Similarly, the conduct of the company must be in accordance with the provisions in the Articles of Association of the company. These are public documents. Anybody who deals with the company is supposed to be acquainted with the provisions of these two documents. So the banker has to examine these documents carefully to know the powers of the company, the powers of the directors, the rights of the shareholders and so on. The banker, before opening the account in the name of the company, must ask for the latest copies of these documents duly certified. By examining these documents, the banker will be able to know the powers of the company to contract debts, to pledge or mortgage the properties of the company, the powers of the directors in this behalf, and so on. He should ask the company to notify to him the changes that may be made in these documents from timc to time.

(3) Then the banker must ask for a copy of the resolution of the Board of Directors appointing him the banker of the company. He should definitely ascertain the person or persons authorised to conduct bank transactions, to sign cheques, to accept bills of exchange, to entrust valuables for safe custody, and so on.

(4) The banker must also examine the Certificate of Commencement of Business. After obtaining the Certificate of Incorporation, the company issues a prospectus. After the minimum subscription is collected and the directors have paid all their dues in full, the Registrar issues the Certificate of Commencement of Business.

A company cannot begin to operate until this certificate is obtained. Hence the banker must satisfy himself that the company has been authorised to commence business.

(5) If a company which has been operating for some time asks for the opening of a bank account, the banker should also examine the balance sheets and the profit and loss accounts of the company for the last two or three years.

Private Limited Companies:

Some of the restrictions imposed on public limited companies do not apply to private limited companies. Provisions relating to the convening of Statutory Meeting, submission of the Statutory Report, submission of balance sheet to the Registrar, etc. are not applicable to private limited companies. Private limited companies can commence business immediately after obtaining the Certificate of Incorporation without obtaining the Certificate of Commencement of Business. A private limited company must file with the Registrar the Articles of Association.

A banker, while opening an account in the name of private limited company, must also examine the Memorandum, Articles, resolution appointing him as banker, etc. in the same manner as opening an account in the name of a public limited company.

Other Companies:

Non-trading and non-profit making associations may also be incorporated under the Indian Companies Act. They are established for promotion of arts, literature, music, religion, charities and so on. These companies also have distinct legal entity and perpetual succession. The word "limited" is not found at the end of their names. The principle of limited liability applies to the members of these companies also. The banker must follow the same procedure when opening accounts in the name of these companies as in other cases.

Precautionary measures regarding the rights and duties of directors of the company: The rights and duties of directors are laid down in the Articles of Association of the Company. The banker must examine this document with reference to his own responsibilities in the matter. Although a particular act may be *ultra vires* the Board of Directors, but *intra vires* the company, may ratify the act of the Directors at its general meeting. But if the company itself has no such power, it cannot be valid even if all the shareholders ratify such an act.

When a company is under liquidation, the powers of the directors automatically cease. No director can issue cheques or endorse bills etc. All these powers vest in the official liquidator appointed by the Government.

Precautionary measures regarding advances to companies: When a company applies for a loan from a bank, the bank must examine Memorandum and Articles of Association to ascertain whether the company has the power to borrow and if so to what extent. In the case of trading companies, there is an implied power to borrow. In the case of non-trading companies the power to borrow must be conferred upon the company by its Memorandum and Articles. Where there is an implied power to borrow as in the case of trading companies, there is implied power to furnish the necessary security, to pledge or mortgage the property of the company and so on. Generally, it will be mentioned in the Articles that the company has the right to borrow. Sometimes the right to borrow vests only with the shareholders, in which case the resolution to borrow must be passed at the General Meeting. The banker should not grant advances to a company beyond the limits, if any, prescribed in the Articles. The banker may lose if he grants a loan beyond the limit specified in the Memorandum of Association. Although the advances may exceed the borrowing power of the Directors, they may be ratified by the shareholders provided they are within the limits prescribed in the Memorandum. The banker must ascertain whether loans have been obtained from other sources, thus exceeding the limit prescribed in the Articles. An examination of the balance sheet of the company will reveal such transactions.

The banker should also be careful in regard to the securities offered for the loan. No registration is necessary if the loan is granted on the security of stock exchange securities of the company or of the personal security of the directors. The banker should also find out whether there is any prior charge on the securities to him.

When a loan is applied for on the security of fixed assets of the company, the banker should see whether such securities are registered under Section 125 of the Indian Companies Act. The securities obtained by the banker must be registered according to the provisions of that Section. Companies cannot lend or borrow on the security of their own shares. A company may borrow by issuing debentures.

According to Section 292 of the Companies Act, loans secured otherwise than by the issue of debentures must be supported by a resolution of the Board of Directors. The amount of the loan is indicated in that resolution. According to Section 293, loans exceeding the paid up capital and reserves must be approved by the shareholders in the General Meeting. These restrictions, however, do not apply to temporary loans obtained for business purposes.

When a company applies for a loan, the banker should see whether the company has already issued debentures. If the company has issued mortgage debentures previously, the banker must ask for other securities. If that is not possible, the bank must ask the directors to give their personal security. When large loans are granted, the banker should obtain fixed charge on fixed assets and floating charge on moveable assets. The banker should examine whether the fixed assets are already mortgaged.

If a promoter of a company asks for a loan before the incorporation of the company, the loan must be granted on the personal security of the promoter. The company cannot ratify the action of a promoter in obtaining a loan after it is incorporated.

Precautionary measures regarding cheques in favour of the company: Cheques drawn in favour of a company may be asked to be credited to the personal accounts of directors or the employees of the companies. In such cases the banker should act with extreme care as otherwise he may be held guilty of negligence, and lose the protection given to the collecting banker under Sec. 131 of the Negotiable Instruments Act.

Precautions to be taken by a banker when a sole trader concern or a partnership is converted into a private limited company: Sometimes a sole trader may convert his concern into a private company and ask for loan on the security of the company's assets. If the debts of the previous sole trader concern have not been completely paid off, one of the creditors may bring an action against the trader. It is an act of insolvency for a trader to transfer all the assets of the business to a company. The banker should therefore ascertain whether all the debts of the previous concern have been completely liquidated.

The banker must satisfy himself about the following while opening an account in the name of the company.

1. Examination of Documents:

As a company is an artificial person, its constitution, powers and objectives, rules and regulations etc. are contained in the following important documents. The banker should thoroughly and carefully examine those documents.

(*i*) Certificate of Incorporation and Certificate of Commencement of Business. The certificates issued by the Registrar of Companies provide a conclusive proof that the company is duly incorporated body and all the necessary formalities regarding its formation have been fulfilled by the promoters.

(*ii*) The banker should examine the Memorandum specially to note the objectives for which the company is incorporated because any contract entered into by a company which serves an object other than the objects mentioned in the Memorandum is unenforceable at law and *ultra vires*.

(*iii*) The Articles of Association contain the rules and regulations of a company regarding its internal management. It contains in detail all matters which are concerned with the conduct of day-to-day business of the company.

The banker should scrutinize these documents very carefully.

2. Copy of the Board's Resolution:

Along with the application to open an account in the company's name, the banker should obtain a certified copy of the resolution passed by the Board of Directors of the company.

3. The Borrowing Powers of the Company:

All joint stock companies engaged in trade or industry have the implied powers to borrow money for the purpose of carrying on their business. The borrowing power of the company may be restricted by its Memorandum of Association. The banker should be very careful in ensuring that the total borrowing of the company does not exceed the limit.

Precautions to be taken by the banker:

(*i*) The banker should ascertain that the company borrows only for the purpose mentioned in its Memorandum of Association and within the limits, if any, specified therein.

(*ii*) A certified copy of the resolution of the Board of Directors should be obtained by the banker for his own record.

(*iii*) The Board of Directors should also pass a resolution certifying that the company's borrowings including the proposed borrowings are within the limit specified by the Companies Act or the limit sanctioned by the shareholders at their general meeting.

Directors' Personal Accounts:

The banker of a company having personal accounts of the directors of the company must handle the latter with care. If a director deposits cheques drawn in favour of the company to be credited to his personal account, the banker should first enquire the purpose for which such cheques are intended to be credited to his personal account and on being satisfied about the genuine reason, credit them to his account. If the banker does not make an enquiry in such case or credits the amount in the personal account of the director despite unsatisfactory reasons given by him, he shall be liable to refund the money credited to the director's account.

5.13. PARTNERSHIP

According to Section (4) of the Indian Partnership Act, a partnership is "*the relation between persons who have agreed to share the profits of a business, carried on by all or any of them acting for all*". There are no legal formalities for starting a partnership firm. Registration is not compulsory. The agreement of the partners need not necessarily be in writing. It may be oral or written.

There should not be more than 10 partners in a firm doing banking business and not more than 20 persons in a firm doing other kind of business. A partnership has no separate existence of its own, apart from the existence of the partners. Therefore if a partner dies or becomes bankrupt, or retires from the firm, the partnership comes to an end. If the remaining partners continue the business under the old firm name, even then a new partnership is deemed to have taken the place of the old.

Precautionary measures:

Opening of a bank account: Since each partner has an implied right to act on behalf of the firm, any partner has the right to open a bank account, unless otherwise stated in the partnership agreement. If there are any provisions regarding the bank account in the partnership deed, bank transactions must take place accordingly. But if there is nothing in the partnership deed regarding the matter, any partner has the right to operate upon the bank account by issuing cheques. Similarly, each partner has the right to countermand any cheque issued under the firm name.

The account must be opened in the name of the partnership firm, but not in the name of the partner himself. A partner has no implied right to open the firm's bank account in his own name. If an account is opened in the name of any partner, other partners are not liable in respect of transactions therein. This has been decided in Alliance Bank vs Kearsley. Section 19 (2) (b) of the Indian Partnership Act says that unless there is custom to the contrary, no partner has the implied right to open a bank account in his own name.

Although any partner can open an account in the name of the partnership firm, it is desirable that the bank should insist on all the partners signing on the Account Opening Form. There will not arise any disputes later if the banker ascertains in writing the person or persons who are authorised to operate the bank account. If there is any partnership deed, the banker must examine it carefully and note the name of the firm, its business, the names of the partners, their addresses, their rights and liabilities and so on.

The right of drawing cheques given to a partner may be withdrawn by others at any future time. When the banker is notified of the withdrawal of such right, he should not honour cheques presented subsequently. Any partner can countermand a cheque issued in the name of the firm.

Death of a partner: When a partner dies, the partnership comes to an end. The legal heir of the deceased partner does not automatically become the partner of the firm. The legal heir has only the right to recover the money due to him from the partnership firm. The banker may continue the bank account if by the date of the death of the partner there is a credit balance in the account. But if there is a debit balance, the banker must stop the account and start a fresh account. The banker thus will secure for himself the right to recover the amount from the estate of the deceased partner also.

Bankruptcy of a partner: The partnership also comes to an end when one of the partners becomes bankrupt. The banker should not honour cheques drawn by the bankrupt partner, unless it bears the signatures of the other partners as well. The banker may continue the bank account in so far as it may be necessary to wind up the affairs of the firm, which is dissolved owing to the bankruptcy of a partner. In such a case, the assets of the partnership may be transferred to one of the partners, who acts as a trustee of such assets. There is the danger of the banker being held guilty of negligence unless he acts with utmost care and caution in such cases.

Insanity of a partner: A partnership is not dissolved when one of the partners becomes insane, but it becomes a sufficient reason for the dissolution of the firm. The relations of the insane partner may file a petition in the court for ordering the dissolution of the firm.

Retirement of a partner: When a partner retires from the partnership firm, he must notify the same to the banker. Otherwise, he also becomes liable for the debts incurred by the firm. After the receipt of retirement notice, if the partnership is indebted to the bank, the bank must stop the account and start a fresh account. In this case, the retiring partner also will be liable for the debt owing by the partnership firm at the date of retirement. If the partnership assets had been given as security for the advance granted to the firm, the bank account may be continued on the basis that transactions are being continued for the purpose of winding it up.

Bank Transactions: The banker must act with care and caution in respect of transactions relating to partnership business. Cheques drawn in favour of the partnership firm should not be credited to the personal account of a partner. But it has been decided in Backhouse vs Charlton that cheque issued by the firm in favour of a partner may be credited to the partner's personal account and the banker is not bound to examine such transactions. But even in such cases, the banker may have to act with circumspection. For instance, the partner may be heavily indebted to the bank, and the bank might be pressing him for repayment. In such cases, if a cheque drawn by the firm is deposited by him in his personal account, the banker has to make an enquiry.

Sometimes, a person may approach a bank with a request to open the bank account in his own name, representing that he is the sole proprietor of the concern. The banker will have to make discreet enquiries in such circumstances. If he does not do so, there is the danger of the cheques belonging to the partnership firm being credited to his personal account. In such cases, the banker may not be able to get the statutory protection given to the collecting banker.(Hampstead Guardians vs Barclays Bank Ltd., 1923.) But if the banker takes reasonable care and opens the account after due enquiry, he will be entitled to statutory protection (Smith and Baldwin v. Barclays Bank Ltd.).

Advances to partnership firms: When a trading partnership applies for a loan, the banker should call for the balance sheets of the firm for the preceding two or three years. The banker will be able to form an idea of the creditworthiness of the firm, but he will be able to know the other partners in the firm and other relevant information.

Unless otherwise mentioned in the partnership deed, a trading firm has the implied power to borrow. Each partner has the right to pledge the properties of the firm, to borrow money on behalf of the firm, to deal in bills of exchange, and so on. A non-trading firm will not have such rights. But it is usual for bankers to obtain a definite mandate from all the partners whether they are partners of a trading firm or non-trading firm. When properties are pledged, all partners must sign the documents. When fixed assets are mortgaged, all partners must necessarily sign. When one of the partners is entrusted with the responsibility of conducting banking transactions, his rights, especially his right to obtain an overdraft, must be clearly ascertained. These rights must be exercised only for the benefit of the partnership firm, but not for personal gain. The banker must keep his watchful eye on all the transactions of the partnership with himself.

The partnership deed contains the details of the agreement reached between the partners. A banker should take the following precautions while operating an account in the name of a partnership firm:

1. Number of Partners: The banker should very carefully examine the partnership deed which is the charter of the firm. The banker should see that the number of partners does not exceed the statutory limit.

2. Title of the Firm's Account: A firm's account should always be opened in the name of the firm and not in the name or names of the individual partner/partners.

3. Opening of an Account: An account in the name of a firm may be opened by a banker on receipt of an application from one or more of the partners. Banker, however, insists that all the partners should join to open the firm's account. If any partner has gone out of the country, the rest of the partners can open a bank account in the name of the firm. Specimen signatures of all the partners should be obtained for the purpose of record. In case any of the partners is deprived of the right to open an account in the firm's name and this fact is within the knowledge of the banker he should not therefore, open an account in the name of the firm at the request of such partner. The banker should therefore, confirm the right of the applicants to open an account in the name of the firm from the partnership deed or from any other available evidence, e.g. the authority letter signed by all other partners.

4. The Partnership Letter of Mandate :

The banker should take a letter signed by all the partners stating,

(*i*) the name and addresses of the partners,

(*ii*) the nature of the business undertaken by the firm, and

(*iii*) the name/names of the partner/partners who will operate the account on behalf of the firm and will have the authority to draw and accept bills etc. and to sell and mortgage the property of the firm.

5. Revocation of Authority to operate the Account :The authorities given in favour of a particular partner/partners to operate the firm's account may be withdrawn by any of them by giving a notice to the banker. In such circumstances the banker should stop payment of cheques signed by all such partners and pay the cheques which are signed by all the partners. A partner can also stop the payment of a cheque issued by any other partner on the firm's account.

6. If a cheque payable to the firm is endorsed by a partner in his own favour and is deposited by him to be credited to his personal account, the banker should do so after making an enquiry about it from other partners and after being satisfied about it.

5.14. JOINT ACCOUNTS

When an account is opened in the names of two or more persons, who are not partners in a firm or who are not joint trustees, it is called a joint account. When a joint account is opened the banker should obtain comprehensive mandate. The mandate should cover all points because the right to draw cheques conferred upon a person does not automatically confer upon him the right to deal in securities, to contract debts, or to deal in bills of exchange. If one of the joint account holders obtains an overdraft, the other does not have any liability.

Precautionary measures:

1. Issuing of cheques: It should be clearly specified as to who is authorized to draw cheques. If nothing is stated in the mandate, all the joint customers must sign the cheques. Although the right to draw cheques may be conferred on one or more of the parties, any one of the joint account holders can countermand a cheque. In this case, the right to sign the cheques conferred on one of the parties is deemed to be temporarily withdrawn.

If a third party, not being a joint account holder, is authorised to draw cheques, the arrangement must be approved by all the parties. Similarly, if a power of attorney is given to a third party, not being a joint account holder, the power of attorney must be signed by all the parties.

2. Death of joint account holder: If one of the joint customers dies, according to English Law, the survivors can continue to transact the business relating to the joint account. But according to Indian Law, the surviving joint customers, along with the heir of the deceased joint customer, must transact the business. Clear instructions must be included in the mandate given to the banker.

3. Joint debts: The right to draw cheques given to a joint customer is limited to the credit balance available in the bank account. If cheques are drawn in excess of the amount, all the joint customers become indebted to the bank. But the right to draw cheques does not extend to contract debts. So the banker must ascertain whether the person who has the right to draw cheques has also the power to overdraw the account.

4. Joint and several liabilities: According to Indian Law, joint liability means joint and several liabilities. If one of the joint customers dies, and if the account is overdrawn by that time, the banker must stop that account and open a fresh account in order to make the estate of the deceased customer liable for the debt. Otherwise, the banker would lose his right to recover the amount from the estate of the deceased party on account of the operation of the rule in Clayton's case.

5. Safe custody deposits: If joint account holders deposit valuables for safe custody with the bank, no one of them can take delivery of them. The banker should return the securities only on the requisition of all the joint customers. Similarly, no one of the joint customers can stand surety on behalf of all the joint customers. No single joint customer can pledge the fixed property of the joint parties without a power of attorney granted to him. When shares or valuables belonging to the joint parties are sold by the banker, the sale proceeds should be handed over to the joint holders and the legal representatives of the deceased party or reimbursed in accordance with their instructions.

6. Death, insanity or bankruptcy of a joint customer: When the banker is duly informed of the death of one of the joint customers, the banker should not thereafter honour cheques presented for payment. Similarly, when a notice is given to him of the insanity or bankruptcy of one of the joint customers, the banker should not honour cheques subsequently presented. The balance should be paid only to the legal representative of the deceased or insane customer and to the other joint customers.

7. Garnishee order: If the banker received a garnishee order in respect of one of the joint account holders asking him not to make any payment out of the joint account, he should inform the Court that it is a joint account and request the Court to withdraw the garnishee order.

8. Trust accounts: If the joint account relates to a Trust, but the banker is not informed of the same, the banker need not take cognisance of the fact. After he comes to know that it is a trust account, he should be careful to see that it is not overdrawn at any time.

9. Joint accounts of husband and wife : A joint account may be opened in the names of husband and wife. If the account is in the name of the husband and he predeceases his wife, the balance will devolve on his legal heirs but not on his wife. To avoid legal formalities, a husband usually opens a joint account with his wife with the term 'either or survivor'. In this case, on the death of one of the parties, the survivor can draw the amount.

10. Others: The banker should take the following precautions in opening and dealing with a Joint Account:

1. The application for opening a joint account must be signed by all the persons intending to open a joint account.

2. The banker should obtain clear instructions in writing signed by all the joint account holders regarding the operation of the account. The joint account may be operated in any of the following ways:

(*i*) By all the depositors jointly.

(*ii*) By either or survivor of them.

(*iii*) By former or survivor of them.

The mandate must include the name or names of the persons who are authorised to operate the joint accounts and must specify the extent to which they are authorized to take advances or to pledge the securities etc. In the absence of such instructions the banker should honour only those cheques which bear the signature of all the persons in whose name the account stands.

3. Any joint account holder can stop payment of a cheque issued on a joint account. Banker must honour such order even if an agent or attorney has been appointed to operate the account.

4. The full name of the account must be given in the entire document furnished to the banker, even if the account is to be operated upon by one or a few of joint account holders.

5. The banker should also take a mandate to ascertain whether the persons operating the joint account are also authorized to overdraw the account. If so, it is desirable to establish separate individual liability of all the joint account holders in addition to their joint liability.

6. The authority to operate the account can be revoked by any of the persons giving such authority. It is automatically revoked if any of the joint account holders dies, becomes bankrupt or is of unsound mind. The banker must stop payment in such cases.

7. The banker should be given clear instructions regarding the withdrawal of securities in the joint account and the power conferred upon the person operating the account to lodge the securities.

9. A joint account may be operated by either of the joint account holders.

But if cheque is drawn and signed by one of them, any alterations therein should also be done by the same person and not the other one. The alteration should bear the signature of the drawer.

In times of death of a joint account holder, the balance in the joint account shall be payable to all the joint account holders together if there is no instruction. If either or survivor condition is included, the balance is payable to the survivor or survivors.

5.15. BANKRUPTS

In case a customer gives notice of his intention to suspend payment of his debts to his creditors or has suspended repayment or filed in the court a declaration to the effect that he is unable to pay his debts, a banker should stop all business transactions with him. The whole property of the debtor will be vested in the Official Receiver, or in the case of Presidency towns, in the Official Assignee who will administer it for the benefit of the creditors generally; the object of it is to protect the property from the debtor and also from the individual creditors who may seek to obtain preferential treatment. Special care should be taken in the case of undischarged bankrupts, as he cannot obtain credit for more than Rs. 50. The bankrupt will be guilty of misdemeanour if he does any business under any other name without disclosing the fact of his bankruptcy.

QUESTIONS

1. What precautions should a banker take in opening and conducting accounts in the names of minors and married women ?
2. What steps should a banker take (a) to open an account of a partnership firm and (b) to close the account of an undesirable customer ?
3. What precautions should a banker take while opening current accounts in the names of (a) joint stock company, (b) Secretary, Madras University Students Union and (c) Ram aged 12 years.
4. What precautions should a banker take in opening account of (i) a partnership firm and (ii) a 'pardanashin' lady ?
5. State the procedure for opening an account of illiterate person as also precautions as may be considered necessary before and after opening of such account.
6. State and explain the formation to be completed and precautions to be taken while opening accounts in the names of
   (a) Minors,
   (b) Trust,
   (c) Public Limited Company, and
   (d) Club, School or College.

Negotiable Instruments

6.1. MEANING

Although negotiable instruments in India are governed by the Negotiable Instruments Act of 1881, the said Act does not define negotiable instruments. As such, Section 13 of the Negotiable Instruments Act merely specifies certain instruments which, when drawn up in a particular manner, would be regarded as "Negotiable Instrument".

Justice K.C. Wiltis defines a negotiable instrument as "*one the property in which is acquired by anyone who takes it bona fide, and for value*" notwithstanding any defect of title in the person from whom he took it.

Another useful definition is given by Thomas in his book "*Commerce, its Theory and Practice (8th Ed)", who states that " an instrument is negotiable when it is, by a legally recognised custom of trade or by Law, transferable by delivery or by endorsement and delivery, without notice to the party liable, in such a way that (a) the holder of it for the time being may sue upon it in his own name, and (b) the property in it passes to a bona fide transferee for value free from any defect in the title of the person from whom he obtained it.*"

These definitions clearly reveal the true nature of a negotiable instrument.

The words "Negotiable" and "Instrument" denote transferability by delivery and a written document by which a right is created in favour of some person. The term negotiable instrument, is therefore, literally a document transferable by delivery. (The term negotiable means transferable with immediate effect).

Though this definition does not give the characteristics of Negotiable Instrument, it states that the three instruments, viz., promissory note, bill of exchange and cheques, are negotiable instruments. A negotiable instrument is a transferable document and passes on freely from one person to another. The three instruments stated above are negotiable instruments by statute. However, there are also certain negotiable instruments by the custom of trade. Thus in India, government promissory notes, hundies, delivery orders and railway receipts have been held as negotiable instruments by usage or custom of trade.

6.2. ESSENTIAL CHARACTERISTICS OF NEGOTIABLE INSTRUMENT

(*i*) Transferability: The basic feature of a negotiable instrument is that it is easily transferable from person to person by mere delivery or by endorsement and delivery. In the case of bearer instrument, the property passes by mere delivery to the transferee and in the case of an order instrument, it passes by endorsement and delivery. Though transferability is an essential feature of a negotiable instrument, but all transferable instruments are not negotiable instruments, but all negotiable instruments are transferable.

(*ii*) Good title to the transferee (Negotiability) : A person who takes delivery of a negotiable instrument in good faith and for value (i.e. a holder in due course) gets a better title than the transferor has got. A person who takes a negotiable instrument from another person, who had stolen it from somebody else, will have absolute and undisputable title to the instrument, provided he has received the same for value and in good faith without knowing that the transferor was not the true owner of the instrument. That is, a bona fide transferee for value is not affected by any defect of the title on the part of the transferor or of any of the previous holders of the instrument. This feature of the negotiable instrument confers absolute and good title on the transferee. But in case X purchases a pen or some other article from Y against payment of its full value. But Y has stolen the pen from another person Z. If the thief i.e., Y is caught for the theft then X has to return the same to the true owner of the pen to Z, because the title to X to the pen is not deemed to be better than the litle possessed by Y. In fact Y had no title thereto and hence X will also stand on the same footing.

(*iii*) Right of Action : The holder of a negotiable instrument being a holder in due course, gets the right of action to sue upon the instrument in his own name.

Every instrument, apart from the three instruments, viz. promissory note, bill of exchange and cheque which will satisfy all the above three features can be called as negotiable instrument. Therefore, any instrument which entitles a person to a sum of money and which possesses the characteristic of negotiability is a negotiable instrument.

Though a bill, a promissory note or a cheque represents a debt, the transferee is entitled to sue on the instrument in his own name in case of dishonour, without giving notice to the debtor that he has become its holder.

6.3. PRESUMPTIONS AS TO A NEGOTIABLE INSTRUMENT

Sections 118 and 119 lay down certain presumptions which the court presumes with regard to a negotiable instrument. Until the contrary is proved, the following presumptions shall be made :

(*i*) Every negotiable instrument is drawn, accepted and endorsed, made or transferred for consideration.

(*ii*) The date it bears on it is the date on which it is drawn or made.

(*iii*) Every transfer of the instrument is made before its maturity.

(*iv*) The instrument is accepted within a reasonable time after its date and before its maturity.

(*v*) The endorsements appearing upon a negotiable instrument are in order in which they appear thereon.

(*vi*) The instrument is duly signed and stamped.

(*vii*) Every holder of a negotiable instrument is a holder in due course unless it is proved otherwise.

(*viii*) In a suit upon a dishonoured instrument, the court shall, on the proof of the protest, presume that it was dishonoured until this fact is disproved.

6.4. TYPES OF NEGOTIABLE INSTRUMENTS

There are two types of negotiable instruments, viz (i) instruments negotiable by law, *i.e.* by the Negotiable Instruments Act, 1881, and (ii) instruments negotiable by usage or custom of trade.

Thus in India, the following are treated as negotiable instruments:

The instruments negotiable by law are:

(*i*) Promissory note

(*ii*) Bill of exchange

(*iii*) Cheque

The instruments negotiable by custom of trade are:

(*i*) Govt. promissory notes

(*ii*) Dividend warrants

(*iii*) Share warrants

(*iv*) Bearer debentures

Exceptional Cases of Negotiable Instruments : Generally every negotiable instrument should possess all the essential features discussed earlier. But at certain times, the drawer or the holder may remove the essential characteristic of negotiability and thus the instrument ceases to be a transferable or negotiable instrument. For example, if a cheque is payable to a specified person only and not to his order or to the bearer, it cannot be transferred to any other person and hence it loses its negotiability. In case if a cheque is crossed 'not negotiable' it can be transferred but without conferring on the transferee absolute and good title to it. The transferee in this case will stand at par with the transferee of any other article and shall not possess title better than that of his transferor.

6.4.1. PROMISSORY NOTES

According to Section 4 of the Negotiable Instruments Act of 1881, "*Promissory note is an instrument in writing containing an unconditional undertaking by the maker to pay a certain sum of money only to or to the order of a certain person, or to the bearer of the instrument.*"

The specimen of a Promissory Note is given below :

Rs. 10,000 =

Chennai-600001

May 18, 2006

Three months after date, I promise to pay Ram or order the sum of Rupees Ten Thousand only for value received.

To

Stamp

Ram

Sd. Laxman.

A promissory note may be drawn by more than one person also who may undertake to pay the amount both in their individual capacities as well as jointly. The specimen of a promissory note with joint and several liability is given below :

Rs. ....

Chennai

On demand we joinly and severally promise to pay to .... or order the sum of Rupees. .... , together with interest on such sum from this date at the rate of .... per cent per annum for value received.

Stamp

Signatures across the stamp

Address..........

Essentials of a promissory note: The above definition gives the following essential features:

(1) Thc instrument must be in writing.

(2) Mere acknowledgement of debt is not sufficient. There must be an undertaking of promise to pay. An I.O.U. (I owe you) therefore is not a promise to pay.

(3) The promise to pay must be unconditional, because a conditional promise destroys the negotiable character of an otherwise negotiable instrument. But a promise to pay at a particular place or after a specified time or on the happening of an event certain to happen is not conditional. For example, I promise to pay Rs. 1000, ten days after X's retirement " is not conditional.

(4)The instrument must be signed by the maker. In the case of an illiterate, he may fix his thumb mark or any other mark. The signature may be indicated by a facsimile or by stamping the name.

(5) The promise to pay must be a certain sum of money in legal tender. For example , a promise to pay Rs. 5000 and such other sums as may become due is not a promissory note. But where the promise is to pay the money at a specified rate of interest it is considered as certain sum of money.

(6) The payee must be certain.

Usually promissory notes bear date and place but they are not required under the law. But a stamp is necessary as is required under the Indian Stamp Act.

6.4.2. BILLS OF EXCHANGE

A bill of exchange is "*an instrument in writing containing an unconditional order, signed by the maker, directing a certain person to pay a certain sum of money only to, or to the order of, a certain person or to the bearer of the instrument*".

Specimen of an Inland Trade Bill

Stamp

Coimbatore
1st Jan. 2002

Three months after date pay M. Kannan or order the sum of one thousand rupees only, for value received.

S. Senthil

To
L. Kumar
D.B. Road,
Coimbatore

There are three parties here.

1 S. Senthil is the Drawer of the bill.

2 M. Kannan is the payee of the bill, i.e., the person to whom the value of the bill is to be paid.

3 L. Kumar is the Drawee, i.e., the party on whom the bill is drawn. He becomes the acceptor when he indicates his acceptance of the instrument.

Essentials of a bill:

(1) The instrument must be in writing.

(2) It must contain an unconditional and express order to pay.

(3) There are three parties in the bill i.e., Drawer, Drawee and Payee. All of them must be certain and definite individuals. Sometimes the drawer and payee may be the same person.

(4) It must be signed by the drawer.

(5) A bill may be payable on demand in which case it is called a demand bill or it may be payable after a specified period and such bills are called time bills. In the case of time bills, the bill matures for payment three days after the day on which the bill is expressed to be payable. These additional days are known as days of grace.

(6) In the case of demand bills, instruments payable on demand, no acceptance is required . But in the case of time bills the drawee must testify his willingness to pay the bill. Without such acceptance, a time bill cannot be negotiated.

(7) The amount of money to be paid must be certain and the payment must be in legal tender.

(8) The bill may be payable to payee or his order. Such a bill is called order bill. When it is payable to bearer, it is called a bearer bill.

Types of Bills:

A. Inland and Foreign Bills:

Inland Bill : A bill which is drawn and payable within the same country is called an Inland bill. It may be a demand or time bill. Demand bills are exempt from stamp duty whereas the stamp duty varies according to length of time and the amount in the case of time bills.

Foreign Bills : They are bills (1) drawn in India but are payable by a person resident outside India and (2) drawn outside India but are payable in India.

Bills in sets : Foreign bills are drawn in sets. This is because in the case of foreign bills they have to be sent over long distances and therefore, there is the possibility of loss or delay.

Rules regarding Bills in sets:

(1) Bills of exchange may be drawn in parts of 2, 3 or 4 as the case may be. All the parts together make a set and the whole set constitutes one bill. Each part must be numbered and stamped.

(2) Each part must contain a provision that it shall continue to be payable only so long as others remain unpaid. In other words, payment of one part discharges the entire set.

(3) Where a person accepts or endorses different parts of the bill to different persons, he and the subsequent endorsers of each part are liable on each such part as if it were a separate bill. Therefore, the acceptor should accept only one part of the set.

(4) Each part should contain reference to the other parts. Where in a particular part there is no such reference, that part in the hands of a bona fide holder is treated as a separate bill. This is so because the reference in each of these parts to the other parts of the set is in the nature of a condition of payment.

(5) If two or more parts are negotiated to different holders in due courses, the person who first acquired title to his part is entitled to the other parts. He also is entitled to the money represented by the bill.

B. Clean and Documentary Bills:

Clean bills are those unaccompanied by any document. Documentary bills are used specially in foreign trade. The exporter ships the goods and obtains a bill of lading. The cargo is also insured by him and policy obtained. He prepares the Invoice and draws a bill of exchange on the importer for the amount covered by the Invoice. The bill of exchange accompanied by the bill of lading, Insurance policy and the Invoice are sent to the banker in the importing country. Such bills are called Documentary bills.

They are called D/A bills (documents against acceptance) if the documents are passed on to the importer after he gives the acceptance. If the documents are handed over only after the payment is made by the importer, they are termed as D/P (documents against payment).

C. Trade and Accommodation Bills:

Trade bills are drawn in the course of trade transaction. When a wholesaler sells goods on credit to the retailer, the relationship between them is one of the creditor and debtor. It is convenient for the wholesaler as creditors to draw the bill on the retailer. He can discount such bill with the banker and realise money immediately without waiting for the payment from the retailer, which can be obtained only after the period of credit expires.

Accommodation bills are drawn and accepted without consideration with a view to provide funds to one or more parties. An example will illustrate this. A, who is in need of money, draws a bill on B, who has credit in the market. B accepts the same without consideration. A discounts the bill with a banker and obtains money. On due date, he provides the necessary funds to enable B to meet the bill.

D. Fictitious Bills:

As stated already, the drawer and payee must be certain and definite persons. When they are fictitious , the bills are called fictitious bills, where the drawer is a fictitious person but the acceptor is genuine and real and the holder in due course can enforce payment of such a bill. This is subject to the condition that the first endorsement and signature of the supposed drawer are in the same handwriting.

E. Ambiguous Instruments:

Instruments which can be interpreted either as a bill of exchange or as a promissory note are called ambiguous instruments. The scope of such interpretation arises because of faulty drafting of the instruments. For example, A draws a bill on B, a non-existent person, and the bill is payable to the order of A himself. Then he negotiates the bill to C. As B is a non-existent person, A becomes primarily liable and therefore it can be treated as a promissory note also, although it is worked as a bill.

The holder in this case has the option to treat it either as a bill or promissory note. But once the option is exercised, it is final.

F. Inchoate Instrument:

It is an incomplete negotiable instrument duly signed and stamped which the holder can complete and make it into negotiable instrument up to the value mentioned or up to the value covered by the stamp affixed on it. Any person who signs such an instrument in a particular capacity becomes liable to the holder in due course in that capacity for such amount. But persons who are not holders in due course cannot recover more than the intended amount.

For example, A instructs B, his agent, to make purchases and signs a promissory note without specifying the amount. B is instructed to complete the amount of purchase. B makes a purchase for Rs.8000 but fills it up for Rs.10000. The promissory note is given to the shopkeeper C, who negotiates it to D. If D is a holder in due course, he can recover the amount of Rs.10000 from A, but C, who is aware of the circumstances, cannot recover more than Rs.8000 which was the amount intended.

G. Escrow:

A bill delivered conditionally or for a special purpose is called Escrow. There is no liability to pay if the conditions are not fulfilled or the special purpose for which the bill is delivered is not satisfied. But the rights of a holder in due course are not affected.

6.4.3. CHEQUES

The Indian Negotiable Instruments Act defines a cheque as "*a bill of exchange drawn on a specified banker and not expressed to be payable otherwise that on demand.*"

A cheque is an order on the bank to pay a certain sum of money to the payee mentioned in the cheque. The same Act defines a bill of exchange as:

"*An instrument in writing containing an unconditional order, signed by the maker directing certain person to pay a certain sum of money only to or to the order of a certain person or to the bearer of the instrument*".

Every person opening a current account with a bank will get a cheque book free of cost from the latter. This book contains a number of cheque leaves which can be used by the customer to draw money. Dr. Herbert L. Hart defines a cheque "*as an unconditional order in writing drawn on a banker signed by the drawer, requiring the banker to pay on demand a certain sum of money to or to the order of the specified person or to the bearer and which does not order any act to be done in addition to the payment of money.*"

A cheque is a written order, technically a mandate, whereby the customer orders the bank to pay the sum of money specified therein. In the eyes of law, however, a cheque, apart from being an authorisation, is a negotiable instrument and it is only a particular type of bill of exchange. Section 6 states, "*A cheque is a bill of exchange drawn on a specified banker and not expressed to be payable otherwise than on demand.*" That is, a cheque as a legal instrument is a particular type of bill of exchange which the customer requires his banker to repay the money lent to him. A negotiable instrument which does not express any time of payment is payable on demand. The main characteristics of a cheque thus are:

(*i*) It is an order of the customer without any conditions, i.e., an authorization.

(*ii*) It is drawn upon a certain banker.

(*iii*) The banker has always to pay it on demand.

(*iv*) It is payable to certain person or to his nominee or to the bearer of the instrument.

The person who draws a cheque, i.e., the customer of the bank, is called the 'drawer' and he must sign his name on the right hand bottom corner. The bank upon whom the cheque is drawn is known as the 'drawee' and the person to whom it is made payable is known as the 'payee'. Sometimes the drawer makes the cheque payable to "self" when he wants to withdraw money from the bank for himself. In such a case, the identities of the drawer and payee are merged into one.

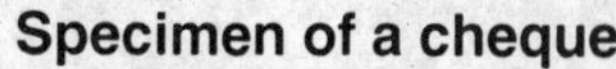

Specimen of a cheque

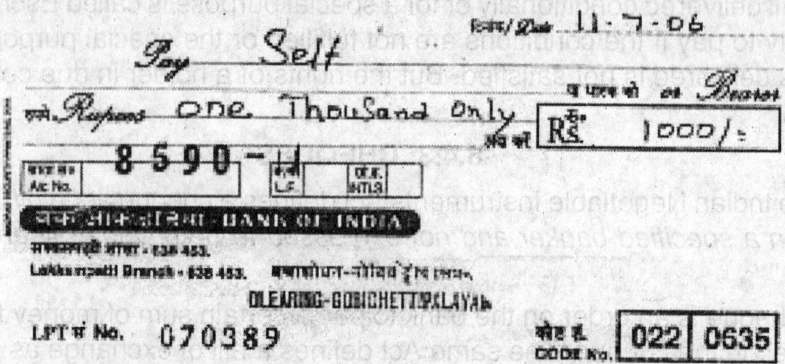

Date 11-7-06

Pay Self or Bearer

Rupees One Thousand Only Rs. 1000/-

8590-II

A/c No. L.F. INTLS

BANK OF INDIA

Lakkampatti Branch - 638 453.

CLEARING-GOBICHETTIPALAYAM

LPT No. 070389 CODE No. 022 0635

Advantages of using Printed Cheques:

A customer of a bank cannot draw cheque on ordinary slips. It is, however, not legally necessary to use any specific form to direct the banker to pay the money provided the wording of his order is such as to satisfy requirements of a valid cheque having all requisites. A cheque may be written on a sheet of paper, but it should be in a suitable form as to make the mandate clear and not to grouse any reasonable suspicion. Thus, it is usually agreed upon between a banker and his customer that for withdrawal of amounts, the customer shall use the particular form of cheques supplied by the banker.

Reasons for use of cheque slips:

1. The use of a printed form is convenient and useful because it relieves the drawer of the trouble of drafting the contents of the cheque according to legal requirements.

2. It helps in preventing the possibilities of forgeries which may invalidate a cheque.

3. All the cheques are (forms) consequently numbered and facilitate ready reference

4. Mistakes and alterations are easily detected, if cheques are drawn in printed forms.

5. Reference to the drawer and the countermanding of the cheque by the drawer would be possible with cheques drawn in a set form.

6. Every cheque form has a perforated counterfoil which serves as a record for the customer.

7. The printed forms mentioning the name and situation of the drawee banker, are a sort of advertisement for the banker.

8. It makes the uniformity in size of the cheque form.

9. Cheque forms are printed on a high quality paper which is durable and it can

be easily detected, if any alteration is made on the cheque due to fine texture of the paper.

10. It avoids the ambiguous and suspicious writing on the cheque.

Hence, cheques are usually drawn on prescribed printed forms supplied to the customers by the bank. The following are the benefits of the cheque system:

1. It is the safe and convenient mode of making a payment. It removes the risk of carrying hard cash.

2 It is also a suitable method for receiving payment.

3 The use of cheque avoids the necessity of demanding acknowledgements from the payee for having received the amount.

4. The transactions through cheques are readily recorded in the paying banker's books which can be adduced as a legal proof, whenever need arises.

5. In case wrong payments are made by chance of mistake, the same can be countermanded by the drawer under intimation to the banker.

6. Crossing of cheques restricts the possibilities of wrong payments being made under forgery and similar offences.

7. Cheque is a negotiable instrument and can be used as a substitute for money in settlement of mutual debts through endorsements and delivery.

8. Since it is a suitable way of transfer of money, it economises the use of other forms of money viz. coins and currency notes.

9. The use of cheques encourages the banking habits and by which banks can play an important role in the economic development of the country.

10. The use of cheques monetises all the dealings in the economy by which monetary and fiscal policies can be effectively implemented.

Thus, the cheque system is beneficial to each and everyone.

Essential features of a cheque:

The aforesaid definition brings out certain distinctive features which are common to all, and may be taken note of as below:

1. Instrument in writing: A negotiable instrument has to be in writing, though the form of writing is not stipulated i.e., it may be typed, handwritten, or printed. Neither does it stipulate any particular language or languages to be used in drawing them.

2. Drawn on a specified bank: The cheque can be drawn only on the banker of the customer and on none else. Also the cheque should be drawn only on the branch of the bank at which the account of the drawer is maintained and the amount in the account should be sufficient to pay the cheque.

3. Payable on demand: The cheque should not be expressed to be payable otherwise than on demand. It is not necessary that the words "on demand" should appear on the cheque. A cheque is presumed to be payable on demand unless an express provision is made in the cheque disturbing this feature. An instrument drawn payable after a certain period of time from the date appearing on the face of it is not a cheque. For example, an instrument dated 30-4-1982 and expressed to be payable on or after 31-5-1982 is not a cheque.

4. Unconditional order or Promise: A negotiable instrument is always unconditional. It is not contingent upon the happening of an event or the fulfilment of a specified pre-requisite. Therefore phrases such as "on arrival" or "after clearance" or "on arrival of S.S" cannot be inserted in them, because that will preclude their negotiation till the specified condition has been fulfilled. The honouring of the instrument cannot be made to depend upon any such contingency or condition. It is highly important that no notations appear on a bill which may possibly make the order/undertaking conditional *i.e.* the payment is always to be imperative.

5. A certain Amount: In both at sight and usance instruments, the amount to be paid by the drawee must be an amount certain, a definite amount. In a usance bill, no doubt the amount is payable; sometimes in future, but the amount thereof is made known in the beginning itself. The amount of the instrument may preferably be indicated both in numerals and spelled out, and it should not bear notations like "plus collection charges", "plus interest", "plus interest at 10 per cent". Unless the length of time has been specified, notations of this character not only destroy the validity of the instrument but they are also not well received by the drawee.

6. The Drawee: Every instrument has a drawee who is its addressee. While in a cheque the drawee is always a banker. Any person, partnership, company or association could be a drawee in bills of exchange and promissory notes. The identity of the drawee is, however, to be made certain by indicating his (their) name, address, etc. Although there is need for the drawee to be named with reasonable certainty, it can very well be addressed to two or more drawees whether they are partners or not. But an instrument addressed to two or more drawees in the alternative or more drawees in succession cannot be a negotiable instrument.

7. Payable to Order or to Bearer: The instrument may be payable "to order" or "to bearer". Bearer instruments are similar to "cash" as these can be negotiated by mere transfer and without signatures of the transferor. When, however, the proceeds of an instrument are to be paid to a designated person or to his nominee, it must contain the words "or order" which makes it transferable by endorsement. While a bearer instrument passes from hand to hand without further formality, an order instrument is payable to a particular payee. However, the original payee may transfer his right to receive payment to some other person by mere signature on the instrument viz. the endorsement.

8. Payee a certain person: A negotiable instrument must be payable to a definite person named or to anyone to whom he in turn directs payment to be made. In a bill of exchange and cheque, the payee is often the drawer because the drawer wants the money to be paid to himself, or wants to transfer it to a third party who will give him value for it.

9. Payee to be certain: The person to whom the cheque is drawn payable should be certain. He need not be an individual as is understood generally, but can be any legal person recognized under law like corporations, etc. The cheque can be drawn payable to a certain person or his order or it may be drawn to a certain person or the bearer of the instrument. Order cheque should contain the name of the payee. It may be omitted in the case of bearer cheques. However, in practice, the name of the payee is written in all cases.

A cheque payable to a certain person and not specifying whether payable to his order or to the bearer is payable to order provided the cheque does not contain words prohibiting transfer [Section 13(1) of the Negotiable Instruments Act]. This provision justifies the treatment of bearer cheques with the word "bearer" struck off as order cheques.

A cheque payable to a fictitious or non-existing person may be treated as a bearer cheque. If a person is mis-spelt or wrongly designated, yet the payee is certain, provided there is no genuine ambiguity about the identity of the payee.

A cheque can be drawn payable to two or more persons jointly, or it may be made payable in the alternative to one or two, or several payees [Section 13(2) of the Negotiable Instruments Act].

10. Time of Payment: An instrument may be payable on demand or at a fixed or determinable future time. Without a definite time element, such instruments could not be negotiated because the payee would not know when they are to receive payment. The validity of a negotiable instrument is entirely lost when the date of payment is made uncertain by the addition of such phrases as "on arrival" or "on arrival of merchandise" or "on arrival of steamer Uvaraja" etc.

11. Signature of the Maker: Every instrument has a maker who in a promissory note is called the "promisor" and in a bill or a cheque the "drawer". Maker, therefore, is the person who addresses the instrument to someone. It need be reminded that the word, the person, applies to corporations, partnerships, and trade names as well as to natural persons. An instrument may be drawn jointly or severally, but actual signatures be made in pen and ink. Where the drawer of the bill is an individual, there is no difficulty. But if it is drawn by a company, it has to be seen as to whom the board of directors have granted the signing authority. When the instruments are issued by partnerships, the partnership signature may be made by any of the several partners.

12. Delivery: Delivery means "transfer of possession, actual or constructive, from one person to another" The title to a negotiable instrument is passed to another by mere delivery or endorsement and delivery. The negotiator merely writes his name on the back of the instrument and delivers it to the party who is to discount or purchase it. If the instrument is non-negotiable, title to it cannot be passed by a mere endorsement, but the instrument must be assigned and the assignment must recite the receipt of "consideration".

6.5. DIFFERENCES BETWEEN A PROMISSORY NOTE AND A BILL OF EXCHANGE

Promissory Note	Bill of Exchange
1. A promissory note contains a promise to pay.	1. A bill of exchange contains an order to pay.
2. In a note, there are only two parties viz. the maker (debtor) and the payee (*i.e* creditor)	2. In a bill there are three parties *viz.*, the Drawer, Drawee and Payee. But one person can assume two capacities e.g. : The drawee and payee may be the same person.
3. In the case of a promissory note, the liability of the maker who signs the note is primary and absolute.	3. But in the case of a bill, the drawer becomes liable only if acceptor fails to make the payment. Thus his liability is secondary and contingent. If the bill is not accepted, the drawer's liability is primary.
4. In the case of note, as the marker himself is liable, the need for acceptance does not arise.	4. A bill which is payable after sight and bill drawn payable after specified period from the date of bill require acceptance before they can be presented for payment.
5. A promissory note is payable only to the payee named therein or to his order.	5. But a bill can be made payable to bearer.
6. Notes are not prepared in sets.	6. Foreign bills are drawn in sets.
7. The promise to pay in the case of promissory note and the order to pay in the case of bills are unconditional.	7. But in the case of bills, they may be accepted conditionally. If the holder does not object to it such qualified acceptance does not amount to dishonour. However, other parties to the instrument are discharged from the liability.
8. No noting and protesting is necessary for dishonour.	8. It is necessary for bill. However, it is essential to note that protest is compulsory only in the case of foreign bills.
9. Parties in immediate relation in the case of promissory note are maker and payee.	9. But in the case of bills, they are the drawer and acceptor.
10. No notice of dishonour is required to be given to the drawer and endorsers.	10. In the case of bills, the holder should give notice of dishonour to the drawer and endorsers otherwise they are discharged from their responsibility.

6.6. DIFFERENCES BETWEEN A CHEQUE AND A BILL OF EXCHANGE

Cheque	Bill of Exchange
1. A cheque is always drawn on a banker.	1. A bill may be drawn on any person including a banker.
2. A cheque can only be drawn payable on demand and not otherwise.	2. A bill may be drawn payable on demand or the expiry of a certain period after date or sight.
3. A cheque does not require the acceptance and is intended for immediate payment	3. Acceptance is necessary for Usance Bill.
4. In the case of cheques, no grace period is allowed.	4. Three days of grace are allowed in the case of bills.
5. Cheques can be crossed generally or specially.	5. There is no crossing in the case of bills.
6. The holder need not give notice of a dishonour to make the previous parties liable.	6. In the case of bill the holder must give such a notice to all the previous parties, whom he wants to hold responsible.
7. The drawer of a cheque is not discharged by any delay in presentation for payment unless he suffers any damages by such delay.	7. The drawer for a bill is discharged if there is any delay in presenting a bill.
8. The payment of a cheque can be countermanded by the drawer.	8. This is not possible in the case of a bill.
9. A cheque is supposed to be drawn on the funds of the drawer.	9. There is no such presumption in the case of bills.
10. Cheques are exempt from stamping.	10. It requires stamping depending on value and duration of the bill.
11. They do not require noting or protesting when dishonoured.	11. Protesting is compulsory in the case of foreign bills.

6.7. DIFFERENCES BETWEEN A PROMISSORY NOTE & A CHEQUE

Promissory Note	Cheque
1. It contains a promise to pay.	1. It contains an order to pay.
2. There are two parties in the case of Promissory note, namely, the maker and the payee.	2. There are three parties in the case of cheque, namely, Drawer, Drawee and Payee.
3. The liability of the maker of note is primary.	3. The liability of the drawer of a cheque is secondary.
4. There is no crossing of promissory note.	4. Cheques can be crossed.
5. Promissory notes require stamping.	5. Cheques are exempt from stamping.
6. A promissory note is payable only to the payee mentioned.	6. Cheques can be made payable to bearer.

6.8. SIMILARITIES BETWEEN PROMISSORY NOTES AND CHEQUES

1. Both the instruments do not require acceptance as they are payable on demand.

2. The practice of noting and protesting is absent.

3. The parties in immediate relation are the maker of the instrument and the payee.

4. Notice of dishonour is not required.

6.9. DIFFERENCES BETWEEN A FIXED DEPOSIT RECEIPT AND A CHEQUE

A fixed deposit receipt is a receipt issued by a bank acknowledging the receipt of a deposit from the customer which is repayable after the expiry of a certain period. Usually it is in a printed form containing the name of the depositor, the sum deposited, the rate of interest, duration of the deposit, the due date and the terms of payment of interest and the principal. It contains the words "not negotiable" at the top. It must be returned duly signed by the customer to obtain payment on the due date.

The Negotiable Instruments Act defines a cheque under Sec. 6 as follows : "*A cheque is a bill of exchange drawn on a specified banker and not expressed to be payable otherwise than on demand.*" Therefore a cheque must satisfy all the conditions of a bill of exchange, i.e., it must be an instrument in writing, it should contain an unconditional order and the amount must be certain. Besides these, the cheque contains an order on a specified banker only, directing him to pay the amount to or to the order of the person named in it. The following are the differences between a fixed deposit receipt and a cheque:

1. The cheque originates from the customer, ordering the banker to pay a certain amount to the order of the person specified in the cheque, but a fixed deposit receipt is issued by a banker acknowledging the receipt of the amount from the customer to be repaid to him with interest after a fixed period.

2. A cheque is a negotiable instrument and as such it can be freely transferred from person to person by proper endorsement and delivery. A fixed deposit receipt is not a negotiable instrument under law. Further, it contains words 'not negotiable' which means that the transferee cannot get a better title than what the transferor has.

3. With regard to cheque, the payment has to be made by a banker on demand by the holder of the cheque, but in case of a fixed deposit receipt, the payment will be made only after the expiry of the fixed term.

4. In case of a cheque, the amount specified in the cheque alone will be paid, but in the case of a fixed deposit receipt, the principal amount together with the unpaid balance of interest will be paid on the due date.

5. It is the practice of bankers to refuse payment of a cheque if it becomes stale. In India cheques become stale after six months from the date of drawing of the cheque. But there is no such restriction for a fixed deposit receipt and the amount

can be drawn at any time within three years from the due date as the law of limitation applies.

6.10. HOLDER IN DUE COURSE

Meaning of Holder and Holder in due course: Holder : Section 8 of the Negotiable Instruments Act defines a holder as a person entitled in his own name to the possession of the instrument and to receive or recover the amount due thereon from the parties thereto. Clause (2) of the same section provides that when an instrument is lost or destroyed, the person entitled as above at the time of such loss or destruction will be the holder. From the definition, it will be seen that a holder must satisfy the following conditions : (1) He must be in possession of the instrument; (2) He should have the right to receive or recover the amount thereon. That is, a finder of a lost instrument, a person prohibited by law to receive the money, an agent acting on behalf of another person, a person having an instrument with a forged endorsement or a person who has stolen the instrument are not holders within the meaning of the section; (3) The holder's name must be found in the instrument; otherwise, although he may be entitled to receive the money on the instrument, he is not a holder; and (4) Although not mentioned in this section, the heirs of a deceased holder or the official assignee or official receiver of a holder who has become insolvent are also holders of the instrument.

6.10.1. HOLDER FOR VALUE

A banker becomes a holder for value of a cheque in the following circumstances :

1. When he pays the amount of the cheque to the customer in anticipation of collection.

2. When he permits the customer to draw against it before it is collected.

3. Where he receives a cheque in specific reduction of the amount owing to him by the customer.

4. Where the banker has a lien on the cheque.

When a banker becomes a holder for value, his rights are the same as of any other holder for value. In other words, he will be entitled to receive the amount of the cheque from the drawee in his own right and in case of dishonour, from one or all of the endorsers. In case one of the instruments is forged, he will be liable to the true owner, but can recover the amount from the endorsers subsequent to the forgery.

6.10.2. HOLDER IN DUE COURSE

Section 9 defines a holder in due course as '*any person who, for consideration, became the possessor of the promissory note, bill of exchange or cheque, if payable to bearer or the payee or endorsee thereof if payable to order, before the amount mentioned in it became payable, and without having sufficient cause to believe that any defect existed in the title of the person from whom he derived his title.*'

Thus a holder of a negotiable instrument will be a holder in due course, if he fulfils the following conditions :

(*i*) He must be a holder as defined in Section 8 of the Act. That is, he must be in possession of the instrument, he must have the right to sue on the instrument in his own name, and he must have paid consideration for it.

(*ii*) The instruments must be complete and regular in all respects.

(*iii*) He must acquire the instrument before it became due for payment. If he takes it after the due date, he will receive the instrument with all the defects in the instrument. If the instrument is payable on demand, he should have acquired it within a reasonable time after it is issued.

(*iv*) He should not have had sufficient cause to believe that any defect existed in the title of the person from whom he acquired it. A holder in due course acquires a good title to the instrument notwithstanding the defective title of any one of the customers. He cannot, however, acquire a good title when one of the signatures of the endorsers is forged because forgery conveys no title. According to Section 9, the transferee of a negotiable instrument should act with honesty and diligence.

(*v*) The instrument must have been obtained for valuable consideration, i.e., paying its full value. That means, a person who receives a cheque as a gift will not be called its holder in due course for want of consideration.

6.10.3. CIRCUMSTANCES IN WHICH A BANKER BECOMES A HOLDER IN DUE COURSE

The banker who receives a cheque from the customer becomes a holder in due course in the following circumstances :

(1) When he makes payment to the customer in anticipation of the collection of the cheque. When the banker has to make payment to the customer, it is desirable from him to take an undertaking from the customer that he will reimburse the amount paid if the cheque is not collected for any reason. Although the banker has the right to recover the money by virtue of his position as a holder in due course, still it is desirable for him to obtain an undertaking from the customer to that effect.

(2) When the amount of the cheque is credited to the amount of the customer and when the customer is permitted to draw against the amount, such a permission must be in pursuance of an agreement between the banker and the customer. In Lloyds v. Horn, a customer opened an account with a crossed cheque for £ 250 and the amount was permitted to be withdrawn by the customer. The cheque could not be collected as it was countermanded by the drawer. The banker took out an action in his capacity as a holder in due course. The decision was in favour of the collecting banker. It was held that it was irrelevant whether the banker was guilty of negligence or not.

(3) When the banker has received the cheque not for the reduction of the balance of an overdraft in the ordinary course of business, but in settlement of an advance granted to the customer previously.

(4) When the banker has a lien on the cheque deposited for collection. Suppose a customer has paid in a cheque and drew the money and suppose further that the cheque is dishonoured and when the amount of the cheque is debited to the account of the customer, the customer's balance is thrown in debit. In such circumstances, the banker has a lien on that cheque.

When a banker becomes a holder in due course, he will have all the rights of a holder in due course. That is, he can recover the amount of the cheque in his own name. If the cheque is dishonoured, he can recover the amount from all or any of the endorsers. If one of the signatures of the endorsers is forged, he will have the right of recovering the amount from any of the subsequent endorsers. If the signature preceding the customer's signature happens to be forged, the banker can recover the amount from the customer.

6.10.4. DIFFERENCES BETWEEN HOLDER AND HOLDER IN DUE COURSE

The following are the differences between holder and holder in due course:

(*i*) **Consideration :** It is not essential to have consideration in the case of a holder, but a holder in due course should have obtained an instrument for valuable consideration. That is, a cheque is issued to provide a gift or donation to a college, the college does not become a holder in due course. On the other hand, tuition fee is paid to the college, the college acquires the status of holder in due course.

(*ii*) **Possession :** The person entitled to be called holder in due course must become the possessor of the instrument before it became payable. That is, if it is obtained after the due date, the possessor will not be called its holder in due course. But in the case of holder, neither actual possession nor any time limit within which it must be acquired is required.

(*iii*) **Defect in the Transferor's Title :** The person claiming to be a holder in due course should have obtained the instrument in good faith, i.e., without the knowledge of the defective title of the transferor. But this condition is not essential in the case of a holder.

6.10.5. RIGHTS AND PRIVILEGES OF THE HOLDER IN DUE COURSE

The holder in due course enjoys the following privileges under various sections of the Negotiable Instruments Act:

1. Better Title : A holder in due course possesses better title free from all defects. That is, he always obtains a better title than that of his transferor or any of the previous parties.

2. Purging of Prior Defects : The defective title of the previous endorsers will not affect adversely the rights of the holder in due course.

3. Transfer of Better Title : Once an instrument passes through the hands of a holder in due course, it is purged of all the defects and he can give to the subsequent parties the good title that he possesses.

4. Liability of Prior Parties to Holder in Due Course : According to Section 36, every prior party to a negotiable instrument, i.e., its maker or drawer, acceptor or endorser, is liable thereon to a holder in due course until the instrument is duly paid.

5. Right of the Holder in due course in case of Inchoate Instrument : The drawer of an instrument cannot claim invalidity of the instrument against the holder in due course on the ground that the instrument was originally an inchoate, i.e., incomplete instrument.

6. Right in case of Fictitious Bills : If a bill of exchange is drawn on behalf of a fictitious person and is payable to his order, the acceptor is not relieved of his liability to the holder in due course because of such fictitious name. But it is essential that the holder in due course should prove that the instrument bears the endorsement and that of the drawer with signature in same hand.

7. Right in case of the Instrument obtained by Unlawful means or for Unlawful Consideration : A person liable to pay for the instrument cannot deny payment to a holder in due course on the ground that the instrument was lost or obtained from him by means of an offence or fraud or for an unlawful consideration (Section 58).

8. Estoppel against Denying Capacity of Payee to Endorse : The claim of the holder in due course cannot be denied on the plea that the payee had no capacity to endorse.

9. Estoppel against Denying Signature or Capacity of Prior Party: No Endorser of an instrument is permitted to deny the signature or capacity of any prior party to the instrument in the case of a suit by a holder in due course. For example, X draws a bill on Y in favour of Z who endorses the same in favour of A, a minor. A endorses to B and B to C, who become its holder in due course. On the due date, the bill is dishonoured; C, the holder in due course, can proceed against all parties or any of the parties except A, the minor. In this case, B, the endorser, cannot claim that A was a minor and had no capacity to endorse the bill and thereby the bill is void. But B remains liable on the bill to C.

6.11. LIABILITIES OF PARTIES TO A NEGOTIABLE INSTRUMENT

The liability of the parties in a negotiable instrument is as follows:

(1) Liability of Drawer of a Bill or Cheque :- Section 30 lays down the liability of the drawer of a bill of exchange or cheque. "*The drawer of a bill of exchange or cheque is bound, in case of dishonour by the drawee or acceptor thereof, to compensate the holder, provided due notice of dishonour has been given to or received by the drawer as herein after provided.*" From the above, it is clear that the liability of the drawer of a bill or a cheque arises only when the bill or the cheque is dishonoured and it does not arise earlier. A bill of exchange may be dishonoured by non-acceptance or by non-payment but a cheque is dishonoured by non-payment only. Thus when a bill is dishonoured by non-acceptance by the drawee of the bill, the drawer becomes liable immediately on such dishonour. When a bill or a cheque is dishonoured by non-payment, the holder can give due notice to the drawer and make the drawer liable over the instrument.

The liability of the drawer of a bill or a cheque is thus second to that of the drawee, i.e., he becomes liable to the holder, when the bill or the cheque is dishonoured by the drawee. However, in the case of cheque, the drawer remains liable thereto, even if the cheque is not presented by the holder to the drawee banker as has been provided in Harish Chander vs M/s. Ganga Singh and Sons and others (1974). But the drawer is discharged from his liability, if the drawer suffers damage as a result of delay in presentment of the cheque as provided under Sections 72 and 84.

To make the drawer liable on the bill or the cheque, it is essential that due notice of dishonour is given to or received by him; otherwise he will be discharged from his liability. It is enough if the drawer comes into know of the dishonour of the bill or cheque. In the case of Baijnath Agarwal vs. Ram Kumar Agarwalla and others (1975), it was held that confirmation by the drawer of his knowledge about the dishonour was sufficient compliance with the requirements of the Law.

Whatever be the reasons for dishonour of a cheque, the drawer was subject to civil liability only in respect of the money due on a cheque till 1989. But after passing of the Banking, Public Financial Institutions and Negotiable Instrument Laws (Amendment) Act, 1988, dishonour of cheque for want of sufficiency of funds, it will be a criminal offence for which the drawer may be punished with imprisioment for a term up to one year or with fine up to twice the amount of the cheque or with both. This will be in addition to his liability in a civil suit.

***(ii)* Liability of Maker and Acceptor :** The liability of a maker of promissory note and the acceptor of a bill is definite and unconditional. Their liability is primary as they are the principal debtors to the instrument. They are bound to pay on the date of maturity.

***(iii)* Liability of Bank as a Drawee** : Bank as a drawee of cheque is liable to honour all cheques of the customer till there is a credit balance left in the customer's account.

***(iv)* Liability of various Parties :** The liability of all the parties is completely discharged when the payment of the instrument is made.

6.11.1. RIGHTS OF PARTIES IN SPECIAL CASES

The rights of the parties of a negotiable instrument in some special cases are as follows:

1. Lost Instruments :

(*a*) The finder of a lost instrument does not get a title over the instrument and only the true owner is entitled to recover the instrument.

(*b*) When the payment is made on the lost bill by an acceptor or maker, he is discharged from all liability to the rightful owner.

(*c*) When the lost instrument is transferred to a bona fide transferee for value, the transferee acquires a valid title to it as the holder in due course. He is entitled to receive the payment due from the parties liable to him.

(*d*) If the signature is forged and endorsement is made, such an endorsee does not become a holder in due course.

2. Stolen Instruments : When an instrument is stolen, the thief does not get title to the instrument. The true owner can recover it from him.

3. Instruments obtained by Fraud and Coercion : If a party gets the instrument by means of fraud, coercion or undue influence, he gets a defective title.

4. Instruments by Unlawful Considerations : When an instrument is obtained by unlawful considerations, the person who gets the instrument does not get the title to the instrument.

5. Forged Instruments and Forged Endorsements : The instrument carrying forged signatures does not confer any right nor it creates any liability.

Endorsee gets no title if there is a forged endorsement on the instrument.

6. Instruments without Consideration : If the instruments are made, drawn, accepted or endorsed without any consideration or for insufficient consideration there is no obligation for payment, but in case of a holder in due course, this rule does not apply.

QUESTIONS

1. Give the exact definition of a Promissory note, a cheque and a bill of exchange. Give specimens of each of these instruments.
2. What are negotiable instruments and their characteristics ? Would you consider the following a negotiable instrument ? Give reasons.
   (a) Bill of lading
   (b) Postal order
   (c) A promissory note
   (d) A debenture
3. Examine the term 'negotiability'.
4. Explain fully the privileges granted to a holder in due course under the Negotiable Instruments Act.
5. Discuss briefly the difference between holder for value and holder in due course.
6. What are the essential features of a cheque ?
7. Define a bill of exchange and explain the difference between a cheque and a bill of exchange.
8. All cheques are bills but all bills are not cheques. Discuss.
9. Who is a 'holder in due course'? What precautions should the transferee of a negotiable instrument take to qualify as a holder in due course?
10. Explain the main characteristics of negotiable instrument.
11. Who is called a 'holder of a negotiable instrument' in accordance with the negotiable Instruments Act? What conditions are required to be satisfied by a banker to claim the right of a holder in due course?

7

CHEQUES

7.1. DRAFTING OF CHEQUE

The drafting of cheques includes the following:

1. Dating of Cheques: A cheque should be properly dated if it is to be honoured. If a cheque having no date is presented to the bank, the cheque will be returned with the remark "should bear the date". In case a cheque has not been dated by a drawer, any holder can insert a date. If a cheque dated 1st February 2002 bears at the foot the following words: "Must be presented for payment on or before February 1", the banker can dishonour such a cheque, if the cheque is presented after 1st February 2002. Such a clause will not make the cheque a conditional order. In the case of Griffith Vs Dalton, it was held that a banker is not bound to honour an undated cheque. A cheque dated on a Sunday should not be paid until the following business day. A cheque which bears a date not in the Calendar e.g., "31st April 2001" should be paid on or after 30th April.

An ante dated cheque is one that bears a date before the date of issue; a post-dated cheque is one dated later than the date of issue. If a cheque is post-dated the banker is not correct in debiting his customer's account before the ostensible date of payment. So a post-dated cheque if presented should be returned, with the remark 'post-dated, should be presented on the date mentioned on the cheque'. Payment of post-dated cheque has been considered illegal as decided in the case of Bank of Baroda Vs Punjab National Bank (1939).

A cheque is considered to be stale after six months after the date of its issue and such a cheque is returned, if presented for payment, with the remark "out of date".

2. Payee: Where a cheque is not payable to bearer, the payee's name must be written, or otherwise indicated with certainty ." A normal cheque is one in which there is a drawer, a drawee bank and a payee or no payee but bearer" (Sir John Paget). A cheque may be drawn payable to or to the order of the drawer.

"Pay self or order". If it is drawn pay to.......order" this ordering should be same as "Pay my order". This cheque should be endorsed by the drawer. In case a cheque is drawn pay order, it should be returned with the remark "Payee's name required."

When a cheque is presented for payment without any payee's name upon it, the banker is not safe in asking the holder to insert his own name; but if the holder inserts his own name before presentment, the banker would be protected on the ground that the drawer has misled him. A cheque drawn like "Pay or bearer" must be considered as a bearer cheque and hence paid to any holder. If a cheque is drawn as pay A only "after striking off the words 'bearer' or 'order' it becomes incapable of being transferred as the word 'only' restricts its negotiability to others.

A cheque may be made payable to two or more payees jointly or to one of two, or one or some of several payees, or to the holder of an office. A payee is not liable on a cheque until he has endorsed it. Cheques are sometimes made payable to fictitious person, but in such case they are treated as bearer cheques. e.g. Pay Robinson Crusoe or bearer. Cheques which are drawn as payable to "water rate or order" or income -tax or order" are obviously payable to a water supply authority or the income tax department. These should be endorsed by the heads of respective departments.

3. Amount of the Cheque: The amount to be paid to the payee must be clearly stated, both in words and figures. No blank space should be left before and after the amount stated in words and figures. If the drawer leaves blank spaces carelessly before or after the words and figures, thus facilitating the alteration of the amount, and if the banker pays the amount as altered, the latter is entitled to debit the customer's account with the amount actually paid.

4. Signature: The cheque must be signed by the drawer himself or by the person authorised by him. If the drawer happens to be illiterate, cheques can be drawn by means of the thumb impression of the drawer duly witnessed by a person known to the banker, preferably in the presence of the banker himself.

The signature on the cheque must correspond to the specimen signature of the customer obtained at the time of opening the account. Where the customer authorises another person to sign on his behalf, a letter containing the authorisation must be sent to the banker and also the specimen signature of the person so authorised.

5. Delivery: In order that the drawer of a cheque may be held liable thereon, he must have handed over the instrument, complete in all respects, to the payee with the intention that the proceeds thereof shall be paid to him or his order or to bearer. Unless the cheque is properly delivered, the drawer does not become liable thereon.

Section 46 says: "The making, acceptance or endorsement of a promissory note, bill of exchange or cheque is completed by delivery actual or constructive". The making of a cheque is thus not complete unless it is delivered within the meaning of Section 46 of the Act.

If a cheque is lost in transit, who should bear the loss that may arise? When it is sent through post at the request of the payee and gets into the possession of an unauthorised person who obtains the proceeds, the loss should be borne by the payee on the ground that he employed the post office as his agent. If the drawer sends the cheque through post without a specific request from the payee to do so, the drawer should bear the loss. The mere fact that it is the drawer's practice to send his cheques through post does not mean that the payee has requested that the cheques be sent to him through post.

Open cheques should not be sent by ordinary post. They should be sent by registered post only. If cheques are to be sent by ordinary post, it is desirable that they should be crossed generally.

Types of Cheques:

(*i*) **Bearer Cheque:** A cheque payable to a certain person or to the bearer is known as bearer cheque. A person (whose name need not to be written on it) Who is in lawful possession of such cheque is entitled to receive money payable on it. (He may, however, be required to sign on the back of it as an acknowledgement of receipt).

(*ii*) **Order Cheque:** A cheque payable to a certain person or to his order is an order cheque which can be negotiated by endorsement (i.e., the transferor should sign his name).

(*iii*) **Crossed Cheque:** A cheque is known as a crossed cheque when two parallel lines, with or without the words "& co", "and company" etc. are drawn across the face of the cheque. A crossed cheque is payable through another bank and not payable over the counter. There are various types of crossing in practice, as given below :

(*a*) **General Crossing** : Where a cheque bears across its face an addition of the words " and company" or any abbreviation thereof (& Co) between two parallel transverse lines or two simple parallel transverse lines with or without the words "Not Negotiable", it is known to be crossed generally. The paying banker shall make payment only to a banker in case of a generally crossed cheque.

(*b*) **Special Crossing** : Where a cheque bears across its face an addition of the name of a bank with or without the words "Not Negotiablc", the cheque is said to be crossed specially. The paying banker shall make payment, on such a cheque, only to the banker whose name Is wrltten on the face of a specially crossed cheque.

(*c*) **Restrictive Crossing :** Where a cheque bears across its face such words "Account Payee" or "A/c Payee only" along with general or special crossing it is known as Restrictive crossing or Account Payee crossing (account payee cheque). The addition of these words to the crossing restricts the transferability of the cheque. The payee, in such cheque, should obtain payment through his own account in the bank.

(*d*) **Not Negotiable' Crossing:** Where a cheque bears across its face the words "Not Negotiable" in addition to a general or special crossing, it is known as "Not Negotiable crossing." A chequc with such words looses its characteristic of negotiability. The transferee of such cheque gets no better title than that of his transferor or previous holder. A person in possession of a Negotiable Instrument is permitted to alter it in certain respects without the consent of the drawer or the drawee (acceptor). In the same following respects without the consent of the drawer or of the banker on whom it is drawn:

(*a*) If it is a bearer cheque, he can convert it into an order cheque.

(*b*) If the cheque is uncrossed, he can cross it.

(*c*) If the cheque is crossed generally, he can convert the crossing into a' special crossing by adding the name of the banker to whom alone it can be paid.

(*d*) He can add restrictive words on the cheque, such as, "not negotiable" or "account payee only".

A banker in possession of a cheque which has been given to him by his customer for collection can also convert a general crossing into a special crossing.

Stale Cheque: If a cheque is not presented for payment within a reasonable time, it becomes stale or out-of-date cheque. What is a reasonable time depends upon the arrangement between the various banks and the customers; in India, this reasonable period is *six months.* No payment is made on stale cheque without getting it confirmed by the drawer.

Mutilated Cheque : Mutilated cheques are those cheques which have been damaged or mutilated in course of circulation. Such cheques are not honoured by the bankers, in general, for payment.

Marked Cheques : In some countries (other than India) there is a practice that the cheques are marked or certified by the drawee bankers indicating that on the date of presentation, the banker had sufficient funds for payment of the cheque.

7.2. CROSSING OF CHEQUES

Crossing of cheques : meaning and object of crossing of cheques: Crossing of cheque means drawing two parallel transverse lines on the left hand top corner of a cheque. Crossing on a cheque is a direction to the paying banker by the drawer that payment should not be made across the counter. The payment on a crossed cheque can be collected only through a banker. Therefore, crossing protects the holder of the cheque and reduces the possibilities of fraud.

7.2.1. ORIGIN OF CROSSING

Crossing first originated in England when cheques were sent from one bank to another. There was the possibility that a cheque might fall in the hands of wrong or unauthorised parties and thereby the original holder was likely to be put to a loss or inconvenience. Crossing also ensured safety, in case a clerk, carrying cheques to the Clearing House, was assaulted and robbed. To avoid this disadvantage, the bankers introduced this new system of crossing of cheques. Crossing automatically means that a cheque should be presented for payment through bank.

Legal Recognition of crossing

Till 1856 in England, crossing was considered as an advice to the banker and only in the year 1856, it was felt necessary to enact a legislation whereby a cheque crossed only with two lines with or without the words "& Co.", the cheque must be presented through some banker. In case a cheque crossed in favour of a particular banker, its payment should be made only to that banker or another banker, acting as agent for collection of the banker named in the crossing. The statute of 1856 imposed the obligation on a paying banker to make payment of crossed cheques only to or through a bank, as advised by the crossing. However, in the case of Simmons Vs. Taylor (1857), the Court held that crossing was not an integral part of a cheque, that its erasure did not amount to forgery and this view was also upheld on appeal. Hence inorder to nullify the effect of the above decision, an amendment to the Act was passed in 1858, which declared that crossing was a material part of a cheque, once it was there. The holder of a cheque was recognised to have the power to cross it.

7.2.2. OBJECT OF CROSSING

The main object or purpose of crossing is to ensure that the money should be transmitted safely through the cheque and the amount of the cheque should reach the hands of the rightful owner. In case it is encashed by unauthorised persons, it helps to detect the parties to whom the amount has been paid. Therefore, crossing, in short, protects the holder of the cheque and reduces the possibilities of fraud.

Before a cheque is crossed, it should be an order cheque. If the drawer issues an order, uncrossed cheque to the payee, the payee can cross the cheque generally or specially. In case the payee has crossed it generally, the holder of the cheque can cross it specially. In case the drawer has issued a generally crossed cheque, the payee or the holder of the cheque can then cross it specially. But if the drawer has crossed it specially, no one can then alter the crossing .

Parties eligible to cross the cheque : The following persons are eligible to cross a cheque:

1. Drawer of the cheque
2. Payee of the cheque
3. Holder of the cheque

(*i*) **Drawer:** The drawer of the cheque can make a general, special or restrictive crossing in a cheque before issuing it.

(*ii*) **Holder:**

(*a*) Where the cheque is uncrossed, the holder may cross it generally or specially.

(*b*) Where a cheque is crossed generally, the holder may cross it specially.

(c) Where a cheque is crossed generally or specially, the holder may add the words 'not negotiable'.

(*iii*) **Banker**: Where a cheque is crossed specially, the banker to whom it is crossed may again cross it specially to another banker, or his agent for collection. (sec.125) A cheque can be crossed specially only once except where the second crossing is to a banker as agent for collection.

7.2.3. TYPES OF CROSSING

There are two types of crossing:

(A) General Crossing (B) Special Crossing.

(A) General Crossing : According to Section 123 of the Negotiable Instruments Act, 1881. "*Where a cheque bears across its face an addition of the words "and company" or any abbreviation thereof, between two parallel transverse lines, or of two parallel transverse lines simply, either with or without the words "not negotiable", that addition shall be deemed a crossing and the cheque shall be deemed to be crossed generally*".

Thus the essential requisite of a general crossing is that the cheque bears on its face two parallel transverse lines. The words "and company" or their abbreviation "& Co" are not necessary to constitute a crossing though they usually accompany it. Likewise, the words "Not Negotiable" are also not a must.

The following are examples of general crossing :

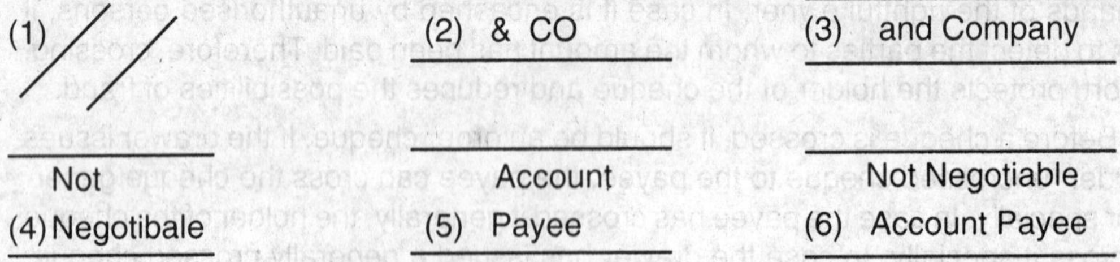

Significance of General Crossing :

A crossed cheque should not be paid across the counter. Even if the payee of a crossed cheque is well known, the paying banker is directed to make payment only through another banker. If the payee does not have a bank account, he can collect it only through someone who is having a bank account. As a result, even if a crossed cheque has been stolen and collected for a party not entitled to it, the person for whom it has been collected can be easily traced. Thus crossing ensures safety and prevents payment into wrong hands.

A generally crossed cheque protects the drawer and also the payee or holder thereof. Whenever a drawer desired to make payment to an outstation party, he can cross the cheque so that even if the cheque is lost, only a piece of paper is lost and nothing beyond that. If by chance, it is encashed by a third and unauthorised person, it is possible to find out to whose account the amount is credited and the unauthorised person can be identified and suitable action take against such person.

Special Crossing : Section 124 defines special crossing as follows: "*Where a cheque bears across its face an addition of the name of a banker with or without the words "not negotiable", that addition shall be deemed a crossing and the cheque shall be deemed to be crossed specially and to be crossed to that banker*".

Here the parallel transverse lines are not essential. But the name of banker to whom payment should be made is to be necessarily written on the face of the cheque. Thus it must be noted that while drawing of two parallel transverse lines is a 'must' for a general crossing, the addition of the name of a banker continues the essential part of a special crossing.

What does not Constitute Crossing ?

Sections 123 and 124 spelt out very clearly in specific lines or what constitute general or special crossings. The inclusion of any other word/words without the essential ingredients of crossing, on the face of a cheque does not constitute crossing. For example (1) A cheque bears the words " not negotiable" or "account payee" **without** two parallel lines or the name of any bank. This is not deemed to be a crossed cheque because the words' not negotiable' within two parallel transverse lines on the face of the cheque are essential in the case of general crossing. The name of a bank with or without two parallel lines is a must for special crossing.

(2) Suppose a cheque is crossed by a single line across its face or simply putting some mark, the cheque is not treated as crossed cheque.

(3) Suppose a cheque is crossed with some irrelevant words within the two parallel transverse lines, the cheque is deemed to be a crossed cheque, example.

Under Rupees hundred **& Co., Chennai**

The following are specimens of special crossing :

Significance of Special Crossing : Here the paying banker should make payment only to the particular banker named as a part of special crossing or to his agent for collection. Thus special crossing is safer than general crossing.

(1) | ABC Bank Ltd. |

(2) | Not Negotiable ABC Bank Ltd. |

(3) | Account Payee ABC Bank Ltd. |

(4) | Account Payee |

(5) | Not Negotiable |

A specially crossed cheque gives additional protection to the drawer of the cheque as it is a direction to the paying banker asking him to pay the amount to that banker whose name is mentioned in the crossing. Special crossing is normally done when the drawer knows fully well that the payee has an account in a particular bank and by special crossing, he is assured of double safety – safety to the drawer and safety to the payee

3. **Not negotiable crossing :** Section 130 of the Indian Negotiable Instruments Act lays down that "*a person taking a cheque crossed generally or specially, bearing in either case the words 'Not negotiable' shall not have and shall not be capable of giving, a better title to the cheque than that which the person from whom he took it in the first instance had*".

Such a cheque can be negotiated as usual by endorsement and delivery. Mentioning of the words 'Not Negotiable' on the face of the cheque makes the cheque loose the basic criteria of negotiability. Once the cheque is crossed in such a fashion, its holder will not get a better title than that of the immediate endorser and, in addition, he is not capable of giving a better title to the parties in whose favour he is likely to endorse. In short, the title of all the future or subsequent endorsers becomes defective. The holder of the cheque, in case he gets the proceeds of the cheque, has to refund the amount to the true owner in due course. Therefore, it is a direction given to the collecting banker to be very careful in respect of such cheques and especially to accept only such cheques for collection where the holder's title is absolutely clean.

It does not mean that the cheque is not negotiable or transferable. The only interpretation of this crossing is that, a person taking a cheque crossed generally or specially, to himself shall not have and shall not be capable of giving a better title to the cheque than that, the person, from whom he took it in the first instance had. Suppose a cheque bearing 'not negotiable' crossing is stolen by A and is endorsed in favour of B. B must receive it subject to the condition that he will return the money covered by the cheque to the genuine payee. Regarding this M.L. Tannan, a great authority on Banking Law has remarked, 'such a cheque is like a stolen fountain pen or watch; the transferee of which does not get a better title than that of the thief".

4. Cheque with Account Payee crossing : The inclusion of the words 'Account Payee' or 'Payee's Account' ensures greater safety to the cheque. According to law such a crossing is a direction to the collecting bank, and the paying banker has no obligation in this regard provided the endorsement is in order. The collecting banker is to see that the proceeds go to the payee's account only. If such a cheque is collected for some other person other than the payee, the collecting bank is responsible for conversion and is bound to make good the loss the payee suffers on account of such conversion. An uncrossed cheque marked 'account payee' and presented across the counter for payment should not be paid by the banker. A cheque payable to bearer and marked 'Account payee' is treated as a bearer cheque and shall not require any endorsement. Regarding the words "account payee" on a cheque, the Indian Institute of Bankers has expressed the following opinion:

(*i*) The paying banker is under no obligation to obtain a certificate to the effect that the payee's account has been credited;

(*ii*) The onus is on the collecting banker who must take steps to credit the amount of the cheque to the payee's account;

(*iii*) If the cheque bears any endorsement other than that of the payee, there is still no obligation on the paying banker to obtain a certificate.

The words 'Account Payee' are not recognised by Negotiable Instruments Act, but are in usage as a matter of practice. Such words are directions to the collecting bank, to collect the cheque to payee's account only. Sir John Paget remarks that "the question has never been settled whether the paying banker can absolutely or with impunity ignore the words 'account payee' or the like, where endorsements on the cheques show obviously that it is not being collected for the account indicated. It is a point that may be well argued in support that a banker who pays a cheque crossed by his customer 'Account Payee' when it bears evidence of having been negotiated otherwise than the account of the payee, has not obeyed the mandate of his customer and cannot claim to have paid the cheque in due course and in these circumstances the court would be hardly justified in expressing the view that in no case whatsoever the words 'Account Payee' are to be found on the crossed cheques made payable to bearer or order. To quote Sheldon 'these words are the nature of a direction to him, and if he places the money received to an account other than that of the payee specified, he stands to lose his statutory protection on the ground of negligence."

7.2.4. DOUBLE CROSSING

A specially crossed cheque is to be collected only through the banker specified therein. Therefore, a specially crossed cheque cannot be crossed specially again to another banker i.e., a cheque cannot be crossed specially twice, because the very purpose of first special crossing is frustrated by the second one.

However, there is an exception to this rule for a specific purpose. If the banker on whom a cheque is specially crossed does not have a branch at the place of the paying banker, he may cross the cheque specially to another banker who acts as his agent for the purpose of collection of the cheques. In such a case, the banker crossing it again must specify that the banker on whom it has been specially crossed again shall act as the agent of the first banker for the purpose of collection of the cheque.

For example,

State Bank of India
to
Bank of India
as Agent for collection

It is necessary, that the words "as agent for collection" must be included in the special crossing. Section 127 provides that *"where a cheque is crossed specially to more than one banker, except when crossed to an agent for the purpose of collection, the banker on whom it is drawn shall refuse payment thereof*". Thus a cheque bearing a double crossing shall be honoured as given below by the paying banker.

State Bank of India
Bank of India

7.2.5.OBLITERATING A CROSSING

According to Section 89, "*where a cheque is presented for payment which does not at the time of presentation appear to be crossed or to have had a crossing which has been obliterated, payment thereof by a banker liable to pay and paying the same according to the apparent tenor thereof at the time of payment and other-*

wise in due course, shall discharge such banker from liability thereon and such payment shall not be questioned by reason of the cheque having been crossed."

Thus, the paying banker is given protection, provided the following conditions are fulfilled:

(*a*) The cheque does not appear to be a crossed one at the time of presentation or obliteration of the crossing is not apparent, and

(*b*) The payment is made according to the apparent tenor of the cheque and in due course.

7.2.6. PARTIES ELIGIBLE TO CROSS

The following persons are eligible to cross a cheque.

(i) Drawer of the cheque,

(ii) Payee of the cheque, and

(*iii*) Holder of the cheque.

If the drawer issues an uncrossed order cheque to the payee, the payee can cross the cheque generally or specially. If the payee crosses it generally, the holder of the cheque can cross it specially. In case the drawer has issued a generally crossed cheque, the payee or the holder of the cheque can across it specially. But if the drawer has crossed it specially, no one can then alter the crossing. The authority of cancelling the crossing made by any party is vested only in the hands of the drawer and not on anybody else. He has to put the words 'crossing cancelled, pay cash' at the place of crossing and affix his full signature as token of confirmation. In this case the banker should be careful to ascertain that the crossing is cancelled by the drawer only.

7.2.7 LIABILITY OF THE PAYING BANKER ON CROSSED CHEQUES :

Section 126 lays down that the paying banker on whom a crossed cheque is drawn must make payment thereof in accordance with the crossing. The duty of the paying banker is as follows :

" *Where a cheque is crossed generally, the banker on whom it is drawn shall not pay it otherwise to a banker and where a cheque is crossed specially, the banker on whom it is drawn shall not pay it otherwise than to the banker to whom it is crossed or his agent for collection.*"

Thus the payment of a crossed cheque is to be made to a banker only. Suppose a crossed cheque is presented for payment at the counter of the paying banker, the latter is justified in refusing payment of the cheque. If the payee of a crossed cheque has an account with the paying banker and presents a crossed cheque for payment at the counter, the banker should not comply with the request and the cheque should be paid through his account.

The paying banker's liability is provided under section 129 which is as follows:

" *Any banker paying a cheque crossed generally, otherwise than to a banker, or a cheque crossed specially, otherwise than to the banker to whom the same is crossed, or his agent for collection being a banker, shall be liable to the true owner of the cheque for any loss he may sustain owning to the cheque having been so paid*". Thus the paying banker shall be liable to the true owner of the cheque and to the drawer as follows :

(1) Liability to the true owner of the cheque : Generally, the paying banker is not responsible to the true owner of the cheque, i.e., the payee or the holder of the cheque, as there is no contract between the two; but if the paying banker makes payment of a crossed cheque in contravention of the direction of the drawer shall be liable to the true owner of the cheque for any loss sustained by him as a result on such payment. If a crossed cheque is lost by the true owner and its finder get its payment at the counter of the paying banker, the true owner is entitled to recover the amount of the cheque from the person who received its payment from the bank. Whatever is the loss suffered by the true owner or are the expenses incurred by him will be reimbursed by the banker.

2. Liability to the drawer : Suppose the banker fails to make payment of a crossed cheque in accordance with section 126, the payment is not deemed to be made as per the direction of the customer. The banker will, therefore, not be entitled to debit his customer's account with the amount of such cheque, if the payment happens to be made to a wrong person. Furthermore, the paying banker shall loose the statutory protection[1] granted to him under section 128 as such payment is not deemed to be payment in due course.

7.2.8. ADVANTAGES OF CROSSING

1. If payment is made by means of a crossed cheque, receipt need not be obtained.

2. 'Account payee' crossed cheque makes sure that only the particular person to whom the cheques are drawn can receive payment.

3. If a crossed cheque is lost, the finder of the cheque cannot encash it without the help of a banker.

4. Payments made through cheques particularly crossed cheques enable an automatic record of the amount in the pass book.

7.2.9. IMPACT OF CROSSING

Crossing serves the purpose of direction to the bank only or to a particular bank, as the case may. Crossing may be written, stamped or printed. Whenever two parallel transverse lines appear on the cheque, bank will not make payment to its holder at the counter of the bank.

The payment of a crossed cheque can only be obtained through the bank of the holder. Thus, crossing affords security and protection to the true owner of the cheque. The object of crossing is to secure payment to a bank in order to easily trace for whose benefit the money was received. Crossing is done to avoid losses arising from open cheques falling into the hands of wrong persons. However,

1. Elaborately discussed in chapter 9.

crossing of a cheque does not affect its negotiability. Crossed cheque is negotiable by mere delivery if it is payable to bearer and by endorsement and delivery in case, it is payable to order but where the words 'not negotiable' are added to the crossing, the cheque is not negotiable, though transferable.

7.3. MARKING OF CHEQUES

7.3.1. MARKING OF CHEQUES – MEANING

Marking or certification refers to the practice of indicating on the cheque that there are funds in the account of the drawer to meet the cheque.

When the payee who is unknown to the customer of the bank hesitates to accept a cheque for the goods supplied, the customer may require the banker to mark the cheque as good for payment. The authorised officer to the bank writes the words 'Good for payment' or 'Approved' or 'Certified' and then puts his signature on behalf of the bank.

Marking a cheque means making remarks by the banker testifying to the adequacy of the resources of the drawer to meet its effects. The banker certifies that the drawer of a cheque has sufficient funds in his account and hence it can be honoured on presentation by any legitimate holder.

7.3.2. ADVANTAGES

1. Marked cheques are useful to traders because they increase their credit-worthiness.

2. If a trader wants to buy goods from a stranger against payment by cheque, marked cheque will convince the seller about the payment of the cheque.

3. It gives additional currency by showing on its face that it was drawn in good faith on funds sufficient to meet its payment.

4. It adds credit of the drawer as well as the banker on whom it is drawn.

7.3.3. PROCEDURE OF MARKING CHEQUES

1. Marking may be done by the banker at the instance of:

(*a*) Customers (Dawers)

(*b*) At the request of holders and

(*c*) At the request of another banker.

If the marking is done on the request of the drawer, the banker has to honour the cheque on its presentation by the holder. The banker marking the cheque at drawer's request is entitled to earmark money out of drawer's account for the purpose of honouring such cheque. It has to be irrespective of death, insanity or insolvency of the drawer that might occur during the interval between marking of the cheque and its present for payment.

When the marking is done by the banker at the request of the holder, the banker's liability is limited on presentation. It may be honoured if the funds are sufficient. If before the payment of such a marked cheque, the drawer countermands payment of the cheque or himself withdraws money or due to any other reason and the cheque cannot be paid, the holder of the cheques so marked cannot hold the banker liable.

If the marking is done for another banker, it is construed as a promise to pay. The banker is entitled to take into account the cheques so marked, in estimating the balance available for meeting other cheques presented after the marked cheques.

2 Marking of post-dated cheque is held to be anomalous and invalid in India.

3 When the cheque is marked by a banker, he should make note of it in the respective account in the ledger.

Thus, marking is a kind of certificate from the paying banker that sufficient funds of the drawer are available to meet the cheque.

7.3.4. EFFECT OF MARKING

Unless the practice of the place or the usage of traders gives marking the effect of acceptance and consequently binds the banker to pay the cheque when presented, marking in other cases only indicates that the cheque has been drawn in good faith against sufficient funds. "When such marking by usage amounts to a undertaking by the bank to honour it, it adds the credit of the banker to that of the drawer" (Gadden vs Newfoundland Savings Bank).

The effect of marking is to give a cheque additional currency by showing on the face of it that the cheque was drawn in good faith and on funds sufficient to meet its payment by adding the credit of the banker to that of the drawee (Gadden vs Newfoundland Savings Bank).

Marking may be done at the instance of the drawer of the cheque or at the instance of the holder.

Marking at the instance of the drawer : In this case, the banker is entitled to appropriate the amount of the cheque from the balance standing to the customer's account. He is justified in treating the balance in the customer's account after the deduction of the amount of the marked cheque as the effective balance standing to the customer's credit; as such he is entitled to dishonour a customer's cheque when the effective balance is insufficient to meet it. The banker has the right to debit the customer's account with the amount of the cheque even after the occurance of an event, which has the legal effect of stopping the account such as the death or insolvency of the customer.

When marking is done at the request of the drawer, the drawer cannot countermand payment of the cheque.

The banker can set aside sufficient funds standing to the credit of the customer to meet the cheque he has certified.

He is also entitled to dishonour cheques presented subsequently if the balance remaining after providing for the certified cheque is insufficient to pay them.

It must be understood that the banker only certifies the genuiness of the drawer's signature and sufficiency of funds at the time of marking the cheque.

The banker is under no statutory obligation to certify a cheque.

Marking at the instance of the holder : If the marking is done at the instance of the payee or holder, the banker does not bind himself to make payment on presentation. The leading case in India on this point is, *Punjab National Bank Ltd., vs The Bank of Baroda Ltd.* The facts of the case are as follows: On 13th June, 1939, the Manager of the Calcutta Branch of the Bank of Baroda marked a crossed post-dated cheque for Rs.2,75,000 bearing the date 20th June, 1939, with the words 'Marked good for payment on 20.6.1939' The cheque was drawn by a person who had an account with the Bank of Baroda as well as with the Punjab National Bank. The cheque, after marking, was paid into the Punjab National Bank by the customer, who obtained payment of the amount of the cheque. On 19-6-1939, the Manager of the Bank of Baroda was suspended for some irregularities committed by him, and the notice of the cancellation of his power of attorney was duly given to all the banks concerned. When the cheque was presented to the Bank of Baroda on 20th June, it was dishonoured. Thereupon the Punjab National Bank filed a suit against the Bank of Baroda for the recovery of the amount of the cheque on the ground that the marking of the cheque rendered it obligatory on their part to honour the cheque on the date mentioned in the marking.

It was held that the Punjab National Bank could not recover the money from the Bank of Baroda. In the course of the judgment, the following points were brought out:

(1) Marking of a cheque does not amount to acceptance, since a cheque does not require acceptance at all. The holder of a cheque had neither the need nor the authority to require the acceptance of the drawee bank. A cheque differs from a bill exchange in that a bill requires acceptance before the drawee can be made liable, while a cheque does not require acceptance because the banker is always under the obligation of honouring the customer's cheques provided all the conditions are satisfied. Acceptance of a cheque is therefore superfluous. But if marking is done at the instance of the drawer, the banker has the right of setting aside the amount of the cheque from the funds belonging to the customer.

(2) There was no commercial practice or custom according to which marking was treated as acceptance.

(3) Certification could not be taken as a promise to pay enforceable at law, as there was no consideration supporting the promise.

(4) Certification can be taken as a representation as to the genuineness of the cheque and the signature of the drawer. But as a representation regarding the sufficiency of funds at a future date, it has no meaning. The plea of estoppel is of no avail, as certification is not a representation regarding an existing fact, while estoppel must be one.

(5) The Manager has no ostensible authority to certify post-dated cheques.

(6) It is true that when a cheque is certified, the certifying banker has a moral obligation to honour it when presented. But this is quite different from saying that he is legally bound to make the payment.

In view of the above, the practice of marking cheques are favoured by bankers and such a practice, except for clearing purposes, should be put an end to. A bank may instead of marking his customer's cheque, offer its cheque provided the customer has sufficient balance or credit limit.

In Sita Ram Jhunjhun Walla vs. Bombay Bullion Association Ltd. and others (1965). The Supreme Court explained that "*Certification is a method adopted when a bank on which a cheque is drawn verified the customer's account on which it is drawn and indicates on the cheque that there are enough funds in his account to meet the cheque.*"

Marking at the instance of the collecting banker : A banker who receives a cheque too late for inclusion in that day's clearing may send it to the drawee bank for certification. If such a cheque is certified, the certifying bank is bound to honour it. But the marking or certification is not acceptance, as acceptance creates a negotiable liability, while marking is inconsistent with further negotiation.

Marking as between bankers : Marking between bankers has been recognized as a judicially established custom. They do it for the purpose of clearance and they become bound to each other. When a cheque is presented for clearing after clearing hours, it may be marked. The banker in effect undertakes to pay the cheque the next day when clearing business is resumed.

7.4. MATERIAL ALTERATION

Alteration means making change in the negotiable instrument. Any alteration in a negotiable instrument which effects or introduces basic changes in the instrument such as, alteration in date, or place of payment, or amount payable or mode of payment or rate of interest, or its legal character is known as material alteration. It is considered material alteration only if it affects the operation of the instrument substantially and the liability of the parties concerned is changed significantly.

7.4.1. DEFINITION

A material alteration is one which materially or substantially alters the operation of the instrument and the liabilities of the parties thereto. In Aldous Vs Cornwell, (1868), *it* was held that an alteration is material which alters the business effect of an instrument which causes it to speak a language different in legal effect from the one which it originally spoke; or which changes the legal identity or character of the instrument either in terms or the relation of the parties thereto, is a material alteration. A cheque with a material alteration is not a cheque at all. Under the Indian Law, it is void (Section 87 of the negotiable Instruments Act, 1881.)

The important case in this regard is Slingsby and Others Vs. The Westminster Bank Ltd. (1931). In this case, Cumberbirch, a solicitor, made out a cheque in favour of John Prust & Co., a firm of stock-brokers and got it signed by the executors as drawers. There was a blank space left after the name of the payee and before the words 'or order'. After obtaining the signature of the drawers, Cumberbirch filled the blank space after the payee's name with the words 'Per Cumberbirch and Potts', without the knowledge of the drawers. He then endorsed the cheque as 'Cumberbirch and Potts' and paid it into the Westminster Bank, with instructions that the proceeds be credited to the account of Palatine Industrial Financial Co. Ltd., to whom he was indebted. In an action brought against the Westminster Bank by the executors for wrongful conversion of the cheque, it was held that no action could be brought on it against the Westminster Bank as the document, when it came into their hands, was not a cheque at all by reason of the unauthorised alteration made in it. There was no question of any negligence because there was no contractual relationship between the plaintiff and the Bank".

Slingsby and others Vs The District Bank: Thereupon, the executors sued the paying bankers, the District Bank for the amount of the cheque again on grounds of wrongful conversion. They pointed out that the endorsement on the cheque was irregular. They alleged that the defendants were guilty of negligence and breach of duty in as much as they paid the cheque without proper enquiry. It was held that the instrument was not a cheque at all, and even if it was one, the endorsement was irregular. The bankers could not therefore debit the account of the Executors with the amount of the cheque.

The defendants put forward the plea that the drawers of the cheque were guilty of breach of duty in leaving blank space after the payee's name, thus facilitating forgery. It was held that to leave blank space after the payee's name was not breach of duty, as it was not the usual practice at that time to draw a line after the payee's name.

Examples : Alteration in the cheque can be effected chemically also. Examples of material alterations are as below:

(i) Alteration of the date of the cheque or negotiable instrument:– By altering the date the holder of the cheque can secure payment of a post dated cheque or a stale cheque. The bank is not empowered and authorised to make such payments, if detected.

(*ii*) Alteration of place of payment.

(*iii*) Altering the amount of the cheque

(*iv*) Altering the names of the parties

(*v*) Substituting the word 'bearer' in the place of 'order' cheque.

(*vi*) Making alteration of the crossing of a cheque.

(*vii*) Alteration of the rate of interest;

(*viii*) Alteration of the number of parties to the instrument and

(*ix*) alteration of the relation of the parties to the instrument or their legal character.

7.4.2. ALTERATIONS (IMMATERIAL)

Undermentioned alterations, additions, changes in an instrument or cheque are not accepted as material alterations:

(*i*) Converting a blank endorsement into a full endorsement.

(*ii*) Crossing a cheque, including converting a general crossing into a special crossing.

(*iii*) Filling up blanks in an instrument.

(*iv*) Addition of words like 'not negotiable' to a crossing in a cheque.

(*v*) Qualifying an acceptance, or

(*vi*) An alteration made accidentally or innocently.

The following are not material alterations: (1) filling up blanks of an inchoate instrument: (2) conversion of a blank endorsement into an endorsement in full. (3) qualifying an acceptance and (4) crossing a cheque.

7.4.3. EFFECTS OF MATERIAL ALTERATIONS

Section 87 of Banking Law and Practice says, "*any material alteration of a negotiable instrument renders the same, void as against anyone who is a party thereto at the time of making such alteration and does not consent thereto unless it was made in order to carry out the common intention of the original parties.*" Any alteration if made by an endorsee, discharges his endorser from all liability to him in respect of the consideration thereof'. Therefore the material alteration as mentioned above on a negotiable instrument or cheque shall have the following effects:

(a) The instruments become void. The liability of a person who becomes party to the instrument after the alteration has been made is not affected.

(b) If material alteration is made with the permission or consent of the parties to the instrument shall not become void one.

In certain circumstances an alteration though made is not considered as material alteration if it does not vitiate a fatal flaw, in the negotiable instrument.

The following are the circumstances: –

(*a*) If alteration is made merely for correcting the mistake.

(*b*) If alteration is made before the actual execution of the instrument.

(*c*) If alteration is made purely to carrying out the common intention of the original parties to the instrument.

Protection to the Banker: Undoubtedly a material alteration in the negotiable instrument makes it void; but Section 89 grants protection to the bank that makes the payment as under:

"*Where a promissory note, bill of exchange or cheque has been materially altered but does not appear to have been so altered, payment thereof by a person or banker liable to pay and paying the same according to the apparent tenor thereof at the time of payment and otherwise in due course shall discharge such person or banker from all liability thereon and such payment shall not be questioned by reason of the instrument having been altered*'.

The banker who is responsible for payment of cheques which have been materially altered , may therfore avail of the statutory protection under section 89, provided:

(*a*) The atteration is not apparently clear, *i.e.*, it can not be detected with reasonable care, prudence and scrutiny. For example, if the drawer of the cheque has written the amount so carelessly by leaving sufficient space before the amount (both in words and figures) and the holders or any other person alters so carefully by inserting some words and figures which cannot be detected with due care and scrutiny by the banker, the latter shall not be held responsible for paying the amount so altered. In the case of Bank of Maharashtra Vs. Automative Engineering Co. (1993), the Supreme Court held that there is nothing in the Act, which makes it obligatory for the 'bank to subject every cheque to examine under ultraviolet ray lamp, though it could be prudent to examine under the said light. The bank will not be deemed as failed to take reasonable care in passing the cheque for payment without the cheque being examined under ultraviolet ray lamp.

(*b*) If the payment has been made in due course as per section 10, the paying banker is discharged from his liability on the cheque and he can debit the account of the drawer with the amount of the cheque.

7.5. ENDORSEMENT

7.5.1. DEFINITION OF ENDORSEMENT

When the maker or holder of a negotiable instrument signs the same otherwise than as such maker, for the purpose of negotiation on the back or face thereof or on a slip of paper annexed thereto........ he is said to endorse the same and is called the endorser. "Endorsement " is derived from the Latin term "dorsum", meaning "upon the back" which indicates that the usual place of an endorsement is on back of the instrument. Suppose the space available is not sufficient due to rapid circulation of an instrument, a piece of paper – called allonge – is pasted to it and subsequent endorsement made thereon.

Section 15 of the Negotiable instruments Act defines endorsement as Follows:

" *When the maker or holder of a negotiable instrument signs the same, otherwise than as such maker, for the purpose of negotiation, on the back or face thereof or on a slip of paper annexed thereto, or so signs for the same purpose a stamped paper intended to be completed as a negotiable instrument, he is said to have endorsed the same and is called the endorser.*"

Thus, an endorsement consists of the signature of the maker (drawer) of a negotiable instrument or any holder thereof but it is essential that the intention of putting the signature on the instrument should be negotiation, otherwise it will not constitute an endorsement.

The person who signs the instrument for the purpose of negotiation is called the "endorser" and the person in whose favour instrument is transferred is called the "endorsee". The endorser may sign either on the face or on the back of the negotiable instrument. However, it is the normal practice that endorsements are made on the back of the instrument. In case the space on the back of the instrument is not sufficient for this purpose, a piece of paper, known as" allonge" may be attached thereto for the purpose of recording the endorsements.

7.5.2 LEGAL PROVISIONS REGARDING ENDORSEMENT

1. Effect of Endorsement: Section 50 provides that the endorsement of a negotiable instrument followed by delivery transfers to the endorsee the value therein with the right of further negotiation. Thus the endorsee acquires the property and also the right in the instrument as its holder and he can also negotiate it further.

Where a negotiable instrument is endorsed for any purpose, the endorsee becomes its holder and the property therein is passed on to the endorsee. In Kunju Pillai and others vs. Periaṣami (1969), the trial court held that the endorsement for collection created the relationship of Principal and agent between the original payee, and the endorsee and on the death of the payee, the agency came to an end in terms of section 201 of the Indian Contract Act, 1872. But on appeal, the High Court held that a holder of a negotiable instrument, who secures the same by endorsement, does not lose the right of his action by the reason of the original payee. In another case, viz, Mothireddy vs. Pothireddy (1963), the Andrah Pradesh High Court held that "the right based on endorsement survives notwithstanding the death of the endorser. The endorsement having been made for a specific purpose, namely, collection of the amount, will be valid till that purpose is 'served." Hence the ordinary Law regarding agency does not, therefore, apply in such cases.

2. Endorser : Every sole maker, drawer, payee or endorsee of a negotiable instrument may endorse and negotiate the same. Seciton 51 provides that this is subject to the condition that the right to negotiate has not been restricted or excluded. In case the endorsement is held jointly by a number of persons, endorsement by all of them is essential. One cannot represent the other.

Even if the words "or order" in the instrument or endorsement thereon are not found, it does not restrict further negotiation. For example, a bill is drawn payable to X or order. X endorses it to Y but the endorsement does not contain the words "or order"or any equivalent words. This does not restrict Y from further negotiation of the instrument.

3. Time : As per section 60 a negotiable instrument may be negotiated until its payment has been made by the banker, drawee or acceptor at or after maturity but not thereafter.

4. Endorsement for a part of the amount : Section 56 provides that if an endorsement is made on the instrument for transfering only a part of the amount appearing to be due on the instrument, the endorsement is not valid. Therefore, the instrument must be endorsed for its entire amount. But in case an instrument has been partly paid, it may be negotiated for the balance of the amount provided a note to that effect is given on the instrument.

If the endorser intends to transfer the document to two or more endorsees separately it will not constitute a valid endorsement.

5. If the endorser dies after endorsing the instrument payable to order but without delivering the same to the endorsee, such endorsement shall not be valid and his legal representative cannot complete its negotiation by mere delivery thereof.

6. Unless contrary is proved, it is presumed under section 118 that the

endorsement which appears on an instrument first has been made earlier to the second one.

Rules for endorsement or essentials of a valid endorsement: The rules regarding valid endorsements are given below:

1. The endorsement must be written on the instrument itself or on a slip of paper annexed thereto.
2. It must be made by the holder of the instrument and not by a stranger.
3. It must be signed by the endorser. The endorser must sign his name in the same spellings as appearing on the face of the cheque.
4. An endorsement written on an allonge is deemed to be written on the instrument itself.
5. The endorser should endorse the instrument in full and not in part.
6. If an instrument is payable to the order of two or more payees or endorsees who are not partners, all must endorse unless the one endorsing has authority to endorse for all others.
7. Endorsement is complete only when the instrument is delivered. The delivery must be made by the endorser himself. If the delivery is conditional, endorsement is not complete until the condition is fulfilled.
8. Endorsements can be made by the endorser merely by signing his name on the instrument or by adding the name of a specified person to whom the endorser likes to endorse.

7.5.3. KINDS OF ENDORSEMENTS

According to the Negotiable Instruments Act, 1881, endorsement may take any of the following terms :

1. **General or Blank Endorsement :** If the endorser just puts his signature without specifying the name of the endorsee, the endorsement is said to be blank. (Section 16). The effect of such an endorsement makes the instrument payable to bearer even though originally payable to order and negotiation takes place at mere delivery. For example: A cheque payable to

Mr. B. Senthilnathan may be endorsed as :"B.Senthilnathan", i.e., merely signs on its back.

According to Sec.54 a cheque which is endorsed in blank becomes payable to bearer even though it was originally payable to order. But if a cheque is a crossed one, its payment cannot be made at the counter of the bank, even if it is endorsed in blank. If the endorsement in blank is followed by endorsement in full, it becomes payable to or to the order to the person mentioned in the last endorsement.

2. **Special or Full Endorsement :** If the name of the endorsee is specified in whose favour it is being endorsed, along with the signature of the endorser, the endorsement is called endorsement in full (Section. 16). If in the above illustration the words "pay to A Kumaran" or "pay to A. Kumaran or order" are made, such endorsement is called endorsement in full. If such an endorsement is made, the banker should make payment either to the endorsee or to his order. The instrument

having such endorsements shall be negotiated by means of endorsement and delivery.

An endorsement in blank may be converted into 'endorsement in full' by the holder by merely adding above the endorser's signature, a direction to pay to any other person.

According to Sec. 55, " if a negotiable instrument after having been endorsed in blank is endorsed in full, the amount of it cannot be claimed from the endorser in full, except by the person to whom it has been endorsed in full or by one who derives title through such person. For example a cheque is endorsed in blank by B Senthilnathan and transferred to A Kumaran who endorses it in favour of B. Raman. The latter transfers it A. Sita without any endorsement. If the cheque is dishonoured, A. Sita cannot sue A. Kumaran or B. Raman. But she can sue B. Senthilnathan only.

3. Conditional Endorsement : It is an endorsement under which the endorser lays down some condition to be fulfilled by the payee before making the payment. This type of endorsement involves a special problem because, according to the definition of a cheque, it is an unconditional order payable on demand. That is, a cheque cannot be made payable on the happening of certain conditions and therefore it ceases to be a cheque. For example, endorsement, 'pay to X after he signs the enclosed receipt'.

4. Sans Recourse Endorsement : In this case, the endorser makes it clear to the endorsee that the endorser would not be liable in case the instrument is dishonoured. This means that further recourse cannot be taken against the endorser. For example: Pay to X without recourse to me.

5. Restrictive Endorsement : Restrictive endorsement, by written words, restricts the right of further negotiation. In this case, an endorser specifies that the banker should pay the amount to a particular endorsee only. Example : Pay to X only.

6. Facultative Endorsement : The endorser waiving the right of 'notice of dishonour' of the instrument, while making the endorsement is called facultative endorsement. It means that future endorsers need not serve a notice of dishonour to the endorser who has made such facultative endorsement. In this case, the endorser makes the endorsement with the words, "Notice of Dishonour is waived". Usually, whenever a negotiable instrument is dishonoured on presentation, it is the first duty of the holder of the instrument to serve a notice of dishonour to all the provious endorsers. But in this case, the endorser makes it clear that he need not be served a notice of dishonour. Example : Pay to X or order – Notice of dishonour waived.

7. Partial Endorsement : If an endorsement is made for the part of the amount of the instrument, it is called "partial endorsement". But such an endorsement is not valid.

7.5.4. FORGED ENDORSEMENTS

If an instrument is endorsed in full, it cannot be further endorsed or negotiated except by an endorsement signed by the person to whom the instrument is payable. Thus, if such an instrument is negotiated by way of a forged endorsement, the endorsee will acquire no title even though the instrument is purchased for value and in good faith, because the endorsement nullifies further negotiation.

THE RULE OF ONCE A BEARER OF THE INSTRUMENT ALWAYS A BEARER

The view that once a bill of exchange is issued as bearer, it remains always a bearer. This view had been in vogue in India untill in Forbes, Forbes Compell & Co. Vs. The Official Assignee of Bombay (1925), wherein it was held that once a bearer hundi is endorsed in favour of a payee or his order, it ceased to be a bearer hundi and was payable to the third person or his order only. The above ruling so completely upset the ordinary banking practice in India. To remedy the defect, the Negotiable Instruments (Amendment) Act. 1934 was passed based on the principle, "once a bearer, always a bearer". The amendment introduced as sub-section (2) to Section 85 of the Negotiable Instruments Act. 1881, reads as follows:

"*Where a cheque is originally expressed to be payable to bearer, the drawee is discharged by payment in due course to the bearer thereof, notwithstanding any indorsement whether in full or in blank appearing thereon, and notwithstanding that any such indorsement purports to restrict or exclude further negotion.*"

Therefore the bank is not required to look into the regularity of endorsements on a bearer cheque.

1. A cheque originally expressed to be payable to the bearer can be paid to the bearer and the drawee banker is discharged by such payment, even if such a cheque contains some endorsement in full or blank. This rule does not apply to a cheque which becomes bearer subsequently because of blank endorsement.

2.Where an instrument is endorsed in blank or is payable to bearer, it can be negotiated by delivery. If a holder endorses it specifically to a person and makes its payable to the person, the endorser in full cannot be sued by anyone except the person in whose favour he endorsed it. As regards parties prior to the endorser in full, the instrument remains transferable by delivery.

For example Mr.A, the payee, endorses a bill in blank and delivers it to Mr.B. Mr.B endorses it to Mr.C or order. Mr.C without endorsement transfers it to M.X. M.X is no doubt entitled to payment as the bearer of the instrument. When the bill is dishonoured, Mr. X is entitled to sue the drawer, the acceptor and also Mr.A the endorser in blank and all endorsers 'prior' to Mr.A; but he cannot sue either Mr.B or Mr.C.

7.5.5. ENDORSER'S LIABILITY

The liability of an endorser of a bill and other negotiable instrument is stated in section 35 of the Negotiable Instrument Act. This section lays down the following points.

1. Every endorser of a bill of exchange before maturity is liable to every subsequent holder in case the bill is dishonoured by the acceptor or drawer.
2. This can be excluded by a separate contract to the contrary.
3. The person making such endorsement may expressly exclude his own liability to the subsequent parties eg. Sans Recourse Endorsement.

4. Such endorser is liable only if due notice of dishonour is given to him.

5. These provisions will apply to demand bill also. Here it must be noted that the endorser's liability is that of a surety but he is also the principal debtor to his immediate endorsee. For example A draws a bill payable to C on B, who accepts the bill. C afterwards endorses the bill to D and D to E. As between E and B, B is the principal debtor and A, C & D are his sureties.

As between E & C, C is the principal debtor and D is the surety.

7.5.6. BANKERS PRACTICE REGARDING ENDORSEMENT

Before a cheque is paid, the banker should ensure that all the endorsements are regular. This is one of the conditions to be fulfilled for obtaining statutory protection by the paying banker in case of order cheques. It is not necessary that the endorsement should be genuine. It is to be regular and valid only when it is in accordance with the practice of bank. The following principles are followed in this regard:–

1. Incorrect Spelling: If the name of the payee or endorsee is mis-spelt, the endorsement must correspond to the mis-spelt name. For e.g. if a cheque is made payable to S.L.Raam or order, the correct spelling being S.L.Ram, the proper endorsement should be:

S.L.Raam

(S.L.Ram,).

2. Individuals: In the case of individuals, complementary prefixes, suffixes and other courtesy titles or professional designations should not form part of an endorsement. Thus endorsement such as : Mr. Senthil.

Dr. Saravanakumar

Sir M.J.Prakash

are irregular.

The proper endorsements are :

a. Senthil

b. Saravanakumar

c. M.J.Prakash

3. Women: In the case of unmarried woman the endorsement consists of her first name and surname. Therefore a cheque endorsed to Miss. Seetha Kishore must be endorsed as Seetha Kishore. If the cheque is payable to a woman in her maiden name, but now married, the endorsement should be as follows:

Vidya Lakshmi

(Now Mrs. Vidya Lakshmi)

or

Vidya Lakshmi

Nee Vidya Lakshmi)

The meaning of Nee is formerly.

4. Illiterate persons: Endorsement must be made by thumb impression which should be duly attested or witnessed.

Thumb mark by Ram Gopal
Witnessed and attested by:
Sridharan
Advocate,
Coimbatore-10.

The witness must be an independent party who is known to both parties.

5. Clubs, Schools, and Colleges etc: In the case of cheque made payable to clubs, schools etc., they must be endorsed by the persons authorised to deal with such cheques. The proper endorsement in the case of a cheque payable to ABC college would be:

For ABC College.
xxxxxxxxxxx
Principal.

Here, the name and designation and the name of the person are important.

6. Firms : In the case of cheques payable to a firm, the cheques must be endorsed in the name of the firm by a partner or manager who is duly authorized to sign on behalf of the firm. The name of the firm must be mentioned in full. For e.g. a cheque payable to "Vasanth Trading Company" may be endorsed to any one of the following ways:

1. Vasanth Trading Company,
   Vasanth
   Partner.
2 Vasanth Trading Company
3 for Vasanth Trading Company,
   M.Laxman
   Manager.

7.Joint Payees : In the case of cheques drawn, payable to two or more persons, the cheque must be endorsed by all of them. For *e.g.* If the cheque is payable to Laxman and Kumar the proper endorsement would be :

Laxman
Kumar

In this case, an endorsement must be in one handwriting. Laxman and Kumar usually require confirmation as there is nothing to show that the two are partners or one has authority to sign for the other.

8. Agents : As stated under partnership, in the case of agent, they derive the authority to endorse under a power of attorney and the usual form of endorsement is:

"Per Pro M. Laxman,
J.Prakash.

9. Joint Stock Companies : In the case of a company the endorsement will be made by the officials who have the authority to sign, as for instance directors or secretary or the General Manager or Accountant. An endorsement by the cashier is generally not accepted.

e.g. for "XYZ Corporation Limited "
T.Rajan.
(Secretary & Accountant)

10. Executors and Administrators : Executors have the power to delegate the authority among the one self but not outside the oneself. Therefore if a cheque is drawn payable to "The Executors of late Mr. S. Kumara Dhunga, the correct endorsement would be as follows:

1. for Self & Company Executors of the late
S. Kumara Dhunga
S. Ranga Raj.

2. S. Ranga Raj } Executors of late S. Kumara Dhunga
M.Mubarac }

11. Trustees : They have no power to delegate their authority even among the oneself. Therefore in the case of a cheque payable to the trustee of late S. Kumara Dhunga, the endorsement must be made by all of them as follows:

T.Johnson } Trustees of late S. Kumara Dhunga
H.Abdhul Kadhar }

12. Official Payees: In the case of cheque payable to official payees, the endorsement must also state their official capacity. For example, a cheque payable to Income-Tax Officer, Coimbatore must be endorsed as :

Anand Keerthan,

Income-tax Officer,
Coimbatore.

13. Impersonal Payees: In the case of cheques made payable to "Income-tax or order" the endorsement must be :

Anand Keerthan,
Income-tax Officer,
Salary Ward,
Coimbatore.

14. Deceased Persons: In the case of deceased persons, the endorsement must be made by legal representative. For examble a cheque drawn payable to late Mr. Kumara Mangalam can be endorsed as follows:

B.Hariharan,
Legal heir or son of late Mr.N.Kumara Mangalam

Endorsement and Identification of Holders of Bearer Cheques:– In England endorsement of a bearer cheque is not insisted upon by the paying banker.

But whereas in India, banks ordinarily insist that the person presenting even bearer cheques for payment to endorse them. Though it is not legally required and if the holder of a bearer cheque refuses to sign, the paying banker may insist upon having a stamped receipt for the amount paid to him. Though the paying banker need not insist for identification of the holder of a bearer cheque, in case of large amount, the banker may, if possible, ask through telephone, for the drawer's confirmation. In practice, the paying banker insists on the holder of a bearer cheque to sign on the back of the cheque to establish the payment has been made. In case of bearer cheques made payable to companies, it is well advised to make inquiries before paying them at the counter.

Effect of Endorsee's death before payment

In Kunju Pillai & others Vs. Periasami (1969), it was held that a holder of a negotiable instrument who secures the same by endorsement does not lose his right of action by reason of the death of the original payee. He (the endorsee) secures the title to the instrument which is enforceable by him in the ordinary course of the law. Such a title is vested in him and cannot be denied by reason only of the fact that the original payee died after making the endoresment.

QUESTIONS

1. What are the contents of a cheque ?
2. What is an endorsement ? Explain and illustrate the different kinds of endorsements.
3. Define endorsement. Explain types of endorsements. Explain and illustrate the effect of partial endorsement.
4. Explain the meaning of the following terms :

   (a) Allonge

   (b) Sans Recourse.
5. Define general crossing. What are its essentials ?
6. Distinguish between general crossing and special crossing ?
7. What is double crossing ? Is it valid ?
8. What is 'marking' of cheque ? Bring out clearly the Significance of marking when it is done,

   (i) at the request of a drawer

   (ii) at the request of another banker.
9. Discuss the legal implication of marking of a post-dated cheque with a relevant case Law on this subject.

8

COLLECTION OF CHEQUES

Collection of cheques and other negotiable instruments deposited by his customers is an important service rendered by a modern commercial bank. When a customer receives a cheque, particularly a crossed cheque drawn on any other bank, he has to send it to his banker for the purpose of collection from the drawee bank. The bank which has been deputed to collect the amount of the cheque from another bank is called the collecting banker. However, a bank is under no legal obligation to collect is customer's cheques. But collection of cheques has now become an important function of a banker with the growth of banking habit and with wider use of crossed cheques which can hardly be dispensed with.

The term "Collecting Banker" refers to the function of receiving cheques by a banker from customers for the purpose of collecting the proceeds and crediting them to the respective customer's account. In other words, the banker who is deputed to collect the amount of the cheque from another banker, is called the collecting banker. Thus, collecting banker can be described as a link between the payee of a cheque and its drawee (paying banker).

The collecting banker accepts the cheque, bills of exchange, and other negotiable instruments issued or endorsed in favour of his customer and forwards them to the paying banker to collect the amount specified therein and credits the respective accounts with the proceeds thereof.

8.1 CAPACITY OF THE COLLECTING BANKER

When a banker collects his customers' cheques, he acts in any one of the following capacities:-

(*a*) Holder for value

(*b*) Agent of the customer

When a customer receives cheques drawn on other banks, he deposits them in his own bank and requests the banker to collect them and credit the proceeds to his account. The bank performs this service for the customer.

In receiving a cheque for collection from the customer, the banker acts as the agent of the customer. But he becomes a holder when he pays the amount of the cheque or credits the amount of the cheque to his customer in anticipation of collection. He becomes a 'holder in due course' if the conditions attaching to the term are satisfied.

(a) Collecting Banker as Holder for Value : In the case of outstation cheques, the collecting banker cannot get the amount of the cheques immediately and it will take sometime. Sometimes, in order to oblige a customer, he may pay the amount of the cheque or may credit his customer's account and allow him to withdraw the amount even before he realises the cheque.

If it is done, the collecting banker is regarded as a holder for value as was held in the case of *A.L. Underwood Ltd. Vs. Barclays Bank* (1924). But the collecting bankers should get an undertaking from the customer to the effect that the latter shall reimburse the former in the case of dishonour of the cheque.

As Sir John Paget (Laws of Banking) put it, a banker becomes its holder for value by giving its value to the customer in any of the following ways:

(*a*) by lending on the strength of the cheque;

(*b*) by paying the amount of the cheque or part of it before it is cleared;

(*c*) by agreeing to allow the customer to withdraw before the cheque is cleared, so that an existing overdraft is reduced.

(*d*) by giving cash over the counter for the cheque at the time it is paid in for collecting.

(e) by accepting the cheque in avowed reduction of an existing overdraft.

In any of the above circumstances, the banker becomes the holder for value and also the holder in due course.

(*b*) Collecting Banker as an Agent : If the collecting banker credits with the amount of the cheque after the cheque amount is actually realised, the banker is deemed to be acting as agent of his customer. In this case, the customer will be allowed to withdraw the amount of the cheque after the payment is realised from the drawee bank. As an agent of his customer, the collecting banker does not get a better title than that of his customer. Suppose the customer has a defective title, the collecting banker cannot have good title to the cheque. In case the cheque collected by him did not belong to his customer, he will be held liable for "Conversion of money" i.e., illegally interfering with the rights of the true owner of the cheque.

Therefore, conversion means wrongful or unlawful interference with another person's property. However, the right of the true owner is a restricted one and cannot be exercised in case the goods reached hands of one who (i) receives it in good faith (ii) for value and (iii) without the knowledge that the other party has no authority thereon. Excepting these circumstances, the true owner of the negotiable instrument can file a suit for conversion.

Bankers, duty and agency Functions : While collecting a cheque for a customer, the relationship between the banker and the customer is converted into the agent and customer. As an agent, he has certain duties to be performed as stated below:

(1) **Presentment of cheque without delay** : It is the duty of the bank to present the cheques for payment without delay. It must be presented to the drawee bank within a reasonable period of time. In case the collecting and the paying bankers are in the same place, the collecting banker should present the cheque the next day after receiving the same. In case of outstation cheques, he should mail them to the drawee banker on the day after it is received by him. If cheque is presented through clearing house, delay in presenting a cheque entrusted for collection may occur in more than one way. If for instance, some cheques meant for collection are misplaced and traced a few days later and sent for collection and if in the meantime the customer relying on the clearance of his cheque, has issued cheques on this account, and they are dishonoured by bank, the bank will be liable for wrongful dishonour. What is reasonable time is a pertinent question which might strike to the minds of readers. Reasonable time depends upon the circumstances of each case. Reasonable time is determined having regard to:

(i) The nature of the credit instrument,

(*ii*) Usage of trade and bankers,

(*iii*) Facts of a particular case.

The practice being followed is stated in the preceding sentences above.

Section 72 and 84 lay down the consequences of non-presenting the cheque before the drawee within a reasonable period of time as follows "*where a cheque is not presented for payment within a reasonable time of the issue and the drawer or person on whose account it is drawn had the right, at the time, when presentation ought to have been made, as between himself and the banker to have the cheque paid suffers actual damage through the delay, he is discharged to the extent of such damage, that is to say, to the extent to which such drawer or person is a creditor of the banker to the larger amount than he would have been if such cheque had been paid*'.

2. **To serve notice of dishonour** : In case a cheque is returned to the collecting banker without payment for one reason or the other, the banker must serve a notice of dishonour on his customer to enable the latter to claim the amount from previous parties including the drawer. If the banker fails to send such notice within reasonable time, he will be liable to the customer for any loss suffered by him as a result of such omission on the part of the banker.

As per Section 93 of the Negotiable Instruments Act, the notice of dishonour should be given by the holder of the dishonoured instrument to all other parties whom he intends to make liable, stating the fact of dishonour, the date of presentation, the reason given, if any, for the dishonour. As per Section 96 of the above Act, when the instrument is deposited with an agent for presentment, the agent is entitled to give notice of dishonour to his principal, who can in turn serve such notice of dishonour to other parties sought to be made liable.

If the banker is holder for value and is not an agent of the customer while collecting the cheque, he must give notice of dishonour to all parties to the cheque so as to make all or any of them liable for the payment of the amount of the cheque.

3. Duty to make over the proceeds : In crediting the proceeds of a draft paid into the bank for collection, to the account of the customer, there should not be any delay on the part of the collecting banker. The draft should be issued strictly in accordance with the instructions of the customer. If the banker is negligent in this behalf, he would be held liable. In Bank of Bihar Limited vs. Tata Scob Dealers, Calcutta Limited, it was held that the bank was negligent in having sent the draft by ordinary post. The drafts should, therefore, be sent by registered post only or according to the instructions given to the collecting banker.

The Collecting banker is given statutory protection subject to the fulfillment of the following Conditions :

1. The Cheque must be a crossed cheque : The statutory protection is available to the banker only in case of cheques crossed generally or specially to himself. He can claim no protection in case of open cheques, i.e., in the case of uncrossed cheque or an uncrossed cheque which is crossed by the collecting banker himself after having received it. It is essential that all cheques received by bankers, are usually crossed by them with a rubber stamp as a precaution against their being stolen and cashed, before they are deposited with the collecting banker; otherwise the banker will be liable for conversion if the title of the customer proves to be defective or the endorsement thereon is a forged one.

2. Collection must be on behalf of customers : Secondly, the statutory protection is available only when the banker collects the cheque on behalf of a customer. A customer is one who has an account with the banker and his dealings with the banker are in the nature of banking business. Suppose a cheque has been collected for a person who has not been a customer of the banker, then the banker is not entitled to claim protection under this section, if found after that the cheque has been collected otherwise of the true owner of the cheque. The statutory protection is available to the banker if he collects the cheque as an agent of the customer and not as its holder for value. As the holder for value, the collecting banker becomes its rightful owner and cannot avail of the statutory protection. Section 131 explains further that" a banker receives payment of a crossed cheque for a customer within the meaning of this Section notwithstanding that he credits his customer's account with the amount of the cheque before receiving payment thereof." This is very important as it is extends statutory protection to a banker in all such cases where the customer's accounts are credited with the amounts of the cheques before their actual realisation. In such cases the banker is deemed to be the agent of his customer for collection and not holder for value. Thus the collecting banker does not lose statutory protection if he credits his customer's account with the amount of the cheque before its actual realisation but the customer is allowed to draw the amount only after its realisation.

However, the question whether the bill is taken from a customer for collection or as security or is discounted by him has been decided in the case of Dena Bank vs. The Madhya Pradesh National Textiles Corporation Ltd. (1982). In this case, the Madhya Pradesh High court held that if the bills and the relevant documents presented by its drawer were accpeted by a banker with endorsement in its favour and the same were immediately discounted by the banker without waiting for their realisation by giving full credit for the entire amout of the document so presented, the banker itself becomes the purchaser and holder thereof for full value. Thus, the banker is not entitled to have statutory protection as the collecting banker, as the bill has been collected not for the customer but the banker acted as the holder the value.

3. Payment must be received in good faith and without negligence : Lastly, the collecting banker can claim protection only if he received payment "in good faith and without negligence". A thing is deemed to be done in good faith when it is in fact done honestly whether negligently or not. And at the same time he should not be negligent in receiving payment. The *ouns* of proving that he is not negligent in collecting the cheque lies on the banker himself.

Negligence depends upon the circumstances of each case. Generally, negligence indicates lack of care which is ought to be taken in any circumstances. In the Central Bank India Ltd, Bombay vs.

V Gopinathan Nair and others, the Kerala High Court observed that *"the test of negligence under Section 131 is whether the payment considered in the light of the circumstances, antecedent and present, was so much out of ordinary course that it ought to have aroused doubt in banker's mind and caused him to make enquiries*".

Suppose the circumstances of a case create doubt or suspicion about the right of the customer to the cheque, the banker must make proper enquiries and take adequate precautions. Failure to do so will constitute negligence on his part. Though the banker owes a duty to his own customer, the Law also makes him responsible to the true owner of the cheque. Thus the privilege of statutory protection can be availed of by the banker if he fulfills his statutory duty towards the true owner of the cheque and exercises due care in safeguarding the latter's interest.

8.2. PRECAUTIONS TO BE TAKEN BY THE COLLECTING BANKER

The collecting banker should take due precautions in collecting cheques of customers in order to avoid the risk involved. They are as under:

1. He must have received the payment only for a customer and not for a stranger.
2. He must receive payment in his capacity as an agent of his customer.
3. The title of the customer to the cheque should be closely examined by verifying the regularity of endorsement and the correctness of other contents of the cheque.
4. He must have acted in good faith and without negligence.
5. The cheques must have been crossed before it came into the possession of the collecting banker.

Therefore, to avoid personal liability in case of fraud, the collecting banker should fulfill the conditions as per Section 131 of the Negotiable Instruments Act.

Statutory Protection to a collecting banker : A collecting banker may obtain protection under the Negotiable Instruments Act which states as follows: "*A banker who has in good faith and without negligence received payment for a customer of a cheque crossed generally or specially to himself shall not, in case, the title to the* *cheque proves defective, incur any liability to the true owner of the cheque by reason only of having received such payment*" (Sec. 131). The Act also gives protection in respect of collection of crossed bank drafts.

A banker should be careful when requested to cash a cheque where the crossing has been cancelled; otherwise by paying such a cheque he should render himself liable to its true owner who took the cheque in the crossed condition. To conclude , it can be stated that a banker must not collect a crossed cheque for a person who is not his customer, as by such collection he should render himself liable and lose protection under Negotiable Instruments Act.

The drawer of a cheque at the time of issuing it can cross it. If he has issued it in an uncrossed state , the holder can cross it specially. Where a cheque is crossed specially, the banker to whom it is crossed may cross it specially to another bank, which acts as his agent for collection.

Cancellation of crossing or opening of a crossed cheque: Sometimes, the payee or the holder of a crossed cheque may not have a bank account. Under such circumstances, it becomes very difficult, rather impossible, for him to get the amount. To avoid such a difficulty the payee or holder of the instrument would be keen to get the crossing cancelled so that he can obtain the necessary cash immediately at the counter. The authority to cancel the crossing is vested only in the drawer and no one else. He has to put the words 'crossing cancelled pay cash' at the place of crossing and affix his full signature as a token of confirmation. The banker has to be careful in such cases to ascertain that the crossing is cancelled by the drawer only.

Where the crossing is cancelled and the words "pay cash" is found on a cheque along with customer's signature, the banker pays the cheque across the counter. No cancellation of crossing on a cheque should be recognised unless the full signature of the drawer be attested to such an alteration. A banker should be on his guard when requested to cash a cheque where the crossing has been cancelled. Otherwise by doing so he should render himself liable to the true owner who took the cheque in the crossed condition.

Bankers' position in case of uncrossed cheques for collection : Crossed cheques are invariably pass through the hands of the collecting banker enroute to the paying banker, because crossed cheques are not encashable on the paying banker's counter. But there is no necessity of such a procedure in case of uncrossed cheques since they are encashable on the paying banker's counter. The collecting banker cannot claim protection in case of uncrossed cheques because they need not be channelled through a collecting banker. The banker in case of uncrossed cheques received for collection should take the following precautions:

1. The banker should act as an agent of the customer for value rather than holder for value.

2. Payment must be received in good faith and without negligence. He should verify the title to the cheque, endorsements, etc. The collecting banker is liable to the true owner in respect of open cheques, the proceeds of which are received for a customer with defective title.

3. Cheques received for collection should be sent to the drawee bank within a reasonable time.

4. The banker must advise the customer whether the cheque received for collection is collected or not. In case of dishonour, collecting banker should give notice of the same to his customer, within a reasonable time. Usually, the collecting banker returns the dishonoured cheques to the customer, who may act upon it to enforce his right against prior parties.

5. In case of acting as holder for value, the collecting banker should take an undertaking from the customer to the effect that the customer will reimburse the banker in case of dishonour of the cheque.

Thus, collecting banker should follow the same procedure that is followed in case of crossed cheque for the purpose of collecting uncrossed cheque to safeguard his interest.

8.3. NEGLIGENCE

It may be stated at the outset that negligence arises only when there is a duty. There cannot be any negligence where there is no duty. The banker has a duty towards the customer, but not towards third parties. But the law imposes such a duty on the collecting banker.

The term negligence has been defined in *Blyth v. Birmingham Water Works Co. as follows : "Negligence is the omission to do something which a reasonable man, guided upon those considerations which ordinarily regulate the conduct of human affairs, would do, or doing something which a prudent and reasonable man would not do."* In another case, it was said, *"The test of negligence is whether the transaction of paying in any given cheque, coupled with the circumstances antecedent and present, was so out of the ordinary course that it ought to have aroused doubts in the bankers' mind and caused them to make enquiry"*.

8.3.1. CIRCUMSTANCES IN WHICH THE BANKER HELD LIABLE

The following are the circumstances in which the collecting banker may be held guilty of negligene and so lose statutory protection.

(1) Omission to obtain reference from a new customer when opening the current account : It was decided in many cases that it is negligence to open an account in the name of a customer without obtaining reference .The facts of *Ladbroke v. Todd* have been given in an earlier chapter. It was held in that case that if the banker simply obtains specimen signatures of the customer and does not obtain satisfactory references about him, he is guilty of negligence. The decision in the case was that the banker was liable to the true owner for the amount of the cheque collected for the customer. In *Hoarding v. London Joint Stock Bank,* the facts were: A person approached a bank with a request to open an account with a cheque payable to his employer. He was duly introduced by another customer of the bank. The bank asked the prospective customer to get a written confirmation of his right to deal with the cheque. The customer furnished the required confirmation, forging the signature of the employer. The Court held that in the circumstances further enquiry by the bank was necessary and the bank was negligent in not making such further enquiry.

In *Lloyds vs. Savory & Co.*, two clerks of a company paid in two crossed bearer cheques in the Head Office of the Bank and requested that the proceeds be credited to two accounts at different branches. One of the accounts was in the name of the clerk and the other in the name of the wife of the other clerk. The names of the clerks' employers or the employers of the customer's husband were not obtained by the bank when these accounts were opened. It was held that the bank was negligent. From this it appears that the bank, while opening an account of a married woman, will have to enquire the name of her husband's employer. In Guardians of S. John's Hampstead v. Barclays Bank, it was held that the bank would be negligent if he opens the account on the basis of a reference from a person unknown to the bank. In Turner v. London and Provincial Bank, the banker was held guilty of negligence in not taking up a reference furnished by a new customer.

(2) Omission to verify the correctness of endorsement on cheques payable to order: The collecting banker has to ensure that all the endorsements on cheques presented to him are regular. It was held in one case that the collecting banker was negligent in not detecting that an endorsement and a signature to a receipt on a cheque did not correspond with the name of the payee.

In the case of per pro. Endorsements, the banker is put on enquiry. (Bissel & Co., Vs Fox Bros. & Co). Although in a subsequent case it was held that the words per pro. did not put the banker on enquiry, it is desirable that the banker should make enquiries when there are per pro endorsements on cheques.

(3) Omission to verify per pro. signatures : The banker should be very careful in accepting for collection of cheques bearing per pro. signatures. He should make an enquiry in cases where an agent draws on behalf of his principal and pays them into his own account. In *Underwood V. Bank of Liverpool*, the sole director of 'one man' company paid into the bank cheques endorsed in favour of the company for credit to his personal account. The bank collected the cheques and credited the proceeds to the director's personal account. The bank was held guilty of negligence and was held liable to the payee for the amounts so collected.

(4) Collecting for a private account of an official or agent, a cheque made payable to his company or firm and endorsed by him as agent on its behalf: This has been considered to be an act of negligence in several cases.

(5) Disregard of warning on the face of the cheque by a person who had authority to do so if it is paid into his personal account : In *Rekitt Vs Barnett Pembroke & Stater Ltd. case, the facts were* : The plaintiff gave Lord Terrington power of attorney to conduct his business, including the right to draw cheques ' without restriction' in his name Lord Terrington purchased a motor car from the defendants for his own use and paid for it by drawing a cheque in the name of the principal. The Court held that the power of attorney did not confer upon Lord Terrington the authority to draw cheques for paying his private debts, and the defendants, having notice on the face of the instrument that the plaintiff's money was being misapplied, were not entitled to hold the proceeds of the cheque.

In another case, Midland Bank Ltd. Vs Reckitt, Terrington, who held the power of attorney to draw cheques on Reckitt's account paid cheques drawn by him in the name of Reckitt into is private account. It was held that Lord Terrington was applying Reckitt's money for his private purposes and the bank was held guilty of negligence in collecting it for Terrington.

(6) Collecting for a partner's private account cheques payable to the partnership: The banker has no right to assume that a partner is entitled to present in his own account cheques payable to the firm.

(7) Placing to a customer's personal account cheques payable to him in an official or fiduciary capacity: If cheques are drawn in favour of his official capacity and he says that they be credited to his private account, the banker should enquire into the circumstances of the transaction.

(8) Collection of crossed cheques bearing Account Payee crossing: The banker should not disregard the directions conveyed by general or special crossing. In the case of a cheque marked 'account payee' the banker should make proper enquiries when collecting it for a person other than the payee. In Akrokerri (Ashanti) Mines Ltd. V. Economic Bank, it was held that the addition of these words constituted a direction to the collecting banker to collect the cheque for the payee. This direction is to be followed whether it is an order cheque or bearer cheque. This view was confirmed in Underwood V. Bank of Liverpool and Martins. The banker, however, is freed from the duty of making enquiries where he cannot be expected to be in position to do so.

(9) Collecting cheques paid in at one branch for a customer who had an account at another branch of the same bank: In Lloyds Bank Ltd., Vs E.B. Savory & Co.,crossed bearer cheques drawn by Savory & Co., in favour of third parties misappropriated by two of the bank's employees and paid into a branch of the Lloyds Bank, to be credited to their accounts kept at other branches. It was held that the branch receiving credits was negligent in not communicating all the facts in its possession to the branches where the customers had their accounts.

(10) Accepting for a customer's private account cheques drawn per pro. or by him and endorsed by him as agent : In Mortson Vs London and County and Westminster Bank Ltd., it was held that the banker was negligent in accepting for an employee's personal account cheques drawn by him per pro on his firm's account either at the same bank or another bank, the cheques being payable either to the employee himself or being endorsed by him in his own name or 'per pro'. the firm.

In Lloyd's Bank Vs Chartered Bank of India Ltd. the collecting bank was held guilty of negligence in collecting for the private account of an employee cheques drawn by him and another on the plaintiff's account.

The collecting banker should lose no time in taking steps for the collection of the customer's cheques entrusted to him for collection the following day, and in case they are entrusted to an agent for collection, he can keep the cheque for one more day. However, it is the practice of bankers to send the cheques for collection on the day of receipt.

8.3.2. EXAMPLES OF NEGLIGENCE

(*i*) Opening of Accounts without introduction: In Guardians of S.John's Hampstead Vs. Barclay's Ltd (1923), a person unknown to the bank opened an account after giving the name of a stranger as reference. The bank didn't take any steps to check the reference and hence it was held that the bank was negligent.

Similarly, an account was opened without getting proper introduction, the bank was held negligent as decided in the case of Ladbroke & Co. Vs. Todd.

(*ii*) Irregularity of endorsements : The collecting banker should verify the correctness or regularity of the endorsements on the order cheques.

(*a*) If the collecting banker doesn't take note of the endorsements that the endorser has not signed in the same spelling as it appears on the instrument, the endorsement will be held irregular.

(*b*) If two or more endorsements on a cheque are in the same handwriting, their genuineness may be easily doubted and enquiry should be made. Failure to do so will constitute negligence on the part of the banker.

(*c*) A cheque in favour of a partnership firm was endorsed by one of the Partners on behalf of the firm and was paid into his private account for collection with the bank, the bank was held negligent (*Bevan Vs. National Bank Ltd., 1906).*

(*iii*) **Collection of Account Payee cheque for any other person :** A cheque crossed "Account payee" is supposed to be collected only for the payee. Thus, in House Property Co. Ltd. Vs. London Country and Westminster Bank, 1915, a cheque crossed 'A/c Payee' was collected by the defendant bank for a third party without any enquiry. The bank was held liable for conversion on the basis of negligence.

(*iv*) **No enquiry being made in doubtful cases** : If a person of ordinary means deposits a cheque for a large amount, the banker should properly enquire into the matter in order to ascertain the good title of the depositor.

(*v*) **Failure to take note of 'not negotiable' crossing** : The collecting banker should carefully examine the title of the prior parties before accepting, for collecting a cheque with 'Not Negotiable' crossing.

8.4. DUTIES AND RESPONSIBILITIES OF A COLLECTING BANKER

(1) Due care and diligence in collection of cheques : As an agent of the customer, the collecting banker is bound to show due care and diligence in the collection of cheques given to him. If the banker fails in this regard and as a consequence, the customer suffers a loss, the collecting banker shall be required to compensate that loss.

(2) Reasonable Time : The collecting banker should present the cheques deposited by his customers for collection within a reasonable time. If the banker and the drawee bank are in the same place, the collecting banker should present the cheque the next day after he receives it.

In the case of out station cheques, the collecting banker should despatch the same to the paying banker on the day after it is received by him. If a cheque is presented for payment with undue delay and the customer suffers loss, the banker has to make good the losses and moreover, loses the statutory protection provided by law. Further, where a cheque is not presented for payment within a reasonable time of issue and in the meanwhile the drawer of the cheque suffers damage, the drawer is discharged to the extent of "such damage". For example, A draws a cheque for Rs.2000 and the drawee bank fails before the cheque is presented after long delay, the drawer of the cheque is discharged.

(3) Advising the Customer about collection : It is the duty of the collecting banker to inform his customer immediately about the collection if the cheque is collected. As soon as the proceeds are collected he can debit his customers account in respect of his commission and credit the gross proceeds to the customer's account. The banker should then inform the customer through a credit slip. Only on receipt of this slip, the customer would come to know that the cheque has been collected.

(4) To Serve Notice of dishonour : If the cheque deposited for collection stands dishonoured and the collecting banker gets the information in writing from the paying banker, the collecting banker should immediately intimate his customer in writing giving reasons thereof. Along with his this notice, he must also return the dishonoured cheque to the concerned customer to take necessary steps such as serving notice of dishonour to the drawer of the cheque.

8.4.1. PROCEDURE FOR COLLECTION

The collecting banker should follow the following procedures while collecting the proceeds of the cheques deposited by his customers:-

1 The person depositing the cheque must be a customer of the bank and must have an account.

2. The cheque must necessarily be a crossed one.

3. If it is endorsed, it should be a regular endorsement to show that the customer has a clear title.

4 If the banker suspects upon the clear title of the customer, he must insist upon proper proof in this regard.

5. There should not be any delay in presenting the cheque to the drawee bank.

6 Until and unless information is received from the paying banker about the payment, the customer's account should not be credited.

8.5. CONVERSION

"Conversion is the unlawful taking, using, disposing or destroying of goods, which is inconsistent with the owner's right of possession".

Conversion is unauthorised interference with another person's property, which is inconsistent with the owner's right of possession. It is defined as follows : "*Any person, who, however innocently, obtains possession of the goods of a person who has been fraudulently deprived of them and disposes of them whether for his own benefit or that of some other person is guilty of conversion*" The plea of innocence is of no avail in actions concerning conversion; nor the plea that the person charged did not derive any benefit from it. The charge of conversion cannot also be avoided by exercising extra-ordinary care and skill.

The true owner of a cheque always can maintain a suit for conversion in all cases but the following : (1) where there is no forgery and the instrument comes into the hands of the holder in due course; (2) where there is forgery and the instrument is a cheque payment whereon has been made in due course by the banker.

8.5.1. COLLECTING BANKER AND CONVERSION

The banker who receives the amount of a cheque for which the customer has no valid title is held liable for the unlawful act or what are legally termed as 'conversion .

8.5.2. DEFINITION OF THE TERM CONVERSION

"*Conversion is a legal term signifying wrongful interference with another person's property inconsistent with the owner's right of possession*".

"The unlawful taking, using or destroying of goods, which is inconsistent with the owner's right of possession".

Dr. H. L. Hart has defined the term thus: "*Conversion consists in wrongful intermeddling with the goods of another for the purpose of taking them away from him or for exercising some domain or control over them*".

From the above definitions, it is clear that the collecting banker has to be very careful while accepting his customer's cheques for collection. It is obligatory on every banker to see that his customers possess clean titles or there should not be any defect in their titles. If the banker collects the proceeds of a cheque for a person who has either no title or a defective title, he will be held liable for the act of conversion.

A cheque or a bill is also included in the term 'goods'. Therefore when a banker collects a cheque for his customer whose title to his defective, he will be held guilty of conversion. He is answerable to the true owner of the cheque in the same way as a thief or a buyer of a stolen article is answerable to the true owners.

The plea of innocence cannot be raised in action concerning conversion. Even an innocent agent for sale can be held liable for conversion. But in the case of a negotiable instrument, when there is no forgery and it comes into the hands of a holder in the due course, the true owner has no right to maintain a suit for conversion.

Section 131 of the Negotiable Instrument Act gives limited protection to a collecting banker against the charge of conversion if he:

(*i*) collects a crossed cheque,

(*ii*) for his customer,

(*iii*) in good faith and without negligence.

Thus a banker would escape the charge of conversion only in the case of collection of crossed cheques for his customer. As for the bills, promissory notes or open cheques, the plea of conversion can be successfully maintained against him if he has collected them bearing forged endorsements. For example if the bill he has collected bears a forged endorsement, the true owner can claim the amount of the bill from the banker.

A banker who takes as a holder for value a bill or a cheque marked 'not negotiable' will be liable for conversion, since no protection is available to him in such circumstances in which an action for conversion would lie against a banker.

8.5.3. CIRCUMSTANCES WHEN CONVERSION IS SAID TO HAVE BEEN DONE

The following points are to be considered in this regard:

1. Collection of a cheque for a customer who has no title or a defective title.

2. Collection of a cheque bearing forged endorsement.

3. In case of 'not negotiable' crossed cheques, where the title of the parties is defective.

8.5.4. LIABILITY OF THE COLLECTING BANKER FOR THE ACT OF CONVERSION

1. The collecting banker would be liable to the true owner and has to indemnify the losses, if any.

2. The collecting banker would lose the statutory protection granted by law.

8.5.5. INSTRUCTIONS TO THE PAYING BANKER AND COLLECTING BANKER

The following are the general instructions for the paying and collecting bankers:

1. Instructions on Generally Crossed Cheques:

(*a*) To the paying banker:

(i) No Immediate cash payment at the counter.

(*ii*) Amount should be credited to a customers' account who has an account with the banker provided the cheque is alright in all respects.

(*b*) To the collecting banker:

(*i*) See that the customer who deposits the cheque is the customer of the bank.

(*ii*) Credit the proceeds of the cheque only after realization.

2. Instructions on Specially Crossed Cheques:

(*a*) To the paying banker:

(*i*) No immediate cash payment at the counter.

(*ii*) Account should be invariably credited to a customer's account.

(*iii*) Send the proceeds of the cheque to the banker whose name is mentioned in the crossing.

(*b*) To the collecting banker:

(*i*) The cheque received for collection should belong to one of the customers of the bank.

(*ii*) Credit the proceeds of the cheque only after realization of the cheque.

(*iii*) Cheque should be forwarded through the banker whose name is mentioned in the crossing.

QUESTIONS

1. Explain the term, "Collecting banker". What are his duties and responsibilities in the collection of his customer's cheque ? Does the law give him any protection in this connection ?
2. What are the conditions that must be satisfied before statutory protection available to a collecting banker in India ?
3. What are the instances where a collecting banker in India may lose his statutory protection on the ground of negligence ?
4. Discuss the significance to the collecting banker with regard to "Account Payee only" and" Not Negotiable" crossing on the cheque.
5. State and explain the protection offered by the Negotiable Instruments Act, 1881, to the collecting banker.
6. Discuss the position of a collecting banker who collects for a customer a cheque which was open when delivered to him and crossed by him before collection ?
9. What should a banker do in case he gets an uncrossed cheque for collection ?
10. What constitutes negligence on the part of a collecting banker ? what are its legal consequences?
11. Discuss the position of a collecting banker as (i) a holder for value and (ii) an agent of his customer.
12. What is Conversion ? What are the Safeguards which a banker should adhere to in the collection of cheques for its customers, if it were to claim statutory protection in this regard as against the true owner ?
13. Define 'negligence' as contemplated in section 85 and section 131 of the Negotiable instruments Act. Bring out cases of negligence of banks under the above sections separately.
14. Comment on the statement "the main risk the banker runs in collecting cheques for a customer is that of conversation".
15. Explain the conditions to be fulfilled by a banker to get protection from liability for conversion for collection of cheques under section 131 of the Negotiable Instruments Act.
16. What is the effect of a material alteration in a negotiable instrument? Give three examples of material alterations.

9

Payment of Cheques

It is already noted that one of the legal obligations of a banker towards his customer is to honour the cheques drawn by the latter on the former. According to Section 31 of the Negotiable Instruments Act 1881, "*The drawer of cheque having sufficient funds of the drawer in his hands, properly applicable to the payment of such cheques must pay the cheque when duly required to do so, and in default of such payments, must compensate the drawer for any loss or damage caused by such default*". From the above it is clear that this obligation of the banker, as the drawee of a cheque is very delicate and of crucial importance. If the banker were to honour cheques not in order, he loses the statutory protection but also would be liable for damages. Therefore, the duty of paying banker is of great importance and call for great care, caution of prudence and presence of mind on his part.

9.1. PAYING BANKER

The term "Paying Banker" is used to denote the position and duties of the drawee bank in regard to the payment of cheques drawn on it by its customer. The money of the customer in his bank account is payable on demand by honouring the cheques drawn by the customer and presented by the legitimate holder. This obligation of the bank is regarded as an implied contract between the banker and the customer. Thus, the paying banker is the drawee bank who pays on the cheques of his customers.

9.2. ROLE OF A PAYING BANKER

A banker's role is important because he performs two roles, *viz.*,

(*a*) as a paying banker; and

(*b*) as a collecting banker.

Between these two, the role of the paying banker is more vital as the customers are prepared to open their accounts and deposit their savings provided the banker is ready to return their deposits as and when demanded. As a matter of fact, this is the basis on which banking business is carried on.

According to Section 31 of the Act, "*The drawee of a cheque, having sufficient funds of the drawer in his hands, properly applicable to the payment of such cheque must pay the cheque when duly required to do so, and in default of such payment, must compensate the drawer for any loss or damage caused by such default*".

Thus, a paying banker who has sufficient funds belonging to his customer, should honour his cheques. Good cheques (i.e., cheques which are prefect in all respects) should be honoured and bad cheques should be dishonoured. If the banker were to honour bad cheques, he loses the statutory protection and also loses the amount. Similarly, if he was to dishonour good cheques, not only does he lose the statutory protection, but also would be liable for damages (nominal or substantial). Therefore, a banker has to be very careful while dealing with customer's cheques.

9.3. DUTIES OF A PAYING BANKER

1. According to the provision of Section 31, if the drawee of a cheque has sufficient funds of the drawer in his hands which can be properly used to pay the cheque, he must pay the cheque when required to do so. If he fails to do so, he will be liable to compensate the drawer for any loss or damage caused to him by such non-payment of the cheque so drawn.

2. The paying banker is expected to pay the cheque to the genuine payee as per the direction of the customer.

3. The payment should be made during banking hours.

4. He has to honour the cheque that is drawn against the account maintained at that branch of the bank where the cheque is presented.

5. He should not make payment of crossed cheque at the counter. i.e., crossed cheques should be paid through a banker if cheques are crossed generally or through the specified banker in case of special crossing.

Thus, the paying banker must make the payment as per the provisions of the Negotiable Instruments Act. The paying banker should act with care and caution and prudence in honouring the cheque.

9.4. PRECAUTIONS BY THE PAYING BANKER

While making payment of a cheque, the banker has to be extremely vigilant while handling cheques on a payment basis. No doubt, in the absence of pre-existing arrangements between the banker and the customer that is, in case, the account of the customer shows a debit balance, the banker is under no obligation to pay such cheques. This regularity has to be examined, apart from the sufficiency of funds with regard to the following:

(1) Crossing of the cheque.

(2) Drawing branch of the bank.

(3) Presentation of the cheque.

(4) Proper form of the cheque.

(5) Drawer's signature.

(6) Correctness of the amount stated both in words and figures.

(7) Material alterations, if any.

(8) Whether the cheque is mutilated or torn.

(9) Balance in the customer's account.

(10) Time of presentation after it is drawn.

(11) If it is endorsed –its regularity.

(12) Other relevant items.

The banker will have to examine all the points mentioned above very carefully. The banker's responsibility in the matter of honouring cheques is a difficult one. On the one hand, the banker may lose the money if he makes an irregular payment. On the other hand, he may be held liable for wrongful dishonour. Therefore the banker must carefully examine the cheques presented to him for payment.

1. Crossed Cheques

The banker should see whether the cheque presented to him for payment is an open cheque or crossed cheque. If it is an open cheque, he may make the payment across the counter provided that the other conditions are satisfied. If it is a crossed cheque, he should pay it only when it is presented through a banker

The following are the relevant sections of the Negotiable Instruments Act :

Section 126: "*Where a cheque is crossed generally, the banker on whom it is drawn shall not pay it otherwise than to a banker.*

Where a cheque is crossed specially, the banker on whom it is drawn shall not pay it otherwise than to the banker to whom it is crossed or to his agent for collection."

Section 127: "*Where a cheque is crossed especially to more than one banker, except when crossed to an agent for the purpose of collection, the banker on whom it is drawn shall refuse payment thereof*".

Section 129: "*Any banker paying a cheque crossed generally otherwise than to a banker, or a cheque crossed specially otherwise than to the banker to whom the same is crossed, or his agent for collection, being a banker, shall be liable to the true owner of the cheque for any loss he may sustain owing to the cheque having been so paid.*"

Cheques crossed generally: Crossing is a direction to the paying banker not to pay the cheque across the counter. A banker does so at his own risk. If he pays the cheque in contravention of the crossing, he will be responsible to the true owner, if the payment happens to have been made otherwise than to the true owner. The true owner can proceed against him notwithstanding the fact that there is no privity of contract between him and the banker.

When the banker pays a crossed cheque across the counter, he cannot debit the account of the customer, since there is a disregard of the mandate given to him, which amounts to negligence. He also loses the statutory protection given to him under Section 128 of the Negotiable Instruments Act, because it is not a payment in due course.

When a customer of the paying banker presents a crossed cheque for payment, the proceeds should be credited to his account and he should be asked to issue a fresh cheque in his own favour for the amount. The banker will not be justified in making payment across the counter either to his own customer or to another, however well known to him they may be.

Section 126 applies only to cheques drawn upon the paying banker himself. It does not apply to cheques drawn upon other banks or upon other branches of the same bank. So if a crossed cheque drawn upon some other bank is paid by the banker, he does not lose his rights against the person to whom the payment was made. But he will be liable to the true owner, if the cheque happened to have gone into the possession of a person not entitled to receive payment.

Specially crossed cheques: Where a cheque is specially crossed, payment should be made only to the banker to whom it is specially crossed. If it is crossed specially to two bankers, the drawee banker should refuse payment. The only exception to this rule is where the banker to whom it is specially crossed may cross it again specially to another banker as his agent for collection. A cheque which is crossed to two branches of the same bank is not treated as specially crossed to two bankers as both constitute the same bank.

Crossing is an integral part of the cheque. The Act permits an uncrossed cheque to be crossed, a generally crossed cheque to be specially crossed, to add the words 'not negotiable' to the crossing. So a cheque not originally crossed may become a crossed cheque in course of time.

'Not Negotiable' and 'Account Payee" crossing: As has been explained earlier, when the words 'not negotiable' are added to the crossing of a cheque, it does not mean that the cheque cannot be negotiated. The only effect of the whole words is to take away the character of negotiability from the cheque, with the result that the transferee of the cheque cannot get a better title than the transferor. When the cheque payable to A with a 'not negotiable' crossing is endorsed to B, who presents it through the bank, the drawee banker is not justified in refusing payment.

The words 'not negotiable' form an integral part of crossing. So when the words are found struck off, there is a material alteration and the banker should refuse payment unless the alteration is confirmed by the drawer. The words 'not negotiable' do not have any legal significance unless they accompany with a crossing. Hence an uncrossed cheque bearing the words 'not negotiable' can be paid across the counter.

On the other hand, if a cheque is drawn payable to B only, the paying banker should not pay it except to B. If B presents the cheque for payment, he should be properly identified by a person known to B and the banker.

When a cheque is crossed with the words 'account payee' added, and is presented for payment through another banker, there is no special responsibility which the paying banker has to assume. The mandate contained in those words is addressed to the collecting banker. These words might have been added by the drawer of the cheque himself or the payee, or any of the endorser. As a cheque is drawn payable to '...... or order', the addition of the words may be considered contradictory and hence ignored by the paying banker. But if one of the endorsements happens to be forgotten, the true owner may contend that the payment is not a payment in due course, or he may take action on the ground of conversion. The paying banker runs no risk at all in making payment of a cheque with 'account payee' crossing as the mandate is intended to the collecting banker.

Duties of the Paying banker in respect of crossed cheques:

The paying banker on whom a crossed cheque is issued (drawn) must make the payment thereof in accordance with the crossing. If he makes a default in paying the crossed cheque otherwise than as stated in the crossing, he shall be liable to the true owner and the drawer of the cheques. Therefore the banker's duty in case of crossed cheques is as under:

(*i*) Crossed cheques shall not be paid cash on the counter.

(*ii*) Crossed generally shall be paid when presented through a banker.

(*iii*) Crossed specially shall be paid only to the banker specified thereof.

(*iv*) Cheques paid contrary to crossing entails serious legal disabilities for the paying banker, i.e., he cannot debit drawer's account and liable for true owner and he cannot claim statutory protection for payment not being made payment in due course.

Thus, the paying banker is liable to the parties as follows:

(a)True owner: If the payment is made in a manner other than the one conveyed to him in the crossing, he shall be liable to the true owner of the cheque for any loss sustained by him as a result of such payment.

(b)The Drawer: The banker fails to make payment in accordance with the direction of the drawer, when a crossed cheque is paid at the counter or to a banker other than the banker specified in special crossing, he will not be entitled to debit his customer's account with the amount of such cheque, if the payment is made to a wrong person.

Thus, the banker should refuse payment of a crossed cheque presented for payment at the counter with the remark "Present through a banker" or the named banker in case of special crossing. In case of the payee of the crossed cheque is also a customer of the paying banker, the latter should not pay him cash directly but by crediting his account with the amount of the cheque. The customer, thereafter, withdraw the amount through his own cheque.

2. Drawing branch of the bank

A customer has no right to draw cheques on a branch of his bank except on the one where he keeps his account. The branch of a bank should not pay cheques drawn on another branch because it has no means of verifying the drawer's signature or the state of his account.

Sometimes a customer may ask that he be permitted to draw cheques on the branch of the bank situated at a place he is visiting. In that case he may be authorized to do so under intimation to the branch concerned. The branch on which the customer is permitted to draw cheques must be supplied with the specimen signature of the customer and must also be informed the limit upto which cheques may be paid. A note must be kept of such authorization when made and the funds must be treated and ear-marked for the purpose. It is advisable that the customer is instructed to present his cheques at the new place for payment personally. If the customer expresses his inability to comply with this instruction, he should be asked to give an indemnity against payment of cheques issued by him if they happen to bear forged endorsements.

The customer can draw cheques only on the branch of the bank where he has his account. If the payment of a cheque has been made in another branch, it will not be considered as a payment made by the drawee banker. This can be explained with the help of an example : Mr. A had an account with the X bank at its Q branch. Mr. A gave a cheque for Rs.50000/- to B. B presented the cheque at the Z branch of the X bank and obtained payment. When the cheque was sent to Q branch, it was found that Mr. A's account had not sufficient balance for the cheque to be honoured. The manager of the Z branch brought an action against B for the recovery of the amount of the cheque. It was held that the Z branch was not bound to honour Mr. A's cheques and could not be considered to have paid the cheque as his bankers. Z branch had been acting as the agent for collection, and having failed to do so, it was entitled to be repaid the money (Woodland Vs Fear). *But now-a-days, taking advantage of internet banking, cheques are being honoured by other branches of the bank, as the balance available in the customers's account and his specimen signature can be downloaded by all the branches.*

3. Presentation of cheques during working hours

Cheque should be presented for payment during working hours. In India, cheques should be presented before 2 p.m. (except regional offices and some special branches) and on Saturdays before 12 noon. But now-a-days fixed banking hours are not being followed and every branch follows different working hours based on local requirements and hence cheques are to be presented during the working hours only of the concerned branches. Cheques presented after the business hours should not be paid, because such a payment may not be considered payment in due course, resulting in the banker's losing statutory protection given to the paying banker. There is also another danger. The cheque may be countermanded by the drawer, and he may contend that on the date the cheque was issued there was no possibility of the cheque being encashed because it was given in such a way that it could not have been presented on the same day for payment. But in a slight margin may be allowed for the banker. In Baines Vs National Provincial Bank case , a cheque was presented and paid at 3.05 p.m., while the bank normally closed at 3 p.m., it was held that the bank did not act out of the way in making the payment.

4. Drawing of cheque in proper form

The cheque drawn by the customer must satisfy all the requisites of a valid cheque. Otherwise, the banker does not enjoy the protection given to the paying banker. The difficulty is to a large extent obviated by requiring the customer to make use of the printed cheque forms supplied to him. If any conditions are attached to payment it is not a valid cheque.

5. Amount stated in words and figures

Where the amount stated in words and figures is different, it is the usual practice of bankers to dishonour the cheque giving that as the reason. Section 18 of the Negotiable Instrument Act provides that where the amount is stated differently in words and figures, the amount stated in words shall be the amount to be paid. So the banker does not run any risk in paying the sum stated in words. Still it is advisable for him to return the cheque unpaid. The banking practice justifies such action. Where the amount is stated in words only, the banker should honour the cheque; but where it is stated in figures, he should return it requiring the amount to be stated in words. Where the cheque once rejected on this ground is presented again with the words filled in with the handwriting of someone other than that of the drawer, he should require the drawer's confirmation.

6. Mutilation of cheques

A cheque which is torn in such a way that the intention to cancel it is apparent should be returned without payment with the remark that the cheque is mutilated. Where it is accidentally torn by the drawer, the confirmation of the drawer is required. Where it is accidentally torn by the holder, the drawer must confirm it; or the collecting banker must undertake to indemnify the paying banker. A cheque which is soiled or torn at the corners on account of protracted circulation can be paid. Similarly, a cheque which is torn into two or four equal parts on account of frequent folding can be paid.

7. Post-dated or stale cheques

Post-dated cheques: A banker should not honour post-dated cheques. If he does so, he runs the following risks:

(*a*) The customer may countermand the cheque before its ostensible date.

Where a cheque is countermanded by the drawer, the banker is obliged to refuse payment of the cheque. The banker will not be able to comply with the drawer's direction if he had already paid it

(*b*) Similarly, circumstances may arise necessitating the closure of the customer's account before the ostensible date of the cheque, eg death, insolvency or insanity of the customer, receipt of the court's order, etc. Obviously, the banker will be in a difficult position if he has already paid the cheque

(*c*) Although, he may pay a post-dated cheque in advance, he cannot debit the account of the customer till the date of the cheque. He cannot therefore deduct the amount of the cheque to arrive at the balance standing to the customer's credit. He cannot dishonour any cheque drawn by the customer if the balance of the customer's account, before the deduction of the amount of the post dated cheque in the question, is sufficient to cover it.

(*d*) The banker cannot claim the statutory protection given to the paying banker because the payment of a post-dated cheque is not a payment in due course.

Stale cheques: It is the practice of the bankers to require the drawer's confirmation in the case of stale cheques. A cheque is usually regarded as 'Stale' if it is drawn six months before the date of presentation of the cheque for payment.

8. Balance in the customer's account

The banker must see whether the customer has sufficient credit balance in his account to permit the payment of the cheque. He is not bound to honour the latter's cheque unless there is sufficient credit to the latter's account or unless he has agreed to grant an overdraft facility which covers the cheque in question. In computing the available balance, the banker need not take into account balance standing to the credit of the customer in some other account, although he may transfer funds from one account to another for the purpose of meeting the cheque, under intimation to the customer, provided that both the accounts are opened by the customer in the same capacity. Moreover, cheques paid in for collection by the customer need be credited to his account only after realization, unless there is an agreement by which he undertook to treat them as cash.

The banker should not offer a part of the amount of the cheque. The credit balance of the customer must be sufficient to meet the entire amount of the cheque. The banker should not intimate the balance available in the customer's account, for this will enable the payee to pay the difference into the drawer's account and obtain payment of the cheque (Foster Vs Bank of London).

Another case bearing on the subject is Rockitt Vs Numburnholme. The facts of the case are as follows: T was the solicitor of N. He took from her (N) a cheque for £ . 5000/-. He knew that there was not sufficient balance in her account. He drew a cheque for a large amount on R's account (for which he had power of attorney) and paid the amount in N's account, and obtained payment. R took out an action against N for the amount drawn by T on his account. The case was decided in R's favour. It was held that N's bankers acted as her agents in receiving money from R. It was also decided that the bankers should not accept any payment from the payee except in special circumstances.

When cheques and bills are deposited in the bank, sufficient time must be allowed to the banker for collection and credit, before they are drawn against. The banker is not bound to honour cheques against uncleared effects unless there is an agreement to that effect. When the amount of the uncleared cheques is credited to the customer's account either as a result of an agreement or for the banker's own convenience, the customer is entitled to draw against the amount credited to his account.

In computing the amount standing to the credit of the customer, the banker should not deduct payments to be made on future date. For instance, if a banker has accepted a bill of exchange on behalf of the customer, he should not deduct the amount of the bill from the available balance in arriving at the balance to the credit of the customer.

Sometimes, a number of cheques might be presented and the credit balances might not be sufficient to meet all of them. The question arises, what is the order in which the cheques should be paid. There is no decision of the courts on this point. Some banks pay the larger cheques first, while others pay as many of the small cheques as possible. But it is desirable to obtain a mandate from the drawer, since it is contended that where there is ambiguity, the banker cannot rely on his own interpretation of the intention of the customer.

9. Material alterations of cheque

Section 89 of the Act lays down that where a cheque has been materially altered but does not appear to have been altered or where a cheque is presented for payment which does not at the time of presentation appeared to be crossed or to have had a crossing which has been obliterated, the paying banker cannot be held liable if he makes the payment of the cheque in due course. In other words, the paying banker can claim protection provided that the alteration is not apparent and payment was made in due course.

10. Alterations in the amount of cheques

The general position in respect of cheques with the sum payable altered is as follows: Where the amount of the cheque is altered and the alteration can be detected by the exercise of reasonable care on the part of the banker and the banker has failed to exercise that degree of reasonable care which is expected of him, he can debit the customer's account only with the original sum and not with the altered amount. If, on the other hand, the customer has acted negligently in drawing the cheque thus facilitating fraudulent alteration of the amount, the loss will have to be borne by him, and therefore the banker can debit the customer's account with the altered amount. What constitutes negligence is a question of fact, to be decided from the surrounding circumstances.

The important cases in this regard are as follows:

(*a*) Young Vs Grote: Young gave his wife five cheques signed in blank to be used by her for his business as and when necessary. Mrs. Young gave one of the cheques to a clerk to be filled up for $50. The clerk filled up the cheque for the amount and showed it to Mrs. Young. But he filled it in such a way that he could alter the amount both in words and figures to £ 350. The alterations were so made that they could not be detected. It was held that the customer acted negligently and therefore had to bear the loss.

But in *Colonial Bank of Australia v Marshall*, the decision was reversed and the judgement was given in favour of the customer. The earlier decision in Young v. Grote seemed to have been set aside. But the original position was restored in The *London Joint Stock Bank v. Macmillan and Arthur,* the facts of which are as follows: A clerk in the firm of Macmillan and Arthur prepared a cheque for £ 2 with spaces left before and after the figure 2, and with no amount written on the body of the cheque. After obtaining the signature of the partner in the firm, the clerk altered the amount to £ 120. He then encashed the cheque at the bank and absconded. It was held that the banker was entitled to debit the customer's account with £ 120 because the alteration was not apparent and the customer, by his carelessness in drawing the cheque had facilitated the alteration. It was also held that the customer was bound to exercise proper care and take proper precaution against forgery.

The learned judge observed in the course of the judgement, "*The relation between banker and customer is that of debtor and creditor with a superadded obliga-*

tion on the part of the banker to honour the customer's cheques if the account is in credit. A cheque drawn by a customer is in point of law a mandate to the banker to pay the amount according to the tenor of the cheque. It is beyond dispute that the customer is bound to exercise reasonable care in drawing the cheque to prevent the banker from being misled. If he draws the cheque in a manner which facilitates fraud, he is guilty of a breach of duty as between himself and the banker and he will be responsible to the banker for any loss suffered by the banker as natural and direct consequences of this breach of duty."

Where there is no negligence on the part of the customer who had taken sufficient precautions against forgery, but still the amount is altered, his account cannot be debited with the amount for which the cheque was originally drawn. Further, the customer need exercise reasonable care, and he need not exercise extraordinary care. We have already seen that leaving a blank space after the payee's name does not constitute negligence on the part of the customer. In *schofiled vs The Earl of Londesborough,* the defendant was not responsible for a higher amount. There was space before the figure of 500. After securing the acceptance of the drawee, the drawer changed the amount to £ 3,500, and passed it on to a bona fide holder for value. It was decided that the defendant was liable only for £ 500 and that he was not responsible to the plaintiff for his negligence.

If blank cheques are given to an agent, the banker is entitled to debit the customer's account with the amount entered therein by the agent. The banker has nothing to do with the fact that the agent has exceeded his authority in filling the amount in the cheques.

To prevent the raising of the amounts of the cheques, it has become a recent practice to note on the cheque 'Under Rs......... The amount of the cheque cannot be raised beyond the amount so noted.

11. Customer's signature in the cheque while drawing payment

The banker must see whether the cheque is drawn by the customer himself for his duly authorized agent. He must also see whether the signature on the cheque is that of the drawer himself. He should see whether the signature corresponds with the specimen signature supplied to him by the customer. In the case of joint accounts, all the joint customers must sign, unless there is a different understanding between them and the banker.

The banker cannot debit the customer's account if the customer's signature is forged. Even if the signature is very cleverly forged such that the banker cannot detect that it is a forged signature, he cannot debit the customer's account, *(Bhagwandas v Creet)*. This is because a cheque with the signature of the customer forged is not mandate given by the customer at all.

The following are the circumstances when the customer cannot object to the cheque without his signature being debited to his account:

(1) Estoppel : In certain circumstances the customer may be stopped from denying that the signature on the cheque is his. For instance, if the banker, being in doubt as to the genuineness of the drawer's signature has referred the matter to the latter and the latter has confirmed, no plea subsequently that the signature was forged would be available. In *Leach v. Buchanan,* the acceptance to a bill of exchange was forged. A person who wished to become the holder of the bill, being doubtful about the drawee's handwriting, sent to ask him if the acceptance was his and received an affirmative reply. The drawee afterwards refused to pay and pleaded forgery. It was held that the person was estopped from denying that the acceptance was his.

In *Greenwood v. Martins Bank*, it was held that it is the duty of the customer to inform the banker of the forgery as soon as he came to know of it. If he fails to do so, he is stopped from complaining of the forgery subsequently. The facts of the case were: Mr.Greenwood had an account with Martins Bank. His wife obtained his cheque book and forged as many as forty-four cheques. When this was known to Mr.Greenwood, his wife requested him not to report the matter to the bank, and assured him that the money would be repaid by her sister to whom she advanced the money. After some time, she asked for more money and Mr.Greenwood refused to oblige and threatened to take the matter to the bank. Mrs. Greenwood committed suicide. Mr. Greenwood sued the bank for honouring forged cheques. Held that the banker was entitled to debit Mr. Greenwood's account since he maintained silence when he first came to know the facts and his silence, when there was a duty to speak, stopped him from making any claim on the bank.

Ratification : An unauthorised signature might be ratified and it would become legally equivalent to a genuine signature. The right to debit the account depends simply on proof of ratification. It is not clear from decided cases whether a forged signature can be ratified.

When the customer authorizes another person to sign on his behalf, either by executing a power of attorney in his favour or by giving him a letter of authorisation, and when the power so given is exceeded by that person, his action may be ratified by the customer. The person signing indicates that he his signing by virtue of the power conferred upon him. His signature may be as follows:

A by his attorney, B.

p. p. A, B.

The above forms of signature by B indicate that he is signing on behalf of A. The banker must examine the power of attorney or the letter of athorisation to see that the power delegated is not exceeded. The banker is not concerned with the manner in which the money drawn by cheque is actually utilised.

Negligence: The banker can debit the customer's account when it can be established that the customer acted negligently, facilitating forgery. What constitutes negligence? An idea can be had from the following cases:

(*a*) In one case, it was held that 'before a banker can debit his customer's account with the amount of the forged cheque, he must prove negligence on the part of customer which was intimately connected with the drawing and encashment of the cheque book and the rubber stamp used on the cheques without proper custody.

(*b*) There is no duty cast on the customer to exercise extraordinary care to prevent the possibility of his signature being forged. The customer is not negligent in keeping the cheque book in an unlocked drawer. Even though the customer might have signed a firm undertaking to keep the cheque book under lock and key, it is not negligence if he fails to do so.

(*c*) It is not negligence to repose trust in an employee who was previously convicted forging. In *Lawes Sanitary Laundry Co. Ltd. v Barcley Bevan & Co.*, the secretary of the company was previously convicted of forgery. The Chairman of the Directors knew this. The company's cheques had to be signed by one director and the Secretary. The Secretary was in charge of the cheque book and the pass book. He forged the signature of the director on a number of cheques, appended his own and obtained payment. The plaintiffs (the company) sued to recover the money paid by the bank on these cheques. The judgment was in favour of the company. It was observed that it was not enough for the banker to show that the customer's conduct had enabled fraud to be committed, they must show that the loss directly resulted from such conduct.

(*d*) **In Keptigalla Rubber Estates Ltd. Vs National Bank of India,** the facts were: Cheques had to be signed by two directors and the Secretary. The Secretary forged the signatures of the two directors, appended his own and obtained payment by changing the word 'order' to 'bearer'. The plaintiff claimed to recover the amounts so paid to the Secretary. The defendants alleged negligence on the part of the plaintiffs. It was held that the plaintiffs were under no duty to organise their business that forgeries of cheques could not take place. It was further held that it is no negligence on the part of a customer if he fails to examine the pass book from time to time with a view to seeing whether there are any forged cheques debited to his account.

12. Regularity in endorsement

Negotiable instruments are transferred by delivery or by endorsement and delivery. While bearer instruments can be transferred by mere delivery, order instruments require endorsement and delivery.

When a cheque is presented for payment, the banker will have to see whether all the endorsements on the cheque are regular. He cannot claim statutory protection if one or some of the endorsements are irregular for payment of a cheque with an irregular endorsement is not a payment in due course.

In the case of bearer cheques, the rule 'once a bearer always a bearer' applies. The rule was being followed in India until the decision in Forbes Compbell & Co. Vs The Official Assignee of Bombay in 1925. Doubts were expressed regarding the correctness of that procedure in the decision of that case. The original position was restored by the addition of clause (2) to Section 85 of the Negotiable Instruments Act, which reads as follows:

"*Where a cheque is originally expressed to be payable to bearer, the drawee is discharged by payment in due course to the bearer thereof, notwithstanding any endorsement, whether in full or in blank, appearing thereon, and notwithstanding that any such endorsement purports to restrict or exclude further negotiation*".

Blank endorsement: An order cheque with an endorsement in blank becomes a bearer cheque. It can be transferred by mere delivery. So the banker can pay such a cheque to the person presenting it. Blank endorsement can be converted into endorsement in full. If the bearer cheque is crossed and the words 'account payee' are added, it becomes payable only to the payee mentioned in the cheque.

Endorsement of order cheques: Order cheques can be transferred by endorsement and delivery. When such a cheque is presented for payment, the banker should see whether there are endorsements on the cheque, and if so they are regular. Payment of cheque with irregular endorsements is not payment in due course. In the case of conditional endorsements, payment should be made only on the fulfillment of the conditions imposed. In England, the paying banker can disregard the conditions in the endorsement, but in India, payment can be made only on the fulfillment of conditions.

Endorsement can be made in ink or with pencil. But since endorsement in pencil can be easily altered, banks do not accept endorsements in pencil. If the endorsement has been made with a rubber stamp, the bank can pay the cheque only if it has been done with the permission of the customer.

Endorsements by diverse persons: General considerations-All endorsements must be made in ink, although endorsements in pencil are legally valid. Bankers insist on endorsements being made in ink because endorsements made in pencil can easily be altered. In the case of endorsements made by means of rubber stamps or in printed characters, the banker has to satisfy himself that they are made under proper authority.

(1) Individuals: Endorsement should ordinarily be in the form of ordinary signature of the payee or endorsee. Complimentary prefixes, suffixes and other courtesy titles should not form part of the signature. Descriptive additions such as P.N. Nasarulla Basha, M.D., or K.K.Amarnath, Capt., are permitted. The signature of the payee or endorsee must be in the same spelling as given in the cheque. If the cheque is payable to K.K.Amar Nath, but is spelt in the cheque as K. K. Amar Nath , he must sign as K. K. Amar Nath, only, but may affix his signature with the usual spelling in brackets.

(2) Women: In the case of unmarried women, the full name must also be given. For instance, if the payee is Miss. Kumar, she should sign as Seetha Kumar. In the case of married woman, as for example, Mrs. Ratha Kannan, the signature should be 'Ratha Kannan,' wife or widow of Kamalakkannan. If a cheque is payable to Mrs.Dr.Sankar, the endorsement should be such as Sujata Sankar, wife of Dr.Sankar. If a cheque is payable to an unmarried woman, since married, the endorsement should give the name after marriage and the former name also.

(3) Joint Payees: If a cheque is payable to joint payees, all the joint payees must endorse. The signature of one of the joint payees is not sufficient, unless one has the authority to sign on behalf of the other or others, as the case may be. If both the signatures are in the same handwriting, the endorsement requires confirmation.

If one of the two payees dies, the cheque is payable to the survivor, provided he can produce satisfactory evidence of the death of the other party.

(4) Agents: The agent endorsing must indicate that he is signing as agent. As per procreation, signature indicates that the signatory is acting as agent within limited authority. It is not the duty of the paying banker to enquire about the extent of the limit of authority and whether the limit has been exceeded. It may be noted that a firm may act as the agent of an individual.

(5) Deceased Persons: An endorsement made by the son of a deceased payee or endorsee is irregular, unless authority is established by producing succession certificate or a valid order of the court.

(6) Partnerships: In the case of partnership, the endorsement must literally follow the description given in the cheque. No abbreviation or addition or alteration of a firm's name is permitted. The endorsement by a partner must indicate that he is signing on behalf of the firm.

(7) Joint Stock Companies: The signature of the Managing Director or Secretary or a person authorised to sign on behalf of the company must be accompanied by a description of the capacity in which he signs.

(8) Joint Stock Companies (in liquidation) : The liquidator must sign in his capacity as official liquidator.

(9) Schools and Clubs : The designation of the payee or endorsee must be given.

(10) Executors : Executors and administrators have authority to sign on behalf of their co-executors or administrators.

9.5. STATUTORY PROTECTION TO THE PAYING BANKER

It is the duty of the paying banker to honour the cheques issued by his customers as and when they are presented for payment. Payment should be made to the right person and also the banker should have the orders from his customer for debiting his account. But he cannot make detailed enquiries before making the payment. Therefore, the Act provides him some legal protection provided the banker fulfils the obligations laid down in the Act.

Sections 85, 85A, and 128 of the Negotiable Instruments Act accord protection to the paying banker.

A banker cannot be expected to know the signatures of all the persons who may deal with a cheque. All that he has to do is to see that the endorsements that are appearing on the cheque are regular. He is protected even if one of the endorsement is a forgery provided the endorsements appear to be regular and the banker has taken due care in paying the cheque. Section 85 of the Act provides:

(1) Where a cheque payable to order purports to be endorsed by or on behalf of the payee, the drawee is discharged by payment in due course.

(2) Where a cheque is originally expressed to be payable to bearer, the drawee is discharged by payment in due course to the bearer thereof notwithstanding any endorsement thereon, and notwithstanding that any such endorsement purports to restrict or exclude further negotiation.

The section does not apply to bills or promissory notes.

The protection is extended to payment of bank drafts with the addition of section 85A to the Act. It reads 'where any draft that is an order to pay money drawn by one office of the same bank for a sum of money payable to or order on demand, purports to be endorsed by or on behalf of the payee, the bank is discharged by payment in due course.

The protection is available for crossed cheques also "*where a banker on whom a crossed cheque is drawn has paid the same in due course, the banker paying the cheque and (in case such cheque has come to the hands of the payee), the drawer thereof shall respectively be entitled to the same rights, and be placed in the same position in all respects as they would respectively be entitled to and placed in if the amount of the cheque had been paid to and received by the owner thereof*'(section 128).

The banker is protected for payment of cheques which when they came into his hand, were not crossed or did not appear to have been crossed. Section 89 provides that where a cheque is presented for payment which does not at the time of presentation appear to be crossed or to have had a crossing, which has been obliterated, the banker liable to pay according to the apparent tenor, thereof in good faith without negligence, discharges the banker from all liability thereon and such payment shall not be questioned by reason of the cheque having been so crossed.

9.5.1.Conditions for Statutory Protection :

(1) Entitles the banker to protection only in case of cheques that turn out to be wrongly endorsed.

(2) It offers no protection to the banker if the drawer's signature is forged.

(3) There must be payment in due course.

Payment in due course :

All the above provisions apply only when payment is made in due course. Payment in due course is defined by Section 10, of Negotiable Instruments Act, "*as payment in accordance with the apparent tenor of the instrument in good faith and without negligence to any person in possession thereof under circumstances which do not afford a reasonable ground for believing that he is not entitled to receive payment of the amount therein mentioned.*"

Thus, the essentials of payment in due course are :

(1) The payment must be in accordance with the apparent tenor of the instrument. Thus a paying banker cannot claim protection in the case of post-dated cheques. Further he should not honour a cheque presented outside the banking hours.

(2) The payment must be made in good faith and without negligence. The paying banker must ensure that all the endorsements are regular. Where a cheque is endorsed by a person on behalf of another, the banker should satisfy himself that the person signing had the authority to do so.

(3) He should make the payment only to the person who is in possession of the instrument.

(4) There should be no reasonable ground for believing that the person presenting the cheque is not entitled to receive payment of the amount therein mentioned.

Payment in due course includes the following three elements:

1. Payment according to the apparent tenor of the instrument.

2. It should be made in good a faith and without negligence.

3. The banker should not have any doubt in his mind that the person claiming or receiving the amount is not entitled to receive payment in respect of the instrument.

(*i*) Payment in accordance with the apparent tenor: Payment should be made in accordance with the intention of the parties as it appears on the face of the instrument. For example, if a cheque is post-dated, the intention of the drawer is that it should not be paid before the ostensible date. Payment of a post-dated cheque is clearly contrary to the intention of the parties and as such it does not constitute payment in due course. That is, the paying banker is therefore, not entitled to the statutory protection if the endorsement of the payee later turns out to be a forged one. Similarly if a crossed cheque is paid across the counter, payment cannot be said to have been made according to the apparent tenor of the instrument.

(*ii*) Payment in good faith and without negligence: "Good faith" means acting honestly and banks are always presumed to act in good faith; but they should take care not to be negligent in the performance of their duties. For example, failure to see whether all the endorsements are regular, or failure to verify whether the person signing an instrument per pro has the necessary authority to do so, will constitute negligence.

In this connection, it would be appropriate to quote the case of Madras Provincial co-operative Bank Ltd. Madras Vs. the Official Liquidator of South Indian Match Factory Ltd. (1944). The facts of the case were that the Official Liquidator of the company did not open an account with the bank as required under the Companies Act and Rules framed by the Madras High Court. A cheque drawn payable to the Official Liquidator was presented by him for payment over the counter. The bank called for his order of appointment and after seeing the same paid the amount. The Official Liquidator misappropriated it. In a suit by the succeeding the Official Liquidator against the bank for recovery of the amount, the Madras High Court held that the bank must be deemed to have known that it was improper on the part of the Official Liquidator to ask for payment over the counter, and he could collect the amount only through his bank. The payment was not made in due course within the meaning of Section 85 of the Negotiable Instruments Act and the bank was, therefore, liable for the amount.

In Union Bank of India Vs. Sales-Tax officer, Emforcement Branch, Greater Bombay and others (1979), the Bombay High Court held that in order that a payment should be held to be made in due course, it should be, firstly in accordance with the apparent tenor of the instrument; secondly, it must be made in good faith and without negligence; thirdly payment must be made to a person in possession of the instrument, and fourthly, while making the payment, care should be taken to see that no circumstances exist which afford a reasonable ground for believing that the instrument-holder is not enlitted to receive payment of the amount mentioned in the instrument.

(*iii*) Person in possession of the instrument: Payment should be made to a person who is in a possession of the instrument. But here possession of a cheque does not entitle him to receive payment. If the surrounding circumstances raise a reasonable suspicion in the mind of the banker that the holder is not the real owner, the banker is put on enquiry; he should not pay without proper verification. For example the holder of a cheque, payment of which has been stopped by the drawer is not entitled to receive the amount.

Forgery of Drawer's signature: Every time a cheque is paid, the banker should verify the signature on the cheque to make sure that it has been issued by the customer. The banker is not entitled to pay a cheque on which the customer's signature is forged. Such a cheque is not an order from the customer and the banker is not entitled to debt its amount to the account of the customer. Even if the forgery is so clerverly made that it cannot be detected, the banker has to bear the loss if he pays such a cheque. The provision is made to protect the interests of the customer. Otherwise the banker would be entitled to debit any cheque drawn on the customer's account without his authority and the balance in the account would disappear without his knowledge.

The only exception to this rule is where the customer's negligence has contributed to the forgery or where the customer by his conduct has caused the banker to believe that the signature on the cheque is genuine. The term negligence is not defined in law and will depend upon the fact and circumstances of each case.

The legal position regarding forged cheque is summarised very clearly in Abbu Chettiar vs. Hyderabad State Bank.

(*i*) It is for the customer to establish affirmatively that the signature on the disputed cheque is not that of the customer but a forgery.

(*ii*) If the drawer's signature is forged or unauthorised, however clever the forgery is made, the banker cannot debit his customer's account in case he pays the sum unless he establishes adoption.

(*iii*) What amounts to adoption is dependent upon the circumstance of each case.

(*iv*) In order to make the customer liable for the loss, the neglect on his part must be intimately connected with the transaction itself and must have been the proximate cause of the loss.

(*v*) The banker cannot set up either estoppel or adoption if his own conduct or negligence has occasioned or contributed to the loss. The well settled principle of that where one or two innocent parties must suffer for the fraud of a third, that party should suffer whose negligence facilitated the fraud.

Thus on the basis of the above provisions, the statutory protection available to the paying banker can be summarized as follows:

(a) **Protection in case of order cheques :** According to Section 85 (1) "*when a cheque payable to order purports to be endorsed by or on behalf of the payee, the drawee is discharged by payment in due course*".

According to this section, the paying banker is granted protection if he makes payment of an order cheque with forged endorsement on behalf of the payee. However, two conditions must be fulfilled to avail such protection:

(1) Endorsement must be regular. It is essential that endorsements are regular though not necessarily genuine or valid. For example if a cheque payable to 'Ravindran' is endorsed with the signature of the same name and in the same spelling, it is a regular endorsement. But if the endorser signs as 'Ravi', the endorsement will be irregular. Hence the banker need not verify the identification of the person who signs on the cheque as the endorser.

(2) Payment must be made in due course : Section 10 of the Negotiable Instruments Act, 1881 reveals that the following conditions must be satisfied before a payment of a negotiable instrument; then only it can be called as payment in due course.

(i) Payment must be in accordance with the apparent tenor of the instrument. That is, it is necessary that a payment to constitute a "payment in due course should be made at or after maturity. A payment before maturity is not payment-in-due course. For example, payment of a post dated cheque is not a payment in due course."

(ii) The payment must be made in good faith and without negligence. When there exists suspicious circumstances and the paying banker does not make any enquiry as to them, the payment is not in due course. So also payment is not in due course, where a banker makes payment on a cheque materially altered, without exercising due care.

(iii) Payment must be made to the person in possession of the instrument. A finder of a lost instrument or a thief is not said to be in possession of the instrument. Thus, in the event of suspicious circumstances, payment should not be made without the drawer's confirmation.

(iv) Payment must be made under circumstances which do not afford a reasonable ground for believing that he is not entitled to receive payment of the amount mentioned therein. So when a peon of a company presents a cheque for a big amount on behalf of the company, which is contrary to the past experience, the banker should make proper enquiry before making payment of such a cheque.

(v) Payment must be made in money only. That is, payment must be made in the form of money which, of course includes bank notes or currency notes but excludes cheque, bill of exchange, promissory note and goods.

(*b*) **Protection in case of bearer cheques :** Section 85 (2) provides protection to the paying banker in respect of bearer cheques. According to this section, a cheque originally issued as a bearer one continues to be a bearer cheque irrespective of the fact that it bears endorsement in full or in blank or whether any endorsement restricts further negotiation or not. Thus the banker need not verify the regularity of its endorsements. If a bearer cheque is stolen and the banker makes its payment without the knowledge of such theft, he will be discharged and will be protected under section 85(2).

(c) **Protection in case of crossed cheques :** According to sec 128, the protection also extends to crossed cheques. Section 128 says "*where a banker on whom a crossed cheque is drawn has paid the same in due course, the banker paying the cheque and (in case such cheque has come into the hands of the payee) the drawer thereof, shall respectively be entitled to the same rights and be placed in the same position in all respects, as they would respectively be placed if the amount of the cheque had been paid to and received by the true owner thereof.*"

The paying banker shall be given protection under Section 128 if he makes payment of a crossed cheque after fulfilling the following two requirements.

(i) He has made payment in due course i.e. in good faith and without negligence and according to the apparent tenor of the cheque.

(ii) The payment has been made in accordance with the requirements of the crossing i.e. through any banker in case of general crossing and through the banker mentioned in the crossing in the case of special crossing.

9.6. REFUSAL OF PAYMENT OF CHEQUES

A banker can refuse to honour the customer's cheque in the following cases :

(1) When the customer does not have sufficient funds belonging to him, the banker can refuse to honour his cheque. It must be noted that the term 'funds belong to the customer includes the sum covered by the overdraft granted to the customer. A banker is not bound to pay a part of the amount of the cheque. Thus if a customer draws a cheque for Rs.1,000, but has only Rs.990, to his credit, the banker is not bound to pay Rs.990 representing a part of the amount of the cheque.

(2) When the cheque is not drawn in proper form;

(3) When the cheque is post-dated and is presented before the ostensible date of issue;

(4) When the cheque is stale, that is, it is presented six months after the ostensible date of issue;

(5) When the cheque is not presented during banking hours;

(6) In case of trust funds, when the banker has knowledge that the cheque was drawn in breach of trust;

(7) When there are material alterations in the cheque;

(8) When the signature on the cheque does not correspond with the specimen signature;

(9) When one or more endorsements are irregular;

(10) When the cheque is presented at a branch of the bank different from the one where he has the account;

(11) When the banker receives notice of the customer's insolvency;

(12) When the customer has countermanded the cheque;

(13) When the banker has a notice of the customer's death;

(14) When the banker receives a Garnishee order from the court;

(15) When the banker has got a general lien on the customer's funds and there are no funds belonging to the customer after the exercise of the lien.

The banker can refuse payment of cheques without incurring any liability under the following circumstances.

(1) **When the Drawer countermands payment :** The drawer of a cheque is competent to cancel or withdraw such order at any time before its payment is made. The banker should obey the countermand order issued by the drawer without enquiring any reason thereof. The following points must be noted in this regard.

(*a*) It should be in writing, i.e. oral instruction cannot be and should not be accepted by the banker.

(*b*) The written instruction should be received by the banker before the cheque is actually presented for payment.

(*c*) The written instruction should contain all particulars such as date of the cheque, number of the cheque, the amount, payee's name, whether crossed or otherwise etc.

(*d*) The order stopping payment should be signed by the drawer of the cheque.

(*e*) The order to stop payment of a cheque can be made only by the drawer of the cheque and not by the payee or the endorsee as there is no contractual obligation on the banker towards the payee or the endorsee.

(*f*) The countermanding order should be duly served on the banker before the payment of the cheque is made.

(*g*) A telephonic message of stopping payment is also valid, provided the banker is able to identify the voice of the customer. Whenever a banker receives stoppage instructions by telegram or over the telephone, he should request the holder of the cheque to present it again after 2 to 3 days so that he could wait the drawer's confirmation in the meantime.

(h) The banker shall be liable to the drawer if he pays the cheque by oversight after the receipt of countermand order.

(i) The stop-payment order remains effective until it is revoked by the drawer.

(2) Death of the Drawer : As soon as the banker comes to know officially about a customer's death, the customer's mandate stands, terminated and the account becomes inoperative. Therefore, no cheques on that account can be honoured. If the banker is not aware of the death of the customer, the banker is justified in honouring the cheques issued by the customer even after his death.

(3) Insolvency of the Customer : When a customer is declared insolvent, the whole property of the insolvent person vests in the court. Therefore, the banker must stop payment from customer's account as soon as he receives the information of insolvency of the customer.

(4) Customer's Insanity : The banker is not bound to honour the cheques of his customer on receipt of information about the latter has become absolutely insane or of unsound mind. In case he is not aware, the banker is justified in honouring the cheques.

(5) Notice of Assignment of Credit Balance : The credit balance in the account of the customer can be transferred by the customer to another person. On receipt of a notice of such assignment, the banker must stop payment of the cheque drawn by the assignor, as the latter ceases to be the owner of such funds.

(6) Receipt of Notice of Garnishee Order : A banker is bound to obey the order issued by the court restraining him from paying the money from a customer's account. Once such a garnishee order is received, the banker should with-hold the customer's funds and refuse payment of cheques presented.

(7) Defective title of the party : Suppose the person presenting a cheque has defective title to the cheque and the banker knows it, the banker can refuse payment of such a cheque.

(8) Breach of trust : Suppose the customer is operating a trust account and the banker comes to know that the customer uses the funds of the trust account in breach of trust, the banker can stop payment of the cheque drawn on such account.

(9) Insanity of the customer : When the banker receives notice of the insanity of a customer, he should note the fact and stop honouring cheques drawn on his account. If such a notice is received from the court, the banker should act accordingly to the terms and conditions contained in the notice. The banker should not honour the cheques drawn by the customer until he receives a certificate to the effect that the customer has regained his sanity. The banker should write 'Refer to Drawer' on the cheques dishonoured.

(10) Usual Answers for dishounoring cheques : Usually, the drawee banker attaches a slip to dishonoured cheques and marks the number of the appropriate answer. When refusing payment, he should not enter into any discussion with the payee, instead, the appropriate letters from the bank may be stamped on the cheque as the answer.

Mistakes : It is likely that banker may pay money to or for the customer by mistake, and he would like to restore his position by rectifying it, e.g. money payable to M. Laksman was by mistake, paid to N.Laksman and if the cheque is for Rs.560 and if by mistake the banker pays Rs. 650.

Whether the banker can recover the amount so paid or not depends upon the actual circumstances. The law and practice regarding the right to recover a payment made by mistake is not well settled and clear. In order to recover the amount paid by mistake the following conditions should be fulfilled.

(*a*) If he can prove that the payee received the amount 'Malafide' knowing that it was not actually due to him.

(*b*) The mistake must relate to the fact and not to general law.

(*c*) The mistake must be only between the party paying and the party receiving.

For example, if the cheque is for Rs.580 and if by mistake the banker pays Rs.850, he can recover the excess amount paid before the payee leaves the bank premises. If the payee leaves the premises, the banker has to prove that the payee received the amount knowing it was an excess payment. In the case of "Skyring Vs. Green Wood" an army major has been overpaid in respect of his salary, who spent it without knowing that it was an over payment and believing that it was actually due to him. It was held that money was not recoverable though it was a payment by mistake. In case of Holt Vs. Markbam, it was held that the amount paid by mistake could be recovered, as the mistake was due to wrong interpretation of war office order.

Therefore, the banker cannot recover the money paidy mistake as under:

1. If it is the mistake relating to general law.

2. If the agent receives the payment on behalf of the principal and returns the amount to his principal.

3. If a bank pays a bill of exchange before it matures due to mistake with regard to the due date.

4. If the money is paid in good faith to the holders, and the holders in good faith received the same and during some interval may alter their position accordingly. In other words, money paid in excess on a negotiable instrument is not recoverable under a notice of claim after unreasonable delay .

Thus, recovery of money paid by mistake depends upon the actual circumstances.

Precautions to be taken by a banker before he honours a cheque presented to him :

It is said that a banker is between the deep sea and the devil, when a chequs is presented to him for payment, because a wrongful payment will not entitle him to debit the account of the customer. Nor can he wrongfully dishonour the cheque as the customer can sue the banker for damages for the loss of his credit. So the banker should exercise utmost care in passing the cheque for payment. He will do well to take the following precautions:

1. He should compare the signature of the drawer on the cheque with the specimen signature with him and he should not pay if it does not tally. Even on the slightest doubt, he should return the cheque as there is no protection to the banker, if he pays a cheque on which the drawer's signature is forged.

1. The balance at the credit of the customer must be carefully computed and any overdraft arrangements should be examined. He should pay the cheque if only there is sufficient balance in the account. If the balance is not sufficient, he should not make part payment.

2. He should examine whether the cheque is a crossed cheque or an open cheque. A crossed cheque should not be paid over the counter, but it should be

credited to the account of the payee.

3. The cheque should have been drawn on the same branch of the bank in which the customer has his account.

4. The cheque should have been properly dated. He should not pay a post-dated cheque or stale cheque. In India a cheque remaining in circulation for more than six months or over is considered as stale cheque.

5. The amount in worlds and figures on the cheque should be the same. If they differ the bank should refuse payment. He should not pay even the lower amount in the cheque.

6. He should examine that the cheque is not torn, altered or multilated. He should reject payment of such cheques.

7. He should pay cheques only during the working hours of the bank. Otherwise he will lose the statutory protection.

8. He should ensure that the endorsements on the cheque are regular and correct. Otherwise he should not pay the cheque.

9. Finally the cheque should have been drawn in the correct form and should satisfy the legal definition of a cheque. The banker should insist that the cheque must be drawn on the printed forms supplied to the customer. The customer cannot draw on cheque supplied to the another as cheques are serially numbered and the numbers are noted in the ledger account of the customer when a new cheque book is supplied.

QUESTIONS

1. A banker has honoured the following cheques:
   (a) An order cheque with a forged endorsement of the payee
   (b) A crossed cheque on which the drawer's signature is a forged one
   (c) A post-dated cheque.
   What are the risks a banker runs in each of these cases?
2. State and explain the protection offered by the Negotiable Instruments Act, 1881 to the paying banker.
3. Discuss the position of a banker if he pays the following cheques:
   (a) when the signature of the drawer is forged.
   (b) when the signature of the payee is forged.
4. What is meant by payment in due course ? What is the protection afforded to a banker under section 128 of the Negotiable Instruments Act, 1881?
5. Under what circumstances is a banker justified in refusing payment of cheques drawn upon him ? What risk does he run in case of unjustified dishonour ?
6. What the precautions available to a paying banker that have been provided under the Negotiable Instruments Act, 1881.
7. What are the main requirements which a drawee bank should fulfil before it can claim statutory protection in the payment of cheques?

LOANS AND ADVANCES

The main function of bankers is to receive deposits and lend the same. But while lending money, bankers will think of the assets which will yield maximum return. Thinking of the return on investments is an important point for the bankers. According to Crowther, the secret of successful banking is to distribute the resources between various forms of assets in such a way as to get a sound balance between liquidity and profitability so that there is enough cash to meet every claim and at the same time, income to pay its salary and interest liabilities and earn profits for share holders, "thus bearing in mind two principles viz., profitability and liquidity". The banker invests his funds mainly in the following scheme of assets.

(*a*) Liquid Assets :

(*i*) Cash on hand,

(*ii*) Cash with other banks,

(*iii*) Cash with Reserve Bank of India

(*b*) Semi-liquid Assets :

(*i*) Money at call and short notice

(*ii*) Bills discounted

(*c*) Earning Assets :

(*i*) Investments

(*ii*) Loans and Advances

The banker cannot invest all the money, because some deposits of the customers are demand liabilities. So daily he has to meet the demands of the customers. For this purpose, it is necessary for him to keep some amount of cash with him. Apart from this, he has to maintain a minimum cash reserve of 3% of the total time and demand liabilities with the Reserve Bank. This is compulsory for all the scheduled banks.

10.1. THE LIQUID ASSETS OF A BANKER

In allocating the funds by a banker in various assets, the banker is also guided by statutory requirements, the Reserve Bank's directive and other considerations.

The main deciding consideration is the nature of sources from which the funds have been mobilised.

Sources of Bank funds: Like any other business undertakings, the banking institutions have funds either by way of (1) their own funds consisting of paid up capital, reserve funds and other reserves and (ii) the borrowed funds, consisting of deposits of various types and borrowings from other banks and apex banking institutions like RBI, etc. The owned funds belong to the owners, viz., the owners of the banks i.e., the shareholders in the case of private sector banks and the Govt. in the case of nationalised banks. Thus, they are the capital contributed by the members of the Govt. and the reserve funds appropriated out of the profits of the bank. The unique feature of the banking companies vis-a-vis other companies is relatively small proportion of the owned funds to the total funds of the banking companies. Thus the borrowed funds of the banking companies, mainly the deposits of the public, constitute the bulk of a bank's funds.

Capital Adequacy Norms : In April 1992, the Reserve Bank of India prescribed that all banks in India which had international standing had to maintain the capital adequacy norm of 8 per cent by March 1994. All other banks were to maintain 4 per cent by March, 1993 and 8% by March, 1996. The RBI has further raised the minimum capital to risk asset ratio from 8% to 9% with effect from March 21, 2000. Thus the capital adequacy ratio is modified or raised based on the changing needs of the economy by the RBI.

Banker's obligations to Depositors: By Accepting deposits of money from the public, banks take upon the following obligations and responsibilities towards the depositors.

(i) obligation to return the amount of the deposit on demand or as per the terms of the deposits, and (ii) obligation to pay interest on the deposits at the prescribed rates.

Both these obligations are significant and have an impact on the pattern of employment of a bank's funds. The pattern of deposits thus, determines the pattern of employment of the bank funds.

Significance of Liquidity in Banking : The concept of "liquidity" to a banker is a significant one which is used to describe the ability of the banker to satisfy the demands of cash by the depositors. In case a banker is not able to meet the demand for cash of a depositor, for any reason whatsoever, will lead to disastrous consequences. That is, the public may lose confidence in the bank and it will ultimately lead to failure of the bank. Hence the bank should maintain adequate cash with himself or with other banks or in the form of assets which can be readily converted into cash without any loss. Such assets are called the liquid assets which include (i) Cash in hand and balances with other banks, (ii) money at call and short notice and (iii) investments in govt. and semi govt. securities. The significance and urgency of maintaining the liquid assets is recognised by the Banking Regulation Act, 1949. Section 24 requires that every banking company has to maintain liquid assets of not less than 25% of its net demand and time liabilities

Liquid Assets such as cash in hand and balances with other banks in current accounts are idle assets that do not earn any income to the bank. But for certain other liquid assets like money at call and short notice, the earnings are lower as compared to other profitable uses of a bank's funds, viz., loans and advances. In order to enable the bank to meet its obligation to pay interest on deposits and to earn adequate profits, the bank should employ the funds in more profitable channels. As the proportion of interest bearing deposits viz., savings and fixed deposits to total deposits increases, the obligation to pay interest thereon also increases and this necessitates the employment of funds in higher income yielding assets. Thus, a banker has to allocate the funds at his command in such proportions as to maximize profits and also to meet his obligation to meet the demands of the depositors. Hence it is important to discuss the various forms of liquid assets of banks, their significance to the bank and the factors that determine their size.

1. Cash Balances

The most liquid asset of a bank is cash held with itself and with RBI and other banks in current account. By having this type of liquid asset, the banker is able to meet the demand of the customers immediately which indicates solvency, reputation and goodwill of the bank. A prudent banker should be able to maintain a balance between the two extremes of maintaining excess cash or shortage of cash. In case he keeps cash balances much above his requirements, he loses interest on the excess portion. If the cash reserves are short of his actual needs, he may find himself in an embarrassing position. Hence, maintaining adequate size of cash balances is an important task faced by a banker. Though the banker has to abide by the legal requirements, he is also guided by the conventions followed by the banking community in this regard.

Important factors that determine cash Reserve : The principal factors that govern the quantun of cash balances maintained by a banker are as follows :

1. Habits of the Customers and Business conditions of the locality: The amount of cash balance required by a bank depends upon the habits of the customers and the business conditions of the locality in which the bank is serving. Thus, a bank serving in a manufacturing and commercial locality, might have to maintain a larger cash reserve, as the transactions would be numerous and rapid. But a bank serving mostly to agricultural community need not maintain much cash balance, as their transactions are less frequent. But however, during busy agricultural season, maintenance of a larger reserve is required so as to finance the agricultural activities.

2. Use of cheque Currency : Where the cheque currency is popular, the need for hand to hand currency is less and consequently smaller reserves will be sufficient, because payments will be made by transfer entries in the books of the bank.

3. Existence of Banker's Clearing House : Wherever clearing houses are available, cheques received for collection are passed through clearing house and hence a banker is not required to find funds for all the cheques drawn upon him and held by other bankers. In India clearing houses exist in most of the towns and are managed largely by the State Bank of India and its subsidiary banks. Now-a-days other nationalized banks have been for certain towns/cities for clearing the cheques.

4. Nature of Accounts : If a large majority of the current accounts are of a fluctuating nature, as is the case with the accounts of share brokers, cotton merchants and bullion dealers, the banker will require a comparatively larger cash reserve because there is the chance of most of them withdrawing the major portions of their balances at a time when there are heavy variations in the prices of shares, cotton and bullion. Similarly city banks have to maintain high cash reserve than those of smaller local banks as there may be a few withdrawals only in small towns/villages.

5. Size of Deposit Accounts : A bank which has a few large deposits has to maintain a larger reserve than a bank with a large number of small accounts because the larger the number of customers of a bank, the less is likely withdrawal of deposits.

6. Nature of advances and Availability of Refinance : Banks generally depend on the central bank of the country for securing re-finance on the basis of credit already granted by them. A bank which has employed its funds in discounting of bills keep less cash balances as they can be rediscounted with Reserve Bank of India. As the RBI is the lender of the last resort to the banks, its credit policy determines the availability and cost of refinance to the banking system. Thus the size of their cash balances is determined by the borrowing facilities available with the Central Bank of the country.

2. Statutory Cash Reserve with the RBI

As per section 42(1) of the Reserve Bank of India Act, 1934 every scheduled bank is required to maintain with the RBI a minimum cash reserve equal to 3% of their net demand and time liabilities. The RBI can vary the cash reserve ratio (CRR) from 3% to 20% of the net demand and time liabilities. With effect from August 11, 2001 banks are required to maintain at least 50% of average amount of C.R.R. during the first 7 days of the fortnight. During the next 7 days of the reporting fortnight the minimum will be 65% without any exception.

It is to be noted that statutory minimum cash reserve with the RBI. though considered as liquid asset of a bank, is in reality not a liquid asset because the maintenance of such reserve is a statutory obligation on the banks. Failure to do so will attract penalties. Withdrawal of such reserves is not permitted except for a few days. The RBI pays interest at a rate equal to the bank rate on the eligible cash balances held with it by banks.

3. Balance with other Banks

Besides the statutory reserves with the RBI, the scheduled banks maintain certain amount of balances with other banks in current account. Section 18 of the Banking Regulation Act, 1949 imposed a duty on every non-scheduled banking company to maintain a certain percentage of demand and time liabilities by way of cash reserve with itself or in current account opened with the RBI/SBI or any other bank notified by the central government in this behalf. The balances held with other banks in current accounts are as liquid as the balances held by the non-scheduled banks themselves and may be withdrawn at any time as it wants.

4. Money at call and Short Notice

It is the second most liquid asset of a banker and it is generally called as the second line of defence. It happens that some banks may have surplus cash over and above the statutory reserve and a few other banks might be short of funds to maintain the statutory reserve. In such cases the banks which are short of funds borrow funds to meet the deficit from the banks which have surplus funds. This may be requested just for a overnight or for a few days. Such loans are repayable on call or at a short notice. The rate of interest on call and short notice loans varies from time to time according to the liquidity positions of banks, i.e., depends on the supply of and demand for funds.

The quantum of such funds in this category is a very insignificant portion of their total resources. The State Bank of India is the main lender in the call money market. The LIC of India and Unit Trust of India also have been placing their surplus funds in the call market. But however, the RBI has restricted the lending under this category by prescribing ceiling limits on borrowings with effect from April 29, 2002. That is (i) Daily lending of a bank is restricted to 25% of their owned funds as at the end of March of the previous financial year, and (ii) Daily borrowings of a bank shall be restricted to 100% of their owned funds or 2% of the aggregate deposits at the end of March of the previous financial year whichever is higher.

10.2. INVESTMENT IN SECURITIES

Besides the above, banks employ a significant portion of their funds in securities. Significance of investments of funds in securities is evident from the fact that such investments of scheduled commercial banks accounted for 37.9%. of the total assets as at the end of March, 2000, whereas loans and advances constituted 40% of the total assets.

Banks' investments are in the following six categories :

(i) Government Securities.

(ii) Other approved securities.

(iii) Shares.

(iv) Debentures and Bonds.

(v) Subsidiaries and /or joint.

(vi) Others viz., certificates of deposit, Mutual Funds

Investments in government and other approved securities account for the bulk of the banks' investments. The investment in stock exchange securities mainly the government securities is significant for two reasons : First the banks as a statutory obligation have to maintain not less than 25% of their demand and time liabilities in liquid assets including the approved securities. Secondly, banks find these securities a convenient medium of employing their surplus funds. Usually the ratio of investment of aggregate deposits goes up during the slack season and falls during the busy season.

As they invest the borrowed funds, their prime concern is the safety of the funds invested. Hence the banker has to consider the following for choosing of the securities for the investment of bank funds: they are safety of the Principal, liquidity or marketability and profitability of the securities.

10.3. GENERAL PRINCIPLES OF SOUND LENDING

1. Safety : As the banks deal with funds entrusted to them by the depositors, they have to ensure the safety of the funds lent. Safety means that the borrowers should be in a position to repay the loan along with interest. The repayment of the loan depends upon the borrower's (i) capacity to repay and (ii) willingness to pay. Capacity of the borrower depends upon his assets and the success of his business. The willingness to repay depends upon the honesty and character of the borrower. Therefore, a borrower should be a person of integrity, good character and reputation. In addition the safety of funds can also be ensured by requiring the borrowers to furnish collateral security.

2. Liquidity : Liquidity means a bank's ability to meet the claims of its customers, *viz.*, cash on demand. It is the capacity of a bank to honour its obligations. As a banker does his business on borrowed funds, he has to ensure liquidity while lending money. In case of need, the banker should be able to convert assets into cash. Depositors develop faith in a bank on the basis of its liquidity. Therefore, the principle of liquidity is as important as that of safety.

3. Profitability : Commercial banks are profit earning concerns and hence they must employ their funds profitably so that they can earn sufficient income to pay interest to the depositors, salaries to the staff and to meet various other expenses and distribute dividends to the shareholders. A bank should always ensure that funds that are lent bring in a reasonably good return. At the same time, they should also possess liquidity. The sound principle of lending is not to sacrifice safety or liquidity for the sake of higher profitability.

4. The Purpose of the Loan : While lending, the banker enquires of the borrower, the purpose for which the money is being borrowed. Repayment of loans depends to a large extent on the purpose for which loans are taken. Loans advanced for productive purpose would increase the earnings and hence repayments are guaranteed. Therefore, the chances of recovery are better. Suppose, loans are given for unproductive purposes, there is lot of uncertainty about recovering such loans. Therefore, loans are not advanced for speculative and unproductive purposes like social functions and ceremonies or for the repayment of a prior loan. Particularly after nationalisation, the purpose of a loan has assumed more significant.

5. The Principle of Diversification of Risks : Since every loan has its own risk, it is always better to give advances for different purposes and spread the risk. It is dangerous to give advances in any particular area or field of business or sector. To safeguard his interest against unforeseen contingencies, the banker follows the principle of diversification of risks based on the principle of "do not keep all the eggs in one basket". The advances should be spread over a reasonably wide area, in terms of the number of borrowers, number of sectors, geographical area and securities.

6. Security : Any valuable given to support a loan or advance is known as security. A large variety of securities may be offered against loans ranging from gold or silver to immovable property. The security accepted by a banker as a loan cover must be adequate, readily marketable, easy to handle and free from any encumbrance. Sometimes the banker is compelled to lend against personal security of the borrower. Anyhow the suitability of the security is specified from the bankers' ability to use it as a cushion in times of need.

7. Borrower's Financial Standing : A banker cannot ignore the repaying capacity of the borrowers. This in turn depends upon the character, capacity, financial standing and willingness of the borrowers. A borrower may have sound financial position but his integrity may be questionable. Then there is remote chance of repayment. However, it is very difficult to judge the character of the borrower. Borrowers with good paying capacity would not be honest in repayment. At the same time inspite of adverse paying capacity, certain individuals somehow, manage to repay the loans in time. Repaying capacity of farmers and small businessmen cannot be easily assessed.

8. Proper Balance of Advances : It is preferable to invest moderate sums of money in a large number of small advance than big sums of money in few big loans. Banking history has proved that bankers were embarrassed due to investment of majority of their funds to a few and their subsequent failures.

9. Margin : The security offered to cover the advance must be judged from the aspect of economic value and legal aspect. The market value of the security must be higher than the advance proposed, giving enough margin for fluctuation in prices and interest accumulation, after an appropriate valuation of them. In case of constant fall in the market price of the securities given, the banker should insist upon the production of additional security to maintain the margin.

10. National Policies : Commercial banks play pivotal role in developing an economy especially in a country like India. Security and return alone cannot influence the lending policy of a bank. Government policies and national interests impose certain social responsibilities on commercial banks. Therefore sometimes, advances are to be made even to weaker and underprivileged section of the society at concessional rates. Lending policies of commercial banks of developing nation, are to be modified from time to suit the needs of the economy.

Investment in Govt. and Trust Securities

The commercial banks in India invest predominantly in Government and Semi-Government securities considering the following factors.

1. **The Statutory Requirement:** Section 24 of the Banking Regulation Act, 1949 requires every scheduled and non-scheduled bank to maintain cash, gold or unencumbered approved securities at any day of the close of business an amount not less than 25% of their net demand and time liabilities in India. This is in addition to the minimum cash balances with the Reserve Bank of India. This minimum

requirement may be raised to 40% by the Reserve Bank of India. Approved securities include Central and State Government securities, the securities issued by municipal bodies, port trusts and city improvement trusts. As the cash and gold reserves don't yield any return, banks invest in approved securities to fulfil the statutory bligation at present banks are required to maintain Statutory Reserve Ratio (SLR) at 25% of their net demand and time liabilities. Therefore the commercial banks are the predominant investors in government securities.

2. **Stability in Prices:** From the point of view of price stability the prices of government securities are considered quite stable as compared to the prices of preference shares and variable dividend securities. Even among the government securities, banks prefer to invest in short dated securities maturing within 5 years, as they are easily marketable and their prices do not fluctuate much when compared to the long dated securities.

3. **Regular yield:** Though the government securities used to earn the lowest yield when compared with corporate securities, the regularity of return makes government securities attractive for the bankers. Now since 1992–93 there has been an upward shift in the yield of government securities and it is around 13.5 to 14.1.

4. **Facilities of Accommodation from the Reserve Bank:** Under Section 17(4) (a) of the Reserve Bank Act, 1934, whenever refinance facility from RBI is required, the government securities can be given as security to secure accommodation.

INVESTMENT IN TREASURY BILLS

Commercial Banks also invest their surplus funds in the Treasury Bills issued by the RBI on behalf of the Central Government. The sale of treasury bills helps the government to absorb any excess liquidity in the money market and also it provides short term finance to the government. Treasury Bills are being issued for maturities of 14 days, 91 days, 182 days and 364 days. During slack season and whenever the commercial banks have surplus funds, they resort to buy these treasury bills which are available in auctions. Since May 14, 2001, auctions of 91 day Treasury Bills on weekly basis and auctions of 364 days bills on fortnightly basis are only available and the treasury bills of 14 days and 182 days have been discontinued.

Investment in Treasury Bills is advantageous, as they are for short periods and they may be rediscounted with the RBI when the banks are in need of money. Investment in Corporate Shares, Debentures and Public Sector undertakings' Bonds:

As per the guidelines of the RBI, the banks are permitted to invest their surplus funds in the corporate shares, debentures and in the bonds of Public Sector undertakings under certain limitations. Now Banks are allowed to invest 5 per cent of their deposits by purchasing shares and debentures in the secondary market. But investments in Units of the Unit Trust of India and other Mutual Funds are included therein.

10.4. CLASSIFICATION OF LOANS AND ADVANCES

According to the Banking Regulations Act, 1949, the loans and advances granted by banks can be broadly classified into (i) secured and (ii) unsecured advances. A secured advance or loan means an advance or loan made on the security of assets and the market value of such asset has to be more than the amount of loan at any time till the loan is repaid. An unsecured loan is one in which the banker grants a loan without any security. Advances made against personal security of borrower , discounting of bills and advances made against guarantees come under this category. Therefore, the unsecured advances are given on the credit worthiness of the borrowers (*i.e.*) on the basis of his character, capacity and financial standing.

Thus, the unsecured advances or those which are granted against the Promissory Note of the borrower and the no tangible security is offered to the bank. These are sanctioned against the general credit of the borrowers. Unsecured advance must be granted by the banker only after analysing the credit worthiness of the borrower. It is granted for a short period and with a nominal interest. Among these advances the following are important.

(i) Cash Credit
(ii) Overdraft
(iii) Loans
(iv) Discounting of Bill of Exchange

(*i*) Cash Credit : Under this system, the banker permits his customers to borrow money upto a particular limit against the security of tangible assets or guarantees. The customer withdraws cash from this account as and when he needs funds and deposits any amount of money which he finds surplus with him. The cash credit account is thus an active and running account to which deposits and withdrawals may be made frequently. The bank will charge interest only on the actual amount withdrawn by the customer. Cash credit is the main method of lending by banks in India and accounts for about 70% of the total credit.

The following are the other features of cash credit arrangements with a bank:

(*i*) The banker takes into account features like the production, sales, inventory levels, etc. of the borrowing concern while fixing the cash credit limit. Thus, the banks relate the limits of cash credit to the security offered by their customers.

(*ii*) As there is no specific date of repayment, it is being practised that they "roll over" a period of time. It is actually found that in the case of large number of accounts, no credit balance will be available and only debit balances are found as if they are loans.

(*iii*) Under this system, the banker has to always keep sufficient cash balances so that the banker will be able to meet the demand of his customers as and when they demand. But the customer will be charged interest only on the actual amount utilized by him. In order to neutralize the loss of interest for keeping idle amount kept by the banks within the cash credit limit, the banker normally charges on the unutilized portion of the cash credit limit.

Commitment charges : As the customers are at liberty to draw against the cash credit limits, banks charge interest only on the basis of withdrawals on daily basis. Therefore, the bankers incur loss for keeping sufficient balances as idle for the unutilized portion of the credit limit. In order to avoid the loss caused, a charge known as commitment charge is made by the banks in recent years. The RBI had made it oligatory for the scheduled commercial banks to buy commitment charge at the rate of one percent per annum on the unutilized portion of the credit limit in excess of Rs. 10 lakhs with effect from 18th April 1970. However, this mandatory requirement to buy the commitment charge on the unutilized portion of the cash credit limits was withdrawn with effect from July 1, 1996 and the banks have been advised by the RBI to evolve their own guidelines to discipline the credit limits and levy of commitment charges.

The advantages of the cash credit system is that first the borrowers need not keep their surplus funds idle with themselves by remitting them in the banks and as and when they require funds, they can utilize the cash credit limit by withdrawing the funds from the banks and secondly, as the banks maintain one account for all the transactions of a customer, the repetitive documentation can be avoided.

There are also demerits in the system of cash credit (*i*) The limits are prescribed once in a year and this gives rise to the practice of prescribing large limits than is required. (*ii*) There will be no built in mechanism for the banks to verify the end-use of funds. (*iii*) The level of advances is determined not by how much the banker can lend at a particular time but by the borrower's decision to borrow at that time.

(*ii*) Overdraft : When a current account holder is permitted by the banker to draw more than what stands to his credit, such an advance is called an overdraft. This arrangement of overdraft facility may be extended to the current account holders either on giving some collateral security or on the personal security of the borrower. The customer may withdraw as and when he needs funds and repays it by means of deposits. Interest is charged on the exact amount overdrawn and for the exact period of its actual utilization.

Overdraft is not granted as regularly as cash credit. It is granted only occasionally and for shorter periods.

(*iii*) Loans : Sanctioning of a specified lump sum amount by the banker to a customer is called a loan. Once a loan is sanctioned and transferred to the customer's current account, the customer is required to pay interest on the full amount irrespective of the fact that the amount is used or not. A loan once repaid in full or in part cannot be withdrawn again by the borrower unless the banker sanctions a fresh loan. This is the aspect which differentiates it from the cash credit.

The commercial banks mainly provide short term loans for meeting the capital requirements of trade and industry. But during recent times, particularly after the nationalization of commercial banks, a new innovation has taken place and the banks have now come forward to grant medium and long term loans to industries. These loans are called term loans.

Under this system, credit is given for a definite purpose and for a predetermined period. These loans are normally repayable in instalments. The loan system of advancing funds to the borrowers ensures a greater degree of self-discipline on the borrowers as compared to cash credit system as, the amount of loan and the number of instalments are fixed in advance and the banker gets an opportunity of automatically reviewing the loan account. However, there are certain drawbacks in this system. There is no flexibility as the loan amount is already fixed and also the banks have no control over the end use of the funds borrowed by the customers.

(*iv*) Discounting of bills of Exchange : Advances are also given by discounting of bills of exchange. Under the scheme of Bill of Exchange the holder of the bill will receive payment mentioned therein on the maturity of the bill (i.e), not exceeding three months. Suppose the holder of the bill is not able to wait till the date of maturity and requires cash urgently, he can sell at a discount. Though this type of loan business is very common in advanced countries like U.K, U.S.A. etc. In India, this has not developed much. However, efforts are being taken to develop such a market in India.

New forms of Advances

In recent years, new forms of advances have come into existence. They are:

(*i*) Consortium Advances and

(*ii*) Participation Certificates

Many banks joining together and providing loans to one single project according to their capacities is called consortium advances. They grant advances on a consortium basis. Some projects require huge capital and the loan requirements of those projects cannot be met by a single bank. Therefore to share the risk and to facilitate large borrowing for a big project, such types of consortium advances are granted jointly by some banks.

A participation certificate is an instrument through which a banker, which has granted credit to its borrowers, can share with other institutions having surplus funds, a part of the credit given to its borrowers. A bank gets finance from other banks in respect of loans already granted. In other words, a bank can purchase the loan granted by another bank.

10.5. CREDIT INFORMATION

Before sanctioning loans and advances, the banker is required to assess the credit worthiness of the borrowers; and a banker has to collect necessary information about the borrower. In advanced countries, there are specialized institutions engaged in the collection of credit information. In India the RBI has set up a Credit Information Bureau. This bureau collects information regarding all advances of Rs.5 lakhs or more and unsecured advances of Rs.1 lakh or more from all banks. Such information collected are consolidated and supplied to banks on request.

Apart from this there are other sources from which credit information may be collected. They are :

(1) Information from the borrower himself.

(2) Exchange of information among banks.

(3) Market reports.

(4) Tax returns.

(5) Profit and loss account and Balance sheet and,

(6) Records of the Registrar of Companies.

Classification of Loans and Advances : Secured and Unsecured

The loans and advances granted by banks can be broadly classified into (*i*) secured and (*ii*) unsecured advances. Section 5(a) of the Banking Regulation Act. 1949 defines as "*secured loan and advance means a loan or advance made on the security of assets, the market value of which is not at anytime less than the amount of such loan or advance; and unsecured loan or advance means a loan or advance not so secured.*"

Thus, the important features of a secured loan or advance are:

(*i*) The loan should be made on the security of tangible assets like goods, land and buildings, gold or silver and government securities. A charge on any of the above should be offered as security for borrowing. (*ii*) The market value of such security should not be less than the amount of the loan at any time till the loan is repaid.

Under the sound banking principles of lending, the banker should assess not only the borrowing capacity and security of the borrower but also the integrity of the borrower. Even in the case of unsecured loans, though there is no security that is being offered, the banker has to assess the borrower's credit worthiness. In fact, unsecured loans are granted to persons of sufficient means, possession of tangible assets and with sound financial position.

10.6. LEVEL OF ADVANCES

The capacity to lend money is limited. The level or size of advances sanctioned by a banker depends upon the following factors:

(1) The size and maturity pattern of deposits.

(2) Credit control policy of RBI.

(3) Seasonal variations in bank credit.

(4) The demand for credit.

(5) Government's policy, and

(6) General business conditions.

10.7.SECURED ADVANCES – MODES OF CREATING CHARGE

Charging a security means making it available as a charges for an advance. Not only has the security to be good but the method of charging it should be legal and perfect. It is therefore, important that the charge must be complete and all the necessary formalities are complied with so that in case of default by a borrower, the security will be available to the banker. It should, however, be noted that whatever form the charge may take, the banker does not become the absolute or exclusive owner of the property. He has only certain defined rights in it, until the debt due to him is repaid.

Secured advances are those advances which provide absolute safety to the banker by means of creating a charge on the assets of the borrower in favour of the banker. By creating charge the banker gets certain rights in the assets offered by the borrower as security. There are several modes of creating a charge (*i.e*):

(*i*) Lien
(*ii*) Pledge
(*iii*) Hypothecation
(*iv*) Mortgage and
(*v*) Assignment

10.7.1. LIEN

Lien means the right of a person to retain any property of another person until the demands of the person holding the lien are satisfied as per the contract. The banker is empowered to retain any property offered as security for granting advances till the entire loan is repaid. Though the banker has got the right to retain the property offered as security, he cannot sell it, unless otherwise stated expressly in the contract.

There are two kinds of lien, viz. particular lien and general lien. A particular lien is related to those specific goods on account of which the debt was created. A general lien, on the other hand, gives a person right to retain possession of goods of the person for the general balance (i.e. any debt) due from the latter. A banker has a general lien.

A banker may also create a 'Negative lien' under which the banker does not get the right to retain any asset of borrower. The borrower gives a declaration to the banker that his assets specified are free from any charge or encumbrance. Also he gives an undertaking that he shall not create any charge or dispose of the assets without the permission of the banker. However, it will be very difficult for the banker to realise debts in case it is a negative lien. The banker's interests are partly safe by securing such negative lien. A banker, therefore, prefers a general lien.

10.7.2. PLEDGE

Pledge is the bailment of goods as security for payment of a debt or performance of a promise. Bailment is the delivery of goods by one person to another for some purpose, under a contract that the goods shall, when the purpose is accomplished, be returned or otherwise disposed of according to the directions of the person delivering them. The person delivering the goods (bailor) as security is called the pledgor or pawnor. The persons to whom the goods are delivered (bailee) is called the pledgee or pawnee.

From the above definition, we observe that :-

(a) Pledge means bailment of goods.
(b) The bailment must be for and on behalf of the debtor or intending debtor.

(c) It must be the intention of the parties that the goods will serve as Security for a debt or performance of a promise.

A pledge may be in respect of goods, stocks and shares, documents of title to goods and any other moveable property.

Importance of Possession : A pledge is said to be created, when the goods are handed over by the borrower or the prospective borrower to the lender or to someone on his behalf, with the intention of their being treated as security for the repayment of the advance. Legal delivery – actual or constructive – is an essential part of a contract of pledge. The contract need not necessarily be expressed in writing. It may be implied from the nature of the transaction or the circumstances of the case. It would, however, be conceded that an agreement reduced to writing facilitates understanding of the terms and conditions thereof, leaving no doubt about the intention of the parties.

Advantages of pledge : Of all the methods of charging a security, pledge is the most satisfactory one because of the following:

(*i*) The goods under pledge being in the possession of the bank, it is easy to dispose them of, (if necessary), at short notice.

(*ii*) If proper precautions including periodical inspections are taken, there is hardly any possibility of the same goods being charged elsewhere.

(*iii*) It is always easy to know the extent of the turnover of the goods by reference to the stock register

(*iv*) Manipulation of stocks is difficult as they are under the banker's full possession and close supervision.

(*v*) There would be little difficulty in preferring or proving an insurance claim, in the event of loss or damage to the pledged goods, say, by fire, as the goods are in the bank's possession.

(*vi*) In the case of insolvency of the borrower, it is always open for the bank to sell the goods and prove for the balance of the debt, if any.

Parties involved in a valid pledge: Generally, any one who is in legal possession of the goods can pledge them. The parties who can make a valid pledge are:-

(a) Owner of the goods.

(b) Mercantile agent, who, with the consent of the owner is in possession of the goods or the documents of title to goods, and acts in the ordinary course of business of a mercantile agent, provided that the pledgee acts in good faith and has not at the time of the pledge, notice that the pledgor has no authority to pledge.

(c) Person in possession of goods under a contract which is voidable at the option of the lawful owner, on the ground of fraud, misrepresentation, coercion or undue influence. Though possession so obtained is not by free consent, nevertheless the person in possession of such goods may make a valid pledge of the goods, provided the contract has not been rescinded at the time of the pledge. This such a case of a de facto contract, though voidable on the ground of fraud and the like. The pledge in this case is valid provided the pledgee acts in good faith and without notice of the pledger's defect in title.

The position would, however be different where goods have been obtained by means of theft. A thief has no title and can give none.

(d) Seller of the goods who, after having sold the goods, is or continues to be in possession of the goods or documents of title to goods. The pledgee in this case must have received the goods in good faith and without notice of the previous sale.

For example, A sells goods to B. B for his convenience leaves the goods with A. A pledges the goods to a banker who accepts them in good faith and without notice of the sale to B. The pledge is valid.

(e) A pledgee of the goods. Where a person pledges goods, the repledge is valid only to the extent of his interest in the said goods. In other words, repledge of the pledged goods is permitted in law, but the re-pledge should not exceed the pledgee's interest in the security. Further, if the original pledgor repays the debt to the pledgee, he should immediately return the pledged goods though they may be in the hands of the repledgee who may not have been paid his debt by the repledger. Because of the limited extent of the pledgee's interest in the goods, bankers do not usually favour this type of business.

It has also to be emphasized that because of various difficulties which are likely to arise, as indicated above, bankers avoid accepting goods in pledge in cases falling under categories (c) and (d) . It is, therefore, advisable to make detailed enquiries about the title of the pledgor to the goods before accepting them as security. The banker should also inspect the original invoices or cash memos to ascertain the title of the pledgor.

Rights and obligations of pledger : The pledger has a right to redeem the security pledged on his repaying to the pledgee the debt with interest and other charges. In case of a forced sale of the goods by the pledgee, the pledgor is entitled to receive from him any surplus that may remain with him after the debt is completely paid off. The pledgor has also a right to redeem the goods pledged even after the time stipulated for payment, but before they have been actually sold by the pledgee.

A pledger must disclose to the pledgee any material faults or extraordinary risks in the goods to which the pledgee may be exposed. If he fails to do so, he may be responsible for damages to the pledgee. The pledgor must also reimburse the pledgee for any expenses incurred by the later for the preservation of the goods. After the pledgee has exercised his right of sale of goods, if there is any shortfall, the pledgor is liable to make good the balance.

The pledger is responsible to the pledgee for any defect in his (pledger's) title to the goods. In other words, he guarantees his clear title to the goods pledged. It follows that the pledgor will be responsible to the pledgee for any loss which the pledgee may sustain by reason that the pledger was not entitled to make the pledge.

Rights and obligations of pledgee: Rights :– (*i*)The pledgee has a right to retain the goods pledged not only for the payment of the debt due to him but also for the interest on the debt and necessary expenses incurred by him in respect of possession or for the preservation of the goods pledged. He can also claim for any extra-ordinary expenses incurred by him in the preservation of the security. A pledgee has the same remedies against a third person as the owner himself would have if he is deprived of the goods.

(*ii*) If the pledger makes default in payment of the debt in respect of which the goods are pledged, the pledgee may sell the security on giving the pledgor reasonable notice† of sale. What is reasonable notice depends upon the circumstances of each case. The notice has to be clear and specific in language indicating the intention of the pledgee to dispose of the security. In case the proceeds of the sale of the goods are less than the amount due in respect of the debt including interest and other charges, the pledgee is entitled to recover the balance from the pledgor. The pledgee may also bring a suit against the pledgor for the debt including interest and other charges and retain the goods pledged as security. The pledgee will not ordinarily exercise this right of filing the suit, unless the security has become unsaleable.

(*iii*) The Pledgee is entitled to know the defects, if any of the goods pledged, if they are known to the pledger and in cash the pledgee suffers any damage as a result of non-disclosure of such fault by the pledger, the latter shall be responsible for it.

(*iv*) In case the title of the goods pledged is found defective and the pledgee suffers any loss due to this, the pledger shall be responsible for such loss.

(*v*) If the pledgee is induced to enter into the contract by fraud or misrepresentation with regard to the pledger's interest in the goods pledged, the contract becomes voidable at the option of the pledgee and hence it cannot be enforced in the court of law.

(*vi*) The pledgee's rights are not limited to the interest in the goods pledged but also have remedies as the owner of the goods against a third party for the injury, if any caused. In the case of Morvi Merchantile Bank Ltd. Vs. Union of India, the Supreme Court held that the pledgee (the bank) was entitled to recover the full value of the consignment from the Railways, *viz.*, Rs. 35,000 and not Rs. 20,000 which was due to its from the customer.

Obligation:–

(*i*) The pledgee must take as much care of the goods pledged to him as a person of ordinary prudence would, under similar circumstances, take of his own goods of a similar nature. (*ii*) The pledgee cannot make an unauthorised use of the goods pledged, incontravention of the terms of the pledge. (*iii*) He must return to the pledger the goods pledged when the debt is repaid. (*iv*) In the absence of any contract to the contrary, any accruals to the goods pledged belong to the pledger who is the owner of the goods. For example, if the security consists of equity shares and the company has issued bonus shares to the equity shareholder, the bonus shares are the property of the pledger and not the pledgee.

(*v*) Any surplus sale proceeds remaining in the hands of the pledgee after the debt, interest, charges etc., have been fully recovered, have to be returned to the pledger; but by a special agreement of set-off entered into between the parties, such surplus can be made available for set-off against any other indebtedness of the pledger.

Features of Pledge :

In case of a pledge, the following features are found :

(*i*) There should be bailment of goods. That is, two important requisites have to be fulfilled. First delivery of goods is essential for a contract of bailment. Delivery may be either physical delivery or constructive (symbolic) delivery. The second requisite is that the bailee should return the goods to the bailer or dispose them of according to his instructions after the purpose for which the goods were delivered is fulfilled.

(*ii*) It is essential that the bailment of the goods is done with the object of securing the repayment of a debt or performance of a promise. Suppose the goods are left with the banker for safe custody or for any other purpose, it does not constitute a pledge.

(*iii*) The pledger should be the owner of the property that is pledged.

(*iv*) There should be an agreement between the pledger and pledgee for creating a charge.

10.7.3. HYPOTHECATION

Hart describes hypothecation as a "*charge against property for an amount of debt where neither ownership nor possession is passed to the creditor*". In hypothecation, the goods remain in the possession of the borrower and are equitably charged to the lender under documents signed by the borrower. He, however, binds himself under the hypothecation agreement to give possession of the goods to the lender when called upon to do so. After the possession is handed over to the lender, the charge is converted from hypothecation into pledge.

Hypothecation Facility granted only to first class Customers :

In Gopan Singh Hira Singh Vs. Punjab National Bank (1976), the Delhi High Court observed as follows:

"*a borrower is in actual physical possession but the constructive possession is still of the bank because, according to the deed of hypothecation, the borrower holds the actual physical possession not in his own right as the owner of the goods but as agent of the bank.*" The High Court concluded that in law there was no difference between pledge and hypothecation as the hypothecated goods are also not only constructively but actually in possession of the bank. Hence inorder to enforce its claim, the bank should take possession of the hypothecated property on its own or through the court. In case the banker fails to take possession of the hypothecated property and chooses to seek a simple money decree, the bank is deemed to have waived its right as hypothecatee.

In Syndicate Bank Vs. Official Liquidator, Prashant Engineering Co. Pvt. Ltd. (1986), the bank failed to take possession of the property but filed a suit for the recovery of money only. It was held that the Bank was considered as an unsecured creditor along with other creditors of the company.

In Bank of Baroda Vs. Babari Bachubhai Hirabhai & others (1987), the Gujarat High Court held that the Bank has no title over the vehicle but it has only a right to recover its due by the sale of the vehicle and so long as there was no default in payment, it would not exercise that right to sell the vehicle.

In the case of State Bank of India Vs. S.B. Shah Ali (1994), the Andhra Pradesh High Court held that it was open to the bank to take possession of the hypothecated property on its own or through the court as per the hypothecation agreement. If there is any specific clause in the Hypothecation Agreement empowering the hypothecatee to take possession of the goods and sell the same in the event of default in payment, the hypothecatee can proceed ahead without the intervention of the Court.

Being only an equitable charge on moveable property without possession, hypothecation facility is granted only to parties of undoubted means with the highest integrity. The facility is also allowed in special cases when it is not practicable or convenient to take possession of the goods securing the advance. The opportunity and the temptation of charging fraudulently the goods to another banker and borrowing against them, or disposing them of to the lender's detriment, offer themselves in a greater measure in a hypothecation account than in a pledge account. Hypothecation is sometimes granted side by side with pledge. For example, in a factory, the bulk of the raw materials and finished products could be conveniently kept in possession of the bank by way of pledge, under its lock and key. There may, however, be stocks-in-process, which are in the course of manufacture and cannot be taken possession of by the banker. If an advance is required against such stock-in-process, it can be considered only on hypothecation basis. In such circumstances, a reasonably small limit commensurate with the credit worthiness of the party is granted by way of hypothecation, along with the pledge limit. Such a limit is usually allowed with a higher margin and at a higher rate of interest because of the difficulties in verification and valuation of the security.

The banker may open two accounts separately – one for the pledge and the other for hypothecation – or he may open one cash credit account for the entire limit, calculate the drawing power separately against stocks and stocks-in-process and then combine these two for the purpose of the total drawing limit.

Sometimes, an advance on hypothecation basis is granted to highly creditworthy parties against goods in a shop or a show-room. Hypothecation may also be given against goods which require constant handling as in a factory such as groundnuts or husks or paddy. The same consideration applies to advances to factories processing cashew nuts, roasting tea or curing coffee as it would be highly impracticable in such cases to keep the goods in process in the bank's exclusive possession. Hypothecation is the only convenient method of charge in such cases.

Precautions of Hypothecation: The following precautions are to be taken to safeguard the position of the banker:

(*i*) Hypothecation should be allowed only when the borrower is unable to effect a pledge.

(*ii*) Financial soundness and business integrity of the borrower should be carefully studied before granting him loan.

(*iii*) An undertaking should be obtained from the borrower regarding the clear title to the goods hypothecated.

(*iv*) Obtain a letter of hypothecation.

(*v*) The goods hypothecated should be fully insured against fire and other risks.

(*vi*) Mention should be made on the goods about the fact of the hypothecation of such goods.

(*vii*) The borrower should be required to submit periodical statement of accounts giving correct position about the stocks and its valuation.

(*viii*) In case of a joint stock company, a banker should get the charge registered under section 125 of the Companies Act.

(*ix*) The banker should see that no hypothecation charge is not already created on the same goods or assets with another banker.

10.7.4. THE DIFFERENCE BETWEEN LIEN AND PLEDGE

Lien	Pledge
1. Right to retain the property	1. Bailment of property by the borrower.
2. Property can be retained either for a specific debt or for a general balance.	2. Property can be retained only for specific debt.
3. Lien by usage of trade or by law.	3. Created by an agreement between the borrower and lender.
4. No right to sell the property though the property can be retained.	4. Right to sell the property is provided in the agreement.
5. Once the property is lost by the creditor, there is an end to lien.	5. Even if it is lost, the pledge continues till the debt is settled.
6. Less secured	6. More secured.

10.7.5. THE DIFFERENCES BETWEEN PLEDGE AND HYPOTHECATION

Pledge	Hypothecation
1. Actual or constructive delivery of goods is essential.	1. There is no delivery of goods.
2. Pledgee can sell the property without the order of court, if provided in the agreement.	2. Hypothecate cannot sell the property without the order of the court.
3. Pledge is more safe	3. Hypothecation is less safe.

10.7.6 MORTGAGE

A mortgage is a charge created by offering immovable property like land and buildings as security for a loan. Section 58 of the Transfer of Property Act 1882 defines mortgage as "the transfer of an interest in specific immovable property for the purpose of securing the payment of money advanced or to be advanced by way of loan, an existing or future debt, or the performance of an engagement which may give rise to a pecuniary liability". The person who transfers the interest in property is called a mortgager and the person who gets the interest in property is known as the mortgagee.

Main Features of a Mortgage :

1. A mortgage can be effected only in case of immovable property.

2. A mortgage is a transfer of some interest in the specific immovable property. However, the right of ownership in the property is not transferred to the mortgagee. The property cannot be sold without the consent of the mortgagee.

3. The actual possession of the property need not always be transferred to the mortgage.

4 When the payments due along with interest are complctely paid by the mortgager, he gets back all his interest and rights in the property mortgaged.

5. If there are more than one co-owners of a property, every co-owner has got the right to mortgage his share of property

6. The object of mortgage must be to secure a loan or to ensure the performance of promise which results in monetary obligation.

Types of Mortgages : Section 58 of the Transfer of Property Act, 1882 gives the following forms of mortgages:

1. Simple mortgage
2. Mortgage by conditional sale
3. Usufructuary mortgage
4. English mortgage

5. Mortgage by deposit of title deeds/Equitable mortgage

6. Anomalous mortgage

(1) Simple Mortgage : Where, without delivering possession of the mortgaged property, the mortgagor binds himself personally to pay the mortgage money, and agrees, expressly or impliedly, that, in the event of his failing to pay according to his contract, the mortgagee shall have a right to cause the mortgaged property to be sold and the proceeds of sale to be applied, in payment of the mortgage-money, the transaction is called a simple mortgage. Or the mortgagee may file a suit for recovery of the whole amount without selling the property.

(2) Mortgage by conditional sale : Where the mortgagor ostensibly sells the mortgaged property, on the condition that in default of payment of the mortgage-money on a certain date, the sale shall become absolute or on the condition that on such payment being made the sale shall become void, or on the condition that on such payment being made, the buyer shall transfer the property to the seller, the transaction is known as mortgage by conditional sale; provided that no such transaction shall be deemed to be a mortgage unless the condition is embodied in the document which effects or purports to effect the sale.

If the mortgage-money is not repaid on the agreed date, the ostensible sale will become absolute upon the mortgagee applying to the court and getting a decree in his favour, since the right to redeem is then lost. The mortgagee can sue for foreclosure but not for the sale of property. This type of mortgage is not usually taken by the banks as there is no personal covenant for repayment of the debt.

(3) Usufructuary Mortgages : Where the mortgagor delivers possession or binds himself expressly or by implication to deliver possession of the mortgaged property to the mortgagee, and authorises him to retain such possession until repayment of the mortgage-money, and to receive the rents and profits accruing from the property, or any part of such rents and profits and to appropriate the same in lieu of interest or in payment of the mortgage-money, or partly of both, then the transaction is known as an usufructuary mortgage and the mortgagee an usufructuary mortgagee. Unless there is a personal covenant for the repayment of the mortgage-money, the usufructuary mortgagee cannot sue the mortgagor for repayment of the mortgage debt; nor can the mortgagee sue for the sale or foreclosure of the mortgaged property. The only remedy for the mortgagee is to remain in possession of the mortgaged property and pay himself out of the rents and/or profits of the mortgaged property. No one can say when the mortgagee will fully recover the mortgage money through this process. Banks hardly entertain advance proposals of this type.

(4) English Mortgage : Where the mortgagor binds himself to repay the mortgage-money on a certain date, and transfers the mortgaged property absolutely (i.e. conveys all interests in the property) to the mortgagee, subject to the proviso that the mortgagee will retransfer it to the mortgagor upon repayment of the mortgage-money as agreed, the transaction is called an English mortgage.

It is characteristic of the English mortgage that the personal liability of the mortgagor remains notwithstanding the absolute transfer of the property to the mortgagee.

Further, in case of default in repayment of mortgage-money, the mortgagee has a right to sell the mortgaged property outside the court in special circumstances mentioned in Section 69 of the Transfer of Property Act, 1882.

Mortgage by deposit of title-deeds or equitable mortgage : Where a person in any of the following towns viz., the towns of Kolkatta, Chennai and Mumbai and in any other town which the State Government concerned may, by notification in the Official Gazette, specify in this behalf, delivers to a creditor or his agent documents of title to immovable property, with intent to create a security thereon, the transaction is called a mortgage by deposit of title-deeds. This type of mortgage is popular equally with the banks and the borrowers. The borrower saves the stamp duty on the mortgage deed and registration charges. Further, except in the case of a limited company where the charge on immovable property requires registration under Section 125 of the Companies Act, 1956, nobody other than the bank and the borrower is in the know of the transaction. This type of mortgage is dealt with at some length in a subsequent part of the chapter.

Sometimes the deposit of the title deeds is accompanied by a memorandum of deposit which is registered at the office of the Sub-Registrar/Registrar of Assurances. The document states, inter alia, the maximum amount to be secured, that the mortgage covers all present and future advances and the mortgagor agrees to execute a mortgage deed as and when desired by the bank. The memorandum does not, however, incroporate the entire terms of the mortgage and represents only the 'bargain' between the parties. The document requires to be stamped but the stamp duty is less than that payable on a simple mortgage.

(5) **Anomalous Mortgages** : A mortgage which is not a simple mortgage, a mortgage by conditional sale, an usufructuary mortgage, an English mortgage or a mortgage by deposit of title-deeds is called an anomalous mortgage.

An anomalous mortgage must, however, satisfy the definition of mortgage as given in Section 58 of the Transfer of Property Act, 1882 (see above). There are two kinds of anomalous mortgages which are often noticed in practice. They are firstly a simple-cum-usufructuary mortgage and secondly a usufructuary mortgage accompanied by conditional sale. We do not propose to deal with such mortgage as they are generally not accepted by banks.

Difference between the legal mortgage and equitable mortgage

English or Legal Mortgage	Equitable Mortgage
1. Created by registering the mortgage deed	1. Created by merely depositing the title deeds of the property.
2. As it is subject to stamp duty, it is costly	2. As no registration is required, it is cheap. But now the Govt. of Tamil Nadu has made it mandatory to register so as to enable to the Govt. to collect stamp duty and hence it now becomes costly.
3. As registration is compulsory, reputation of the mortgager may be affected.	3. As there is no registration, it does not affect the reputation of the mortgage.
4. The mortgage can sell the property without going to the court.	4. He cannot sell the property without going to the court.
5. Legal interest in the property is transferred in favour of the mortgagee.	5. Legal interest in the property is not transferred.
6. It involves lot of time and trouble. trouble.	6. It does not involve much time and trouble.

Rights of Mortgagor : The following are the rights to mortgagor.

1. Right of redemption : The mortgagor has a right to redeem the property on payment of the mortgage money after the principal money has become due, provided the right of redemption has not been extinguished by an act of the parties or by decree of a court. A suit to enforce this right is called a suit for redemption.

The mortgagor who has redeemed the mortgage is entitled on redemption to the following rights:

(*a*) to get back from mortgagee the mortgage deed and all other documents relating to the mortgaged property in the possession or power of the mortgagee.

(b) to obtain possession of the mortgaged property from the mortgagee, as in the case of an English mortgage.

(c) to have the mortgaged property re-transferred at his cost to him or to such third person as he may direct. (Section 60).

2. Accession to mortgaged property : Where the mortgaged property is in the possession of the mortgagee and has, during the continuance of the mortgage, received any accession (addition to the property), or if the mortgagee has voluntarily made any improvement in the property, the mortgagor upon redemption, is entitled as against the mortgagee to such accession and improvement unless there is a contract to the contrary. (Section 63 and 63 A).

3. Right to get mortgage transferred to third party : The mortgagor who is entitled to redeem the mortgaged property, may require the mortgagee, that instead of retransferring the property to him, to assign the mortgage debt and transfer the mortgaged property to such third person as the mortgagor may direct. (Section 60 A).

4. Right to inspection and production of documents : The mortgagor as long as the right of redemption exists, has a right to require the mortgagee to allow him inspection and make copies of or extracts from the title-deeds in the custody of the mortgagee. (Section 60 B).

Rights of Mortgagee : The following are the some important rights of mortgagee.

1. **Right to sue for mortgage money :** The mortgagee has a right to file a suit in a court of law for the mortgage money in the following cases only :

(*a*) Where the mortgagor binds himself to re-pay the mortgage money.

(*b*) Where the mortgagee is deprived of the whole or part of his security by or in consequence of the wrongful act or default of the mortgagor.

(*c*) Where, by any cause other than the wrongful act or default of the mortgagor or mortgagee, the mortgaged property is wholly or partially destroyed or the security is rendered insufficient and the mortgagor has not provided enough further security.

(*d*) Where the mortgagor fails to deliver the mortgaged property to the mortgagee in case he (the mortgagee) is entitled to it.

2. Right of Sale : The right of filing a suit against the mortgagor accrues to the mortgagee after the mortgage money has become due to him. The mortgagee in case of a simple, equitable and English mortgage has the right to have the mortgaged property sold after he has filed a suit against the mortgagor and has obtained a decree from court.

A mortgagee has a right of sale without the intervention of the court under certain circumstances mentioned in Section 69 of the Transfer of Property Act, 1882.

3. Right of foreclosure : After the mortgage money has become due and before decree has been passed for the redemption of the property, the mortgagee, in the absence of a contract to the contrary, may obtain from the court a decree for foreclosure against the mortgagor, that is to say, the mortgagor should be absolutely debarred of his right to redeem the property. The mortgagee under a simple, English or equitable mortgage is, however, not allowed the right of foreclosure.

4. Right of possession in certain cases : The mortgagee is entitled to the possession of the mortgaged property where he is, so entitled under the mortgage deed, for example, in an usufructuary mortgage. The right of possession is, however, not available to the mortgagee in the case of a simplc or equitable mortgage.

5. Accession to mortgaged property : If any accession (addition) is made to the mortgaged property after the date of the mortgage, the mortgagee, in the absence of a contract to the contrary, is for the purposes of the security, entitled to such accession. For example, A mortgages a certain plot of land to B and afterwards erects a house on the plot. For the purpose of his security, B is entitled to the house as well as the plot.

Precautions to be taken by the Banker :

When a proposal for an advance against an immovable property is received, the following points should be carefully considered:

(*a*) **Borrower's Title :** The original title-deeds i.e. sale deeds, sale certificates issued by a court if property has been purchased through a court auction etc. should be obtained. The chain of documents must be complete. Not only should the bank ask for the last sale deed/sale certificate but also the earlier ones. For example, if Mohan approaches the bank for an advance against his bungalow, he should produce for the bank's inspection not only the sale deed of the bungalow in his favour but also the previous sale deed in favour of the person from whom he purchased the property. The sale deeds prior to that, if any, should also be obtained as required by the legal adviser, to establish how the title was transferred from one purchaser to another. The law relating to sale, mortgage and charging of immovable property is highly technical and complicated. The inspection of the title-deeds and the verification of the borrower's title require thorough legal knowledge. The title-deeds should, therefore, be passed on to the bank's legal adviser for his inspection and opinion. It is possible that the borrower may have already obtained a report from the same legal adviser. In such a case, the legal adviser should be requested to resubmit his report and address it to the bank. A search will also have to be taken in the office of the Sub-Registrar of Assurances, etc. to verify that there is no prior charge on the property. In order that the bank may entertain the advance, the legal opinion should be positive that the borrower has a clear and marketable title and that the property is subject to no prior encumbrance. The report on the title should be up to date and based on searches carried on as on the date of the creation of the charge, as may be possible.

(*b*) **Freehold or leasehold property :** The bank should ascertain whether the property is freehold or leasehold. In case of leasehold property, the original lease deed in favour of the borrower must be examined to ascertain the unexpired period of the lease. The bank should also study the terms and conditions of the lease to find out if there are any onerous covenans (burdensome conditions) such as the necessity of taking lessor's consent before mortgaging the property. The latest ground rent receipt should be obtained from the borrower to verify that the rent is not in arrears and that the lease continues to subsist. The documents should be examined by the lawyer along with the other title-deeds, if any, and is opinion obtained thereon.

(*c*) Original lease deeds in favour of borrower : If the borrower has given the property to be mortgaged, on lease to a third party, the bank should ask him to submit the relative lease deed, for bank's inspection. This document will serve as further corroborative evidence of the borrower's title to the property.

(*d*) (*i*) **Municipal tax receipts :** The receipts for the payment of house tax should be obtained in case of buildings situated within municipal limits. Municipal taxes constitute a preferential charge on property.

(*ii*) **Copies of revenue records :** In case of agricultural land, the borrower should be asked to produce certified true copies of the latest revenue records.

(*iii*) **Government dues** : The borrower should be asked to produce latest Receipts regarding the land revenue or any other Government dues paid by him.

(*e*) **Valuation :** An estimate of the value of the property is usually arrived at by one or more of the following methods :

(*i*) taking architect's or engineer's certificate if the property consists of buildings. In case of machinery embedded in the earth, the services of special surveyors may have to be requisitioned.

(*ii*) personally inspecting the property.

(*iii*) making enquiries through brokers, neighbours, etc.

(*iv*) scrutinising the valuation certificate issued by a local authority for taxation purpose.

(*v*) calculations based on the net yield by way of rent.

It should be borne in mind that the law gives protection to tenants. In case of a forced sale, a building occupied by tenants will usually fetch a lower price than a vacant building, particularly when old rents are much lower than current rents of a similar property.

(*f*) **Registration necessary except in case of equitable mortgage:** According to Section 59 of the Transfer of Property Act, 1882, where the principal money secured is one hundred rupee or more, a mortgage other than a mortgage by deposit of title-deeds, can be effected only by a registered instrument signed by the mortgagor and attested by at least two witnesses. The document is to be presented for registration at the office of the Sub-Registrar/Registrar of Assurances within four months from the date of its execution. It is advisable to have the registration effected as early as possible, within the stipulated period of four months.

(*g*) **Documentation** : The mortgage deed (except in case of an equitable mortgage where there is no need) must be drafted by the bank's legal adviser/legal department. The document must set out all the terms and conditions on which the money is being advanced/has been advanced or facility provided. It may be stated that the mortgage deed must be attested by at least two witnesses.

Precautions after mortgage is created :

(*a*) **Title-deeds not to be parted with :** The bank should never part with the title-deeds to the borrower or his representative during pendency of the mortgage, as such a course of action is fraught with grave risks. In case an inspection of the title-deeds is requested by the borrower, it may be permitted under the supervision of a bank official. In the alternative, the title-deeds may be sent to the bank's solicitors, and the borrower's solicitors may inspect them at the office of the former. The title-deeds should be kept under dual control.

It may be stated that under Section 78 of the Transfer of Property Act, 1882, where through fraud, misrepresentation or gross neglect of a prior mortgagee, another person has been induced to advance money on the security of the already mortgaged property, the prior mortgagee shall be postponed to the subsequent mortgagee.

(*b*) **Valuation :** The property should be valued at frequent intervals, say, once in a year.

(*c*) **Periodical Inspection** : The property should be periodically inspected to ensure that it is kept in a proper condition of repair.

(*d*) **Insurance :** If the mortgaged property consists of buildings and/or machinery, it should be adequately covered against risk of fire and other specified risks like strike, riot and civil commotion (S.R.C.C), flood, etc., if necessary. The due date of the policy should be properly diarised.

(*e*) **Balance and security confirmation letters** : The balance and security confirmation letters duly signed by the mortgagor should be obtained in the prescribed form every half year/year according to the practice of the bank.

10.7.7. DIFFERENCE BETWEEN HYPOTHECATION AND MORTGAGE

Hypothecation	Mortgage
1. Relates to movable property.	1. Relates to immovable property.
2. Can be created without execution or registration of a document.	2. Cannot be created without executing or registering a document.
3. Legal interest in the property is not transferred.	3. Legal interest in the property is transferred in all mortgages except equitable mortgage.
4. Court decree is necessary for selling the property.	4. No court decree is necessary for selling the property.
5. It is less secured.	5. It is more secured.

10.7.8. DIFFERENCE BETWEEN PLEDGE AND MORTGAGE

Pledge	Mortgage
1. Relates to movable property.	1. Relates to immovable property.
2. The borrower does not transfer the ownership to the lender.	2. Ownership is transferred to the lender.
3. Delivery of the property is necessary.	3. Except usufructuary mortgage, possession of property is not transferred.
4. The property can be sold without court order.	4. In equitable mortgage the property cannot be sold without court order.
5. The pledgee does not have the right of foreclosure.	5. The mortgagee has got the right of forclosure.
6. Less safe when compared to mortgage.	6. More safe when compared to pledge.

10.8. ASSIGNMENT

Assignment means transfer of an existing or future right over property or money by one person to another. The person transferring the right is called the "Assignor" and the person to whom the right is assigned is called the "assignee". Generally it is applicable in the case of claims. Assignment is also of two types, viz., legal and equitable. Legal assignment relates to the execution of deed in writing duly signed by the assignor which makes the claim absolute. The assignor informs in writing the assignee's name and address at the debtor. The assignee also serves on the debtor of the assignment and seeks confirmation of the balance so assigned. If all these requirements are not fulfilled, the assignment is called an equitable assignment.

QUESTIONS

1. What is meant by cash reserves maintained by bankers ? What are the factors governing the maintenance of cash reserves by a shrewed banker ?
2. Discuss the various fields of investments of commercial bank. What are the creteria which a sound banker has to keep in view in the utilisation of funds ?
3. What are the general principles which should guide a banker in making loans and advances to a customer ?
4. What are secured and unsecured advances of the bank ? What precautions should a banker take while making unsecured advances ?
5. Discuss the characteristics of mortgage, a pledge and a lien. As a banker which of these would you prefer as security and in what circumstances ?
6. Discuss the relative advantages and drawbacks to a banker of (a) an equitable mortgage (b) a legal mortgage and (c) a usufrueetuary mortgage.
7. What constitutes a pledge ? What are the advantages over other kinds of charges say Hypothecation and Mortgage ?
8. What is equitable mortgage ? What is the procedure for creating such mortgage ? What precautions would you take before accepting equitable mortgage as security ?
9. An advance to a limited company against stock is generally by way of hypothecation instead of pledge. Why ?

Secured Advances—Types of Securities

Generally, banks advance money against securities. The securities provided by the customers give protection and safety to the lending banker. In spite of these, the banker is liable to suffer losses due to his ignorance, negligence or carelessness. Therefore, the banker should observe some basic principles, while granting advances against securities.

11.1 GENERAL PRINCIPLES OF SECURED ADVANCES

1. Marketability : As security is obtained for the purpose of meeting an emergency in the event of default by the borrower, the main consideration which weighs with the banker is its ready marketability. Articles of necessity, primary commodities, seasonal goods, raw materials, textiles or other manufactured goods in general demand, afford good examples of marketable securities. Articles of luxury or valuables which appeal to only a small section of society have a limited market. For example, pearls and diamonds are not considered good security. A rich business magnate may have spent Rs. 10 lacs on the construction of a palatial bungalow at an out-of-the way hill station. The building may not be a good security at all, as in the event of a forced sale, there may be hardly any purchaser at a reasonable price. Similarly, a building in the occupation of tenants would not be as marketable as a vacant building. Under the present tenancy laws, rents can hardly be increased and the tenants cannot be evicted except through a long-drawn-out legal process. The bank should be able to realise the security quickly and without undue formality, should the occasion demand. This is also the reason why banks prefer to advance against quoted and fully paid shares of good public limited companies and do not lend against unquoted shares, or shares of private limited companies.

2. Easy Ascertainment of Value : There are certain goods and commodities for which market quotations are easily available, such as shares which are dealt on the stock exchange or commodities for which there are organized markets, for example, sugar, oilseeds, grains, etc. A reference to the commercial columns of any standard newspaper would enable the banker to obtain the day-to-day quotations prevailing in the markets for different types of securities of commodities. There may be some articles which are rarely quoted or may be so highly specialised that it may not be possible to make an easy assessment of their value except by making a reference to an expert. It may not be possible to ascertain the exact value of certain articles such as paintings by old masters, buildings located in out-of-the way places, highly specialised machines, etc.

3. Stability of Value : It is not enough that the banker is able to ascertain the value of a particular security. He must also make sure that its value does not fluctuate violently over short periods. Due to the activities of speculators, commodities like pepper and yarn are sometimes subject to such heavy variations in prices and that they may be accepted as security only with a higher margin.

4. Storability : In the case of pledge, the security, if acceptable, should be capable of being stored in a godown or elsewhere so that it can be safely kept in the custody of the banker and it should be possible for him to supervise it. Securities such as timber floating on rivers, and iron ore near the mines present peculiar problems of storage and supervision.

The same consideration apply to goods which cannot be stored except in air-conditioned godowns. Films and certain chemicals are examples on the point. There may be goods and materials which cannot be stored except at considerable risk to other goods stored in the same godown. These also do not constitute a good security. A similar consideration applies to patent medicines which have an expiry date. Advances against such securities are made only to parties of undoubted means and reputation, generally with a fairly high margin, and after taking proper precautions.

5. Cost and Labour of Supervision : Other things being equal, the banker will prefer a security where very little supervision is involved. He will, for instance, prefer a reliable warehouse-keeper's transferable receipt as security, to goods stored under his own lock and key. In the later case, he will have to attend to a number of points e.g. proper conditions of storage, honesty of the godownkeeper, custody of keys, display of bank's name plate, period of inspection, insurance, etc. For the same reason, he would advance against Government securities or fully paid quoted shares, in preference to goods like kapas and cotton in godowns, which require constant supervision and control.

6. Transportability : A security should be of such a nature that it can be moved from one place to another without much difficulty. For instance, if both bales of certain varieties are not easily marketable in one place and it is possible to find a ready market for them in another place, they can be railed to the other place where they can be easily disposed of. If, on the other hand, the security comprises heavy girders or machinery, it is not easy to transport them to some other place for sale as in the case of cloth bales.

7. Durability : A security should be reasonably durable. Articles such as vegetables, fruits and mutton which are easily perishable unless stored under refrigeration, may not be suitable securities. Their cost may not justify the special storage arrangement. Gur, chillies, woollen cloth, etc., require special care in storage; otherwise they depreciate in quality. There are also a few types of grains and oilseeds which can last only for one or two seasons and have to be disposed of before they deteriorate by lapse of time. There are other commodities such as metals and iron and steel goods which do not deteriorate much in quality for many years. These aspects are also kept in view by a banker when making an advance against such goods.

8. Ascertainment of Title : It should be possible for the banker to know that the borrower's title to the security is clear and undisputed. It has, therefore, to be verified if there are any other interests in the security such as prior charges or encumbrances thereon. It may be a case of house property in which a number of members of a joint Hindu family have interest, or a valuable piece of land over which there is a prior charge. In such cases, complications may arise when a banker proceeds to realise the security. There is also one more reason why banks do not usually entertain mortgage loans. The solicitors have to verify the title of the borrower to the property. Even after that is done, litigation may arise because a certain point was inadvertently omitted or an enquiry was not made relating to the claims of one or more persons to the property.

9. Easy transfer of title : The transfer of title of a security should not be difficult when occasion demands it. In the case of shares accompanied by relative transfer deeds, it is easy to get them transferred in the bank's name. The shares can also be easily sold in the market without many formalities. It is different in the case of house property mortgaged to the bank, where an elaborate legal process will have to be gone through before its sale could be effected through a court of law.

10. Absence of contingent liability : A security which carries with it an onerous liability as in the case of partly paid shares, or immoveable property where taxes are heavily in arrears, cannot be considered a suitable security. In the event of the need for sale of the security, the liabilities attached to it might either impair the chances of its sale or increase the burden of the debit at the time when possibly it is least desired.

11. Yield : In addition to all the above qualities, if a security is a source of some steady income, it is considered desirable as it affords an automatic source of repayment of capital and interest either wholly or in part. For example, if the security consists of highly marketable shares on which substantial dividend is regularly received, the banker can take a mandate to collect the dividends and appropriate them in reduction from time to time of the indebtedness in the overdraft account.

In actual practice hardly any security possesses all the desirable attributes mentioned above and such defects as exist in the security are sometimes covered by taking a higher margin or insisting on other safeguards, say a guarantee.

12. Margin : A bank does not meet cent per cent the requirements of a borrower. The borrower should have some stake in the business. In that case he will devote more time and effort to make the business a success than may be the case when he is dealing entirely with borrowed funds. Margin on securities is also maintained as a caution against fluctuations in value of securities, a shortage which may not be discovered by inspection or shrinkage which may arise on account of the nature of the goods charged. Again, in case a borrower makes default in payment of the bank's dues, the bank may have to take steps to sell the security after giving an appropriate notice to them. In case of forced sale, the security may not sell for its full value. To provide for such eventualities, the banker keeps a margin. The difference between the value of the securities and the amount up to which the borrower can draw is known as margin. The percentage of margin depends upon a number of factors including marketability and fluctuation in prices of the security, Reserve Bank's directives, and to a certain extent on the creditworthiness of the borrower.

The value of securities less margin is known as drawable limit or advance value.

11.2. TYPES OF SECURITIES

A prudent banker ensures that advances given to the businessmen and the industries are backed by sufficient collateral securities. These securities must be tangible and easily marketable so that the bank may sell them for realizing the debt in case of default by the borrower. The important types of securities lodged with banker for securing advances are :

A. Goods

B. Documents of title to goods

C. Life Insurance Policies

D. Real Estates

E. Stock Exchange Securities

F. Fixed Deposits Receipts.

G. Book debts

H. Gold, Sllver, etc. (Gilt edged securities)

I. Government Securities

J. Immovable Properties

K. Supply Bills

(A) ADVANCES AGAINST GOODS

Goods or merchandise are accepted as securities by the banks for granting loans to a borrower. The goods may be agricultural products like paddy, rice, wheat, tobacco, cotton, oil seeds and raw jute, industrial raw materials and finished products, plantation products, mining products and so on. The essential characteristic of all these goods is that they are movable.

Precautions: A banker should take the following precautions before granting advances against the security of goods :

1. The borrower should be trustworthy. He should have experience in dealing with the goods offered as security.

2. Advances should not be granted for speculative purposes.

3. The banker should have a working knowledge of the special features of commodities offered to him as security. He must study the market trends on various commodities in order to protect his interest.

4. The banker should accept only those commodities as securities which are readily saleable.

5. The banker should verify the ownership and title for the goods offered as security. The banker should deal only with the owner of goods or the agent in possession.

6. The banker should make proper valuation of the goods offered as securities.

7. The banker should not accept goods which are liable to deterioration by storage for a considerable time.

8. The banker should decide about the nature of the charge to be created on the goods offered as security such as pledge or hypothecation.

9. The banker should decide about the margin to be kept against the value of the goods.

10. In order to safeguard his interest, it is necessary for the banker to see that the goods are delivered to him before the grant of the loan.

11. The banker should take actual or constructive possession of the goods charged. It is not necessary to have the goods removed from the customer's godowns to that of the banker. The handing over the keys of his godown by the customer to the banker and transferring the services of the watchman, if any, by the customer to the banker constitute constructive delivery or transfer of possession.

12. Great care should be taken in storing the produce and goods not only to avoid their deterioration but also to guard against risks or pilferage, etc.

13. In case, it is difficult on the part of the pledger to hand over the key of the warehouse to the bank when the goods have to be processed, the physical possession or handling of the goods may be allowed to the pledger under delegated authority. In such case, it is advisable for the banker to have its name plate displayed in the godown indicating that the goods are pledged to it in order to prevent the subsequent fraudulent pledge of the same goods.

14. When it is not practicable to have constructive possession of the goods at the time of the grant of the loan, the banker may ask the customer to enter into a contract of hypothecation by which he should undertake to pledge the goods subsequently when he is required by the banker to do so.

15. Goods should be insured against fire and other risks unless insurance is specifically waived.

16. Goods must be periodically inspected as to quality, quantity and condition.

17. Dealers are required by Government to take licences for trading in certain commodities. The banker should ensure that these licences are obtained by borrowers.

18. The security documents must be correctly executed.

19. Reserve Bank of India issues directives from time to time imposing restrictions on advances against certain commodities. Bank should follow these directives.

Advantages – Goods as Securities :

1. Tangible Security : These securities enable the banker to fall back upon something tangible, in case of default by customers borrowing against such securities. A banker making an advance against goods and documents of little to goods is, in case of the insolvency of the debtor, will be able to recover the amount due to him by selling the goods, and for the balance, if any, he can prove his claim against the estate of the debtor.

2. Freedom from heavy fluctuations in prices : If the produce and goods against which loans are granted are essential items, their prices in normal times are not liable to wide fluctuation since they have a wide market; prices of commodities like wheat, cotton, sugar etc., unlike those of certain kinds of shares, do not fluctuate very widely.

3. Easy to Sell : Securities of this kind can be sold more easily than certain types of securities such as lands, buildings, etc. Particularly if the commodities are food articles, the banker has practically no difficulty in realising them, since they have a ready demand.

4. Advances only for short periods : Advances against these securities are generally seasonal and consequently for short periods; a banker lending funds against them need not lock up his money for long time.

5. Easy to evaluate : It is easy for a banker to ascertain the present market price of this kind of security. He can keep himself in touch with the markets for staple commodities by studying reports published in the daily newspapers.

Disadvantages : Most of the goods deteriorate and get damaged quickly due to improper storage. The banker may not be having the required experience and knowledge to deal with every kind of goods on which he is to advance. So he may incur losses. Also there are risks of fraud.

General precautions to be taken by banker while advancing on goods :

1. Borrower to be honest and experienced : Although goods and commodities are acceptable banking securities, the borrower-customer unless he is honest, prudent and trust-worthy, the security is of no value to the banker. The borrower should have practical experience of dealing in the goods. Unless he is trustworthy, the banker may fall a prey to the fraud committed by borrower.

2. Banker to be well acquainted with markets for commodities : It is essential for a banker advancing against goods to be familiar with different markets, such as cotton market, wheat market etc. In addition to this he should also have a sound knowledge of the conditions and customs and practices peculiar to such trade.

3. Nature of the Commodity : In order to ensure liquidity of his advances, a banker should accept only such commodities which are readily saleable and which are not liable to deterioration in quality due to storage.

4. Storage : Great care should be taken in storing the produce and goods not only to avoid their deterioration but also to guard against risks of pilferage etc. It is necessary to maintain necessary records of all godowns etc., in a godown register.

Each godown should be given a number and its measurements should be noted so as to have an idea about its capacity.

5. To deal with owner of goods or an agent in possession : In order that the banker's legal title to this class of securities be valid, he should on the one hand, deal with the owner of goods or the agent in possession. Also he should take delivery of the goods charged. This is because a transferee of goods, unlike the transferee of a negotiable security, cannot get a better title than that of the transferor except in certain cases.

6. Banker should take possession of the goods secured : In order to safeguard his interests it is necessary to have the goods removed from the customer's place to the godown of the banker. In such cases the customer hands over the keys of his godown to the banker and transfers the services of the watchman. Usually the banker puts his name plate in front of the godown where pledged goods are stored.

7. Goods or produce offered should be necessaries of life : The banker should see that the goods offered as security should be more or less necessaries of life, which can be easily sold. The risk which a banker runs in advancing moneys against staple goods is less than that in the case of other goods, the prices of which largely depend upon changes in fashion.

8. Proper care in valuation : The banker has to be very careful in estimating the value of goods. He should know the exact quantity of goods pledged as well as their prices. The goods should be loaded to the godowns in presence of a responsible bank staff. Some articles lose weight if they are storaged for long period.

9. Proper storage and insurance of goods pledged : The banker should see that the goods against which money is advanced, are properly stored and insured against loss by theft, fire, etc. The goods must be insured to their full value irrespective of the amount of advance. It should be made clear in the contract of loan that payments like rent of godown, salary to watchman and insurance premium will form part of the loan and liable for interest to be charged by the banker.

10. Strict supervision regarding releases : During the period of advance, if goods are to be released, it should be done under supervision of a responsible bank employee. Only authorised amount of goods should be released and banker should see that the balance of goods are sufficient to cover the loan given by the bank. The banker should make periodic inspection to satisfy that the goods pledged have not deteriorated due to long storage.

(B) ADVANCES AGAINST DOCUMENTS OF TITLE TO GOODS

As per Sec. 2(4) of the Sale of Goods Act, "a document of title to goods is document used in the ordinary course of business as a proof of the possession of goods and authorises, either by endorsement or delivery, the possessor of the document to transfer or receive the goods represented by such document." Documents of title to goods include, a bill of lading, dockwarant, ware-house keeper's certificate, Wharfinger's certificate, railway receipt etc.

The documents of title to goods are bill of lading, dock warrants, warehouse keeper's certificate, railway receipts and delivery orders. These documents of title to goods represent actual possession of goods. The person who possesses such documents can transfer the goods to any person by endorsement or delivery or by both. The transferee is entitled to take delivery of the goods in his own right. However, the advances against documents of title to goods are subject to certain risks and the banker should, therefore, take the following precautions:

Risks inherent in advances against documents of title to goods: While lending money on the security of documents of title to goods, the banker has to duly consider a number of factors, *viz*:

(*i*) He should know that documents of title to goods do not guarantee the quality or the value of the goods mentioned in them. For instance, in the case of bill of lading, a clause is generally introduced to the effect that 'weight and contents unknown". So the banker has to depend upon the integrity of the person sending the goods.

(*ii*) Unlike negotiable instruments, a title to the goods cannot be acquired through a person who has stolen the documents of title to goods or who has obtained the document without the seller's consent.

(*iii*) The banker should be careful as to distinguish real documents of title to goods and documents which are simply receipts, Bill of lading, dock and warehouse keeper's warrants etc., which are examples of real documents of title to goods; whereas warehouse keeper's certificate and delivery orders are just receipts and orders.

Precautions to minimise the risks : The banker should take sufficient precautionary measures, while advancing against documents. He should see that the goods covered by the documents of title are insured. Secondly, he should insist on a certificate from a reliable packer in order to make sure of the contents of the package. Thirdly, the banker should take a letter of hypothecation from the customer giving the documents as security. Fourthly, sufficient margin should be fixed taking into consideration charges accruing on account of storage, rent, insurance premium etc. Finally integrity and honesty of the customer should be taken into consideration.

General precautions to be taken in advances against documents of title to goods:

1. The documents must be carefully examined to see that they are genuine and of a recent date. The entire set of documents, as in the case of a bill of lading, must be obtained by the bank as on presentation of any document out of the set (original, duplicate or triplicate) containing ostensibly regular endorsements, the carrier has to deliver the goods to the consignee, the last endorsee, or the bearer if the last endorsement is in blank. Such delivery by the carrier discharges him from any liability to the transferee or pledgee of any other document of the same set.

2. The terms of the documents of title should be carefully studied to ensure that they contain the usual clauses, and do not carry any onerous and prejudicial

remarks and conditions. For example, if there is an adverse remark in the bill of lading, say, "goods not properly packed", or "drums leaking", the bank will be well-advised not to consider an advance against such a bill of lading except after taking additional safeguards such as a suitable guarantee. Similar is the case when a bill of lading is issued for goods not "on board": the transferee or pledgee of such a bill cannot get any title to goods not shipped (The shipping company can, however, be made liable to compensate for the loss on the ground of estoppel).

3. The goods must be adequately covered by insurance against fire and other risks, as necessary or desirable, for full value (preferably 10% or more, over the full value). The description of the goods in the bill of lading should tally with that in the policy.

4. There is no protection to a banker if packed goods do not conform to the description contained in the bill of lading or railway receipt, or the consignor commits a fraud. For example, the consignor may have despatched saw-dust instead of tea in wooden cases. Obviously, the shipping company or the railway company cannot verify the contents of the packages. The case will be similar if the boxes said to contain machinery are found to contain only junk when opened. To overcome this difficulty, a certificate from an approved packing firm may be obtained, particularly when the contents and value of the goods justify such a course.

5. The document of title to goods should be endorsed in favour of the bank, where ever necessary. For example, if in a railway receipt, the consignor himself is the consignee, he should endorse it in favour of the bank or in blank. A railway receipt where the drawee of the bill is the consignee is of no use as security as the drawee/consignee can take delivery of the goods without production of the relative railway receipt by executing an indemnity bond.

6. The documents of title to goods do not usually give a better title to the transferee than the transferor himself. In other words, they are not negotiable instruments and every transferee derives his title thereto subject to the defect, if any, in the title of the previous transferor. Under no circumstances can a title be acquired through a thief who has stolen the documents.

7. If the goods are delivered by the carriers to some wrong party against an indemnity bond, while the bank holds the railway receipt (and is entitled to the possession of the goods), the bank as a pledgee will be put to great inconvenience and expense of litigation. It is, therefore, advisable for the banker to give the carrier (e.g. railway office at destination) a notice of his interest in the goods with a request not to deliver them without production of the railway receipt duly discharged, particularly when the amount involved is substantial.

8. A letter of authorisation to clear the goods, store them and insure them, at the cost of the borrower, should be obtained.

9. The invoices should accompany the documents and the amount of the bills drawn by the customer should be within the value stated therein. Sometimes the borrower adds the cost of freight and insurance paid, in the amount of the bill, which is permissible.

10. While sanctioning advances against documents of title to goods, an appropriate memorandum of charge (such as a letter of pledge) should be taken, conferring on the bank the power to sell the goods in the event of default by the borrower and apply the proceeds towards reimbursement.

11. The banker should satisfy himself regarding the reliability of the carrier, warehouse keeper, custodian, etc.

Subject to the above observations, advances against documents of title to goods may be treated as advances against goods because, in the last analysis, it is the goods that form the security for such advances. The banker has, therefore, to ensure that the goods are readily saleable and there is an adequate margin not only for the advance but also for clearing and storage charges which may have to be incurred consequent to the non-retirement of the bill by the drawee. The financial position and creditworthiness of the borrower offering the documents of title to goods have to be studied as in the case of any other advance.

Important documents of title to goods :

1. Bill of Lading : A bill of lading is a document issued and signed by the shipowner or master of the ship or agent on his behalf, which states that certain goods have been shipped on a particular ship and which sets out the terms on which such goods have been delivered to and received by the ship. Thus, it is a document issued by shipping authorities acknowledging the receipt of goods for carrying to a port.

A bill of lading generally contains a provision to the effect that weights and contents are unknown. So the banker cannot ascertain the weight and contents of the packages on a bill of lading. However, he may protect himself by insisting on the deposit of an invoice showing the value and description of goods covered by the bill of lading. The banker should also know whether the goods and packages shipped were in good order and condition. When the goods or packages are shipped in good order and condition, a 'clean' bill of lading is issued. Another point to be considered is whether or not the goods are covered by insurance. The banker should see that the insurance policy is attached with the bill of lading. The description of the goods in the insurance policy must tally with that in the bill of lading.

A bill of lading is usually issued in triplicate, and signed by the master on behalf of the ship owner. The master of the ship is allowed to make deliver of the goods to the person who first presents one of the parts of the bill of lading provided such delivery is made in good faith and without notice of any prior claim to the goods. As a rule a condition is included in the bill of lading to the effect that "which one of the three bills is accomplished, the other two are to stand void". To be on safer side, the banker should get all the parts of the bill of lading into his hands. Where this is not possible, he should give notice of his claim to the ship owner as soon as possible, or if the goods have been landed to the shipping company or warehouse keeper. It is always advisable to get the bill of lading endorsed in blank.

When the goods arrive at the port of destination, the banker should hand over the bill of loading to warehouse keeper with instructions to collect the goods and warehouse them in the name of the bankers.

Since a bill of lading represents a receipt for goods upon shipment, it should be signed by some person authorised to sign the same on behalf of the shop owner. It acknowledges the receipt of goods for carrying to a specified port. It also contains the conditions for such transportation of goods and the full description of the goods. The bankers lending against bill of lading should take the following precautions :

Precautions :

(*i*) The banker must be satisfied of the customers business integrity and financial standing before discounting the bill of lading.

(*ii*) In order to ascertain the contents of packages, the banker should depute a representative to supervise packing.

(*iii*) All the sets of the bill of lading should be secured.

(*iv*) It will be in the interest of the banker to get the bill of lading endorsed in blank by the consignee in which case the responsibility for paying the freight will fall upon the customer and not on the banker.

(*v*) The banker should get the insurance policies covering the specified goods, instead of open policies.

(*vi*) The banker should get from the borrower a general stamped letter of hypothecation executed by virtue of which he may take possession of the goods in case the bill is not paid.

2. Dock and Warehouse warrants : A dock warrant is a document issued by a dock company stating that the goods described therein are deliverable to the person named in the warrant or to his assignee by endorsement. A warehouse warrant is a document issued by a warehouse keeper containing the same statement. When such warrants are offered as security, the banker should make it a point to register himself as owner of the goods. He should lodge with the dock company or warehouse keeper a 'stop order' so as to prevent unauthorised dealing with the goods.

It is a negotiable security and document of title should be stamped as a legal document of title. The banker should take the following precautions while advancing loans against dock warrants.

(*i*) The banker should assess the integrity of the parties concerned The financial soundness of the dock company should be weighed by the lending banker.

(*ii*) The warrants when given as security should be endorsed by the person named, and be accompanied by a memorandum of deposit or letter of lien.

(*iii*) The memorandum should give the bank authority, in the event of default of repayment, to sell the goods and out of the proceeds to repay the loan. It should also provide for insurance of the goods against fire, etc.

3. Warehouse keeper's Receipts : Such receipts are mere acknowledgement by warehouse owners. Where the banker advances money on such receipts, he should see that a delivery order is made out in his favour, otherwise he will not be able to obtain possession of the goods and have them stored in his own name.

Precaution to be take while lending against warehouse Keeper's receipt:

(*i*) Since it is not a negotiable instrument, the banker should satisfy himself as to the title of the holder or the transferor. The banker should also take a declaration from the borrower certifying that goods are his absolute property.

(*ii*) The banker should ensure that the warehouse receipt is a genuine one. The signatures of the warehousemen and the endorsee, if any should also be confirmed.

(*iii*) The receipt should be pledged with the banker with a memorandum of pledge.

(*iv*) The banker should inform the warehouseman about his claim over the receipt and latter's acknowledgement be secured by the banker.

(v) The banker should inform the warehousemen not to release the goods without the consent of the banker.

(*vi*) The banker should release the receipt on the payment of the debt. If in the meanwhile a part of the goods is to be released to the customer, the banker should issue a delivery order.

4. **Delivery orders** : A delivery order is a document addressed to the proprietors of the warehouse where the goods are lodged by their owners and convey their instruction regarding delivery. Either the owner himself or his assignee fills in the name of the person who is authorised to take delivery. If the banker simply possesses a delivery order in his capacity as a pledgee, he will not get possession of the goods, in the event of bankruptcy of customer.

It is a document containing the owner's instructions in respect of delivery, addressed to the proprietors of the warehouse where the goods are lodged. The owner fills in the name of the person, either himself or his assign who is authorized to receive the goods. The document is not required to be stamped.

Precautions :

(*i*) A banker making advance against the security of the delivery order should, for safety's sake get the goods registered in his name under advice to the warehouse keeper.

(*ii*) The standing of parties of the value of goods should be considered before agreeing to make any advance.

5. **Railway Receipt** : It is a document acknowledging the receipt of goods specified for the purpose of transportation to a place mentioned therein. It can be transferred by endorsement and delivery. As the receipt is to be produced before the railway authorities to clear the goods at the destination, advances sought against such receipts should be for very short periods.

Precautions :

(*i*) The invoice dealing the goods covered by the R/R is attached.

(*ii*) The invoice is duly signed by the party or his duly authorised agent.

(*iii*) Rates in the invoice do not exceed the market rates of the goods.

(*iv*) The goods are consigned at the Railway's risk and not at the owner's risk. If at the owner's risk and R/R is accepted, it is to be ensured that the goods are insured for door delivery.

(*v*) Railway freight has been paid on the Railway Receipt.

(*vi*) The R/R should be clean and endorsed in favour of the bank.

(*vii*) It should be carefully examined that the R/R is genuine.

Thus, the banker advancing money on Railway receipt should as usual ascertain the status of the customer, his solvency, his business condition, market value of commodities, etc.

6. Wharfinger's Certificates : This certificate like a warehouse keeper's certificate, represents merely the acknowledgement of goods by the owner of the wharf. A delivery order is necessary to effect delivery of the goods represented by the Wharfinger's certificate. If such certificates have to be offered as security to a bank, they must be in the name of the bank; otherwise in the case of borrower's insolvency, the property of the goods may rest in the official receiver.

(C) ADVANCES AGAINST LIFE POLICY

A life policy is taken for two purposes:

1. It provides protection for the dependents of the assured in case of his death.

2. It is also a type of saving and loans can be raised on the policies in times of need.

A life policy is a contract which is entered into between a certain person and an insurance corporation. Under this contract, the latter agrees to pay a lump sum of money to the assured on payment of premia for a fixed number of years or throughout the life of the assured. The policy is called a whole *life policy* when the amount is to be paid on the death of the assured. It is called an *endowment policy* when the payment is to be made on the death or on the attainment of a certain age by the assured whichever is earlier.

Precautions : The following precautions should be taken by a banker while accepting life policies for advances :

1. The bank should study the standing of the company. In India, at present, life insurance business is nationalised and all policies are issued by the Life Insurance Corporation of India. In the case of private insurance companies, the banker should see that the private insurance company in which the policy is taken should be good standing company supported by other sister companies.

2. The surrender value of the policy should be ascertained from the Life Insurance Corporation before the advance is considered. By surrender value is meant the value which the life insurance corporations is prepared to pay to the assured on surrendering the policy. The current surrender value of any policy can always be ascertained from the Corporation. This information should be periodically obtained from the Corporation. The stipulated margin, usually 10%, should be maintained on the surrender value.

3. The bank should periodically ascertain from the L.I.C. or other insurance companies that there are no encumbrances on the policy.

4. The age of the assured should have been admitted by the Life Insurance Corporation. Complications may arise in the event of the maturity of the policy or death of the assured, if his age has not been admitted.

5. The policy must be in force and premia paid up to date. The last premium receipt must be kept on record by the bank. The bank should also take from the borrower a letter containing standing instructions for payment of premium to the debit of his account.

6. The policy accepted as security should be properly assigned by the assured in the bank's favour. The assignment should normally be made on the policy itself which should thereafter be sent to the L.I.C. for registration of the assignment in its books. A separate assignment on a properly stamped paper can also be made. A notice of the assignment to the Corporation signed by the assured should also accompany the policy. The assignment should be made in the standard form which can be obtained from any office of the L.I.C.

It may be pointed out that in case a nomination is made under Section 39 of the Insurance Act, 1938, any subsequent assignment of the policy has the effect of canceling such nomination.

7. The banker should prefer the endowment policies because they have a fixed date of maturity.

8. The banker should satisfy that the party who has taken life insurance policy has an *insurable interest.*

9. The insurable interest should be present at the time of taking a policy.

10. The banker should satisfy that the premia have been paid up to date. For this purpose the banker should call for the latest premium receipt from the borrower.

11. The banker should satisfy that the life insurance policy offered as security has been in existence for a minimum period of 3 years to have a surrender value.

12. The surrender value of the policy should be ascertained from the Life Insurance Corporation. The amount of advance to be granted should be on the basis of surrender value. A margin of 10% is usually maintained.

13. The assignment takes effect only on its being registered with the L.I.C. Hence, the notice of a assignment should be given to L.I.C.

14. Assignment supersedes nomination, if any, made by the policy holder.

15. While assigning, all parties having an interest in the policy must sign the deed of assignment. If the policy taken out by the assured is for the benefit of his wife then the wife, also must concur. If any of the children interested in the policy is underaged the policy is not assignable as a minor has no power to assign.

16. When a banker makes advances against a life policy, the banker should see to it that the assured pays the premia as and when they fall due. The value of the policy also depends on the continued payment of the premia. The covenant

should stipulate that the premia shall punctually be paid by the owner of the policy; or in the event of the owner fails to pay the premium, it should empower the banker to pay the premia and debit the debtor's account in this regard.

17. After the advance is repaid, the policy should be reassigned in favour of the assured and returned to him.

Office Record : Particulars of the policy should be entered in the security register. The last premium receipt must be kept with the documents. If the policy is "with profits", bonus certificates as and when received should be attached to the policy. In case the premium are to be paid by the bank, standing instructions in this regard should be diarised.

Repayment of Advance : On repayment of the advance by the borrower, the policy should be reassigned to him and the reassignment registered in the Corporation's books. The borrower should be asked to give a receipt for the policy and other relative papers when these are handed over to him. The standing instructions regarding payment to the premium should be cancelled in the books of the bank.

Default : A reasonable notice to the borrower should be given before the bank decides to surrender the policy to the Corporation. The bank may in the alternative suggest to the borrower to repay the advance by taking a loan from the L.I.C. so that his interest may not suffer. In case of the death of the insured, the L.I.C asks for the death certificate which the banker will have to obtain from the appropriate source.

Advantages :

1. As Life Insurance has been nationalized in India, the banker need not doubt the policies issued by Life Insurance Corporation of India. The policies can be realized without any difficulty, if the policy and claims are in order. But now, several private sector companies have been set up to undertake insurance business and hence extra care should be taken by the bank.

2. The assignment of the policy in favour of the banker can be effected easily with perfect title to the banker for the policy.

3. The security can be realized immediately on the borrower's default of payment.

4. The policy is a tangible security in the hands of the bank. All that the banker should do is to ensure the regular payment of premium.

Disadvantages :

1. Policy lapses, if premium is not paid regularly. The procedure for reviving the policy is complicated.

2. A contract of insurance is a contract of utmost good faith (Uberrimae fidei), and any fraudulent representation by the insured in the proposal may render the policy invalid. The bank should, therefore, entertain advance proposals against life policies from respectable parties only.

3. The life policy usually contains a number of conditions and special restrictions. For example, almost all life policies have a "Suicide clause" stating that if the

assured commits suicide within a particular period from the date of insurance, the policy will become void.

4. There are certain policies which cannot be legally accepted as security by a banker. Life policies taken under Section 6 of the Married Women's Property Act, 1874, constitute a trust in favour of the wife and children of the insured, and cannot, therefore, form a security for any advance to be made to him. Similarly a policy already assigned/transferred by the insured in the name of his minor wife/children should be accepted as security.

5. Complications, sometimes arise when a duplicate policy is issued by the Life Insurance Corporation and the banker has no knowledge of it. It would be necessary for the bank to verify that no duplicate policy has been issued and there are no previous encumbrances on the policy. An enquiry on this point may be addressed to the Insurance Corporation.

(D) ADVANCES AGAINST REAL ESTATE

Real estates are immovable properties like land, building, factory, premises, etc. Banks do not prefer to advance money against the security of real estate because of many risks and disadvantages.

Difficulties Associated with Real Estates : There are certain drawbacks in accepting real estates as collateral securities. It is very difficult to ascertain the title to the property. It is also not readily disposable. Valuation of property is another important problem for the bank. The banker should get legal opinion about the property which is expensive. Further, the immovable properties are governed by many restrictive laws.

Precautions : When a banker decides to grant advances against such security, it should take the following precautions :

1. Title Verification : The bank should ascertain through legal experts whether the property offered as security has a clear title. Property should be free from any other charge or encumbrance.

2. Lease-hold Property : If the property is a leasehold property, the bank should examine the terms of lease and unexpired portion of the lease.

3. Valuation : Proper valuation of the property should be done with the help of approved valuers.

4. Adequate Margin : A bank should keep adequate margine i.e., it should not advance more than 50% to 60% of the value of the property in order to avoid loss due to fall in the value of the property.

5. Legal Mortgage : Even if it is expensive, the bank should obtain a legal mortgage of the property, duly registered.

6. Insurance : The bank should see that the building or factory etc., is insured against fire and other calamities and the policy should be assigned in favour of the bank.

(E) STOCK EXCHANGE SECURITIES

Stock exchange securities include all securities issued by public and private enterprises, public authorities and governments. They refer to the different kinds of shares and debentures issued by them. Bankers readily accept stock exchange securities as cover for their advances.

Advantages of Stock Exchange Securities :

1. The value of security can be easily ascertained.

2. Gilt edged securities (those which are issued by the government) are less susceptible to violent price fluctuations.

3. There are only a few formalities to be observed when stocks and shares are taken as security for the advance. This does not involve any complicated investigation of title to them. Moreover, stamp duty upon mortgage of stocks and debentures is small.

4. If stocks and debentures remain as securities for the overdraft or the advance extended by the banker and in case the customer fails to repay his dues, the former can easily sell the securities in the market and realise his dues.

5. They are easily marketable. The prices of good securities do not fluctuate widely in normal times.

6. They can be disposed off more quickly and conveniently as compared to any other security.

7. These securities yield income by way of interest and dividend The income received by the banker on such securities is adjusted towards the dues to be recovered from the customer and to that extent the customer's liability towards the banker is reduced.

8. It is convenient for the banker to examine the title of the holder. Their market prices can be easily ascertained by referring to reliable quotations published in the papers, and their transfer to the banker can be effected more easily.

Disadvantages :

1. Although, now-a-days a very few partly paid up shares exist there are additional drawbacks to partly paid up shares, as banking securities. Suppose, a customer has borrowed against the security of partly paid up shares and not able to meet a call made, then, the banker may be faced with difficulties either to advance more money to enable the call to be paid or the failure will result in the forfeiture of shares.

2. The shares of private companies are not quoted on in the stock exchange. It will be very difficult to ascertain the market value of such shares.

3. There are wide fluctuations in the prices of certain kinds of stocks. If the banker does not take sufficient care in this regard, he may have to lose his money.

4. Generally, the Articles of Association will have a clause which may empower the company with a first right over its shares. Therefore, the banker accept-

ing the stocks as covers for his advance should inform the company concerned his interest over the particular stocks. Otherwise, he may lose his priority claim over them.

5. The banker as a transferee of stocks, may have to indemnify the company from any loss which the company may sustain in regard to a forgery in the transferor's title.

Precautions :

(*i*) The banker should ascertain the current market rates of the securities by referring to financial journals, quotations, etc.

(*ii*) The banker should keep adequate margin on the advances he proposes to give.

(*iii*) The banker should intimate to the company of his 'interest' in the securities.

(*iv*) The banker should examine the Profit and Loss Account and Balance Sheet of the company which is given as securities to satisfy himself about the general working.

(*v*) In case of partly paid up securities e.g., shares, debenture etc., the banker should take an undertaking from the customer that he would pay any calls made on the shares deposited with the bank.

(*vi*) Memorandum of deposit should be executed by the customer along with the delivery of share certificates, etc.

Thus, stock exchange securities refer to shares, debentures, stocks, scripts issued by the companies and other documents issued by the government or semi-government bodies, that are listed on the recognised stock-exchanges.

Stock Exchange Securities as Banker's Securities : Prices of stock exchange securities are liable to fluctuations. But generally prices of government securities do not vary widely. The margin required by the bankers for securities of industrial concerns should be higher than in the case of government securities. The margin in the case of equity will be higher than in the case of preference shares.

In the case of the debentures of industrial enterprises, the margin will depend upon the financial position and status of the company. However, the margin for them will be higher than for government bonds. High interest rates of debentures should never be taken to indicate their good worth.

Shares of foreign companies cannot be regarded as ideal banking securities.

Valuation of shares as securities : While ascertaining the value of industrial enterprises, many factors have to be reckoned with. The banker accepting these as cover for his advance should first of all refer to stock exchange quotations. Nevertheless, he has to supplement it with his own valuation. He should analyse the past business record of enterprise concerned. He must completely examine the Balance Sheet of the enterprise. He should take into account the integrity and status of the men behind the enterprise especially, in the case of a private company, and also it's future prospects. When he fears that a depression is going to set in that industry, he shall not accept it's stocks and debentures as cover for his advance. Anyhow, he can readily accept shares which carry steady dividend.

Preference shares are more suitable as cover against advance than equity shares. The former rank before the latter with regard to the payment of dividend. Further, they carry a preferential claim in getting back the capital in the event of company's liquidation. When a company has issued only equity shares, they can serve as better banking securities, other things remaining the same. Because, if the company prospers, the value of it's equity shares may rise sharply. But when disaster overtakes the company, its equity shares will become worthless. It is always advisable for a banker to take fully paid up securities as cover.

Precautions in granting and conducting advances against shares :

(*a*) The general principles of good lending should be followed in particular, advance for speculative purposes or for cornering shares should not be allowed.

(*b*) Lending against unapproved shares should be avoided.

(*c*) Market trends should be watched from time to time (Market quotations appear in reputed newspapers)

(*d*) Risk should be spread. Shares and debentures held in large blocks by a few parties should be avoided.

(*e*) Stipulated margins should be maintained at all times.

(*f*) The conduct of the account should be watched.

(*g*) Drawing limits should be calculated upto date.

(*h*) Adequate number of transfer deeds (according to latest legal requirements – *vide* Appendix 20) duly signed and witnessed, should be taken. It is advisable to have the transfer deeds witnessed by a person who is known and is easily identifiable. The witness should state his complete address on the form. It is preferable to have a separate transfer deed in respect of each marketable lot.

(*i*) As far as possible, third party shares should not be accepted as security. If such shares are accepted, letters of renunciation should be obtained from parties in whose names the shares stand. This restriction is generally waived in the case of advances to sharebrokers in whose accounts shares are expected to move quickly.

(*j*) A mandate addressed to the company for payment of dividend direct to the bank should preferably be taken from the customer.

(*k*) Fully paid shares only should be accepted. The risk in accepting partly paid shares has already been explained above. Partly paid shares may, however, be accepted as security in very exceptional cases where the company has an excellent financial record or the customer is of high financial standing. It should, however, be noted that the Reserve Bank of India has issued a directive that no bank advances should be made against partly paid shares.

(*l*) Third party shares which are received against payment on behalf of a customer should be promptly transferred to his name (or the bank's name under proper instructions). Partly paid shares, if accepted as a special case, should not, however, be transferred to the bank's name.

(*m*) Under Section 19(2) of the Banking Regulation Act, 1949, no banking company can hold shares in a company whether as pledgee, mortgagee or absolute owner of an amount exceeding 30% of the paid-up share capital of that company or 30% of its own paid-up capital plus reserve, whichever is less. Supposing the paid-up capital of Model Bank Ltd. is Rs. 1 crore and its reserve is Rs. 1 crore, the total of paid-up capital and reserve will be Rs. 2 crore : 30% of this comes to Rs.60 lacs. Let us assume that the paid-up capital of V.K.H & Co.Ltd., is Rs. 5 crores : 30% of this will be Rs. 1.5 crores. The lesser of the two figures (Rs.60 lacs and Rs. 1.5 crores) is Rs. 60 lacs. The Model Bank Ltd. cannot hold as pledgee, mortgagee, or absolute owner shares of a total paid-up value of more than Rs. 60 lacs of V.K.H. & Co. Ltd., this being the lower limit of the two.

(*n*) The bank's own shares cannot be accepted as security. This is prohibited under Section 20 of the Banking Regulation Act, 1949.

(*o*) While considering an advance against the security of shares of another banking company, it should be remembered that under the Articles of Association of that banking company, it will probably have its first and paramount lien upon its own shares. A declaration, therefore, should be taken from the customer that he has not borrowed from the relative bank and shall not do so during the period of his indebtedness to the lending bank.

(*p*) Mutilated and damaged share certificates, certificates containing unauthenticated alterations and cancellations, as well as those which do not bear the company's seal should not be accepted.

(*q*) The companies issue temporary receipts when shares are lodged with them for transfer. Banks do not ordinarily lend against such temporary receipts if tendered by a customer as security. Many banks have been cheated in making such advances. Lending against broker's delivery orders should also be avoided.

(*r*) Proper documents of charge should be taken.

(*s*) Balance and securities confirmations should be obtained from time to time.

(*t*) Bank's rubber stamps should be put on shares or transfer deeds. There should be no cutting or over-writing on the transfer deeds.

(*u*) If the shares stand in the name of the customer, notice of the bank's charge on the shares accepted as security, should be given to the companies concerned. It may be noted that many companies have, under their Articles of Association, their paramount lien on their shares for debts due to them from their shareholders. It may, therefore, be advisable to apprise the companies concerned of the bank's charge on the shares pledged. If any company has a lien on such shares, the lien is not rendered inoperative even when the debt due from the shareholder becomes time-barred.

(*v*) In case the Reserve Bank of India has issued any directives in regard to advances against shares, these should be followed (See Appendix No.35).

In the case of joint accounts, the bank should preferably at the time of opening the account, obtain instructions as to the manner in which the account has to be conducted and the party to whom securities may be delivered. The borrowers have the right to amend or rescind the mandate.

The accounts should be looked into periodically to know the names of the parties in whose favour cheques are being drawn and the sources from which credits are forthcoming. Normally no drawings in excess of sanctioned or drawing limits should be permitted.

Debentures of a Company : Debentures are documents issued by a company as the evidence of its debt. Debenture acknowledges the company's indebtedness to its holder. While advancing loans against debentures the banker should take the following precautions:-

(*i*) The integrity of the debenture holder should be assessed by proper enquiries.

(*ii*) The standing of the company, which has issued debentures should be ascertained by reference to its accounts, reports and market quotations.

(*iii*) The borrowing powers of the company should be verified by looking to the M/A and A/A of the company.

(*iv*) The banker should lend only against fully secured debentures. He should examine the mortgage deed executed by the company and make sure that the debenture has a first charge on the assets of the company. Market value of the assets charged should be ascertained to decide about the margin to be maintained.

(*v*) He should inspect the register of the charges to know the nature and particulars of charge created for the debentures in question.

(*vi*) The validity of the title deed of the registered debenture holder should be verified from the relevant records.

(*vii*) The banker should get the memorandum of deposit along with the deposit of debenture.

Thus, the suitability of debentures as security for bank loan depends upon its market price and easy marketability.

Liquidity of Shares : When a banker accepts stock exchange securities as cover for this advances, he should select only liquid stocks and shares. Here liquidity implies easy realisability or shiftability without loss. Liquidity should never be sacrificed at the cost of profitability.

In the case of private limited company's shares as securities the banker should go through the Articles of Association of the company carefully. In general, they are not freely marketable because many restrictions are imposed with regard to transfers.

As such they are not ideal banking securities. But these restrictions are not present in the case of shares issued by a public company.

(F) ADVANCES AGAINST BOOK DEBTS

A customer of a bank may seek an advance against the security of his book debts which will either become due or accrue due in the near future. In other words, the debt which the customer has to realise from his debtor is assigned to the banker. The transfer of Property Act of 1882 permits the assignment of an actionable claim to any one. "*Actionable claim*" means a claim to any debt or any beneficial interest in movable property not in the possession of the claimant. A debt secured by mortgage of immovable property or by hypothecation or pledge of movable property is not included in actionable claim. The person who assigns an actionable claim is called the assignor and the person to whom it is assigned is called the assignee. Assignment of debts may be with or without consideration.

Precautions : A banker should take the following precautions before granting a loan on the security of a book debt :

1. The banker must enquire into the solvency of the party owing debt to the customer and also the validity of the debt.

2. The assignment of a book debt must be effected by the execution of an instrument in writing, signed by the transferor or his duly authorised agent clearly expressing his intention to pass on his interest in the debt to the assignee. If the debt is in the form of a promissory note, the assignment must be made on the note itself.

3. The assignor must pass an order to his debtor to pay the assigned debt to the banker.

4. Notice of assignment must be served on the debtor by the banker so as to make the debtor to be liable to make payment to the assignee.

5. The banker should also take an undertaking from his customer to pass on to him the amount received by the customer from his debtor in respect of the assigned debt.

6. After the assignment of the debt , all rights and remedies of the transferor, whether by way of damages or otherwise, shall vest in the transferee and the latter may sue or institute proceedings for the same in his own name without obtaining the transferor's consent and without making him a party thereto.

7. The transferee of an actionable claim shall take it subject to all the liabilities and equities to which the transferor was subject in this respect at the date of the Transfer.

(G) JEWELLERY AND BUILLION

When a banker advances money on the security of jewellery, he has to take the following precautions :

(1) He should get a declaration from the pledger according to (IA) of Rule 125/ D of Defence of India (Fourth Amendment) Rules 1966.

(2) He should carefully take into account the parity of the jewellery. He can even get the assistance of a goldsmith in this connection.

(3) He can readily lend money up to 45% of the value of the jewellery. This margin will vary from time to time. This is at the discretion of banker concerned subject to directions from the Reserve Bank of India. From February, 1995 banks were permitted to fix their own ceiling on such advances.

(4) The pledger should be the bona fide owner of the jewellery pledged. The banker should get a declaration as to this effect from the pledger.

(5) When stone-studded ornaments are pledged here the banker should take serious note of the value of the stone contents. To be on the safer side, he can approximately reduce the value of the stone contents from the total value of the jewellery.

(6) When he delivers the jewellery to the pledger, the banker should get an acknowledgement from the pledger, as to the details of the jewellery delivered.

(7) When the banker allows part delivery, much care and caution should be exercised.

(8) Advance against such securities shall be made only to people of honesty and integrity.

No banker in India will advance money on the security of bullions. When we assume that a banker advances money on the security of bullions, then he has to take all precautions mentioned above in connection with jewellery.

(H) ADVANCES AGAINST GOVERNMENT SECURITIES

Government papers (securities):

Government securities are of the safest and easily realizable securities for bank advances. Their prices generally do not fluctuate widely and ready market for them exists. Government Securities may be in the form of inscribed stock of promissory note.

Inscribed stock consists of securities issued by the Government in the name of the owner of the stock. His name is registered in the books of the Public Debt Office of the Reserve Bank of India. These certificates contain particulars like the amount, rate of interest, date of redemption etc. There is a transfer form printed on the reverse of the certificate. This transfer form has to be completed by the transferor and the transferee for getting the inscribed stock transferred to the latter. Inscribed stock is not very popular as a security because of the procedure involved in its transfer.

Government promissory note contains a promise by the President of India in the case of Central Government loans and by the Governor in the case of State Government loans to pay the holder the amount mentioned on the face of the promissory note on a particular date after certain notice according to the issue. A Government promissory note is transferable by endorsement and delivery.

Precautions :

The following precautions should be taken before granting advances against Government securities.

(1) While pledging the securities with the banker, the borrower should endorse them in favour of the banker and also execute a letter of pledge.

(2) Borrowers title to the security should be verified.

(3) The banker should ask the borrower to have the securities renewed in his favour, if they bear a number of endorsements and thereafter to endorse in favour of the banker.

(4) The banker should grant advance only against the pledge of Government promissory note. The borrower should execute the agreement of pledge.

(5) The Government promissory note should be duly endorsed in favour of the bank.

(6) The banker should decide about the margin to be maintained. Generally, banks fix a margin of 10% to 15% on the market value of Government promissory note.

(7) When the Government promissory note belongs to partnership firm, the constitution should be registered with the public Debt Office.

(8) If the borrower is a limited company, the lending banker should ensure that the power of attorney of the officer of the company endorsing the promissory notes is registered with the Public Debt Office.

(9) When semi-government securities like bonds and debentures issued by Port Trusts, Municipal Corporation etc., are offered as security, the banker should make proper enquiries about their marketability and fluctuations in prices.

(I) IMMOVABLE PROPERTY

Though immovable property, e.g., land and building, is legally sound and valid security for advances by a bank, it is not popular because of the difficulties involved in Hindu and Mohammedan customs and laws relating to succession and transfer to property place serious obstacles to the banker in accepting them as security for financial accommodation. Further there is difficulty in ascertaining the title of the customer. The valuation of a property is also very difficult. Another problem is the delay and difficulty in the realisation of such security. The banker has also to incur costs on the repair and upkeep of the property.

Precautions : A banker should take the following precautions before accepting the immovable properties as securities for granting advances.

1. Borrower's title to the immovable property must be clear beyond doubt. The banker should satisfy that there is no encumbrance against the immovable property to be mortgaged.

2. In the case of leasehold property, the lease deed of the borrower should be examined for the unexpired period of lease and whether there are any terms in the

lease deed requiring the permission of the lessor before the borrower can mortgage the property.

3. When the buildings are situated within the municipal limits house-tax receipts may be called for to ensure that there are no arrears of tax. The borrower should also be asked to produce the latest receipts of the revenue or any other Government dues.

4. The property should be valued properly by any of the following ways :

(*a*) By employing recognized valuers such as architects or engineers.

(*b*) Sale transactions of neighbouring properties.

(*c*) Valuation of the property by local authorities such as municipalities and municipal corporation.

(*d*) Making enquiries with real estate agents.

5. When limited company creates a simple or equitable mortgage of immovable property, the charges are required to the debited for registration with the Registrar of Companies within 30 days of its creation.

6. The bank should never part with the title-deeds to the borrower or his representative during the pendency of the mortgages.

7. When buildings become securities for bank's advances, the bank should get it insured for their full value at the customer's expenses. The policy should also be endorsed and assigned in favour of the bank. The borrower should undertake to renew the policy regularly till the loan is repaid.

8. With egalitarian attitude, the State Governments are often enacting Tenancy and Land Reform Acts. These invariably affect the mortgage; hence, when the banker advances money against land and buildings, he has to take serious note of the present policy of the Government in general and land, a '*dead security*' in particular. But while enacting new legislations, safeguards are always provided to protect the risks involved in such transactions.

9. The property should be valued and inspected periodically.

(J) ADVANCES AGAINST FIXED DEPOSIT

(*a*) Fixed Deposit Receipts : The banker issues a deposit receipt after accepting the customer's money at the time of deposit. It is a non-negotiable receipt. A fixed deposit made by a depositor with a banker is repayable after the specified period is over. If in the meanwhile he is in urgent need of money, he may take an advance from the banker on the security of the fixed deposit receipt. It is a good type of security being most safe and it represents a debt due from the banker-himself.

Precautions :

1. Banker should not grant an advance on the security of fixed deposit receipt issued by another bank because the latter possesses its paramount lien over the receipt.

2. While handling over the receipt to the banker, the receipt should be discharged by the depositors by signing across a revenue stamp and also sign a memorandum

of pledge.

3. After sanctioning the loan, the banker must make a note of the lien in his Fixed Deposit Register and also on the receipt itself.

4. If the receipt stands in the name of a minor, the banker should not grant a loan to a minor as it is void as per the law.

Advances against Fixed Deposit : Procedures to be followed for collection.

1. Advances should, as a rule, be granted to the person in whose name the deposit stands. If the deposit is in two or more names, a letter of authority should be obtained from all the depositors concerned. They may jointly request the bank to grant an advance to one or more of them according to their own convenience.

2. The deposit receipt should be discharged by the depositor (or all of them if they are more than one) on an appropriate revenue stamp. The signature must tally with that on the bank's record. Whether the receipt is payable "jointly" or to "either or survivor", discharge by all the depositors must be obtained.

3. The discharged receipt must be surrendered to the bank along with a letter signed by the depositor authorising the bank to appropriate the proceeds of the receipt on the due date towards the repayment of the advance.

4. The bank's lien should be prominently noted in the fixed deposit register and ledger, and also on the face of the receipt under the signature of an authorised bank official.

5. No advance should ordinarily be granted against a deposit standing in the name of a minor. In special cases where the bank agrees to make an exception, a declaration is obtained from the guardian that the money belongs to him, but has been kept in the minor's name as a matter of convenience and the amount of the advance is being utilised for the benefit of the minor.

Deposit receipts of branches : The procedure followed by a branch of a bank in granting an advance against a deposit receipt of another branch is the same as above, but as a further precaution, the lending branch should ascertain that no lien is already noted against the deposit receipt at the issuing branch. The branch granting the advance should also get the discharge on the deposit receipt duly verified by the issuing branch before lending against the receipt. The lending branch should, after granting the advance, intimate the branch which issued the deposit receipt to note and confirm its (lending branch's) lien. A letter should be taken from the borrower addressed to the issuing branch to remit the proceeds to the lending branch on maturity.

Before entertaining an advance against a deposit receipt issued by another branch of the bank, the depositor must be properly identified.

Margin and rate of Interest : A margin of 5% to 10% is usually kept while advancing against a fixed deposit receipt. In the case of cash certificates issued by a bank, the margin is calculated on the current value (surrender value) of the certificates. The rate of interest on advances against deposit receipts is ordinarily not linked with the bank rate, as is the case with other advances.

Supervision and control : Confirmation of debit balances are obtained on appropriate revenue stamps every year/half year according to the practice of the Bank. Diary notes should be taken about the maturity of the receipts.

Repayment : Usually advances against deposit receipts are automatically adjusted on maturity from the proceeds of the deposit receipts. If, however, repayment is made before due date, the deposit receipt is returned to the customer after cancellation of the discharge thereon. All notes of lien taken in the deposit register and ledger are also cancelled.

Advances against third party receipts : Some banks allow advances on the security to third party fixed deposit receipts of their own bank. In such a case the usual documents are taken from the borrower along with the fixed deposit receipt duly discharged by the person in whose name the deposit stands. The lien is registered in the bank's books and on the deposit receipt as usual. A letter of consent is also taken signed by the party in whose name the deposit is standing authorizing the bank to hold the receipt as security for the advance and to apply the proceeds of the deposit towards repayment of the advance.

Miscellaneous : As a rule, no advance should be made against a fixed deposit receipt issued by another bank. The bank has a paramount lien on the deposit receipt issued by it and may refuse to register the lien of the lending bank.

In the case of an advance against deposit receipt in the name of a limited company, the same procedure is followed as stated above, except that a duly authenticated copy of the resolution of the directors to borrow against the receipts is to be kept on record.

In the case of advances against bank's cash certificates, the same procedure as already mentioned in the preceding paragraphs should be followed mutatis mutandis.

(K) ADVANCES AGAINST SUPPLY BILLS

Customers sometimes approach banks for advances against bills for goods supplied to or contracts undertaken for Government and semi-Government departments. A party who submits a tender for supply of goods and receives an order to supply them within a stipulated period at an agreed rate is entitled, on supply, to charge the Government or semi-Government body, as the case may be in terms of the contract. Similarly a contractor on completion – partial or whole – of the contract, submits a bill for the amount to the department or body concerned in accordance with the terms and conditions of the contract.

On verification that the goods supplied conform to the terms of the contract, or part or whole of the contract work is duly completed, the bill is passed for payment by the appropriate authority. The procedure, however, of checking and passing the bills takes a couple of months and sometimes even more. Pending such verification and checking, an interim payment of about 80 per cent to 85 per cent of the value of the goods is made by the concerned authority against production of relative documents evidencing the dispatch of goods, say, a railway receipt or B/L., or against delivery of the relative goods. An inspection note issued by a representative of the Government (or semi-Government) authority, certifying the quality and quantity of the goods supplied or the contract work done, has to accompany the supplier's/ contractor's bill.

Procedure for collection: The railway receipt or the bill of lading for the relative goods is sent direct by the supplier/contractor to the concerned department and the bill for the amount is sent for collection through a bank. It is on the basis of this bill accompanied by an inspection note, as stated in the previous paragraph, that an advance is given by the bank to the borrower. Although supply bills are not accompanied by documents of title such as a railway receipt, (which are sent directly earlier), the number of the railway receipt is entered in the bill which is prima facie evidence of the goods having been duly despatched. Secondly, the goods are usually checked by a Government representative before dispatch and an 'inspection note' is issued certifying the quality and quantity of the goods.

Supply bills are not bills of exchange. They do not, therefore, enjoy the legal status of negotiable instruments. A supply bill, however, represents a debt arising out of a bona fide supply of goods etc. An assignment of the debt arising thereunder to the financing banker forms the basis of the advance to the supplier of the goods. Such bills are endorsed for payment to the bank and have to be receipted on a revenue stamp. They are also accompanied by a separate letter of authority addressed to the relative Government or semi-Government department by the supplier/contractor to pay the amount to the bank direct. In law there can be a valid equitable assignment of future debts, and such debts cannot be attached by another creditor to the detriment of a prior creditor who may have advanced money on their security.

The security available to a banker is by way of assignment of debts represented by supply bills. It suffers from the usual drawbacks of assignment of debts as security . There is always the possibility of counter-claim or set-off against the debt. Secondly, the debtor usually the Government in this case, could pay the amount direct to the creditor unless the assignment is registered with the debtor, and the debtor undertakes to pay the amount to the assignee only. Thirdly, the amount claimed by the supplier/contractor may be reduced or the payment refused, if there is a default on his part in observing the terms of the contract.

Precautions: To overcome these drawbacks, the following precautions should be taken in handling advances against supply bills:

(*i*) Great care should be taken in selecting the borrower. He must not only be honest and have enough business experience but also be familiar with the working of the Government department concerned.

(*ii*) The original contract which authorises the contractor to supply goods etc. to Government should be scrutinised. This will give the banker an idea of the amount and size of the transaction, the period within which the goods have to be supplied/contract completed, the rates accepted by the department and other terms of the contract. A strict compliance by the borrower of these conditions will be necessary.

(*iii*) An irrevocable power of attorney should be executed by the borrower in favour of the bank authorising it to collect the relative bills. The power of attorney should be registered with the Government department concerned. Usually while registering the power of attorney, the Government absolves itself of any responsibility in case the amount of the bill is paid direct to the supplier. And it does happen at times that the amount is inadvertently sent direct to the supplier instead of the banker. The banker relies on the integrity of the customer and also takes a formal letter from him undertaking to pay to the banker any amount received by him direct from the Government.

(*iv*) An inspection note or a passing certificate should be obtained. These should certify that the goods are in conformity with the requirements of the contract, say, as to quality and quantity. In some cases the department concerned gives a receipted challan, instead of an inspection note, that the goods have been actually received and are in order.

(*v*) Usually interim bills for 80/85 per cent of the value of the goods are submitted after the dispatch of the goods, the remaining 20/15 per cent being settled after the complete checking of the goods at destination. Bills drawn towards the final settlement are small in amount and are sometimes subject to heavy delay. It is only the bills in respect of 80/85 per cent of the value that are advanced against the bills for the balance being accepted usually for collection only.

(*vi*) An appropriate margin, depending on the creditworthiness of the borrower, the nature of the transaction and the previous experience, if any, in this regard should be maintained while advancing on the security of the interim bills.

(*vii*) The bills should be promptly forwarded by registered post, acknowledgement due, to the respective departments for payment, together with a covering letter which should contain clear instructions to remit the proceeds of the bill to the bank direct. Receipt of acknowledgements from the respective departments should be watched. The bank's stamp should be put on all the bills (including duplicates, triplicates etc. if any). The customer's endorsement for payment of the amount to the bank should appear prominently on the bills. It is even advisable to attach a slip to the bill stating that the amount it represents is assigned to the bank and proceeds are to be remitted direct to the bank. This will minimise the chances of inadvertent remittance to the borrower.

(*viii*) It is necessary for the banker to know the usual time taken for the realization of the bills according to the procedure of the department concerned. A careful watch should be kept and reminders promptly sent in case of delay. There have been instances where amount paid through mistake by the Government to the customers direct posed difficult problems of recovery from them.

(*ix*) The bill should be receipted by the bank on a revenue stamp.

(*x*) The possibility of forged bills being offered for collection, or of payment being held up without any valid reason cannot be ruled out. It has already been pointed out that Government does not undertake any responsibility if payment is made direct to the borrower inspite of the irrevocable power of attorney in the banker's favour registered with it and the assignment of the bills to the banker. Sometimes on account of a defect in the goods supplied or a discrepancy in past supplies, Government may and does detain, reduce, refuse or return any subsequent bills. If the bank has advanced money on the security of such bills, it has to look only to the customer for reimbursement of the amount advanced against such unpaid bills. For all these reasons, it is necessary to emphasis once again the importance of selecting only reliable customers of means for this type of business.

(*xi*) Bills remaining unpaid for sometime, say, two months or more (depending on the usual time a bill takes to be passed) are generally treated by the bank as items for collection and the amounts advanced there against recovered from the borrowers.

An advance against supply bills is a remunerative business which involves lending for short periods. The advance is, however, generally classified as clean because there is no legal or effective charge on any security and the main consideration on which the safety of the advance depends is the creditworthiness of the customer.

QUESTIONS

1. What are the general principles that are to be followed by a banker while granting secured advances.
2. Describe in detail the usual precautions which a bank should observe when granting advances against the security of (a) immovable property and (b) manufactured goods.
3. What precautions should a banker while making advances against: (a) Life Insurance Policies, (b) Commodities and (c) Fixed Deposit Receipt.
4. What are supply Bills ? Describe the procedure, documentation and precautions relating to advances against supply Bills.
5. State briefly the precautions to be taken and the procedure to be followed while granting advances against (1) Govt. Securities (2) Shares of limited companies.
6. What is trust Receipt against which goods under pledge to the Bank are released to the borrower without liquidating the advance?
7. State the precautions required to be taken by a banker in case of advance against the security of goods.
8. What precautions should a banker take while bending against documents of title to goods ?
9. Discuss the suilability of thc following as security for bank advances : (a) Debenture (b) Partly paid up shares (c) unquoted shares.
10. Why are banks reluctant to advance loans against the mortgage of real estate as a security for an advance ? What precautions are necessary in this regard ?

LETTERS OF CREDIT AND GUARANTEES

A letter of credit is a document or order by a banker in one place, authorizing some other banker in some other place, to honour the drafts or cheques of a person named in the document up to the amount stated in the letter and the issuing banker himself binds to pay the money paid. In fact, a letter of credit carries a promise or an undertaking by the issuing banker which is honoured throughout the world.

12.1. TYPES OF LETTERS OF CREDIT:

Letters of credit are of two types.

1. **Travellers' Letter of Credit** : This is issued for the convenience of the travelling public. A traveller incurs great risk if he carries with him sufficient amount of money. The money may be lost during travel. In order to avoid the risk, banks issue travellers' letters of credit to grant protection to the travellers. Under this, the banker giving such a letter of credit ásks another banker to whom it is addressed to place a specific sum of money at the disposal of or to the credit of one in whose favour the letter is issued. When this letter of credit is addressed to more than one banker, it is known as a 'circular letter of credit' and the bankers to whom it is addressed have to endorse on the letter the amount paid by each one of them. With a circular letter of credit, a letter of identification along with the specimen signature of the customer is also issued.

(*a*) Circular Notes : Circular notes are just like cheques but in specific denomination to suit the convenience of the holder. The letter of credit issued along circular notes becomes a letter of identification. The holder of circular notes can get the money by exchanging the circular notes to the bank concerned.

(*b*) Circular Cheques : These are different from circular notes and are issued without the letter of identification. These cheques are issued by the banks to their agents abroad for the purpose of selling these cheques to persons intending to visit the country of the issuing bank.

(*c*) Travellers' Cheques : Travellers' cheques are similar to circular notes. Travellers' cheques can be obtained from any bank but the holder is required to place his signature on all the cheques issued to him. At the time of encashment, he is required to sign once again. The two signatures must tally. If the cheque is lost, it is difficult for the finder to receive its payment.

2. Letters of Commercial Credit : These letters of credit play an important role particularly in international trade. In foreign trade, exporters and importers do not know each other and hence, the exporters might loose if the importers default in accepting the bill of payment. To avoid such risks, the exporter asks the importer to get a letter of credit from his bank in favour of the exporter. Based on the letter of credit, the goods may be exported to the foreign importer.

A letter of credit is a letter issued by the banker of the foreign buyer by which the issuing banker undertakes to accept the bills drawn in respect of exports made to the foreign buyer specified therein. It is usually drawn in accordance with certain terms and stipulations and it has to be made use of within a period of six months. If a letter of credit is drawn without conditions, the document is called an "open or clean letter of credit". On the other hand if documents of title to the goods are to accompany the bills, the latter is called a "documentary letter of credit". By issuing a letter of credit, the issuing bank lends its name and reputation to the buyer, who can import the goods on the basis of the letter of credit.

Parties to Letter of Credit :

1. The importer who is arranging for a letter of credit with a bank is called the opener or applicant. He requests his banker to issue a letter of credit.

2. The bank issuing a letter of credit is called opening bank or issuing bank. This bank gives an undertaking to the exporter to accept and honour the bill drawn by the exporter.

3. The exporter in whose favour a letter of credit is issued is called the beneficiary because he gets the benefit of the undertaking given by the issuing bank to honour the bills drawn on the importer.

4. The issuing bank generally sends the letters of credit to the beneficiary through its own branch in the beneficiary's country or its correspondent banker in that country. Such branch or bank is called the advising bank.

5. When the exporter draws the bill as per the letter of credit, he negotiates the bill with a banker, who pays the amount of the bill to the exporter. Such banker is called the negotiating banker.

Types of Letters of Commercial Credit : Commercial letters of credit are of various types and are classified as under:

1. Documentary Letter of Credit and Clean Letter of Credit : If the issuing bank adds a clause in the letter of credit that the document of title to the goods, such as bill of lading, insurance policy, invoice, consular invoice, certificate of origin etc., have to be attached with the bill of exchange drawn under the letter of credit, such letter of credit is called a documentary letter of credit.

If the letter of credit does not contain any such clause, it is called a clean letter of credit.

2. Fixed Credit and Revolving Credit : If the letter of credit specifies the amount upto which one or more bills may be drawn within the specified period of time, such credit is called a fixed credit.

If the opening bank does not specify the total amount up to which bills may be drawn, but specifies the total amount that may remain outstanding at a time, this type of credit is called revolving credit.

3. Revocable and Irrevocable Letters of Credit : In case of a revocable letter of credit, the opening banker reserves to himself the right or modify the credit at any time without notice to the beneficiary. Such letters of credit do not provide any security to the exporter, who should accept it only from importers of known integrity.

Under an irrevocable letter of credit, the opening bank gives an absolute undertaking to honour bills strictly in accordance with the terms of the credit. Such letters of credit cannot be cancelled or modified in any way by the issuing banker, except with the consent of the beneficiary.

4. Confirmed and Unconfirmed Letters of Credit : If an irrevocable letter of credit issued by a issuing bank is passed through a advising bank by confirming it, the letter of credit is called "irrevocable and confirmed letter of credit". Such confirmation constitutes a definite undertaking that the payment or acceptance will be duly fulfilled. Such undertaking cannot be cancelled or modified without the agreement of all parties to the letter of credit.

If the advising bank does not add his confirmation, the letter of credit remains an unconfirmed one.

5. 'With' and 'Without recourse' Credits : The drawer of a bill of exchange drawn under the letter of credit will be required to pay to the holder of the bill, if the drawee fails to honour it. In order to avoid such liability, the exporter may ask the importer to arrange credit 'without recourse' to the drawer. Under this type of credit, the issuing bank can realise the amount by selling the goods. Asking for such letters of credit are called 'Without recourse credit'.

6. Transferable and Non-transferable Letters of Credit : Under a transferable letter of credit, the beneficiary can transfer his right to draw a bill to somebody else. But it can be done only if the letter of credit is expressly stated as "transferable" by the issuing bank. If a special mention is not made, then it is a non-transferable letter of credit.

7. Back to Back Letter of Credit : When a beneficiary has a non-transferable letter of credit, he may request a bank to open a new letter of credit in favour of some other person on the security of the letter of credit issued in his favour. Such letter of credit is called a Back to Back letter of credit.

12.2. THE LIABILITY OF THE ISSUING BANKER

The liability of the issuing banker is subject to the fulfillment of the conditions laid down in the letter of credit itself. If, on the other hand, the exporter supplies inferior goods and violates his agreement with the importer, the liability of the issuing banker remains unaffected, (case law: *Tarapore and Company, Madras Vs Messrs Shao Tractor Export, Moscow and another)*.

But this does not apply in a case where the seller commits a fraud in complying with the terms of the letter of credit itself.

12.3. BANK GUARANTEE AND LETTER OF CREDIT

A distinction can be made between a letter of credit and bank guarantee. Under an irrevocable letter of credit, a direct relationship between the banker and the seller is created and the bank becomes directly liable to the seller for the payment under the letter of credit. But in a bank guarantee, the banker becomes liable only as a guarantor if the buyer fails to fulfill his obligation.

12.4. ADVANTAGES OF A LETTER OF CREDIT TO THE BENEFICIARY

A letter of credit facilitates trade transactions between importer and exporter who are not known each other. The major advantages derived by the exporter or beneficiary of a letter of credit are as follows:

1. Certainty of Payment and Avoidance of Risk : As the exporter is unfamiliar with the importer, the letter of credit provides him an absolute assurance that the bills drawn under letter of credit will be honoured. The risk of dishonour is totally avoided.

2. Immediate Negotiation of the Bills is possible under Letter of Credit : Bills drawn under L.C. are readily negotiated by the confirming/advising banker, because of the firm undertaking is given by the issuing banker.

3. The issuing banker issues a L.C. after having been satisfied that the exchange control regulations of his own country do not impose any restriction on the transfer of money. Thus the transfer risks are avoided and the exporter need not investigate into the foreign exchange regulations of the importer's country.

4. Advance can be secured by the exporter on the basis of L.C. to meet the expenses in connection with export of goods.

12.5. GUARANTEES

Ordinarily, advances given by a banker must be properly secured. But in exceptional cases, advances may be given on the personal security of the borrower, provided the banker has complete confidence in the integrity and honesty of the customer. If the banker considers that the borrower's personal security is not sufficient, an additional security is required by the banker in the form of a "guarantee" given by a third party. A guarantee is, therefore, the personal security of the third party whom the banker has got confidence. In recent years, the importance of giving guarantee as a security for loans has greatly increased.

Section 126 of the Indian Contract Act, 1872 defines a contract of guarantee as "a contract to perform the promise or discharge the liability of a third person in case of his default". The person who gives the guarantee is called the surety or the guarantor. The person in respect of whose default, the guarantee is given is called the principal debtor and the person to whom the guarantee is given is called the creditor. Hence, it is clear that contract of guarantee is a secondary contract, the principal contract being between the creditor and the principal debtor themselves. Therefore, the existence of a principal contract is essential for entering into a contract of guarantee.

12.6. CONTRACT OF INDEMNITY

Another contract which appears similar to the contract of guarantee is the contract of indemnity. Section 124 of the Indian Contract Act, 1872 defines the contract of indemnity as "a contract by which one party promises to save the other from loss caused to him by the conduct of any other person". The person who makes such a promise is called the 'indemnifier' and the other person is called the 'beneficiary'. For example, if the consignee of goods has lost the lorry receipt, he may take delivery of the goods from the transport company by furnishing an indemnity bond, thereby promising to reimburse the transport company any loss that may be caused to it by giving delivery of the goods without the lorry receipt.

A contract by which one party promises to save the other (beneficiary) from loss caused to him by the conduct of the promissor (indemnifier) himself, or by the conduct of any other person, is called a "contract of indemnity". For example, A contracts to indemnify B against the consequences of any legal proceedings which C may take against B in respect of a certain sum of Rs. 5000/-. This is a contract of indemnity. If the beneficiary is sued, he is entitled to recover from the indemnifier all sums including costs and damages which he may have been compelled to pay in respect of any matter to which his promise to indemnify applied. However, in the case of any sum or costs which the beneficiary may have paid, he should have acted in a prudent manner as if no contract of indemnify existed.

12.7. DISTINCTION BETWEEN A CONTRACT OF GUARANTEE AND A CONTRACT OF INDEMNITY

Though both the contracts seem to be alike, they differ in many respects :

1. In the case of a contract of guarantee, there are three parties, viz., the surety or guarantor, the principal debtor and the creditor. But in the case of contract of indemnity, there are only two parties, viz., the promissory or the indemnifier and the party to be indemnified or insured.

2. In the case of guarantee, the liability of the surety to the creditor is secondary, the primary liability being that of the principal debtor. But in the contract of indemnity, the liability of the indemnifier to the indemnified is primary and independent.

3. In a contract of guarantee, there are three contracts. One between the principal debtor and the creditor, the second between the creditor and the surety and the third between the surety and the principal debtor. But in the contract of indem-

nity, there is only one contract i.e., between the indemnifier and the indemnified.

4. In the contract of guarantee, there is usually an existing debt, the performance of which is guaranteed by the surety. But in the contract of indemnity, the liability of the indemnifier arises only on the happening of a contingency.

5. In the guarantee, it is necessary that the surety should give the guarantee at the request of the debtor. But in the indemnity, it is not necessary for the indemnifier to act at the request of the indemnifeed.

6. The guarantor possesses certain rights which are not available to the indemnifier. For example, the surety has the right of subrogation *i.e.*, he can recover the amount paid by him from the principal debtor. The indemnifier cannot claim such reimbursement from anybody else.

Differences between Contract of Guarantee and Contract of Indemnity

Contract of Guarantee	Contract of Indemnity
(1) There are three parties, *viz.* the l principa debtor, the creditors and surety.	(1) There are two parties, *viz.* indemnifier and the indemnified.
(2) It must be in writing.	(2) It need not be in writing.
(3) The liability of surety is subsidiary.	(3) The liability of the inddemnifier is primary.
(4) The liability of the surety is subsisting	(4) The liability of the inemnifier is contingent.
(5) The surety can sue the principal debtor in his own name after paying the creditor.	(5) The indemnifier cannot sue third party in his name even after making good the loss unless there is an assignment in his favour from the indemnified.

Thus, the test is applied to determine whether the contract is one of guarantee or indemnity is whether the obligation has been undertaken at the debtor's request in which case the contract is one of guarantee. If the obligation has been undertaken without any request, express or implied of the debtor, the contract is one of indemnity.

12.7.1. ESSENTIAL FEATURES OF A CONTRACT OF GUARANTEE

1. A contract of guarantee may be either oral or written. Invariably bankers insist to have a written contract of guarantee as in England, where a guarantee must be in writing.

2. The contract of guarantee requires the concurrence of all the three parties concerned to the contract of guarantee.

3. Under certain special circumstances, a contract of guarantee is implied. For example, the endorser of a bill of exchange is liable to pay, as a surety, the amount of the bill of exchange to the payee in case the acceptor of the bill defaults to fulfill his promise.

4. A contract of guarantee, like any other valid contract, must have consideration. Here consideration received by the principal debtor is sufficient for the surety and it is not necessary that it must necessarily result in some benefit to the surety himself.

Kinds of Guarantee : Guarantees are of two types (kinds)

(*a*) Specific guarantee

(*b*) Continuing guarantee

(*a*) Specific Guarantee : It refers to a specified transaction only. Guarantee will lapse as soon as the specific transaction is liquidated. It relates to one particular debt only and it is not applicable to fresh loan renewed immediately after the first loan.

(*b*) Continuing Guaranee : It is one which extends to a series of transactions, between the banker and customers within an agreed limit. It is not affected by any payments, for it is framed to secure the final debt balance.

It is advisable to the banker to take continuing guarantee so that the surety is made liable for the subsequent advances granted to the customers.

(***a*) Example of specific guarantee:** Anand purchases goods from Bharat on credit. Chandra agrees to stand as a surety which means that if Anand does not pay the price of goods, he will pay.

(***b*) Example of continuing Guarantee** : Ashok, in consideration that Bhagwan will employ Charan in collecting the rents of Bhagwan's zamindari, promises Bhagwan to be responsile, to the amount of Rs. 6000, for the due collection and payment by Charan of those rents.

12.8. LIABILITY OF THE SURETY

1. Nature and Extent of Liability : It is co-extensive. According to Section 128 of the India Contract Act "the liability of the surety is co-extensive with that of the principal debtor unless otherwise provided by the contract". This means that the quantum of liability of a surety is the same as that of the principal debtor, unless there is a contract to the contrary. That is, the liability of the surety can neither be more nor less than that of the principal debtor, though by a special contract, it may be made less than that of the principal debtor, but never greater.

2. Limitations of Surety's Liability : Though the liability of the surety is co-extensive with that of the principal debtor, he may limit his liability.

3. The Time Liability arises : The liability of the surety arises as soon as the principal debtor makes a default. The creditor is not bound to proceed first against the principal debtor before recovering the amount from the surety. In other words, the creditor can sue the surety without sueing the principal debtor. In the *Bank of Bihar Limited Vs Damodar Prasad and Another,* the Supreme Court held that the liability of the surety is immediate and cannot be deferred.

4. Liability of Co-sureties : If there are more than one person guaranteeing a debt, all of them are called co-sureties and are liable to the principal debtor. If one of the sureties paid the entire amount to the creditor, he is entitled to claim contribution from his co-sureties.

12.9. RIGHTS OF SURETY AND THE CIRCUMSTANCES UNDER WHICH A SURETY IS DISCHARGED

Rights of surety can be classified as under :

(*a*) Rights against the principal debtor.

(*b*) Rights against the creditor.

(*c*) Rights against the co-sureties.

(*d*) Right to revoke continuing guarantee.

(a) Rights against the Principal Debtor :

1. Right of Subrogation : When the principal debtor defaults to pay the creditor and the surety pays, the surety steps into the shoes of the creditor and acquires all right of the creditor against the principal debtor (Section 140 of Indian Contract Act, 1872). Thus the surety is entitled to the benefit of every security which the creditor has against the principal debtor provided such security was in existence at the time of the contract of guarantee.

(*i*) The right of subrogation i.e., after discharging the liability of the principal debtor, the surety is entitled to all those rights which the creditor himself exercises against the principal debtor.

(*ii*) The surety can proceed against all those securities of the principal debtor, which the creditor himself can proceed against.

(*iii*) The surety is entitled to be indemnified for all payments rightfully made by him.

(*b*) Rights against the Creditor :

(*i*) The surety may require the creditor to sue the debtor while giving guarantee to the creditor.

(*ii*) In the case of fidelity contracts, he can insist upon the creditor to dispense with services of the principal debtor when principal debtor's dishonesty is established.

(*iii*) He can claim set off or counter claim which the principal debtor could have obtained against the creditor.

(*iv*) On payment of the guaranteed debt, he can require the creditor to assign to him all the securities held by the creditor in respect of the debt.

(*c*) Rights against the Co-sureties :

(*i*) All the sureties shall bear equally the loss caused by the insolvency of the principal debtor.

(*ii*) When the co-sureties agreed to become liable in different sums, they should contribute accordingly.

(*d*) Right to revoke continuing guarantee:

The surety has the right to revoke at any time a continuing guarantee by giving notice of such revocation to the creditor. This right is acceptable only for future transactions, but he remains liable in respect of the transactions which have already taken place.

Discharge of Surety from liability:

(1) When the principal debtor pays the debt in full in case of specific guarantee, the contract of guarantee is discharged.

(2) The surety is discharged by revocation as to future transactions in case of continuing guarantee.

(3) The surety is discharged from liability if the contract of guarantee becomes void or voidable on the ground of misrepresentation or concealment by the creditor with regard to the material fact.

(4) The surety is discharged,

(*a*) By variance of contract.

(*b*) By release or discharge of principal debtor.

(*c*) By composition or compromising with debtor.

(*d*) By act of omission or commission impairing surety's remedy.

(*e*) By loss of security by creditors.

Thus, surety or the guarantor is the third party who undertakes to repay the loan given to a customer, in case the customer fails to repay it to the bank. The banker loses his right to recover the amount from the surety, if the surety is discharged.

12.10. OBLIGATION OF CREDITOR (BANKER) TOWARDS SURETY

The banker as the creditor of the customer (principal debtor) has certain obligations towards the surety under contract of guarantee.

1. The banker as creditor should not change the original terms of the contract, without taking consent of the surety. If he does so without the consent of the surety, the surety is discharged from his obligation as regards the transactions undertaken subsequent to the date of such charge.

2. The banker as creditor should not release the principal debtor or do any thing of which may discharge the principal debtor. If he does so, the surety is discharged from his liability.

3. The creditor should not give any extension of time to the debtor, unless the same is provided for in the contract of guarantee. If the time is extended, it is possible that in the meantime the debtor may die or become insolvent with the effect that the surety may not be able to recover the amount from the debtor.

4. It is the duty, on the part of the creditor to do every act which is necessary to protect the rights of the surety.

5. The banker should not mishandle or make unauthorised dealings in securities belonging to the debtor without the concurrence of the surety.

6. The banker should not release the principal debtor from liability without the prior consent of the surety.

7. The banker should reserve a clause in the contract of guarantee giving the banker necessary authority to deal with the securities as he may think fit so that he

may not be held liable by the surety for any depreciation in those securities due to the mishandling of the customer's securities.

Rights of the Banker against Surety :

1. The banker has a right to recover from the surety all that the principal debtor owes to him in case the principal debtor defaults in payment of the debt.

2. The banker has a right or claim on the estate of the surety, in case he dies. Surety's death does not underline the guarantee and the banker, on default of the debtor, is entitled to recover the money due from the legal representatives of the decreased surety.

Upon the bankruptcy of the surety, the banker can stop the account and demand payment from the principal debtor and default prefer claim on the surety's estate. Similar would be the effect when surety becomes lunatic.

3. If the banker has with him any account of the surety, he has a right of lien on the balance of his account. This right arises when the principal debtor fails to repay him debt.

4. Mere forebearance on the part of the banker to sue the debtors does not affect his claim on the surety.

5. Where there are co-sureties, a release by the banker one of them does not discharge the other surety or sureties.

12.11. PRECAUTIONS TAKEN BY A BANKER FOR GRANTING ADVANCES AGAINST GUARANTEE

Guarantee is an undertaking to perform the promise or discharge the liability of a third person in case of his default. There are two component contracts one between the principal debtor and the creditor and another between surety and the creditor. In the contract of guarantee, the surety is liable only when the 'Principal debtor' commits default.

When a customer is not in a position to offer any collateral security for an advance, the banker can lend on a guarantee. It is easy to obtain a guarantee than to insist for a tangible security. There is no need for lengthy legal formalities like registration etc. A simple signature of the surety on the duly stamped guarantee form is sufficient to constitute the guarantee the banker for the debtor. It is adjustable to different types of dealings and circumstances. Thus, customers who have little or no tangible security of their own to offer as a cover for a proposed advance often inform the bank or lender that they have a relative or friend, who is prepared to guarantee the repayment of the loan.

Precautions to be taken before granting advances against guarantee:–

Bankers have to consider the guarantee proposal form and advance from two aspects; *viz.*,

(*a*) Business Aspect : *i.e.* financial standing of the surety,

(*b*) Legal Aspect : *i.e.* execution of guarantee deed.

It is the primary duty of a shrewd banker to assess the financial position of the security before accepting his guarantee for an advance. The security behind a guarantee is the instant ability of the guarantor to pay, when called upon. The banker should enquire about the integrity and financial strength of the surety. The banker should always keep continuous touch with the financial conditions of the surety, till the guarantee is terminated.

It is advisable for the banker to get the guarantee agreement signed by the surety in the bank itself. He should avoid misrepresentation by the borrower and the banker need not disclose the full state of debtor's account nor should he misrepresent any fact to secure a guarantee.

The deed form should be stamped as per the provision of the Indian Stamp Act. The guarantee forms are detailed documents drafted in consultation with legal experts, to protect the interests of bankers. Banker should not advance money on guarantee contract unless it is strictly in accordance with bank's own forms.

Thus, guarantee serves a supplementary cover to the personal security of the principal debtor. Ease of enforcement is another merit of guarantees. Bankers have to consider the guarantee proposal for an advance from the business and legal aspect. The banker should take into account any prior considerations and conditions attached by the surety in signing the contract of guarantee.

(*i*) The guarantor should be highly creditworthy. An ideal guarantor is one who can be considered good for a clean advance to the extent of the guarantee.

(*ii*) Periodical reports on the borrower as well as the guarantor should be obtained. The value of the guarantee has to be maintained throughout the currency of the advance.

(*iii*) The letter of guarantee should be signed in the presence of an officer of the bank. Sometime back, there was a case where the proposed guarantor, who was a very well-known businessman, happened to be the borrower's relative. The borrower asked the Bank Manager to give him the guarantee form for is relative's signature, to which the Manager agreed. As the debt was not repaid, a notice of demand was sent to the guarantor who denied any knowledge of the transaction. The borrower had obviously forged the signature of the guarantor. The bank lost the case filed against the guarantor.

(*iv*) The banker should not approach any person to give a guarantee for an advance to a borrower.

(*v*) In the case of joint, or joint and several guarantee, no advance should be made until the signatures of all the proposed guarantors are obtained. Suppose, one out of two or more proposed guarantors signs the letter of guarantee and, in anticipation of obtaining the other signatures, the advance is made. If any of the other proposed guarantors refuses to sign the letter of guarantee, the guarantor who has signed the document may avoid his liability on the plea that the guarantee could not be operative unless all the proposed guarantors signed the document (Section 144).

(*vi*) Periodical confirmation of the guarantee should be obtained from the guarantors separately along with balance confirmations duly signed by the borrower to avoid the guarantee agreement becoming time-barred. The period of limitation for filing a suit on the basis of an agreement of guarantee is 3 years. The agreement should be properly stamped before execution. The duty payable is different in different states.

(*vii*) Any amounts received from the guarantor towards repayment of the advance in fulfilment of his obligation should be credited to a separate "Suspense" account and not directly to the credit of the borrower's account if the banker intends to claim on the debtor's estate.

(*viii*) On the death, insolvency or lunacy of the principal debtor or the guarantor, or on receipt of a notice of determination from the guarantor, the account should be broken to avoid the operation of the rule in Clayton's case. In the case of lunacy or insolvency of the guarantor, the principal debtor should be informed and a suitable new arrangement discussed with him. In the meantime, steps should be taken to ensure that the banker's remedy against the guarantor is not prejudicially affected.

(*xi*) The guarantee should be taken on the bank's approved form only.

(*x*) No bank should lend to a customer solely relying on a guarantee. Even if the contract of guarantee is legally valid, it cannot ultimately produce cash from a guarantor who may be incapable of meeting his liability.

12.12.TERMINATION OF THE GUARANTEE

1. It is terminated by mutual agreement of parties.

2. Notice of revocation by the surety as per section 130 of the Contract Act puts an end to the guarantee, as to future transactions.

3. Variation of the terms of the contract by the creditor without surety's consent seals of the guarantee under section 133 of the contract Act.

4. Discharge of the debtor by the creditor without surety's consent automatically operates as a discharge of the surety's guarantee.

5. Compounding or compromising with the debtor by the creditor without surety's approval result in the termination of the guarantee.

6. Notice of surety's death, lunacy or insolvency would amount to determination of the guarantee.

7. Death, Lunacy or insolvency of the principal debtor will entitle the creditor to determine the guarantee.

8. Misrepresentaion of the facts to secure a guarantee entitles the surety to set aside the contract.

9. Giving time to the principal debtor or showing similar indulgence to him without the consent of surety would operate as a terminus to the guarantee contract.

10. Change in the institution of persons to or for whom the guarantee is offered will put an end to the guarantee.

QUESTIONS

1. Discuss the precautions a banker should take in granting loans and advances against guarantee.
2. Distinguish between contract of guarantee and contract of indemnity.
3. State the advantages of accepting guarantee as security for a loan.
4. What do you understand by 'letter of credit' ? What is its significance in the financing of foreign trade ? Explain the liability of the banker issuing a Letter of Credit.
5. Explain the essential features of an irrevocable letter of credit.

PURCHASE AND DISCOUNTING OF BILLS

Purchasing and Discounting of Bills is another form by which a banking institution sanctions loans and advances without any collateral security. Discounting of bill is nothing but purchasing a bill by a bank as transferee for value. The holder of a bill of exchange can get the bill discounted by getting cash from a bank before its date of maturity. The banker charges a small amount as interest for the unexpired period of the bill and compensation for the expense and trouble in realisation.

Generally bills of exchange arise out of commercial transactions both in inland trade and foreign trade. When the seller of goods has to realise his dues from the buyer at a distant place immediately or after the lapse of an agreed period of time, the instrument of bill of exchange facilitates this task with the help of the banker.

The bills of exchange are classified into (i) demand bills and usance bills, and (ii) clean bills and documentary bills. When a bills is payable 'at sight' or 'on demand' or on 'presentment', it is called a sight bill or a demand bill. If a bill is drawn payable after a certain period of time, say 30, 60 or 90 days after date or after sight, it is called a usance bill. No stamp duty is necessary in the case of demand bills whereas the usance bills are to be properly stamped till 1989. But the govt of India remitted the stamp duty chargeable in respect of usance bills of exchange, provided certain conditions are fulfilled.

When a drawer of a bill encloses with the bill the documents of title to goods such as railway receipt or lorry receipt to be delivered to the drawee of the bill on payment or against acceptance of the bill, the bill is called a documentary bill. In the absence of such documents, it is called a clean bill.

By discounting bills of exchange with bank, the person who gets the bill discounted has to part with all rights, title and interest in the bill and its proceeds. The banker becomes the holder for value. He can deal with and part with the bill as he likes. He gets absolute title to the bill which covers the whole face value. Whereas if a bill is pledged, the banker has an interest equal to the amount he has advanced on the security of the bill. The bill remains the property of the pledger.

13.1 ADVANTAGES OF DISCOUNTING OF BILLS BY BANKS

Discounting of the bill is an ideal form of bank leading. It has the following advantages :

(a) Certainty of Payment on Due Date :- It is almost certain that the amount invested in first class bills realised on the due date, because a trader who has accepted a bill would definitely honour it as otherwise his credit suffers and secondly, if the acceptor fails to honour on the maturity of the bill, the banker will get his money from his customer for whom he discounted the bill.

(b) Employment of funds for a definite period :- As the bill is drawn for a definite period, the banker is able to employ his funds for a definite period by discounting bills for that definite period. For instance, if a banker receives a deposit of Rs. 1,00,000 for three months he can use the amount in discounting bills which will mature just a day or two before the deposit falls due.

(c) Stability in value :- The value of bill will not change as in the case of many other securities such as stock exchange securities. Though there may be some fluctuations in discount rate depending on the changes in the credit policies, the variations in value are comparatively small and are of no material consequence even if the banker is compelled to convert his bills into cash.

(d) Liquidity :- Bills are highly liquid assets. In case of urgent or unforeseen demands, the banker can convert the bills held by him into cash, by having them discounted with the central bank of the country. That is the reason why it is said that "prudent banker is one who knows the distinction between a bill and a mortgage."

(e) High and quick yield :- The yield from the discounting of bills is slightly higher than that from loans or advances and further the interest known as discount is deducted at the time of discounting of bills, whereas in the case of other loans or advances, it becomes payable only when the principal falls due or is payable quarterly, half-yearly or yearly.

(f) Simple legal remedy :- In the event of nonpayment of bill on maturity, the legal remedy for recovering the amount is relatively simple. In case of dishonour of a bill on the date of maturity, what the banker has to do is to simply have it noted, protested and then the amount of such bill should be debited to his customer's account.

13.2 Though there are several advantages as stated above in favour of discounting of bills, certain precautionary steps have to be taken before advancing loans by discounting of bills.

(a) Integrity of the Parties :- Firstly, the banker has to satisfy himself regarding the credit standing and integrity of not only the drawer of the bill, but also of the acceptor and other endorsing parties. If the various parties to the bill are the customers of the bank, fairly reliable information can be gathered from its own records.

If the acceptor or endorser happens to have account with another bank an enquiry can be made in the ordinary way and will be obtained easily. Generally banks keep detailed information regarding the credit standing of different customers whose names are likely to appear on commercial bills.

(b) Genuine Trade Bills :- Secondly, the banker should see that the bills he discounts, are genuine commercial bills and not in the nature of accommodation paper, as the former have the advantage of being backed up by goods, while the latter is without any backing. For example, when a cloth merchant in Bombay buys a few packs of nitwares from a Tiruppur manufacturer of nitwares and being unable to pay cash for this purpose, accepts a bill drawn upon him by the Tiruppur manufacturer, he hopes to sell the goods and meet his acceptance with their sale proceeds. Thus the bill is backed up by actual goods, i.e., nitwares. On the other hand, if the bill discounted is a "Kite" or accommodation bill, which is merely a means between the drawer and the acceptor of raising money, it will not have such goods as a backing. Though it seems that it may be difficult to distinguish between the genuine bills and commercial papers, the bankers do not have much difficulty in differentiating them. It should also be noted that bills, given in payment of fixed assets such as buildings or machinery should be avoided, as such bills cannot be regarded as liquid.

(c) Preference to short term bill :- Banks should also prefer the bills drawn for short periods, not exceeding three months to those drawn for long periods. Generally bills drawn for more than three months and above are not discounted.

(d) Bill must be complete and fee from defects :- The banker should see that the bill is complete in every respect i.e., the bill must not be overdue or defective in any other respect. In case the banker comes to know of a defect in the title of his customer to the bill, he should refuse to discount it, as the banker cannot be treated as a holder in due course and consequently his title to the bill will be rendered defective.

(e) Proper endorsements :- While discounting a bill, the banker should see that the bill is in proper form. The endorsement, if any on the bill must be complete and regular, i.e., the bill must comply with the requirements of the law regarding the acceptance and that the customer's endorsement on the bill.

(f) Discounted only for customers :- The banker must also see that the bill is discounted only for his customer and not for others who are not customers. Bankers should provide this service only for their customers.

(g) Customer's Account Credited :- When a banker discounts a bill, he will credit the customer's account with the amount of the bill less discount.

The bill is then entered in the bills receivable book and its date of maternity noted in the bills receivable diary.

(h) Payment of Stamp Duty :- The bill must be duly stamped and conform to the provision of the Indian stamp Act, 1899.

(i) Procedure on the dishonour of a bill :- In case the bill discounted is dishonoured, the banker should follow the following procedure :

(*i*) If the customer has sufficient credit balance, his account should be firstly debited with the amount of the bill plus changes in connection with dishonour. The bill should be returned to him with an advice for debiting the account.

(*ii*) If the customer's account does not have sufficient balance to meet the bill, notice of dishonour and a request/notice for payment should be made to the customer and to all parties liable to the bill. The banker should keep possession of the bill and retain the customers credit balance, adjusting the amount of the bill.

(j) Notice of dishonour :- The banker should also be careful in sending the notice of dishonour. If the customer resides in the locality of the banker, the notice of dishonours should be sent to reach the customer on the same day of dishonour. When they reside in different places, the notice must be despatched at least on the same day after dishonour. Otherwise the banker will lose his rights to claim the amount.

QUESTIONS

1. Write the precautions a banker should take in discounting of bills of exchange.
2. What are the advantages to a banker for lending money by discounting of bills of exchange ?

Model Question Papers

Banking Law & Practice

Time : Three Hours Maximum : 100 Marks

Section A — (10 × 1 = 10 marks)

Answer All the Questions.

All questions carry equal marks.

Choose the best answer for each of the following from the given alternatives :

I. A banker has a particular lien on :

(*a*) Savings deposits

(*b*) Bills of Exchange given for collection

(*c*) Gold ornaments given for safe custody.

(*d*) Goods given as security.

II. When money is deposited for a specific purpose, the banker becomes a :

(*a*) Trustee (*b*) Debtor

(*c*) Creditor (*d*) Bailee.

III. A letter of introduction is very essential in the case of a :

(*a*) Fixed deposit account. (*b*) Recurring deposit account

(*c*) Savings deposit account(*d*) Current account.

IV. In the case of a firm, the account must be opened in the name of :

(*a*) a partner (*b*) all partners

(*c*) the firm (*d*) the firm and a partner.

V. The document which can be used only for making local payment is:

(*a*) a cheque (*b*) a Bill of Exchange

(*c*) a draft (*d*) a Banker's Cheque

VI. The essential element of a special crossing is :

(*a*) two lines (*b*) two parallel transverse lines.

(*c*) words "Not Negotiable". (*d*) Name of a banker.

VII. A banker becomes a "holder for value" When :

(*a*) he collects a cheque

(*b*) he credits a customer's account before collection

(*c*) he collects to a wrong account

(*d*) he collects a crossed cheque.

VIII. The statutory protection is given to a paying banker when he makes :
(*a*) payment in due course
(*b*) payment to a holder
(*c*) payment to a holder in due course
(*d*) payment on a crossed cheque.

IX. Which one of the following is the most liquid asset?
(*a*) Land and buildings (*b*) Bill of Exchange
(*c*) Stock (*d*) Gold.

X. The most suitable charge for an industrialist is :
(*a*) Hypothecation (*b*) Lien
(*c*) Pledge (*d*) Mortgage.

SECTION B — (5 × 6 = 30 marks)

Answer All the Questions

All questions carry equal marks

Each answer should not exceed 300 words.

XI. (*a*) "A banker is a privileged debtor" — Do you agree? Support your answer with valid reasons.

Or

(*b*) Under what circumstances can a banker disclose his customer's account?

XII. (*a*) Discuss any six features of a fixed deposit receipt.

Or

(*b*) Discuss any six features of a fixed deposit receipt.

Or

XIII. (*a*) Distinguish a cheque from a bill of exchange.

Or

(*b*) Discuss the various forms of conditional endorsement.

XIV. (*a*) Explain the concept of "payment in due course".

Or

(*b*) What are the duties of a collecting banker?

XV. (*a*) Bring out any six drawbacks of lending against immovable properties.

SECTION C — (5 × 12 = 60 marks)

Answer All Questions

All questions carry equal marks.

Each answer should not exceed 600 words.

XVI. (*a*) What is banker's lien ? Under what circumstances can he exercise it?

Or

(*b*) Explain the law relating to a banker's obligation to honour his customer's claques.

XVII. (*a*) Bring out clearly the function of a pass book.

Or

(*b*) What precautions should a banker take while opening an account in the name of a joint stock company?

XVIII. (*a*) Define crossing. Bring out its various forms and their significance.

Or

(*b*) Define material alteration and discuss the duties of a banker in respect of a cheque wherein the amount has been altered ?

XIX. (*a*) What constitutes negligence under Sec. 131 of the Negotiable Instruments Act ?

Or

(*b*) Outline the precautions which a paying banker should take before honouring a cheque.

XX. (*a*) Describe the different methods of creating a charge and bring out their features.

Or

(*b*) Discuss the drawbacks of lending against goods and state the precautions which a banker should take while lending money against them.

BANKING LAW

Time : Three hours **Maximum : 100 marks**

SECTION A — (10 × 1 = 10 marks)

Answer All the Questions

Choose the correct answer for each of the following from the given alternatives.

I. A customer of a banker is one who
(*a*) Frequently visits the bank
(*b*) Has transactions with the bank
(*c*) Has an account with the bank
(*d*) None.

II. The general relationship between a banker and his customer is that of
(*a*) Debtor and creditor (*b*) Creditor and debtor
(*c*) Lessor and lessee (*d*) Agent and principal

III. A fixed deposit receipt can be
(*a*) Transferred (*b*) Negotiated
(*c*) Assigned (*d*) Endorsed.

IV. No introduction is necessary for opening
(*a*) Savings account
(*b*) A domiciled bill
(*c*) Account of a registered firm
(*d*) None of the above.

V. If a bill is draw in sets of three copies, it is

(*a*) A foreign bill (*b*) A domiciled bill

(*c*) Inchoate bill (*d*) None.

VI. Crossing a cheque means

(*a*) Cancelling the cheque

(*b*) Putting the "*X*" mark on the cheque

(*c*) Drawing two parallel lines on the face of the cheque

(*d*) Drawing two parallel lines on the back of the cheque.

VII. If the amount of a cheque in words and figures differs

(*a*) The amount mentioned in words should be paid

(*b*) The amount mentioned in figure should be paid

(*c*) Lower of the amounts should be paid

(*d*) The cheque cannot be paid.

VIII. When a banker accepts a cheque for collection, he should follow the instruction of

(*a*) The drawer (*b*) The paying banker

(*c*) The customer (*d*) None.

IX. The sale and purchase of shares on behalf of customer should be executed

(*a*) Through share brokers

(*b*) Through stock exchanges

(*c*) With parties directly

(*d*) Through the head office of bank.

X. Consumer credit loans are available to

(*a*) Salaried persons (*b*) Depositors of the bank

(*c*) Professionals (*d*) Any of the above.

SECTION B — (5 × 6 = 30 marks)

Answer All the Questions

Each answer should not exceed 300 words.

XI. (*a*) Define the term "customer". When does a person become a customer?

Or

(*b*) Explain the rule in Claytons case.

XI. (*a*) What are the features of current accounts?

Or

(*b*) What are the precautions to be taken by a banker when opening an account in the name of a lunatic?

XIII. (*a*) Define "Cheque" and bring out its features.

Or

(*b*) Write a note on "Not negotiable crossing".

XIV. (*a*) Discuss the risks involved in honouring a post dated cheque.

Or

(*b*) What are the precautions to be taken by a banker before granting advances against LIC policies?

SECTION C — (5 × 12 = 50 marks)

Answer All Questions

Each answer should not exceed 600 words

XVI. (*a*) Explain the general relationship between banker and customer.

Or

(*b*) What are the circumstances under which a banker can disclose the state of affairs of the customer's account?

XVII. (*a*) Explain the procedure for opening a bank account.

Or

(*b*) Discuss the effects of entries made in the Pass Book on the banker and customer.

XVIII. (*a*) Distinguish between a cheque and bill of exchange.

Or

(*b*) What do you mean by endorsement? Explain the rules relating to endorsement.

XIV. (*a*) What are the precautions to be taken by a banker before honouring a cheque?

Or

(*b*) Explain the statutory protection granted to the collecting banker.

XX. (*a*) What are the guiding principles of bank lending?

Or

(*b*) What are the precautions to be taken by a banker before lending money on immovable properties?

BANKING LAW

Time : Three hours **Maximum : 100 marks**

SECTION A — (10 × 1 = 10 marks)

Answer All the Questions

All questions carry equal marks.

I. To constitute a customer the following nature of transaction is required.

(*a*) Even a single transaction

(*b*) More than two transactions

(*c*) Many number of transactions

(*d*) None of the above.

II. Which of the following is a feature of general relationship between banker and customer?

(*a*) Debtor and Creditor relationship

(*b*) Trustee and Beneficiary relationship

(*c*) Principal and Agent relationship

(*d*) All of the above.

III. To open a new bank account which of the following is required?

(*a*) Letter of introduction

(*b*) Specimen signatures of the customer

(*c*) Both of the above

(*d*) None of the above.

IV. Which of the following is considered as a special type of customer?

(*a*) Minors (*b*) Lunatics

(*c*) Nontrading concerns (*d*) All of the above.

V. Which of the following is considered as a credit instrument?

(*a*) Cheques (*b*) Bills of exchange

(*c*) Drafts (*d*) All of the above.

VI. A cheque is issued by the following person :

(*a*) By one banker on another banker

(*b*) By a customer of a bank

(*c*) By the borrower of a bank

(*d*) None of the above.

VII. Which one of the following is considered as crossing of a cheque?

(*a*) Which one of the following is considered as crossing of a cheque?

(*a*) Drawing a line of the face of a cheque

(*b*) Drawing two lines one the reverse side of a cheque

(*c*) Drawing two parallel transverse lines on the left hand side corner of a cheque

(*d*) None of the above.

VIII. A banker becomes a 'holder for value' when

(*a*) He collects a cheque

(*b*) He credits a customer's account before collection

(*c*) He collects to a wring account

(*d*) He collects a crossed cheque.

IX. In which of the following situation a banker can dishonour a cheque issued by his customer?

(*a*) When the funds are insufficient

(*b*) When there is material alteration in the cheque

(*c*) When the amount in figures and words do not tally.

(*d*) All of the above.

X. Which of the following is considered as a principle of good leading?

(*a*) Safety of funds (*b*) Liquidity of funds

(*c*) Profitability of the funds (*d*) All of the above.

SECTION B — (5 × 6 = 30 marks)

Answer All the Questions

All questions carry equal marks

Each answer should not exceed 300 words.

XI. (*a*) Explain the obligation of a banker to honour cheques. When he can dishonour a cheque?

Or

(*b*) What is a lien? When a banker can exercise the lien?

XII. (*a*) What is a Pass Book? What are its functions?

Or

(*b*) Define a minor. Explain the precautions to be taken by the banker before opening an account in the name of a minor.

XIII. (*a*) Define a cheque. Explain its characteristic features.

Or

(*b*) What is crossing of a cheque? Explain the different kinds of special crossing.

XIV. (*a*) Who is a paying banker? What are his duties?

Or

(*b*) What points are to considered by a banker before passing a cheque for payment?

XV. (*a*) Define mortgage and discuss its various types.

Or

(*b*) What are the drawbacks in lending money against immovable properties?

SECTION C — (5 × 12 = 60 marks)

Answer All the Questions

All questions carry equal marks

Each answer should not exceed 600 words

XVI. (*a*) Explain the features of special relationship between a banker and a customer.

Or

(*b*) Define the terms 'Banker and Customer'> What is the nature of general relationship between them?

XVII. (*a*) Explain the various types of accounts that are offered by a banker.

Or

(*b*) What precautions a banker should take before opening an account in the name of a Partnership Firm and Trust Accounts.

XVIII. (*a*) Distinguish between a cheque and a Bill of exchange.

Or

(*b*) What is endorsement? Explain the various types of endorsements.

XIX. (*a*) Explain the legal protection given in a collecting banker.

Or

(*b*) Explain the terms 'Payment in Due Course' and 'Holder in Due Course'.

XX. (*a*) Explain the various modes of securing advance.

Or

(*b*) What precautions a banker should take before lending money on Stock Exchange Securities and Goods.

BANKING LAW

Time : Three hours **Maximum : 100 marks**

SECTION A — (10 × 1 = 10 marks)

Answer All the Questions

Choose the correct answer for each of the following from the given alternatives.

I. The banker's obligation to maintain secrecy of customer's accounts

(*a*) arise out of an agreement between the parties

(*b*) is statutory

(*c*) none of the above.

II. Banker's lien is

(*a*) General (*b*) Specific

(*c*) None of the above.

III. A savings account can be opened by

(*a*) a partnership (*b*) a private company

(*c*) none of the above.

IV. Generally a person attains majority

(*a*) after completing 18 years of age

(*b*) after completing 20 years of age

(*c*) after completing 21 years of age.

V. Bearer instruments are negotiated by

(*a*) endorsement (*b*) delivery

(*c*) cannot be negotiated.

VI. Endorsement of a negotiable instrument is done by

(*a*) the holder (*b*) the drawer

(*e*) the holder or drawer.

VII. The obligation of the bank to pay the customer's cheque is determined by

(*a*) the Banking Regulation Act

(*b*) the Negotiable Instruments Act

(*c*) the Reserve Bank of India Act.

VIII. Collection of cheques should be done for

(*a*) the payee

(*b*) the person known to the bank

(*c*) the customer of the bank.

IX. The "Indra Vikas Patras" are payable to

(*a*) the bearer (*b*) the purchaser

(*c*) none of the above.

X. Advance against documents of title to goods may take the form of

(*a*) cash credit (*b*) loan

(*c*) any of the above two.

SECTION B — (5 × 6 = 30 marks)

Answer All the Questions.

Each answer should not exceed 30 words.

XI. (*a*) Explain the special features of the relationship between banker and customer.

Or

(*b*) Write a note on Banker's lien.

XII. (*a*) Explain the risks that a banker runs in opening a current account without obtaining a suitable introductory reference.

Or

(*b*) What precautions should a banker take when opening a joint account?

XIII. (*a*) Define negotiable instrument with suitable examples.

Or

(*b*) Write a note on "Special crossing".

XIV. (*a*) What is meant by "Payment-in-due course"?

Or

(*b*) What is meant by "negligence"?

XV. (*a*) Explain the different methods of creating charge.

Or

(*b*) What are the different types of documents of title to goods?

SECTION C — (5 × 12 = marks)

Answer All the Questions

Each answer should not exceed 600 words.

XVI. (*a*) "A banker is bound to honour his customer's cheques"—Discuss.

Or

(*b*) Explain briefly the ruling in Clayton's case.

XVII. (*a*) Explain the different types of "Time Deposits" received by a bank.

Or

(*b*) When a banker can close customer's account?

XVIII. (*a*) Define a "cheque" and bring out its salient features.

Or

(*b*) Define "crossing". What are the different types of crossing?

XIX. (*a*) Discuss the circumstances under which a banker must refuse payment of a customer's cheque.

Or

(*b*) Explain the instances in which a collecting banker may lose his statutory protection on the ground of negligence.

XX. (*a*) What are secured and unsecured advances of the bank? What precautions should a banker take while making unsecured advances?

Or

(*b*) What precautions should a banker take while advancing money against (*i*) Fixed Deposit Receipt (*ii*) Life Insurance Policy?

BANKING LAW

Time : Three hours **Maximum : 100 marks**

SECTION A — (10 × 1 = 10 marks)

Answer All the Questions

Choose the best answer for each of the following from the given alternatives :

I. When money is deposited for a specific purpose, the banker becomes a

(*a*) Debtor (*b*) Bailee

(*c*) Trustee.

II. No lien is available to a banker in the case of

(*a*) Securities left to cover a loan

(*b*) Securities left by mistake to cover a loan

(*c*) Securities not taken back after repayment of a loan.

III. A current account is best suited to a :

(*a*) Minor (*b*) Lunatic

(*c*) Partnership firm.

IV. The best course to open an account in the name of a minor is

(*a*) Minor and his guardian (*b*) Minor himself

(*c*) Guardian himself

V. The instrument that is used only for making local payment is

(*a*) Banker's cheque (*b*) Draft

(*c*) Bill of exchange.

VI. The following one is absolutely essential for a special crossing :

(*a*) Name of a banker (*b*) Two parallel transverse lines

(*c*) The words & Co.

VII. The collecting banker is given statutory protection against

(*a*) Forged Endorsement (*b*) Conversion

(*c*) Fraud.

VIII. The following payment does not constitute payment in due course

(*a*) Payment of a post-dated cheque on the date of maturity

(*b*) Payment of a crossed cheque at the counter

(*c*) Payment of a generally crossed cheque to a fellow banker.

IX. The most RISKY charge from a bankers point of view is

(*a*) Hypothecation (*b*) Pledge

(*c*) Legal mortgage.

X. The most risky document of titles to goods is

(*a*) Bill of Lading (*b*) Railway Receipt

(*c*) Warehouse Receipt.

SECTION B — (5 × 6 = 30 marks)

Answer All Questions

Each answer should not exceed 300 words.

XI. (*a*) "A banker is a privileged debtor" Discuss.

Or

(*b*) How will you assess damages for wrongful dishonour of cheques?

XII. (*a*) Discuss any six special features of a Fixed Deposit Receipt.

Or

(*b*) State and explain any six general precautions which you will take before opening an account.

XIII. (*a*) Define a Bill of Exchange and distinguish it from a cheque.

Or

(*b*) Define material alteration and explain it with a suitable case law.

XIV. (*a*) What arc the duties of a collecting banker?

Or

(*b*) What do you mean by 'Payment in due course'?

XV. (*a*) Discuss any six principles of Sound leading.

Or

(*b*) Discuss the different kinds of mortgages.

SECTION C — (5 × 12 = 60 marks)

Answer All the Questions

Each answer should not exceed 600 words.

XVI. (*a*) What is Banker's lien? Under what circumstances can he exercise it?

Or

(*b*) Discuss the legal obligation of a banker in keeping secrecy of his customer's account.

XVII. (*a*) What precautions should a banker take while opening an account in the name of a partnership firm?

Or

(*b*) What precautions should a banker take while opening an account in the name of a Joint Stock Company?

XVIII. (*a*) Define crossing an bring out its various forms and their significance.

Or

(*b*) Explain the various forms of Endorsement and bring out their significance.

XIX. (*a*) Examine the nature of statutory protection given to a collecting banker in India.

Or

(*b*) Under what circumstances can a banker dishonour a cheque?

XX. (*a*) Discuss the various modes of creating a charge and explain their features.

Or

(*b*) What precautions should a banker take while advancing loan against stock exchange securities?

BANKING LAW

Time : Three hours **Maximum : 100 marks**

SECTION A — (10 × 1 = 10 marks)

Answer All the Questions

All Question carry equal marks

Choose the best answer from the given alternatives.

I. A banker can exercise his lien on properties

(*a*) Left by mistake

(*b*) Not taken back after the repayment of loan

(*c*) Left for a specific purpose

(*d*) Obtained unlawfully.

II. When gold ornaments are given for the purpose of safety, the banker becomes a

(*a*) Debtor (*b*) Creditor

(*c*) An agent (*d*) Bailee.

III. The convenient deposit from the businessman's point of view is

(*a*) Current deposit (*b*) Savings deposit

(*c*) Fixed deposit (*d*) Recurring deposit.

IV. The best course to open an account in the name of a minor is in

(*a*) Minors name (*b*) Guardians name

(*c*) Joint account in the name of minor and Guardian

(*d*) Minors father's name.

V. The instrument that can be used only for local payment is

(*a*) Cheque (*b*) Draft

(*c*) Bill of Exchange (*d*) Banker's cheque.

VI. The following one is very essential for a special crossing

(*a*) Name of a banker simply

(*b*) Two parallel transverse lines simply

(*c*) Name of banker within two parallel transverse lines

(*d*) Words A/c payee.

VII. A paying banker is given protection against

(*a*) Conversion

(*b*) Forgery of customer's signature

(*c*) Forgery of payee's signature

(*d*) All of the above.

VIII. A collecting banker is given protection only when he acts in the capacity of a

(*a*) Agent (*b*) Holder

(*c*) Holder for value (*d*) Holder in due course.

IX. The most risky advance from the banker's point of view is against

(*a*) Lien (*b*) Hypothecation

(*c*) Pledge (*d*) Mortgage

X. The desirable security for a loan of Rs. 5 lakhs is

(*a*) Life policy for Rs. 10 lakhs

(*b*) Bill of lading for Rs. 10 lakhs

(*c*) Building costing Rs. 10 lakhs

(*d*) Gold ornaments worth Rs. 10 lakhs.

SECTION B — (5 × 6 = 30 marks)

Answer All the Questions

All questions carry equal marks

Each answer should not exceed 300 words.

XI. (*a*) Distinguish between a commercial debt and a banking debt.

Or

(*b*) How will you assess damages for wrongful dishonour of cheques?

XII. (*a*) What precautions will you take while opening an account in the name of a sports club?

Or

(*b*) Discuss the effect of wrong entries in a Pass Book which are favourable to a customer.

XIII. (*a*) Explain the characteristic features of Negotiable Instruments.

Or

(*b*) Distinguish between a general crossing and a speciaı crossing.

XIV. (*a*) Under what circumstances can a paying banker dishonour a cheque?

Or

(*b*) What constitutes negligence under Sec. 131 of the Negotiable Instruments Act?

XV. (*a*) Discuss any six principles of sound lending.

Or

(*b*) Discuss the drawbacks of lending against a life policy.

SECTION C — (5 × 12 = 60 marks)

Answer All the Questions

All questions carry equal marks

Each answer should not exceed 600 words

XVI. (*a*) What is Banker's lien? State the circumstances under which

(*i*) lien can be exercised and

(*ii*) lien cannot be exercised.

(*b*) Under what circumstances can a banker disclose his customer's account and what precautions should he take in such cases?

XVII. (*a*) Explain the legal position of a banker with regard to a fixed deposit.

Or

(*b*) What precautions should a banker generally take while opening an account in the name of a limited company?

XVIII. (*a*) Explain with suitable illustrations the term material alteration and bring out the duties of a paying banker in connection thereof.

Or

(*b*) Explain with suitable illustrations the different kinds of endorsements and bring out their significance.

XIX. (*a*) Discuss the concept of payment in due course.

Or

(*b*) Discuss the nature of protection granted to a collecting banker in India under Sec. 131 of the negotiable Instruments Act.

XX. (*a*) State and explain the different modes of charging a security and bring out their features.

Or

(*b*) What precautions should a banker take while lending against goods?

BANKING LAW

Time : Three hours **Maximum : 100 marks**

SECTION A — (10 × 1 = 10 marks)

Answer All the Questions

All questions carry equal marks

Choose the best answer from the given alternatives.

I. A banker can exercise his lien on properties
(*a*) Left by mistake
(*b*) Not taken back after the repayment of loan
(*c*) Left for a specific purpose
(*d*) Obtained unlawfully.

II. When gold ornaments are given for the purpose of safety, the banker becomes a
(*a*) Debtor (*b*) Creditor
(*c*) An agent (*d*) Bailee.

III. The convenient deposit from the businessman's point of view is
(*a*) Current deposit (*b*) Savings deposit
(*c*) Fixed deposit (*d*) Recurring deposit.

IV. The best course to open an account in the name of a minor is in
(*a*) Minor's name (*b*) Guardians name
(*c*) Joint account in the name of minor and Guardian
(*d*) Minor's father's name.

V. The instrument that can be used only for local payment is
(*a*) Cheque (*b*) Draft
(*c*) Bill of Exchange (*d*) Banker's cheque.

VI. The following one is very essential for a special crossing
(*a*) Name of a banker simply
(*b*) Two parallel transverse lines simply
(*c*) Name of banker within two parallel transverse lines
(*d*) Words A/c payee.

VII. A paying banker is given protection against

(*a*) A conversion

(*b*) Forgery of customer's signature

(*c*) Forgery of payee's signature

(*d*) All of the above.

VIII. A collecting banker is given protection only when he acts in the capacity of a

(*a*) Agent (*b*) Holder

(*c*) Holder for value (*d*) Holder in due course.

IX. The most risky advance from the banker's point of view is against

(*a*) Lien (*b*) Hypothecation

(*c*) Pledge (*d*) Mortgage

X. The desirable security for a loan of Rs. 5 lakhs is

(*a*) Life policy for Rs. 10 lakhs

(*b*) Bill of lading for Rs. 10 lakhs

(*c*) Building costing Rs. 10 lakhs

(*d*) Gold ornaments worth Rs. 10 lakhs.

SECTION B — (5 × 6 = 30 marks)

Answer All the Questions

All questions carry equal marks

Each answer should not exceed 300 words

XI. (*a*) Distinguish between a commercial debt and a banking debt.

Or

(*b*) How will you assess damages for wrongful dishonour of cheques?

XII. (*a*) What precautions will you take while opening an account in the name of a sports club?

Or

(*b*) Discuss the effect of wrong entries in a pass book which are favourable to a customer.

XIII. (*a*) Explain the characteristic features of Negotiable Instruments.

Or

(*b*) Distinguish between a general crossing and a special crossing.

XIV. (*a*) Under what circumstances can a paying banker dishonour a cheque?

Or

(*b*) What constitutes negligence under Sec. 131 of the Negotiable Instruments Act ?

XV. (*a*) Discuss any six principles of sound lending.

Or

(*b*) Discuss the drawbacks of lending against a life policy.

SECTION C — (5 × 12 = 60 marks)

Answer All the Questions

All questions carry equal marks

Each answer should not exceed 600 words

XVI. (*a*) What is Banker's lien? State the circumstances under which

(*i*) lien can be exercised and

(*ii*) lien cannot be exercised.

Or

(*b*) Under what circumstances can a banker disclose his customer's account and what precautions should be taken in such cases?

XVII. (*a*) Explain the legal position of a banker with regard to a fixed deposit.

Or

(*b*) What precautions should a banker generally take while opening an account in the name of a limited company?

XVIII. (*a*) Explain with suitable illustrations the term material alteration and bring out the duties of a paying banker in connection thereof.

Or

(*b*) Explain with suitable illustrations the different kinds of endorsements and bring out their significance.

XIX. (*a*) Discuss the concept of payment in due course.

Or

(*b*) Discuss the nature of protection granted to a collecting banker in India under Sec. 131 of the negotiable Instruments Act.

XX. (*a*) State and explain the different modes of charging a security and bring out their features.

Or

(*b*) What precautions should a banker take while lending against goods?

XXI. (*a*) Differentiate cheque with bill of exchange.

Or

(*b*) What are the remarks given by the paying banker when payment is refused?

XXII. (*a*) What do you mean by 'mortgage'?

Or

(*b*) What is payment by mistake?

XXIII. (*a*) Bring out clearly the risks of honouring a post-dated cheque.

Or

(*b*) Discuss the legal position of a pass-book.

PART D — (2 × 15 = 30 marks)

Answer All the Questions

XXIV. (*a*) What are the statutory protection available to paying banker?

Or

(*b*) What is an endorsement? What are its types?

XXV. (*a*) Explain the duties of a collecting banker.

Or

(*b*) What precautions should a banker take while making loan against (*i*) Goods (*ii*) L.I.C. Policy?

BANKING LAW

Time : Three hours **Maximum : 100 marks)**

PART A — (10 × 1 = 10 marks)

Answer All the Questions

All questions carry equal marks.

I. Choose the correct answer :

The banker has a statutory obligation to

(*a*) Honour customers cheques

(*b*) Maintain secrecy of his customer's accounts

(*c*) Honour customers bills.

II. State whether the following statement is True or False :

Savings deposit is more suitable for business people.

III. State whether the following statement is True or False :

The rate of interest payable on various deposits of commercial banks is determined by the Central Government.

IV. Define the term 'Customer'.

V. What is material alteration in a cheque?

VI. What is stale cheque?

VII. What is crossing of a cheque?

VIII. What is meant by 'common courtesy'?

IX. Give the meaning for the word 'Collateral securities'.

X. Write a short note on 'Mutilated cheque'.

PART B (5 × 4 = 20 marks)

Answer All the Questions

XI. (*a*) Write any four conditions for exercising the right of lien by the banker.

Or

(*b*) Write a note on 'right of set-off accounts'.

XII. (*a*) Briefly note what precautions that the banker should take when opening the account in the name of a married woman.

Or

(*b*) Briefly note what precautions that a banker should take before opening of an account in the name of illiterate person.

XIII. (*a*) What are the features of fixed deposit?

Or

(*b*) Write a note on 'Recurring Deposit'.

XIV. (*a*) What are secured advances?

Or

(*b*) Briefly discuss the circumstances under which a banker can close the accounts of his customer.

Or

XV. (*a*) Define 'Payment in due course'.

(*b*) Define holder in due course.

Part C — (5 × 8 = 40 marks)

Answer All the Questions

Answer not exceeding 2 pages for each question.

XVI. (*a*) Explain the general relationship between banker and customer.

Or

(*b*) Define the term 'Banker'.

XVII. (*a*) What is a cheque? What are its requisites?

Or

(*b*) What is special crossing? Explain with examples.

XVIII. (*a*) Define endorsement. Explain with illustrations the different kinds of endorsements and bring out their significance.

Or

(*b*) Discuss the legal implications of marking of a postdated cheque with a relevant case law on this subject.

XIX (*a*) Under what circumstances, is a banker justified in refusing payment of cheques drawn upon him?

Or

(*b*) What constitutes negligence under section 131 of the Negotiable Instruments Act?

XX (*a*) State the precautions required to be taken by a banker in case of advances against the security of goods.

Or

(*b*) Describe the mechanism and effect of different commercial letters of credit.

NOTES

NOTES